international
review of
social history

Special Issue 31

Punishing Workers, Managing Labour

Edited by Christian de Vito, Adam Fagbore, and Eric Vanhaute

Published by the Press Syndicate of the University of Cambridge
The Pitt Building, Trumpington Street, Cambridge, CB2 1RP
1 Liberty Plaza, Floor 20, New York, NY 10006, USA
10 Stamford Road, Oakleigh, Melbourne 3166, Australia

© Internationaal Instituut voor Sociale Geschiedenis

*A catalogue record for this book is available
from the British Library*

Library of Congress Cataloguing-in-Publication Data applied for

ISBN 9781009421348 (paperback)

Printed and bound by CPI Group (UK) Ltd, Croydon, CR0 4YY

CONTENTS

Special Issue: Punishing Workers, Managing Labour

Edited by
Christian de Vito, Adam Fagbore, and Eric Vanhaute

International Review of Social History, 68:S31 (2023), pp. 1–14
doi:10.1017/S0020859022000840

RESEARCH ARTICLE

Introduction: Punitive Perspectives on Labour Management*

Christian G. De Vito[a]† and Adam S. Fagbore[b]

[a,b]Bonn Center for Dependency and Slavery Studies, University of Bonn, Bonn, Germany
†Corresponding editor, e-mail: cdevito@uni-bonn.de

Abstract
What is the historical role of punishment in the management of labour? This is the central question of this Special Issue of the *International Review of Social History* (*IRSH*), "Punishing Workers, Managing Labour". Through a close reading of the diverse range of articles included in this Special Issue and by addressing the relatively extensive but highly fragmented scholarship on the subject, this introduction argues that the key to labour management lay in the interplay of differentiated forms of punishment with distinct labour relations, rather than in the imposition of one punitive regime onto an undifferentiated workforce. In other words, the effective management of labour required the systematic differentiation of the workforce; to that end, the imposition of diversified forms of punishment did not merely reflect existing labour distinctions, but also contributed to creating them. This point leads us to address broader methodological and theoretical issues about how we can analyse such complex interactions: how we can compare the role of punishment in the management of labour across space and time, and how our findings can be used to explain short- and long-term historical changes.

Rethinking the Entanglements Between Labour and Punishment

The starting point of a comprehensive analytical frame of the role of punishment in labour management lies in a double pluralization. On the side of labour, we should acknowledge that the coexistence of various ("free" and "unfree") labour relations has been the standard throughout history, as global labour historians have

---

*The authors of this introduction would like to thank the contributors, the anonymous reviewers, the co-editor of the Special Issue, and the editors and members of the *IRSH* Editorial Committee for their precious work on this volume and for their feedback on earlier drafts of this introduction. They also express their gratitude to the Bonn Center for Dependency and Slavery Studies (BCDSS) for their generous support and for funding the interdisciplinary conference "Punishment, Labor, and the Legitimation of Power", which was organized by Adam Fagbore on behalf of the research group "Punishment, Labor, and Dependency" of the BCDSS on 18–19 February 2021. Seven articles (Fagbore, Revilla Orías, Avellino, Pearson, Loktionov, Ferraro, and Dimmers) included in this Special Issue derive from that conference; the five other articles (Reid, Rio, Chevaleyre, Lyngholm, and Heinsen) have been included to expand the historical and temporal scope of the volume.

highlighted.[1] Consequently, labour management should be understood as the governing of an articulated and internally fragmented workforce. On the side of punishment, we need to view the multiple punitive practices that have stemmed from various normative sources in any historical or social context. Not only the criminal justice system but also military, religious, and administrative justice, together with other actors such as masters, employers, the guilds, and indigenous communities. Indeed, this volume features an anthropological view of "punishment", which embraces any practices that diverse historical agents have used to retribute and modify the behaviours of other individuals and groups perceived as deviating from (constructed and contested) moral, economic, and political norms. From this perspective, the use of punitive practices as a mode of control over workers has always been plural, and it is precisely this plurality that has given management the necessary flexibility to cope with specific composition of the workforce, within the historical context of shifting imperatives of production combined with changing external circumstances. This means that we need to understand the logic of deployment of, say, incarceration, penal transportation, or capital punishment as differentiated tools for the control of enslaved, waged, and indentured workforces, or the composite workforces of distinct worksites in each specific historical context.[2] To this end, the simultaneous pluralization of labour and punishment that we propose raises new questions regarding the relationship between punishment and labour management, such as: Why and how were forms of punishment differentiated vis-à-vis workers in distinct labour relations? Why and how did some punitive institutions target workers in certain labour relations rather than others? And how were these differentiations in punitive practices legitimized?

At the crossroads of this double pluralization, a new frame begins to emerge, one that views the analysis of the role of punishment in labour management as the investigation of the impact of concurring and shifting punitive practices on multifaceted and changing forms of labour relations. Three processual approaches to labour history echo this agenda and seem suitable to be expanded to include the perspective of punishment.

The first approach includes works that have contended that the management of labour does not imply the imposition of a homogeneous regime of control and coercion on the workforce as a whole but precisely its segmentation and – to use Roediger and Esch's expression – the "production of difference" among workers.[3] Although the original focus of these scholars has been on differentiations by race, citizenship, and gender, this approach seems also well positioned to explore the ways in which and the

---

[1] Tom Brass and Marcel van der Linden (eds), *Free and Unfree Labour: The Debate Continues* (Bern, 1997); Marcel van der Linden, *Workers of the World: Essays towards a Global Labor History* (Amsterdam and Boston, MA, 2008).

[2] We echo and expand here the concept of "logic of deployment", proposed by Jairus Banaji, *Theory as History: Essays on Modes of Production and Exploitation* (Amsterdam and Boston, MA, 2010), pp. 113–116.

[3] David R. Roediger and Elizabeth D. Esch, *The Production of Difference: Race and the Management of Labor in US History* (Oxford, 2012). For other examples on the United States, see Lisa Lowe, *Immigrant Acts: Asian American Cultural Politics* (Durham, NC, and London, 1996); Grace Kyungwon Hong, *The Ruptures of American Capital: Women of Color Feminism and the Culture of Immigrant Labor* (Minneapolis, MN, and London, 1999).

reasons why different punitive practices targeted distinct groups of workers and, by doing so, created and reinforced the distinctions among those workers. The second approach addresses the processes by which labour coercion is constructed and maintained.[4] By suggesting the need for a contextualized and relational study of labour regimes, it invites us to disentangle the specific dynamics of labour coercion.[5] As such, this perspective offers the possibility to view punishment as one of the processes that produce and reproduce labour coercion across all types of labour relations. For example, it highlights how anti-vagrancy policies, backed by punitive practices, produced workers' im/mobility; it foregrounds the connections between debt, punishment, and the fixing of labourers to specific worksites; and it calls attention to the importance of flogging in the control of the enslaved and tributary workforce, and in constructing them as distinct from other fellow labourers. The third approach emerges from various studies that, starting from the empirical observation of the entanglements among distinct groups of workers, have suggested bottom-up categories to describe them as a multifaceted whole. For example, this is the case with Peter Linebaugh and Markus Rediker's "many-headed hydra" and "motley crews", Marcel van der Linden's "subaltern workers", and Peter M. Beattie's "intractable poor".[6] Such dynamic categories match with the equally flexible notions of "coercive networks" and "punitive pluralism" that have been proposed to address the ways multiple punitive practices intervened in the management of composite bundles of workers.[7]

The analytical frame we are suggesting questions prominent theoretical views about entanglements between labour and punishment, and invites us to develop more integrated empirical studies beyond the fragmentation that marks current scholarship. Major criminological and sociological theories, like those of George Rusche and Otto Kirchheimer, Dario Melossi and Massimo Pavarini, and Michel Foucault, have framed the relationship between labour and punishment through a Eurocentric lens. They have described them as shifting linearly across time, and have typically conflated them with connections between a single type of labour relation – wage labour – and a single type of punishment – penal imprisonment.[8] These

---

[4]Christian G. De Vito, Juliane Schiel, and Matthias van Rossum, "From Bondage to Precariousness? New Perspectives on Labor and Social History", *Journal of Social History*, 54:2 (2020), pp. 644–662.

[5]Marcel van der Linden, "Dissecting Coerced Labour", in Marcel van der Linden and Magaly Rodríguez García (eds), *On Coerced Labor: Work and Compulsion after Chattel Slavery* (Amsterdam and Boston, MA, 2016), pp. 291–322.

[6]Peter Linebaugh and Marcus Rediker, *The Many-Headed Hydra: Sailors, Slaves, Commoners, and the Hidden History of the Revolutionary Atlantic* (Boston, MA, 2000); Van der Linden, *Workers of the World*; Marcus Rediker, *Outlaws of the Atlantic: Sailors, Pirates, and Motley Crews in the Age of Sail* (Boston, MA, 2015); Peter M. Beattie, *Punishment in Paradise: Race, Slavery, Human Rights, and a Nineteenth-Century Brazilian Penal Colony* (Durham, NC, 2015). For a similar approach, see also Johan Heinsen, *Mutiny in the Danish Atlantic World: Convicts, Sailors and a Dissonant Empire* (London, 2017).

[7]Taylor C. Sherman, "Tensions of Colonial Punishment: Perspectives on Recent Developments in the Study of Coercive Networks in Asia, Africa and the Caribbean", *History Compass*, 7:3 (1999), pp. 659–677; Christian G. De Vito, "Punishment and Labour Relations: Cuba between Abolition and Empire (1835–1886)", *Crime, Histoire & Sociétés / Crime, History & Societies*, 22:1 (2018), pp. 53–79.

[8]Georg Rusche and Otto Kirchheimer, *Punishment and Social Structure* (London and New York, [1939] 2003); Michel Foucault, *Discipline and Punish: The Birth of the Prison* (New York, [orig. FR. 1975] 1977); Dario Melossi and Massimo Pavarini, *The Prison and the Factory: Origins of the Penitentiary System*

approaches have been empirically proved incapable of explaining not only the reality of ancient, medieval, and colonial punishment – which they did not address – but even the diversity of uses of penal labour in Europe, the role of punitive practices, such as penal transportation in what has been dubbed "the age of the triumphant prison", and the centrality of labour camps in the twentieth century.[9]

However, later empirical works that have also addressed the impact of punishment on labour management have replicated this focus on specific forms of labour relations. Thus, in the field of business and management history, studies of "scientific management" and "lean manufacturing" have addressed only the control of industrial wage labour, besides featuring a standard downplaying of the role of coercion and punishment.[10] Conversely, Robert J. Steinfeld's pioneering work on the "invention of free labor" took a labour history perspective and did include a focus on the role of punishment in the regulation of the master–servant relationship but similarly confined itself to the exclusive analysis of wage labour.[11] More detailed insights have emerged within the field of slavery studies, with specific reference to the Americas in the sixteenth through nineteenth centuries. Bivar Marquese's *Feitores do corpo, missionários da mente* showcases the analytical potential of this set of scholarship due to its extended scope, which spans the normative texts produced by missionaries,

---

(London and New York, [orig. IT. 1977] 2018). See also: Dario Melossi, Máximo Sozzo, and José A. Brandariz-García (eds), *The Political Economy of Punishment Today: Visions, Debates and Challenges* (London and New York, 2018).

[9]For example, Florence Bernault (ed.), *Enfermement, prison et châtiments en Afrique. Du 19e siècle à nos jours* (Paris, 1999); Frank Dikötter and Ian Brown (eds), *Cultures of Confinement: A History of the Prison in Africa, Asia, and Latin America* (Ithaca, NY, 2007); Guy Geltner, *The Medieval Prison: A Social History* (Princeton, NJ, 2008); Lynne Viola, *The Unknown Gulag: The Lost World of Stalin's Special Settlements* (Oxford, 2009); Dominique Moran, Nick Gill, and Deirdre Conlon (eds), *Carceral Spaces: Mobility and Agency in Imprisonment and Migrant Detention* (London and New York, 2013); Nikolaus Wachsmann, *Hitler's Prisons: Legal Terror in Nazi Germany* (New Haven, CT, 2015); Christian G. De Vito, Ralf Futselaar, and Helen Grevers (eds), *Incarceration and Regime Change: European Prisons During and After the Second World War* (Oxford, 2017); Mahon Murphy, *Colonial Captivity During the First World War* (Cambridge, 2017); Christian G. De Vito and Alex Lichtenstein (eds), *Global Convict Labour* (Amsterdam and Boston, MA, 2016); Clare Anderson (ed.), *A Global History of Convicts and Penal Colonies* (London, 2018); Christian G. De Vito, Clare Anderson, and Ulbe Bosma (eds), "Transportation, Deportation and Exile: Perspectives from the Colonies in the Nineteenth and Twentieth Centuries", *International Review of Social History*, 63:SI26 (2018); Zhanna Popova and Francesca Di Pasquale (eds), "Dissecting Sites of Punishment: Penal Colonies and Their Borders", *International Review of Social History*, 64:3 (2019), pp. 415–425.

[10]For some examples: Daniel Nelson, "Scientific Management, Systematic Management, and Labor, 1880–1915", *Business History Review*, 48:4 (1974), pp. 479–500; Stephen P. Waring, *Taylorism Transformed: Scientific Management Theory since 1945* (Chapel Hill, NC, 1991); Daniel A. Wren, *The History of Management Thought* (Hoboken, NJ, 2005); Mikhail Grachev and Boris Rakitsky, "Historic Horizons of Frederick Taylor's Scientific Management", *Journal of Management History*, 19:4 (2013), pp. 512–527; Łukasz Dekier, "The Origin and Evolution of Lean Management System", *Journal of International Studies*, 5:1 (2012), pp. 46–51; M.G.S. Dilanthi, "Conceptual Evolution Lean Manufacturing: A Review of Literature", *International Journal of Economics, Commerce and Management*, 3:10 (2015). Available at: https://ssrn.com/abstract=2678896; last accessed 9 November 2022.

[11]Robert J. Steinfeld, *The Invention of Free Labor: The Employment Relation in English and American Law and Culture, 1350–1870* (Chapel Hill, NC, 1991). On wage labour and legal regimes see also: Simon Deakin and Frank Wilkinson, *The Law of the Labour Market: Industrialization, Employment, and Legal Evolution* (Oxford, 2005); Alain Supiot, *Critique du droit du travail* (Paris, 2011).

political authorities, medical experts, and slaveholders across the Portuguese, Spanish, French, and British empires and the United States.[12] Indeed, Marquese provides us with a unique insight into the elites' reflection on the strategies of control of slaves, and foregrounds the role of the various punitive practices employed by the masters and the state in the management of the enslaved workforce. Moreover, he discusses the changes that occurred from 1660 to 1860 by looking at both ideological motivations and at the increasing but often unsuccessful attempts of the state to limit the masters' power to punish. Marquese's findings at the level of the discourses on labour management can be fruitfully complemented with more specific studies on the practices of control of the enslaved workers produced by several scholars, originally with a focus on nineteenth-century Brazil, United States, and the British Caribbean, and, more recently, also on early modern and post-independence Latin America.[13] However, viewed from the perspective of the question that motivates this Special Issue, even this outstanding scholarship on the punishment of the enslaved iterates the exclusive focus on a single labour relation, besides addressing slavery only in the context of the early modern and modern Americas.

Scattered references to the role of punishment vis-à-vis the management of workers in other labour relations and besides the early modern and nineteenth-century Americas can be found in the specialized scholarship.[14] But there is a clear need for systematic empirical research on the control of the work of servants, indentured labourers, convicts, and independent peasants for the early modern and modern

---

[12]Rafael de Bivar Marquese, *Feitores do corpo, missionários da mente. Senhores, letrados e o controle dos escravos nas Américas, 1660–1860* (São Paulo, 2004).

[13]Philip J. Schwartz, *Twice Condemned: Slaves and the Criminal Laws of Virginia, 1705–1865* (Baton Rouge, LA, 1988); Silvia Hunold Lara, *Campos da violência. Escravos e Senhores na Capitania do io de Janeiro 1750–1808* (Rio de Janeiro, 1988); Thomas D. Morris, *Southern Slavery and the Law 1619–1860* (Chapel Hill, NC, and London, 1996); Diana Paton, *No Bond but the Law: Punishment, Race, and Gender in Jamaican State Formation, 1780–1870* (Durham, NC, and London, 2004); Maria Helena P.T. Machado, *Crime e escavidão. Trabalho, Luta e Resistência nas Labouras Paulistas (1830–1888)* (São Paulo, 2014); Dawn Harris, *Punishing the Black Body: Marking Social and Racial Structures in Barbados and Jamaica* (Athens, GA, 2017); Trevor Burnard (ed.), "The Management of Enslaved People on Anglo-American Plantations, 1700–1860", *Journal of Global Slavery*, 6:1 (Special Issue, 2021); Viola Müller and Christian G. De Vito (eds), "Punishing the Enslaved: Labour, Slavery and Punitive Practices in the Americas (1760s–1880s)", *Journal of Global Slavery*, 6:1 (Special issue, 2021). For broader studies on slavery that address the role of punishment in the management of the enslaved workers, see Eric Williams, *Capitalism and Slavery* (London, 1964); Stefano Fenoaltea, "Slavery and Supervision in Comparative Perspective: A Model", *Journal of Economic History*, 44:3 (1984), pp. 635–668; Robin Blackburn, *The Making of New World Slavery: From the Baroque to the Modern, 1492–1800* (London and New York, 1997); Sven Beckert and Seth Rockman (eds), *Slavery's Capitalism: A New History of American Economic Development* (Philadelphia, PA, 2016).

[14]For an explicit analysis of the role of punishment in the management of labour, see Nitin Varma, *Coolies of Capitalism: Assam Tea and the Making of Coolie Labour* (Berlin, 2016). For some examples related to the control of military labour, see Peter Burroughs, "Crime and Punishment in the British Army, 1815–1870", *English Historical Review*, 100:396 (1985), pp. 545–571; David Killingray, "The 'Rod of Empire': The Debate over Corporal Punishment in the British African Colonial Forces, 1888–1946", *Journal of African History*, 35:2 (1994), pp. 201–216; Kaushik Roy, "Spare the Rod, Spoil the Soldier? Crime and Punishment in the Army of India, 1860s–1913", *Journal of the Society for Army Historical Research*, 84:337 (2006), pp. 9–33; Dominique Kalifa, *Biribi. Les bagnes coloniaux de l'armée française* (Paris, 2009).

periods, and on virtually all groups of workers before 1500. Even this might not be enough. Indeed, it is our contention that the multiplication of empirical works is a necessary but insufficient condition for the analysis of the impact of punishment on labour management. The double pluralization of labour and punishment that we propose is not an empiricist exercise but an analytical necessity to address complex configurations that have existed historically at the crossroads of various labour and punitive regimes. In the following sections, we argue that this approach also offers insights regarding methodological issues on trans-epochal comparisons and shifts in punitive intervention on labour management across time.

Trans-Epochal and Transcultural Comparisons

This Special Issue includes articles on the histories of blinded slaves in ancient Mesopotamia, flogged peasant farmers in pharaonic Egypt, convict officers in the prisons of colonial India, and blacklisted factory workers in the nineteenth-century United States. The contributors skilfully ground their histories in their specific temporal and spatial contexts. Assembling them in a single Special Issue suggests that some common themes can be traced across the articles and that, taken together, they make up a coherent contribution to the understanding of the role of punishment in labour management. From a methodological perspective, the question is whether a comparison is possible at all among the contexts presented here (and beyond), and, if so, which kind of comparison are we proposing as editors of this Special Issue.

Large comparative research projects and syntheses have been offered in the last two decades within the field of global labour history. Contrary to traditional approaches in labour history, these works have taken the multiplicity of labour relations as their starting points and have deliberately expanded the chronological and spatial scope with a view to challenging the Eurocentric and methodologically nationalist approaches that still dominate the discipline. However, global labour historians have predominantly developed these shareable premises in the direction of structuralist comparisons that seek to "cover the world" and reach out across the history of humankind by means of predefined categories and taxonomies. Collective volumes have been built on predefined frameworks that include lists of "factors" and questions that contributors are asked to deal with as they go through their sources or, more frequently, the findings of secondary literature. Or, in the case of databases like that of the Global Collaboratory on the History of Labour Relations, labour relations have been categorized and ordered according to a predefined taxonomy that frames the collection and analysis of the data.[15]

---

[15]For examples of this approach, see Jan Lucassen, "Brickmakers in Western Europe (1700–1900) and Northern India (1800–2000): Some Comparisons", in Jan Lucassen (ed.), *Global Labour History: A State of the Art* (Bern, 2006), pp. 513–571; Elise van Nederveen Meerkerk, "Covering the World: Textile Workers and Globalization, 1650–2000: Experiences and Results of a Collective Research Project", in Marcel van der Linden (ed.), *Labour History Beyond Borders: Concepts and Explorations* (Linz, 2010), pp. 111–138. For a long-term synthesis based on these analytical premises, see Jan Lucassen, *The Story of Work: A New History of Humankind* (New Haven, CT, and London, 2021). For the Global

In structuralist comparisons, predefining concepts, frameworks, and taxonomies have the explicit role of creating homogenous sets of data that can subsequently be compared to uncover universal and long-term structures. From our perspective, preliminary standardization is problematic because it creates a tautological circularity between the premises and outcomes of research. In other words, by standardizing the analytical tools and the data, structuralist approaches create a fictive image of a homogeneous social fabric of human societies, and then use it as a basis for large claims over similarities and differences among regions, as well as continuities and discontinuities across time.[16] In this way, the structuralist approach removes or oversimplifies the very dynamics that lie at the centre of the historical process of labour management. Namely, that the contextualized interactions between multiple forms of labour relations and distinct forms of punishment and their combination generate open-ended configurations that change across time. Moreover, the structuralist approach silences the continuous negotiations and conflicts among the historical actors that concretely shaped those shifting configurations of punitive and labour relations.

In this introduction, we offer an alternative path. Building on the tradition of microhistory, we contend that it is possible to construct trans-epochal and transcultural comparisons of labour management and the punishment of workers by asking common questions and analysing the divergences and convergences among the answers.[17] For us, this is a way to dig deeper into the social meanings that both similarities and differences reveal, and acknowledge that the experiences and ideas that workers had about the "world", work, and punishment might have varied consistently, and that their understanding needs to be grounded in their specific contexts and in the investigation of distinct connections. Moreover, acknowledging the plurality of normative sources allows us to interrogate the very existence of "the state" in certain historical contexts and ask how the conceptualization of "the polity" changed over time. It permits acknowledgement of the multi-normativity that has characterized all human societies, and thus moves away from a Weberian model of the state

---

Collaboratory on the History of Labour Relations, see: https://iisg.amsterdam/en/research/projects/global-collaboratory-on-the-history-of-labour-relations-1500-2000; last accessed 9 November 2022. For a "manifesto" of this approach, see Leo Lucassen, "Working Together: New Directions in Global Labour History", *Journal of Global History*, 11:1 (2016), pp. 66–87.

[16]For critical analysis of structuralist or macro-analytical approaches, see John Hatcher and Judy S. Stephenson (eds), *Seven Centuries of Unreal Wages: The Unreliable Data, Sources and Methods that Have Been Used for Measuring Standard Living in the Past* (London, 2018); Alida Clemente, "Micro e macro tra narrativismo postmoderno e scelta razionale. Il problema della agency e la storia economica come scienza sociale", in Daniele Andreozzi (ed.), *Quantità/qualità. La storia tra sguardi micro e generalizzazioni* (Palermo, 2017), pp. 37–58. For a critical analysis of macro-analytical approaches in global labour history, and the proposal of a micro-spatial perspective, see Christian G. De Vito and Anne Gerritsen, "Micro-Spatial Histories of Labour: Towards a New Global History", in *idem* (eds), *Micro-Spatial Histories of Global Labour* (London, 2018), pp. 1–28.

[17]For this view on comparison, see Giovanni Levi, "On Microhistory", in Peter Burke (ed.), *New Perspectives on Historical Writing* (University Park, PA, 1992), pp. 93–113; Carlo Ginzburg, "Our Words, and Theirs: A Reflection on the Historian's Craft, Today", in Susanna Fellman and Marjatta Rahikainen (eds), *Quest of Theory, Method and Evidence* (Cambridge, 2012), pp. 97–119.

as a monopolist of legitimate(d) violence.[18] Finally, it facilitates the study of jurisdictional and social tensions among various state institutions, or among the criminal justice system and the masters/employers, around the management of the labour force.

Doing trans-epochal and transcultural comparisons also means acknowledging and putting to good use diverse approaches and traditions of distinct academic fields. In particular, the questions that have been raised in one field can be asked in other spatial and temporal contexts and in other fields, following the logic of reciprocal comparison.[19] Take the case of the notion of "patronage" in the scholarships on pharaonic Egypt and on the Spanish empire, and how a dialogue between those two distinct academic fields can help reach a deeper understanding of the relationship between punishment and labour management in both contexts. For the American territories of the Spanish monarchy, historians have underlined that both the royal authorities and the masters legitimized their power vis-à-vis their subaltern describing themselves as their "fathers" and "patrons", and through a discourse and practice of "protection". In a context of legal pluralism, in which both the royal authorities and the masters held the right to punish their subaltern, the punishment of an enslaved African or an indigenous worker by the polity could then trigger complex negotiations and conflicts between them, each based on a different understanding of "protection". Indeed, the Spanish Crown increasingly (but often unsuccessfully) intervened to set a limit on the modes and quantity of the punishments inflicted by the masters; these, in turn, acted during criminal cases as defendants of the enslaved to prevent their slaves and indigenous workers from being sentenced to penal transportation or sold to other masters outside the province.[20] How does this resonate with the punitive practices that arose in pharaonic Egypt from the relationship between the authorities and the masters? Asking this question opens new perspectives, without in any way suggesting structural similarities between the two contexts. It rather pushes us to interrogate the actual capacity of the pharaonic "state" to guarantee "protection" and impose punishment, against the background of a weak process of state centralization; it poses the question of the blurred boundaries between "political" and "economic" elites at the local level; and it allows us to consider how the study of punitive regimes cannot be separated from the analysis

---

[18]This is the theme of the vast and transdisciplinary scholarship on "legal pluralism" and "multi-normativity". For some overviews, see Sally Engle Merry, "Legal Pluralism", *Law & Society Review*, 22:5 (1988), pp. 869–896; Brian Z. Tamanaha, "Understanding Legal Pluralism: Past to Present, Local to Global", *Sidney Law Review*, 30 (2007), pp. 375–411; Lauren Benton and Richard J. Ross (eds), *Legal Pluralism and Empires, 1500–1850* (New York, 2013); Thomas Duve (ed.), *Entanglements in Legal History: Conceptual Approaches* (Berlin, 2014). For empirical works on legal pluralism/multi-normativity in contemporary societies, see Franz von Benda-Beckmann, Keebet von Benda-Beckmann, and Julia Eckert (eds), *Rules of Law and Laws of Ruling: On the Governance of Law* (London and New York, 2009); Julia Eckert, Brian Donahoe, Christian Strümpell, and Zerrin Özlem Biner (eds), *Law Against the State: Ethnographic Forays into Law's Transformations* (Cambridge, 2012); Michael A. Helfand (ed.), *Negotiating State and Non-State Law: The Challenge of Global and Local Legal Pluralism* (Cambridge, 2015).

[19]Gareth Austin, "Reciprocal Comparison and African History: Tackling Conceptual Eurocentrism in the Study of Africa's Economic Past", *African Studies Review*, 50:3 (2007), pp. 1–28.

[20]Christian G. De Vito, "Paternalist Punishment: Slaves, Masters and the State in the *Audiencia de Quito* and Ecuador, 1730s–1851", *Journal of Global Slavery*, 7 (2022), pp. 48–72.

of the ways power is exercised, legitimized, and contested at different levels of society.[21]

Meanwhile, scholars of pharaonic Egypt have highlighted that patronage towards the subaltern shaped relationships within the elites. In the context of labourers attached to the pyramid towns of royal funerary estates, some workers were seemingly protected by royal decree, which, under certain circumstances, guaranteed exemptions from local manpower requirements for especially demanding forms of conscription.[22] Another reading is that the royal decrees also served to limit the mobility of temple workers to seek alternative employment in periods of labour shortages or drought,[23] while others fled from overly punitive conditions or unfair tax demands from revenue collectors (who themselves were local notables acting as agents of the temple), only to be tracked, captured, and returned to a holding centre in the temple village.[24] In Middle Kingdom Lahun, the punishment for flight for those who tried to flee ranged from lifelong labour to holding household members hostage to forcing family members to work overdue labour obligations.[25] These questions of how the protection conceded by the temples resulted in conflicts between the temple authorities and the masters and how that affected the control of the workforce can be compared with the social processes by which the indigenous workers subjected to the colonial *mita* took advantage of the existence of competing economic sectors across the Andean region, and could escape the punishments they experienced in a mine, for example, and seek the protection of other employers in a ranch or a textile manufacturer.[26]

Core research questions can also emerge from the close study of primary sources related to one specific context, and can be posed to (sets of) documents belonging to other contexts.[27] For example, the punitive semantics of Spanish colonial sources sometimes features a distinction between the concept of *castigo* – associated with

---

[21]Christopher Eyre, "How Relevant was Personal Status to the Functioning of the Rural Economy in Pharaonic Egypt?", in Bernadette Menu (ed.), *La Dépendance Rurale dans l'antiquité Égyptienne et Proche-Orientale* (Le Caire, 2004), pp. 157–184; Juan Carlos Moreno García, "La Dépendance Rurale en Égypte Ancienne", *Journal of the Economic and Social History of the Orient*, 51:1 (2008), pp. 99–150; Bruce Routledge, *Archaeology and State Theory: Subjects and Objects of Power* (London, 2014); Juan Carlos Moreno García, *The State in Ancient Egypt: Power, Challenges, and Dynamics* (London, 2020), esp. pp. 1–37.

[22]Nigel C. Strudwick, *Texts from the Pyramid Age*, Writings from the Ancient World 16 (Atlanta, GA [etc.], 1995), pp. 97–129.

[23]Eyre, *La Dépendance Rurale*, pp. 157–184.

[24]Christopher Eyre, *The Use of Documents in Pharaonic Egypt* (Oxford, 2013), pp. 71–74.

[25]For instance: P. Berlin 10021, letter, public collection of the Berlin Museum (= Ulrich Luft, *Urkunden zur Chronologie der Späten 12 Dynastie: Briefe aus Illahun* (Vienna, 2006), pp. 44–45; P. UC 32209, letter, public collection of the Petrie Museum of Egyptian Archaeology, University College London (= Mark Collier and Stephen Quirke, *The UCL Lahun Papyri: Letters* (Oxford, 2002), pp. 129–131; P. Brooklyn 35.1446, administrative document, public collection of the Brooklyn Museum (= William C. Hayes, *A Papyrus of the Late Middle Kingdom in the Brooklyn Museum* (New York, NY, 1955), pp. 34–35, 47–52.

[26]Christian G. De Vito, "Las multiples mitas y la coacción laboral, entre el 'sistema toledano' y sus subversiones", in Paola Revilla Orías and Paula Zagalsky (eds), "Mitas coloniales. Ampliando universsos analíticos", *Dialogo Andino*, Special Issue (forthcoming).

[27]This argument expands the logic of Edoardo Grendi's oxymoron, the "exceptional normal": Edoardo Grendi, "Micro-analisi e storia sociale", *Quaderni Storici*, 12:35(2) (1977), pp. 506–520, 512.

state-administered punishment – and *corrección* – connected to punishment administered by the *paterfamilias* to control the behaviour and work of women, children, servants, and slaves in the household. Starting from this, we can interrogate the sources
produced in other (temporally and spatially connected or unrelated) contexts to
understand the relevance of the separation between "private" and "public" punishment therein. Moreover, looking inside the household, we can observe how the
strength of paternalist relations produced a further overlapping of concepts within
the semantic field of punishment. In pharaonic Egypt, for example, the word *sbAyt*
was used to denote some form of "teaching" or "instruction" that had a connotation
of punishment in the ancient Egyptian language.[28] As elsewhere in the ancient world,
the threat of flogging minors undertaking scribal training is found repeated in didactic instructions, which routinely compare its practice to the domestication of cattle
and herds in "private" contexts.[29]

The Analysis of Historical Change

Traditional theories of the connections between punishment and labour, like the ones
mentioned at the beginning of this article, have not only put an exclusive focus on
connections between incarceration and wage labour, but also promoted the double
teleology of the "modernity" of wage labour and the Western penitentiary.
Focusing on selected experiences of the last few centuries of human history, they
have built the master narrative of a historical tendency (and even necessity) towards
the simplification of both labour relations and punitive practices towards wage labour
and incarceration and postulated that the driving force of that simplification was that
of capitalist "modernity". Meanwhile, as we have seen above, structuralist comparisons are built on predefined concepts, taxonomies, and frameworks that standardize
the procedures of data collection and analysis that can overstate the homogeneity of
underlying social processes.

   In our view, configurations of punitive control imposed on workers changed across
space and time in ways that disrupt linear and predefined models of transition. The
picture sketched in this Special Issue is one of multiple concurring punitive practices
that stemmed from various legal sources and targeted distinct groups of workers in
different ways and for distinct goals. It follows that historical change too is a matter
of shifts in configurations of labour relations and punitive practices.[30] A comparative
approach based on asking the type of common questions raised in the opening section of this introduction and allowing the (diverging or similar) answers to reveal the

---

[28]Hans-Werner Fischer-Elfert, "Education", in Donald Redford (ed.), *The Oxford Encyclopaedia of Ancient Egypt, Volume 1* (Oxford and New York, 2001), pp. 438–442, 439.

[29]John T. Fitzgerald, "Proverbs 3:11–12, Hebrews 12:5–6, and the Tradition of Corporal Punishment", in Patrick Gray and Gall R. O'Day (eds), *Scripture and Traditions: Essays on Early Judaism and Christianity in Honor of Carl R. Holladay* (Leiden and Boston, MA, 2008), pp. 291–318. Papyri Sallier I, 8, 1; Lansing 2.6–7, 3.5–10; and Anastasi III, 4.1–2; all in Ricardo A. Caminos, *Late-Egyptian Miscellanies*, Brown Egyptological Studies 1 (London, 1954).

[30]For a similar suggestion of a processual and contextualized perspective, see Johan Heinsen, "Historicizing Extramural Convict Labour: Trajectories and Transitions in Early Modern Europe", *International Review of Social History*, 66:1 (2021), pp. 111–133.

fabric of each social context can highlight how historical change does not follow a predefined pattern but emerges from concrete forms of collaboration, negotiation, and conflict among social actors within and across specific sites.

There was no single transition from slavery to wage labour, or from corporal punishment to incarceration, but rather several transitions from a mix of labour relations to another, and from an articulation of incarceration, corporal punishment, and fines, for example, to another articulation of specific forms of punishment.[31] These complex shifts varied considerably across space, featured divergent temporalities, and did not proceed teleologically. Indeed, new configurations of punishment, labour, and labour management through punishment were shaped at the crossroads of the visions and practices of various and conflicting elite groups and of the multifaceted and contradictory tactics and practices of multiple subaltern groups.

The outcomes of these social negotiations and conflicts were open-ended and unforeseeable.[32] However, using their privilege of looking back at historical social processes, scholars can reconstruct some of the reasons why certain groups and options prevailed or failed. We can ask ourselves why debt or anti-vagrancy policies took different forms, were backed by distinct forms of punishment, and targeted groups that were constructed differently in various periods. We can interrogate ourselves on the historical meaning of the emergence of certain punitive and labour regimes, and of processes of abolition such as those of the *mita* in the Andean region and slavery in the Americas, or the legal extinction of flogging and the death penalty in certain areas and periods. And we can design research projects that investigate whether and which connections existed between the changes in punitive practices and changes in labour management. The articles in this Special Issue of *IRSH* contribute to this challenging and exciting endeavour that lies before us.

The Articles

Although the articles in this Special Issue are organized chronologically, this section will present them in a way that foregrounds their analytical insights and mutual connections. In this way, we wish to strengthen the arguments proposed in the previous sections and underline the need to move beyond linear views of the transitions in labour and punishment. Moreover, we highlight the questions that arise from sets of contributions in this Special Issue, which might speak to scholars in other fields and contribute to the broader debate on the role of punishment in labour management.

The first issue that cuts across several articles regards the forms of control that punitive practices exerted over distinct groups of workers. In particular, the articles by Fagbore, Chevaleyre, Revilla Orías, Heinsen, and Avellino highlight the flexibility of punishment in dealing with different imperatives of management. Addressing

---

[31]This point has been explicitly made for labour in Steinfeld, *Invention of Free Labour*, p. 9.

[32]For a similar argument, see Maurizio Gribaudi, "Scala, pertinenza, configurazione", in Jacques Revel (ed.), *Giochi di scala. La microstoria alla prova dell'esperienza* (Rome, 2006), pp. 121–122; Idem, "Les discontinuités du social. Un modèle configurationnel", in Bernard Lepetit (ed.), *Les forms de l'expèrience. Une autre histoire sociale* (Paris, 2013), pp. 251–294.

pharaonic Egypt, Fagbore points to the issues concerned in the extraction of revenue from peasants who were at the same time independent workers and tributary subjects. In this case, like in other historical contexts where the tributary relation played a key role, the punitive management of the workers did not entail a direct control in the fields by masters and overseers, but rather a control mediated by revenue collectors who were inscribed into the hierarchical structure of a polity (and therefore subjected to control of the higher echelons of that hierarchy). Conversely, the punitive management of labour took an almost intimate dimension in the contexts of the elite households of late Ming and early Qing China, studied by Chevaleyre, and early modern Charcas, addressed by Revilla Orías. In the late imperial Chinese household, one priority in the disciplining and control of the enslaved and hired workers (*nubi* and *gugong*) was that of preventing the bloodline "pollution" that the incorporation of those outsiders threatened to provoke; in sixteenth- through eighteenth-century Charcas, the issue at stake was the control of minors who worked under "guardianship" (*tutela*) and featured a wide range of backgrounds (orphans, captives, and sons and daughters of *mitayos* and *yanaconas*, enslaved African and Afrodescendants). The flexibility of punitive regimes vis-à-vis the complexity of labour management takes yet different forms in the contexts studied by Heinsen and Avellino. Heinsen argues that in eighteenth-century Denmark, corporal and carceral punishments were strategically combined to control a mercenary military workforce that had to be both disciplined and retained in the context of a permanent shortage of military labour. In the case of the Lombard silk workers (1780–1810), the discourses and practices of punishment had to grapple with the ambiguous status of labourers who were legally "free" but had "nothing to lose on the side of things" and were therefore difficult to control through mere economic coercion.

Meanwhile, several articles foreground various aspects of the coexistence and entanglements between individual and collective punishments. For instance, Reid discusses the punishment of slaves in relation to those that targeted dependent workers and even entire communities, with a focus on ancient Mesopotamia during the Ur III period (*c.*2100–2000 BCE). Avellino, Heinsen, and Pearson join Reid in showing the symbolic function of punishment, or the way that punishing even one or a few workers sent out a disciplining message to many others. Avellino writes of the "dissuasive effect of incarceration", the sequestration of the loom shuttles of absent labourers, and plans to use corporal punishments (literally enchaining the workers to the looms) to control not just those individual workers but the whole of the workforce. Heinsen explores the "semiotics of military punishments", and how the seemingly draconian punishments of the mercenary soldiers were calibrated to communicate nuanced messages about honour to the broader society. And, Pearson discusses the deep psychological and social effects of blacklisting on the targeted individuals and their families, and its threatening power as a "soft technique of repression" for the other workers, and especially for militant workers, in the aftermath of the Southwest Railroad Strike of 1886.

The second broad question raised by the articles in this Special Issue concerns the role of punishment in changes in labour management. The theme is especially prominent in the contributions by Loktionov, Lyngholm, and Ferraro, which share an emphasis on the dialectics between legal regimes and social practices vis-à-vis the production of change. From this common basis, the three articles suggest distinct ways to approach the issue. Working at the crossroads of the ancient Near East and the New Kingdom of Egypt, Loktionov foregrounds the circulation of knowledge about punishment as a tool of labour management and as input for changes in practices and legitimation. Meanwhile, Lyngholm situates her article at the height of the abolition of corporal punishment in Denmark (1854) and reveals the ambiguity of legal change in a context where the manipulation of the category "obedience" allowed for a substantial continuity in the coercion of the servants and the corvee labourers. The article by Ferraro on nineteenth-century Brazil offers yet another approach, insisting on the need to embed the study of change in the punitive management of labour both at the level of interactions between enslaved workers, masters, and the state on the coffee plantations and in broader social processes (abolitionism, rising prices of the enslaved, etc.).

The emphasis on the law as a field of conflict and negotiation among various social actors is the third issue that emerges from this Special Issue. It is an important feature in the articles by Avellino, Revilla Orías, Lyngholm, and Ferraro, and is addressed from especially original perspectives in the articles by Rio and Dimmers. Indeed, Rio observes the paradox of the decreasing interest in the punishment of workers in a period of intensified economic exploitation. From this perspective, she digs deep into the shifting discourses and meanings of "punishment" in a wide range of clerical and royal sources across the early Middle Ages in Western Europe (sixth through tenth centuries). In the concluding article of this issue, Dimmers foregrounds the ambiguous position of the convict officers in colonial India: coerced coercers who navigated between the pressures of the convicts and the prison administration when managing the other convict workers, but who were simultaneously the target of control and punishment by the prison administration.

Besides the three themes highlighted so far, striking trans-epochal and transcultural issues can be observed across some of the contributions, which strengthen some of the points presented in this introduction and are worth further exploration in future research. Connecting to our earlier point on "patronage" in ancient Egypt and early modern Spanish America, paternalism as a flexible mode of social control emerges here as a key entry point into the punitive relations among the masters, the polity, and the (free and unfree) workers in the articles on Mesopotamian and Egyptian antiquity (Reid, Fagbore, Loktionov), in Chevaleyre's article on late imperial China, and in the articles that focus on the late eighteenth and nineteenth centuries in distinct yet connected regions like the United States, Brazil, Lombardy, and Denmark (Lyngholm, Avellino, Ferraro). Meanwhile, the importance of debt and anti-vagrancy policies as social and legal processes that connected punishment to acquiring workers as members of the workforce and then the management of that workforce emerges for contexts as far from each other as ancient Mesopotamia and late eighteenth-century Lombardy (Reid and Avellino, respectively). As scholars working on many other contexts (including Lyngholm here) have highlighted, debt arising at the level of individuals, households, and communities (e.g. arrears of tribute) provided private masters and political authorities with a powerful legitimation to force subaltern workers into punitive relations that regularly implied forced labour. In a similar vein, the "assimilation of [...] workers to idlers" – as Avellino puts it in his article –

appears to have been a highly flexible tool of control of the workforce across history, as the economic and political elites could not only regulate the specific modalities of the immobilization of the workforce, but also manipulate the very category of "the vagrant" to target selectively distinct groups of workers in different places and time.

Taken as a whole, the articles included in this Special Issue resonate with the main argument of this introduction; that is, that effective labour management required a systematic differentiation of the workforce, and that punishment offered a flexible range of coercive measures that both created and maintained those distinctions within the workforce. At the same time, the articles provide concrete examples of how, within each context, the specific punitive regimes imposed on the workers depended on, and shifted according to, contingent circumstances and the continuous negotiations and conflicts among the historical actors. Thus, the ranges of punitive and labour regimes were distinct across the various contexts considered here and changed across time within each historical context. From a theoretical and methodological perspective, this means that even when apparently universal social processes – such as paternalism, debt, and anti-vagrancy – can be observed in cross-temporal comparisons as contributing to labour management, we can only grasp their real forms, operations, and meanings by looking deeply into each context. For this reason, in this introduction we have insisted on the importance of taking a processual and contextualized micro-analytical perspective. This allows us to address large historical questions and compare widely across time and space, while also paying due attention to the contextual production of historical processes and change. At this level, as the articles here show, the investigation of the role of punishment in labour management ceases to be exclusively a specialized subfield of research and reveals itself also as an original entry point into a richer and more capacious global social history of work.

Cite this article: Christian G. De Vito and Adam S. Fagbore. Introduction: Punitive Perspectives on Labour Management. *International Review of Social History*, 68:S31 (2023), pp. 1–14. https://doi.org/10.1017/S0020859022000840

International Review of Social History, 68:S31 (2023), pp. 15–32
doi:10.1017/S0020859022000864

RESEARCH ARTICLE

Punishment for the Coercion of Labour during the Ur III Period

J. Nicholas Reid 🆔

Reformed Theological Seminary, Oviedo, Florida, United States, e-mail: jnicholasr@gmail.com

Abstract
This article traces corporal and collective punishment in relation to the labour control of slaves and other dependent persons during the Ur III period (c.2100–2000 BCE). Slaves and other dependent persons often worked in related contexts with some overlap in treatment. Persons of different statuses could be detained and forced to work. Persons of various statuses also received rations and other benefits, but the evidence suggests that the most extreme forms of corporal punishment were reserved for slaves. This article, however, contextualizes these threats of mutilation and the death penalty, demonstrating that such punishments should be considered the exception and not the norm.

Introduction

Physical punishment in relation to labour coercion was likely common for many children, slaves, and other dependent persons. Just before the Third Dynasty of Ur (c.2100–2000 BCE) [hereafter, Ur III], Gudea, ruler of the Second Dynasty of Lagaš (c.2200–2100 BCE), claimed to have ended certain abuses while building a temple for Ningirsu. On one of his dedicatory statues, Gudea says: "No one was beaten by the whip or hit by the goad, a mother did not beat her child."[1] Further, Gudea states: "I had debts remitted and 'washed all hands.' For seven days no grain was ground. The slave woman was equal to her mistress, the slave was allowed to walk side by side with his master."[2] Although the actual implementation of these particular social reforms is not confirmed in other documents, these claims of pious acts relate to ideals dealing with ritual purity for the purpose of temple building.[3] This idyllic social

---

[1] Gudea Statue B, iv: 10–12, Collection of Antiquités Orientales of the Musée du Louvre, Paris = AO 2; RIME 3/1.01.07, St B dark green diorite statue, c.2200–2100 BCE, column iv: 10–12 (= Dietz Otto Edzard, *Royal Inscriptions of Mesopotamia – Early Periods*, III/I: *Gudea and His Dynasty* (Toronto, 1997)). Translation by Edzard. Unless otherwise stated, translations are mine.

[2] Gudea Statue B, vii: 29–30 (AO 2, diorite statue; RIME 3/1.01.07, St B, column vii: 29–33, translation by Edzard, *Gudea and His Dynasty*.

[3] It should be noted that debt releases by kings are well attested in the documentation for the later Old Babylonian period. On the practice of establishing justice in the land and releases, see Dominique Charpin, "Les édits de 'restauration' des rois babyloniens et leur application", in Claude Nicolet (ed.), *Du pouvoir dans L'Antiquité. Mots et réalités*, Hautes études du monde Gréco-Romain (Geneva, 1990), XVI, pp. 13–

picture reflects a practice of negative confessions by kings that is tied to ritual activity and purity ideals.[4] The text could be intended to reflect a social reform that fits in the tradition of earlier reforms, such as the one of Urukagina.[5] But more particular to the focus of this article, the text distinguishes between the negative and positive treatment of labour, envisioning an ideal that included societal harmony rather than physical abuse.

Again, although it is unknown if Gudea's reforms were ever practised, the text shows that there was, at the very least, a contemplative difference between the good treatment of dependent persons of differing statuses and the poor treatment of said persons. As would be expected, much like today, not everyone was treated poorly, and not everyone was treated well. Life was complicated, and the text cited above gives voice to a royal ideal that involved celebrating the proper treatment of dependent persons of all statuses. So, while it is unknown if the practice was implemented, the concept is clearly present in ancient Mesopotamia and indicates that the difference between good treatment and poor treatment of dependents was known. If the difference was known, and positive treatment was celebrated as a pious act, then it is reasonable to conclude that some dependents of various classes were treated well while others were treated poorly.[6] It was not all bad or all good. The everyday realities of life were complicated. Still, some distinctions do appear to emerge in the treatment

---

24; Dominique Charpin, "L'andurārum à Mari", MARI, 6 (1990), pp. 253–270; William W. Hallo, "Slave Release in the Biblical World in Light of a New Text", in Ziony Zevit, Seymour Gitin, and Michael Sokoloff (eds), Solving Riddles and Untying Knots: Biblical, Epigraphic and Semitic Studies in Honor of Jonas C. Greenfield (Winona Lake, IN, 1995), pp. 88–89; Fritz Rudolf Kraus, Königliche Verfügungen in altbabylonischer Zeit (Leiden, 1984). On purity in Mesopotamia, see Walther Sallaberger, "Reinheit A. Mesopotamien", Reallexikon der Assyriologie und Vorderasiatischen Archäologie, 11 (2007), pp. 295–299; Michaël Guichard and Lionel Marti, "Purity in Ancient Mesopotamia: The Paleo-Babylonian and Neo Assyrian Periods", in Christian Frevel and Christophe Nihan (eds), Purity and the Forming of Religious Traditions in the Ancient Mediterranean and Ancient Judaism (Leiden, 2013), pp. 47–113. Note, too, Beate Pongratz-Leisten, "Reflections on the Translatability of the Notion of Holiness", in Mikko Luukko, Saana Svärd, and Raija Mattila (eds), Of God(s), Kings, Trees, and Scholars: Neo-Assyrian and Related Studies in Honour of Simo Parpola, Studia Orientalia 106 (Helsinki, 2009), pp. 409–427, 414, on judicial aspects of purity in Gudea's temple building inscriptions, such as the selection of the location for clay to make the bricks.

[4]For a study of the negative confession in relation to the later New Year Festival, see Beate Pongratz-Leisten, "Das 'negative Sündenbekenntnis' des Königs anläßlich des babylonischen Neujahrsfestes und die kiddinūtu von Babylon", in Jan Assmann, Theo Sundermeier, and Henning Wrogemann (eds), Schuld, Gewissen und Person. Studien zur Geschichte des inneren Menschen, Studien zum Verstehen fremder Religionen 9 (Gütersloh, 1997), pp. 83–101.

[5]See RIME 1.09.09.1, [Reforms of Urukagina], clay cone, c.2500–2340 BCE, Louvre Museum, Paris, France, AO 03278 (= Douglas R. Frayne, Royal Inscriptions of Mesopotamia - Early Periods, I: Presargonic Period (2700–2350) (Toronto, 1998)); Blahoslav Hruška, "Die innere Struktur der Reformtexte Urukaginas von Lagaš", Archiv Orientální, 41 (1973), pp. 104–132; Piotr Steinkeller, "The Reforms of UruKAgina and an Early Sumerian Term for 'Prison'", in Piotr Michalowski, Piotr Steinkeller, Elizabeth Caecilia Stone, and Richard L. Zettler (eds), Velles Paraules: Ancient Near Eastern Studies in Honor of Miguel Civil, Aula Orientalis 9 (Barcelona, 1991), pp. 227–233.

[6]In the "Laws of Ḫammurapi", §§115–116, there is a distinction made between the natural death of a person held as a distraint and one that was because of mistreatment. When a distraint died because of mistreatment, there were penalties that were attached to the death based on the status of the distraint. If the death occurred without beatings or physical abuse, then the creditor was not held liable. While likely not a "law", this demonstrates that, at least on the conceptual level, there was a known distinction between the good treatment and the poor treatment of dependents and workers.

of persons of differing statuses with respect to punishment and threats of punishment for labour coercion during the Ur III period.

In this article, I will discuss the punishment of slaves and other dependent workers during the Ur III period. While the Ur III period is the focus here, various texts from the Old Babylonian period (c.1900–1600 BCE) will also be referenced at points to elaborate upon practices and discuss some of the social changes that occurred.

To avoid the unintended impression that everything was great in Mesopotamia or that everything was terrible and violent, the present article will discuss the positive and negative aspects of the treatment of dependent persons to provide a fuller social picture. While the focus will be on approaches to and threats of punishment that resulted in and facilitated labour coercion, it should be kept in mind that the more extreme forms of punishment were likely exceptions and not the rule. The reasons for this are several. First, of the many surviving texts dating to the Ur III period, attestations to threats of extreme punishment are decidedly limited. Second, households, most of whom likely only possessed a few slaves,[7] did not want to mutilate or kill a slave and, by so doing, hurt the household. A brief discussion below will use texts from the later Old Babylonian period to offer a potential reason why such severe punishment could ever happen. But, in short, mutilating or killing runaway slaves would have been uncommon. Finally, other than accounting, writing was focused primarily on the exceptions and not the norms.[8] So, when extreme details of threats or expressed desires to punish come to the fore in documents, it is likely because the matter was not part of the usual course of life. With these caveats in mind, this paper contends that both slaves and "state" dependents could receive similar treatment, but the threats of the most severe forms of punishment – at least, as far as the record attests – were directed towards slaves. This suggests that slavery was ill-defined, sharing many features with other persons belonging to the lower stratum while also cautioning against flattening the lower stratum altogether. The primary focus of this article, however, is on how punishment was used to coerce labour during the Ur III period.

Ur III Period and Debate About Slavery

Despite only lasting approximately one hundred years, the Ur III period left a remarkable record of nearly 100,000 texts.[9] Most of these texts are administrative, as administrators sought to keep track of and allocate resources. Of particular interest

---

[7]See discussion below.

[8]For helpful discussions about what was written down and what was not, see Marc Van De Mieroop, "Why Did they Write on Clay?", *Beiträge zur Alten Geschichte*, 79 (1997), pp. 7–18; Marc Van De Mieroop, "On Writing a History of the Ancient Near East", *Biblioteca Orientalis*, 54 (1997), pp. 285–305; Piotr Steinkeller, "Toward a Definition of Private Economic Activity in Third Millennium Babylonia", in Robert Rollinger, Christoph Ulf, and Kordula Schnegg (eds), *Commerce and Monetary Systems in the Ancient World: Means of Transmission and Cultural Interaction: Proceedings of the Fifth Annual Symposium of the Assyrian and Babylonian Intellectual Heritage Project, Held in Innsbruck, Austria, October 3rd–8th 2002* (Stuttgart, 2004), pp. 91–111, 95–96.

[9]See Steven J. Garfinkle, "Ur III Administrative Texts: Building Blocks of State Community", in Paul Delnero and Jacob Lauinger (eds), *Texts and Contexts: The Circulation and Transmission of Cuneiform Texts in Social Space* (Boston/Berlin, 2015), pp. 143–165, 145.

here is how those in positions of authority during the Ur III period exerted control over human resources.

Despite the number of texts dealing with this subject, it is important to remember that only some things were written down and that not everything that was written down has been preserved. While texts like the Gudea above suggest that physical punishment could occur across social relationships in relation to labour acquisition and control, the written record indicates that there were some differences that one might observe when considering the punishment and threats of punishment of persons of different social statuses, but also a complex overlap in terms of context and treatment.

Still, determining social status in the Mesopotamian records is complicated. Degrees of functional overlap create challenges when attempting to distinguish between "slaves" and other lower-stratum workers.[10] This problem is exacerbated by the broad semantic range of the terms related to slavery, such as arad/arad$_2$ and geme$_2$, which can refer to slaves or servants.[11] In the field of Assyriology, legal and economic approaches were taken to solve the problem,[12] as well as attempts to focus on treatment when studying the distinguishing features of slavery.[13] While

---

[10]Igor M. Diakonoff, "Slave-Labour vs. Non-Slave Labour: The Problem of Definition", in Marvin A. Powell (ed.), *Labor in the Ancient Near East* (New Haven, CT, 1987), pp. 1–3, 1.

[11]Ignace J. Gelb, "Prisoners of War in Early Mesopotamia", *Journal of Near Eastern Studies*, 32 (1973), pp. 70–98, 76. See more recently Lorenzo Vederame, "Slavery in Third-Millennium Mesopotamia: An Overview of Sources and Studies", *Journal of Global Slavery*, 3 (2018), pp. 13–40, 19–21; Heather D. Baker, "Slavery and Personhood in the Neo-Assyrian Empire", in John P. Bodel and Walter Schneidel (eds), *On Human Bondage: After Slavery and Social Death* (Hoboken, NJ, 2017), pp. 15–30, 24–25. Baker's article deals with the Neo-Assyrian period, but the overall article is relevant for methodology.

[12]See Robert K. Englund's brief critique of the earlier debate, primarily represented by Diakonoff and Gelb: Robert K. Englund, "Hard Work: Where Will It Get You? Labor Management in Ur III Mesopotamia", *Journal of Near Eastern Studies*, 50 (1991), pp. 255–280, 255–256. Englund stated that the paucity of tools available at the time and the subjective nature of much of the discussion hindered the results. More recently, important attempts to revisit the question include for the Middle Babylonian Period: Jonathan S. Tenney, *Life at the Bottom of Babylonian Society: Servile Laborers at Nippur in the 14th and 13th Centuries, B.C.* (Leiden/Boston, MA, 2011); Jonathan S. Tenney, "Babylonian Populations, Servility, and Cuneiform Records", *Journal of the Economic and Social History of the Orient*, 60 (2017), pp. 715–787. See further the proceedings of the Chicago Symposium on slavery: Laura Culbertson (ed.), *Slaves and Households in the Near East: Papers from the Oriental Institute Seminar, Slaves and Households in the Near East, Held at the Oriental Institute of the University of Chicago 5–6 March 2010*, University of Chicago Oriental Institute Seminars 7 (Chicago, IL, 2011). Recent discussions of the terminology related to slavery for the Neo-Assyrian period include Karen Radner, *Die neuassyrischen Privatrechtsurkunden als Quelle für Mensch und Umwelt*, State Archives of Assyria Studies 6 (Helsinki, 1997), pp. 202–248.

[13]Since such a large semantic range exists for the term *wardum* (slave) and other terms relating to slavery (Muhammad A. Dandamaev, *Slavery in Babylonia: From Nabopolassar to Alexander the Great (626–331 BC)*, rev. edn, ed. Marvin A. Powell, trans. Victoria A. Powell (DeKalb, IL, 1984)), several methods have been employed to determine the status of individuals mentioned in the texts of the ancient Near East. Dandamaev, for example, seeks to determine whether a person can be sold or branded in the Neo-Babylonian period. If such is the case, then Dandamaev considers the individual to be a slave (Dandamaev, *Slavery in Babylonia*, pp. 78–79). Gelb argues against Dandamaev's criteria, since Gelb thinks that his own work renders Dandamaev's method insufficient (Ignace J. Gelb, "Quantitative Evaluation of Slavery and Serfdom", in Barry L. Eichler, Jane W. Heimerdinger, and Åke W. Sjöberg (eds), *Kramer Anniversary Volume: Cuneiform Studies in Honor of Samuel Noah Kramer* (Kevelaer, 1976), pp. 195–

the discussion largely came to an impasse, the most recent approaches tend to deal with the question of slavery in the ancient Near East in relation to the legal question of alienability. In Daniel Snell's view, for example, although some slaves were never sold, the potential for sale was the critical feature of slavery.[14] When dealing with the Neo-Assyrian period, Heather Baker takes a "minimalist approach" in search of what she calls "firmer ground when dealing with those slaves whom we know to have been bought and sold in the 'regular' sale contracts".[15] Still, as described by Laura Culbertson:

> A study that isolates slaves for treatment, positing a uniform definition for "slave" while simultaneously neglecting the relationships around them, risks assuming that slavery is an inherent condition that takes a similar shape across time and place without regard for context. Slavery is not in fact definable without reference to relationships within the broader social, economic, and legal concepts that surround it.[16]

Culbertson's edited volume advanced the state of the discussion by considering the household as offering insight into the nature of slavery through relationships. This article looks at the work context to provide insight into the coercion of slaves and other lower-stratum workers. The context of work outside the household is also where so many questions arise since slaves and other lower-stratum persons were worked in a particular context with singular oversight. This study highlights the overlap in treatment and context, suggesting that slavery was not an "inherent condition".

207, 201). Gelb states that members of the semi-free class (whom he calls serfs) were marked or branded, while Dandamaev views such individuals as slaves on that basis. Gelb ("From Freedom to Slavery", in Dietz Otto Edzard (ed.), *Gesellschaftsklassen im Alten Zweistromland und in den angrenzenden Gebieten. XVIII Rencontre Assyriologique internationale* (Munich, 1972), pp. 81–92, 82) explains his own approach as follows: "Because of the difficulties in defining the terms 'slavery' and 'serfdom' based on such criteria as freedom, salability, legal rights, my own approach to the whole question of labor classes is based not on outside form, as reflected in terminology, but on function, as reflected in the utilization of the labor" (p. 87). In one of his earlier writings, Gelb ("The Ancient Mesopotamian Ration System", *Journal of Near Eastern Studies*, 24 (1965), pp. 230–243, 240–241) rejects the use of the term serf based on its medieval feudal connections, preferring to refer to the guruš class. Gelb, however, in his later writings continues to utilize the term. See, for instance, Gelb, "Quantitative Evaluation", pp. 195–207; Ignace J. Gelb, "Definition and Discussion of Slavery and Serfdom", *Ugarit-Forschungen*, 11 (1979), pp. 283–297. Gelb ("From Freedom to Slavery", p. 87) compares "slaves" with "serfs" using twenty "distinctive features". See Diakonoff's (Igor M. Diakonoff, "Slaves, Helots and Serfs in Early Antiquity", *Acta Antiqua Academiae Scientiarum Hungaricae*, 22 (1974), pp. 45–78, 56–63) interaction with Gelb's categories.

[14]Daniel C. Snell, *Life in the Ancient Near East: 3100–332 B.C.E.* (New Haven, CT, 1997), p. 21. More recently, Snell mentioned saleability as a criterion for a "traditional" definition of slavery, after which he discussed and employed to some extent Orlando Patterson's definition of slavery (Orlando Patterson, *Slavery and Social Death: A Comparative Study*, Cambridge, MA, 1982), only to return to the question of saleability for his conclusion (Daniel C. Snell, "Slavery in the Ancient Near East", in Keith Bradley and Paul Cartledge (eds), *The Cambridge World History of Slavery*, I: *The Ancient Mediterranean World* (Cambridge, 2011), pp. 4–21, 4, 20–21).

[15]Baker, "Slavery and Personhood", pp. 24–25. For a legal definition of slavery, see Raymond Westbrook, "Slave and Master in Ancient Near Eastern Law", *Chicago-Kent Law Review*, 70 (1995), pp. 1631–1676, 1634. Raymond Westbrook, "zíz.da/kiššātum", *Wiener Zeitschrift für die Kunde des Morgenlandes*, 86 (1996), pp. 449–459, 458.

[16]Culbertson, "Introduction", in *Slaves and Households*, p. 2.

Slaves could benefit from working outside the household while earning trust and sharing in community projects. Slaves could be set free, often on the death of their owner. But slaves could also suffer consequences for flight. While most of the repercussions looked exactly like those meted out to other lower-stratum workers, more extreme punishment was sometimes threatened.

But a caveat is in order. Punishment for labour coercion cannot provide the fundamental means of isolating slaves in texts, but it does belong to the necessary groundwork for moving towards a greater understanding of slavery in its varied contexts. While the question of slavery cannot be solved in this brief paper, nor is it even attempted, it is worth noting that whenever extreme threats of punishment for labour coercion appear, one of the terms associated with slavery is present in the sources from the Ur III period.

Labour Context

Lorenzo Verderame summarizes the three primary sources of slaves in the Ur III period: prisoners of war, citizens, and unidentified.[17] Not all prisoners of war became slaves, but taking captives served as one source. Citizens could be reduced to forms of slavery through debt or because of crime. Still, the origin of many slaves in the Ur III period remains unpreserved.

It should be noted that it is generally agreed that slavery in ancient Mesopotamia was not a significant source of labour. As early as 1976, Ignace J. Gelb referred to slavery as a negligible part of the population.[18] This general viewpoint has only grown. As justification for a symposium on slavery and subsequent publication of the results, Culbertson states: "The increasing recognition of slavery's negligible role in labor spheres of the Near Eastern societies also prompts new questions about the place, purpose, and experience of slavery in specific Near Eastern contexts."[19] Verderame writes that for the Ur III period: "The few references to slaves in the vast corpus of Neo-Sumerian documents seems to ground Gelb's statement that their number and impact was limited."[20] Verderame, however, helpfully points to some potential exceptions in the evidence.

In one text, the inheritance of a household is divided. The total number of slaves is twenty-six (seventeen males and nine females).[21] More recently, the data from a construction project at Garšana during the Ur III period has led to further questions and reconsiderations among some scholars about the role of slavery and its impact.[22] In particular, the household of Šu-Kabta had approximately 175 "slaves".[23] Considering

---

[17]Verderame, "Slavery in Third-Millennium Mesopotamia", pp. 21–25.

[18]Gelb, "Quantitative Evaluation", pp. 195–207.

[19]Culbertson, "Introduction", p. 1.

[20]Verderame, "Slavery in Third-Millennium Mesopotamia", p. 33.

[21]David I. Owen, "Widows' Rights in the Ur iii Sumer", *Zeitschrift für Assyriologie und Vorderasiatische Archäologie*, 70 (1980), pp. 170–184; Bertrand Lafont, "Les textes judiciaires sumériens", in Francis Joannès (ed.), *Rendre la justice en Mésopotamie. Archives judiciaires du Proche-Orient Ancien (iiie–ier millénaires avant J.-C.)* (Saint-Denis, 2000), pp. 35–68; Manuel Molina, *La ley más Antigua. Textos legales sumerios* (Barcelona, 2000), pp. 49–51, n. 10. Verderame, "Slavery in Third-Millennium Mesopotamia", pp. 33–34.

[22]See Robert McC. Adams, "Slavery and Freedom in the Third Dynasty of Ur: Implications of the Garshana Archives", *Cuneiform Digital Library Journal*, 2 (2010), §4.1.

[23]Adams, "Slavery and Freedom", §4.

this potentially notable exception,[24] it should be recalled that, given the broad semantic range of the term arad, as discussed above, it is unlikely that all of these "slaves of the household" were slaves instead of "servants" or dependents of the household.[25] At least a couple of reasons can be offered for this viewpoint. As Piotr Steinkeller points out, individuals in these texts from Garšana, such as CUSAS 3: 16, 30, and 33, who are described as $arad_2$ e_2-a-me-eš$_2$ (servants of the household) and lu_2-hun-ga$_2$--me-eš$_2$ (hirelings) are summarized in the total as eren$_2$, who are typically considered as non-slave workers dependent upon royal households.[26]

Further, scribal managers, for example, appear among these individuals described as "slaves/servants". Given the semantic range of the terminology, it is more likely that some, if not many, of these persons were dependents rather than "slaves". But even if it could be demonstrated that all these persons were "slaves", the size of this household would represent the exception of a very large and influential household and not the norm, given the limited references to slaves in the existing corpora.

Rather than an economy that consisted primarily of slave labour, Steinkeller argues that most of the labour force entailed persons who "owed services – primary labour – to the king. In exchange for those services, the éren received various benefits from the crown. Most important, the king granted them the *uso fructo* rights to royal land".[27] Numerous individuals who were not slaves worked for royal and institutional administrative bodies in regions under the governor's control.[28] There were certain benefits to be had by working in these contexts.[29] These dependents were moved around and placed under the authority of overseers to complete specific tasks. The overseers were accountable for the distribution of rations and related production.

---

[24]*Ibid.*, §§4.2–4.5.

[25]See discussion in Piotr Steinkeller, "Introduction: Labor in Early States: An Early Mesopotamian Perspective", in *idem* and Michael Hudson (eds), *Labor in the Ancient World*, International Scholars Conference on Ancient Near Eastern Economies 5 (Dresden, 2015), pp. 1–36, 7, n. 12. When considering the eren$_2$, Natalia Koslova (Natalia V. Koslova, "Bezeichnungen der Arbeitskräfte in Umma der Ur III-Zeit", in Steven J. Garfinkle and Justin C. Johnson (eds), *The Growth of an Early State in Mesopotamia: Studies in Ur III Administration* (Madrid, 2008), pp. 149–206) discussed the term dumu-gi$_7$ in Umma, demonstrating the term is largely synonymous with eren$_2$. Such terms have been considered referring to people who are non-slaves (Koslova, "Bezeichnungen der Arbeitskräfte", p. 152), the free (Piotr Steinkeller, "Corvée Labor in Ur III Times", in Steven Garfinkle and Manuel Molina (eds), *From the 21st Century B.C. to the 21st Century A.D.: Proceedings of the International Conference of Sumerian Studies held in Madrid 22–24 July 2010* (Winona Lake, IN, 2013), pp. 347–424, 350), or based on legal texts "a slave who has been freed" for the dumu-gi$_7$ (Raymond Westbrook, "The Sumerian Freedman", in Walther Sallaberger, Konrad Volk, and Annette Zgoll (eds), *Literatur, Politik und Recht in Mesopotamien. Festschrift für Claus Wilcke* (Wiesbaden, 2003), pp. 333–340; Miguel Civil, "The Law Collection of Ur-Namma", in Andrew George (ed.), *Cuneiform Royal Inscriptions and Related Texts in the Schøyen Collection* (Bethesda, MD, 2011), pp. 221–286, 254.

[26]Steinkeller, "Introduction: Labor in Early State", p. 7, n. 12.

[27]Steinkeller, "Corvée Labor in Ur III Times", p. 351.

[28]*Ibid.*, pp. 347–424.

[29]Note, too, Seth F. C. Richardson, "Building Larsa: Labor-Value, Scale and Scope-of-Economy in Ancient Mesopotamia", in Piotr Steinkeller and Michael Hudson (eds), *Labor in the Ancient World*, pp. 237–328; J. Nicholas Reid, "The Birth of the Prison: The Functions of Imprisonment in Early Mesopotamia", *Journal of Ancient Near Eastern History*, 3:2 (2016), pp. 81–115; Vitali Bartash, "Coerced Human Mobility and Elite Social Networks in Early Dynastic Iraq and Iran", *Journal of Ancient Near Eastern History*, 7 (2020), pp. 25–57.

Slaves, prisoners of war, human booty, and other human resources intersected at numerous points while working for the administrative bodies.[30] Once slaves, prisoners of war, and human booty were enveloped into the administrative oversight, they could be worked alongside other persons of different social statuses in the same context and under the same management. This was true of mature adults as well as children.[31] This intersection between workers of different statuses occurred in changing, non-stagnant contexts driven by needs and various factors.

For example, when fighting males went on campaign,[32] the net loss of workers would have increased the need for human resources, with females sometimes filling roles typically performed by males.[33] When successful campaigns brought an influx of prisoners of war under administrative control, the need for labour sources normalized. Further, an influx of human resources resulted in some males being used to fill jobs typically related to females, for example.[34]

The focus of this article is not on prisoners of war and human booty, however. It should also be noted that the origin or status of an individual is only sometimes recorded in administrative documents. Once fully received into administrative control, human booty could be identified as such but could also simply be referred to by name and denoted as a dependent female.[35] As such, the method for identifying a person was more practical than programmatic, depending on the purpose of writing. So, while much is known about the treatment of human resources, many questions remain. With these qualifications, however, specific differences are evident in the record.

Persons of different statuses and origins were often worked in a singular administrative context. Even if differences are observable, there was also a complex overlap across statuses. Both slaves and other dependents received benefits such as barley

---

[30]For the later Old Babylonian period, it should be noted that house-born slaves became a source of labour but were not treated as belonging to the native population. See discussion in J. Nicholas Reid, "The Children of Slaves in Early Mesopotamian Laws and Edicts", *Revue d'Assyriologie*, 111 (2017), pp. 9–23; Kraus, *Königliche Verfügungen*, pp. 280–284. See also Hallo, "Slave Release in the Biblical World", pp. 88–89.

[31]Benjamin Studevent-Hickman, "The Organization of Manual Labor in Ur III Babylonia" (Ph.D., Harvard University, 2006), p. 137, 161ff.

[32]Agnès Garcia-Ventura, "Ur III Biopolitics: Reflections on the Relationship between War and Work Force Management", in Davide Nadali and Jordi Vidal (eds), *The Other Face of the Battle: The Impact of War on Civilians in the Ancient Near East* (Münster, 2014), pp. 7–23, 7–8.

[33]Garcia-Ventura, "Ur III Biopolitics", pp. 7–8.

[34]See discussion of the broken text MVN 13, 242, which includes over 140 male Amorites working as millers during the second year of the reign of Amar-Suen, and HSS 4, 8, which also includes blind males working as millers, in Wolfgang Heimpel, "Blind Workers in the Ur III Texts", *Kaskal: A Journal of History, Environments, and Cultures of the Ancient Near East*, 6 (2009), pp. 43–48, 45. MVN 13, 242, clay tablet, c.2100–2000 BCE, Free Library of Pennsylvania collection, PA, United States, FLP 2029 (= Marcel Sigrist, David Owen, and Gordon Young, *The John Frederick Lewis Collection*, Part II (Rome, 1984)); HSS 4, 8, clay tablet, c.2100–2000 BCE, Harvard Museum of the Ancient Near East, Cambridge, MA, SM 1899.02.034 (= Mary Hussey, *Sumerian Tablets in the Harvard Semitic Museum – Part II: From the Time of the Dynasty of Ur*, Harvard Semitic Studies 4 (Cambridge, MA, 1915)).

[35]Note discussion of the text on BCT 2, 206 in Garcia-Ventura, "Ur III Biopolitics", pp. 15–16. The primary term, geme$_2$, has a semantic range that can refer to a slave but also to any dependent female. BCT 2, 206, clay tablet, c.2100–2000 BCE, Birmingham Museums and Art Gallery, UK, A. 1390_1982 (= Philip Watson, *Catalogue of Cuneiform Tablets in Birmingham City Museum* (Warminster, 1993)).

rations, provisions such as garments,[36] and even opportunities to improve one's life in some senses. Still, those opportunities for advancement for slaves were at the discretion of the master, who held the primary authority over manumission.[37] So, while a slave might be able to earn trust and even gain access to wealth, the hope of freedom was usually restricted by the decision of their master.[38] Even after release, that individual was vulnerable since others might seek to gain access to their labour.[39] By contrast, persons working for the administrative bodies were obligated to fulfil their roles, as seen in the imprisonment of runaways. Still, it is unlikely that there was a permanent requirement to remain working for their administrative group or overseer.[40] While many were returned to their prior role after living under guard, the relatively short periods spent under guard suggest that service to the administrative bodies was not a "life sentence".[41] For some, service to the "state" also meant benefits for their household, where corvée labour and acting as a "merchant" possibly meant gaining access to land, vocations, and commodities.[42]

With punishment, some non-slaves certainly experienced forms of physical abuse, as they would have in households. But the most extreme forms of punishment, such as mutilation and death, do not appear to be attached to the threats of punishment for labour coercion as they were with slaves. So, while physical punishment likely did

---

[36]See J. Nicholas Reid, "Working for Royal Households and Temples at Girsu During the Third Dynasty of Ur: A New Text", in Laura Quick, Ekaterina E. Kozlova, Sonja Noll, and Philip Y. Yoo (eds), *To Gaul, to Greece and Into Noah's Ark: Essays in Honour of Kevin J. Cathcart on the Occasion of His Eightieth Birthday*, Journal of Semitic Studies Supplement 44 (Oxford, 2019), pp. 139–166.

[37]Reid, "Children of Slaves", pp. 9–23.

[38]See discussion in Westbrook, "Slave and Master", pp. 1648–1651. For the Ur III period, Adam Falkenstein, (*Die neusumerischen Gerichtsurkunden. Einleitung und systematische Darstellung* (Munich, 1956), I, pp. 92–95) has compiled court cases that mention manumission. However, it remains questionable whether these proceedings should be viewed as opportunities for manumission or whether these court cases more accurately reflect the possibility that if one was wrongfully enslaved, the individual may be released based on the ruling of the court. Since these proceedings appear to deal with cases that seek to establish if there was a rightful or wrongful enslavement of someone, there does not appear to be any clear principle of manumission that would remove the authority related to ownership from the master to a legal precedent or some other ruling body. Nevertheless, Steinkeller suggests that the text COS 3.134A, the "Manumission of Umanigar", indicates that there was an unrecorded rule that debt-slaves who were the only heir were set free once the head of the household died (see his treatment of COS 3.134A and 3.134B in the "Manumissions" section of William H. Hallo and K. Lawson Younger, Jr. (eds), *The Context of Scripture* (Leiden [etc.], 2002), III, p. 301. It is also possible for freedom or release to be purchased as is shown in CST 541. CST 541, clay tablet, c.2100–2000 BCE, John Rylands Library, University of Manchester, UK, JRL 541 (= Thomas Fish, *Catalogue of Sumerian Tablets in the John Rylands Library* (Manchester, 1932)).

[39]See the case of Warad-Bunene in CT 6, pl. 29 from the later Old Babylonian Period, for example. Warad-Bunene was recently manumitted. He wanted to perform the *ilku*-service of his father's household and tried to avoid conscription into military service. It seems that once people had their slave mark removed, likely a distinctive hairstyle, their status would have been checked and there was the potential that they would be pressed into service. See Theophilus G. Pinches, *Cuneiform Texts from Babylonian Tablets in the British Museum* (London, 1898), VI).

[40]Note, for example, Steinkeller's discussion of periods of required service relating to 100 days in the record. Steinkeller, "Corvée Labor in Ur III Times", p. 366.

[41]Most stays in "prison" were relatively short term. For a discussion of the lengths of stay as well as explanations for longer term examples, see J. Nicholas Reid, *Prisons in Ancient Mesopotamia: Confinement and Control until the First Fall of Babylon* (Oxford, 2022), pp. 141–150.

[42]See discussion in Steinkeller, "Corvée Labor in Ur III Times", pp. 347–424.

occur, and death and sickness are well attested in relation to workers utilized by the administrative bodies, slaves are the only persons who appear in texts that threaten more severe forms of punishment for labour coercion. While these examples of extreme punishment were likely limited and uncommon, the instances that do appear are only attached to labour coercion when the terminology related to slaves is present.

The following section will discuss the punishment of slaves and contextualize these threats of punishment with other texts. Next, dependents who worked in some capacity for the administrative bodies will be discussed. Finally, examples of punishment for labour coercion that extend beyond the individual offender are considered.

Slaves

A variety of punishments are attested concerning the control of slaves. Extreme physical punishment, such as the death penalty or mutilation, could happen to anyone found guilty of a "crime". With respect to labour coercion, however, the most severe examples of corporal punishment are attested in relation to slaves. For example, the death penalty is the most extreme form of punishment threatened against runaway slaves. In one text, a captured slave was forced to take the following oath in the name of the king: "On the day I flee a second time, may I be destroyed."[43] In another text, a slave takes the oath: "On the day I flee, let it be a (capital) crime."[44] While it might appear to be counterproductive to threaten slaves with the death penalty, as it would result in a loss for the owner, the death penalty was an exemplary punishment.

Not all runaways faced the death penalty as corporal punishment. In one text, a slave of the palace ran away for three years.[45] In response, the slave was to have his nose cut as punishment. This would have been painful and humiliating, and the consequences of his flight would have been a visible mark on his body, which would have likely made it more difficult to blend in should another flight attempt be made. It should be noted that this text is not an idealized threat of punishment. Rather, it was a consequence of flight recorded in an administrative document, indicating that mutilation did sometimes occur and was not just threatened.

---

[43]NRVN 1, 1, clay tablet, Ist Ni 737, Arkeoloji Müzeleri, Istanbul, Turkey (= Muazzez İlmiye Çığ and Hatice Kızılyay, *Neusumerische Rechts- und Verwaltungsurkunden aus Nippur* (Ankara, 1965), I). See further editions: Lafont, "Les textes judiciaires sumériens", pp. 35–68, n. 19; Manuel Molina and Marcus Such-Gutiérrez, "On Terms for Cutting Plants and Noses in Ancient Sumer", *Journal of Near Eastern Studies*, 63:1 (2004), pp. 1–16, 8; J. Nicholas Reid, "Runaways and Fugitive-Catchers during the Third Dynasty of Ur", *Journal of the Economic and Social History of the Orient*, 58 (2015), pp. 576–605, 590, n. 37.

[44]BE 3/1, 1, clay tablet, University of Pennsylvania Museum of Archaeology and Anthropology, Philadelphia, Pennsylvania, United States, CBS 11176 (= David W. Myhrman, *Babylonian Expedition of the University of Pennsylvania, III/I: Sumerian Administrative Documents Dated in the Reigns of the Second Dynasty of Ur from the Temple Archives of Nippur* (Philadelphia, PA, 1910)). On the nature of the šer₇-da as a capital crime, see Miguel Civil, "On Mesopotamian Jails and Their Lady Warden", in Mark E. Cohen, Daniel C. Snell, and David B. Weisberg (eds), *The Tablet and the Scroll: Near Eastern Studies in Honor of William W. Hallo* (Bethesda, MD, 1993), pp. 72–78, 76–78. *Contra* Pascal Attinger, "L'Hymne à Nungal", in Walther Sallaberger, Konrad Volk, and Annette Zgoll (eds), *Literatur, Politik und Recht in Mesopotamien. Festschrift für Claus Wilcke* (Wiesbaden, 2003), pp. 15–34, 27. See discussion in Reid, "Runaways and Fugitive-Catchers", p. 591.

[45]See Molina and Such-Gutiérrez, "On Terms for Cutting", p. 3. See further Reid, "Runaways and Fugitive-Catchers", p. 590.

This evidence attests to differences in punishment practices for labour coercion during the Ur III period. While, as will be seen below, detention is attested in relation to runaway workers in the Ur III period, the more extreme forms of corporal punishment, such as mutilation and the threat of the death penalty, are not attested in cases of the labour coercion of dependent workers. But why would a master ever contemplate hurting or killing their slave who was considered their personal property? Texts from the later Old Babylonian period could provide some insight.

The death penalty is attested in the record from Old Babylonian Mari as an exemplary punishment. One text mentions a servant who ran away with two females. The person who caught the runaway gouged out his eyes and requested permission "to kill this man, let him be impaled so people learn from his example".[46] The text demonstrates that the king had authority over the death penalty,[47] which, in this case, was thought of as an exemplary punishment to dissuade others from running away with human resources. In another text more closely tied to punishment for labour coercion, a letter writer grows frustrated with his inability to gather a group of nomads to be dispatched on a mission. He states that he has waited five days at the prearranged place and that he has written to the towns where they are pasturing their flock. As motivation, he writes: "If within three days they do not gather – and if my lord agrees – a criminal should be killed in jail. His head cut off, it should be paraded among these towns, as far as Ḫutnum and Appan, so that the frightened troops will quickly gather."[48] In this case, the death penalty was a way to motivate troops to gather and be sent on an urgent mission. As such, this writer sought to utilize the death penalty to coerce.

These Old Babylonian texts from Mari dealing with the death penalty are not normative. Since they are written seeking permission to apply the death penalty, it demonstrates that this approach was far from the rule and considered more exceptional. Perhaps these texts help contextualize the more extreme examples of threats of punishment directed towards runaway slaves in the earlier Ur III period. First, the use of oaths to threaten extreme punishment could indicate that the slave owner desired a documented reason for carrying out the penalty should it be needed. Further, the oath adds solemnity to the threat, which indicates both the non-normative nature of such penalties and that the owner would not have wanted to lose his slave. Otherwise, the efforts to pursue and capture and the further

---

[46]See RA 91, 110, clay tablet, Mari Excavation, A.1945 (= Sophie Démare-Lafont, "Un 'Cas royal' à l'époque de Mari", *Revue d'Assyriologie et d'Archéologie Orientale*, 91:2 (1997), pp. 109–119). Translated by Jack M. Sasson, *From the Mari Archives: An Anthology of Old Babylonian Letters* (Winona Lake, IN, 2015), p. 227.

[47]See further, the "Laws of Ešnunna" § 48 states that "a capital case is only for the king". Translation by Martha T. Roth, *Law Collections from Mesopotamia and Asia Minor*, 2nd edn, Society of Biblical Literature Writings from the Ancient World Series (Atlanta, GA, 1997), p. 66. See Raymond Westbrook, "Old Babylonian Period", in *idem* (ed.), *A History of Ancient Near Eastern Law* (Leiden, 2003), pp. 361–430, 366. Further, see the Old Babylonian Mari text, RA 91, 110 (= Démare-Lafont, "Un 'Cas royal'", p. 110). See also Daniel C. Snell, *Flight and Freedom in the Ancient Near East* (Leiden, 2001), p. 57, cited below, which indicates that the death penalty had to be approved by the king for it to be carried out.

[48]Archives royales de Mari [ARM] 2, 48, clay tablet, Mari Excavation (= Jean-Marie Durand, *Les Documents épistolaires du palais de Mari*, II, Littératures anciennes du Proche-Orient [hereafter, LAPO] 17 (Paris, 1998), p. 559). Translation by Sasson, *From the Mari Archives*, p. 226.

opportunity to avoid applying the death penalty do not make sense.[49] In short, it seems that threats of mutilation or the death penalty were extreme, exceptional cases that only seem to make sense as instances of exemplary punishment that sought to deter others from running away. The non-normative nature of these texts is evidenced in other texts, as well, which deal with the capture of runaway slaves.

In one letter, Fs Sigrist 127–128, 1, a man named Nanatum pursues and captures a slave who ran away on more than one occasion.[50] Nanatum apparently caught the runaway slave and returned him to his owner, but the slave ran away again. Nanatum found the slave a second time, who was by this time the slave of another individual. Nanatum purchased the slave from the prior owner to sell the slave to the person who had possession of the slave after the second flight. In this instance, Nanatum was utilized on more than one occasion to capture a slave. Although it is conceivable that the slave was punished in some way, it did not rise to the level of death and likely not mutilation. At the very least, any punishment relating to the first incident did not prevent the slave from fleeing a second time.

In a text from Umma, Fs Sigrist 131, 4, a slave ran away from military service after the death of his owner.[51] The slave was discovered in the town of Anšan (modern-day Tall-i Malyan in the Fars province). A man named Gudea, not to be confused with the king from the earlier period referenced above, was able to identify the slave and take an oath as confirmation. The son of the deceased owner of the slave paid Gudea ten shekels of silver and returned the slave to his military service. The return price was steep, especially in comparison to the average cost of slaves in the Ur III period, typically between five or six shekels of silver for females and, on average, ten shekels of silver for males.[52] In part, the compensation recorded in Fs Sigrist 131, 4 is probably related to the distance to Anšan. More to the point of this paper, since the slave was forced into bowman service after flight, severe physical punishment was not likely implemented and was certainly not recorded in the present text. In short, most runaway slaves did not receive death penalties, and likely were not mutilated, but the potentiality is documented in the above examples, unlike with the treatment of dependent workers.

If the more extreme forms of punishment did not occur regularly, what likely happened when slaves ran away? While captured runaways probably experienced some form of corporal punishment that did not rise to the level of mutilation or the death penalty, it is certain that most runaways were guarded or restrained in some manner while being coerced to work. At Garšana, workers appear to have been housed in locked barracks in certain contexts relating to work projects.[53] This practice

---

[49]See Reid, "Runaways and Fugitive-Catchers", pp. 582–587.

[50]Fs Sigrist 127–128, 1, clay tablet, British Museum, BM 106439 (= Manuel Molina, "New Ur III Court Records Concerning Slavery", in Piotr Michalowski (ed.), "On the Third Dynasty of Ur: Studies in Honor of Marcel Sigrist", *Journal of Cuneiform Studies*, Supplemental Series 1 (2008), pp. 125–143).

[51]Fs Sigrist 131, 4, clay tablet, BM 110379 (= Molina, "New Ur III Court Records").

[52]Piotr Steinkeller, *Sale Documents of the Ur-III-Period* (Stuttgart, 1989), p. 138. Compare the return price above to the two shekels mentioned as a return price in "Laws of Ur-Namma", §16. This "law collection" does not likely include actual laws. On the nature of the law collections of ancient Mesopotamia, see bibliography and discussion in Reid, "Children of Slaves", p. 9, n. 3.

[53]See the situation at Garšana in Wolfgang Heimpel, *Workers and Construction Work at Garšana* (Bethesda, MD, 2009), pp. 60–63, 163–165.

could be related to the status of those workers since many who ran away in that context were also called "slaves/servants of the palace".[54] In short, slaves and other lower-stratum workers were detained during the Ur III period to force them to work.

Dependent Workers

In this period, one consequence of flight from labour assignments was detention. Classic definitions of prisons primarily concern detention as a means of punishment.[55] In Mesopotamia, if detention was ever used as punishment in a strictly legal sense, it was rare and not well-attested.[56] Rather, imprisonment was a multifunctional practice typically related to the judicial process and labour coercion.[57] While imprisoned, labour coercion occurred in a more restrictive context and would have been undesirable since imprisonment is consistently presented as a negative experience.[58]

An example of imprisonment relating to work coercion can be found in the case of Lugal-niĝlagare, who was working as a potter.[59] This individual appears in another text as a runaway in prison, this time called Niĝlagare. In a third text, Lugal-niĝlagare appears again as a potter with his previous crew in the administration.[60] The imprisonment of runaway workers demonstrates one of the coercive options utilized to control the labour of even specialized workers such as a potter.

Detention could be used to control workers who ran away or were considered a flight risk. And while the practice does not necessarily qualify as punishment, in a strictly legal sense relating to crime, the act of detention would have been undesirable and a negative consequence. By detaining and coercing workers who sought to run away, the workforce was compelled to accept the work assignments given to them and any concomitant conditions since the process of flight and likely capture would only result in worse conditions with continued service to be rendered. As seen below, a collective punishment directed at family members adds to the coercive approach.

---

[54]Note the runaways many of whom are described as slaves of the palace at Iri-Saĝrig (conveniently summarized in Heimpel, *Workers and Construction Work*, pp. 62–63); see discussion above.

[55]Norval Morris and David J. Rothman, "Introduction", in *idem* (eds), *The Oxford History of the Prison: The Practice of Punishment in Western Society* (New York/Oxford, 1998), pp. vii–xiv, ix. See discussion in Reid "Birth of the Prison".

[56]Reid, *Prisons in Ancient Mesopotamia*. See also Bertrand Lafont and Raymond Westbrook, "Mesopotamia: Neo-Sumerian Period (Ur III)", in Raymond Westbrook (ed.), *History of Ancient Near Eastern Law*, pp. 183–226, 221; Hans Neumann and Susanne Paulus, "Strafe (im Strafrecht) A", *Reallexikon der Assyriologie und Vorderasiatischen Archäologie*, 13 (2011), pp. 197–203, 201.

[57]Reid, *Prisons in Ancient Mesopotamia*.

[58]*Ibid.*, pp. 126–151.

[59]On the case of this potter, see Jacob L. Dahl, "A Babylonian Gang of Potters: Reconsidering the Social Organization of Crafts Production in the Late Third Millennium BC Southern Mesopotamia", in Leonid E. Kogan, Sergey Loesov, and Serguei Tishchenko (eds), *City Administration in the Ancient Near East: Proceedings of the 53e Rencontre Assyriologique Internationale* (Winona Lake, IN, 2010), pp. 275–305, 286. See further discussion in Reid, "Runaways and Fugitive-Catchers", pp. 596–597; Reid, "Birth of the Prison", p. 94.

[60]Other runaways also appear living under guard in various texts. See discussion in Reid, "Runaways and Fugitive-Catchers", pp. 592–597; Reid, "Birth of the Prison", pp. 90–96.

The pursuit of administrative workers was not a dominant practice in ancient Mesopotamia. While the flight of workers from most administrative contexts appears to have been permissible in the Old Babylonian period, unlike the Ur III period,[61] corporal confinement to coerce labour, however, is attested in the cases of the *bīt asīrī* at Uruk and the *nēparum* of the Mari. Detention in such houses was not like modern prisons used for punishment; these were workhouses that detained human resources.[62] Still, one letter mentions disposing of someone in the workhouse to never hear from them again.[63] The writer mentions the provision of rations of bread and oil. Although the end of the text is broken, the context indicates that, whether the prisoner lives or dies, he is not to be heard from again.[64]

In sources dating to the Ur III period, the most extreme threats of physical punishment appear where terminology related to slaves occurs, and then only as exceptionally rare instances. Mutilation and the death penalty would not have been desirable means to coerce labour since such actions resulted in the loss or damage of human property. Corporal confinement does not appear to have been used in a punitive sense; still, detention was consistently considered an unpleasant experience in the record and was one way in which labour was coerced and controlled in early Mesopotamia. While forms of confinement for coercion existed as preventive measures for slaves, since any overseer working a person belonging to another would be responsible for ensuring that they did not flee, runaways living in prison appeared to have been primarily lower-stratum workers working in administrative contexts.[65] The use of imprisonment in labour contexts seems to have been used more expansively during the Ur III period than in the Old Babylonian period. For the former, the administrative bodies and controlling entities used detention to coerce labour

---

[61]Johannes Renger (in "Flucht als soziales Problem in der altbabylonischen Gesellschaft", in Edzard, *Gesellschaftsklassen im Alten Zweistromland*, pp. 167–182) argues that by the Old Babylonian period, non-slave workers were able to leave their position without pursuit. For the Middle Babylonian evidence, see Jonathan S. Tenney, *Life at the Bottom of Babylonian Society: Servile Laborers at Nippur in the 14th and 13th Centuries, B.C.* (Leiden/Boston, MA, 2011), pp. 93–133.

[62]Marie-France Scouflaire, "Quelques cas de détentions abusives à l'époque du royaume de Mari", *Akkadica*, 53 (1987), pp. 25–35; Marie-France Scouflaire, "Premières réflexions sur l'organisation des 'prisons' dans le royaume de Mari", in Marc Lebeau and Philippe Talon (eds), *Reflets des deux fleuves. Volume de mélanges offerts à Andreé Finet* (Leuven, 1989), pp. 157–160; Reid, *Prisons in Ancient Mesopotamia*.

[63]Another text seeks to dispose of a person in related fashion. The partial logic behind some decisions to condemn a person or persons to indefinite grinding in the workhouse can be accessed in part in this text from Mari. In ARM 14, 78 (see next footnote), the sender is concerned about what to do with three nomads. He frets that if they are sold to a distant people to keep them from ever returning to their land, they could subsequently be sold again to anyone. The sender proposes a different solution that will maintain control over the nomads. He says that they should be mutilated, either by eye gouging or tongue cutting, and condemned to grinding. In this way, the workhouse was being used to dispose of a person in a more secure manner, while also coercing labour. See ARM 1, 57, clay tablet, Mari Excavation (= Jean-Marie Durand, *Les Documents épistolaires du palais de Mari*, III, LAPO 18 (Paris, 2000), p. 1076). See translation in Sasson, *From the Mari Archives*, p. 228 [text 4.6.c.i]).

[64]See ARM 14, 78, clay tablet, Mari Excavation (= Maurice Birot, *Lettres de Yaqqim-Addu, gouverneur de Sagarâtum*, Archives royales de Mari 14 (Paris, 1974); Durand, *Les Documents épistolaires* III, p. 929). See translation in Sasson, *From the Mari Archives*, pp. 226–227.

[65]See Table 1 with over 100 texts from the Ur III period in Reid, *Prisons in Ancient Mesopotamia*, pp. 46–50, and discussion of terminology related to "prisons" at pp. 37–64. It is concluded that most prisoners were lower stratum workers coerced in labour contexts.

from a variety of persons, while the later Old Babylonian examples appear tied more closely to prisoners of war, slaves, and what we would call criminals (in the context of modern judicial processes). While lower-stratum workers in the Ur III period do not appear to have been free to leave their work assignments for the administrative bodies, there were benefits to working for the "state". They and their households gained access to provisions and, in some cases, land and other benefits that required taxes and services to be rendered in return. Perhaps the larger familial and household benefits of working for the "state" provide insight into why collective punishment for labour coercion could extend beyond the individual worker.

Collective Punishment to Coerce Labour

Punishment was not always restricted to the individual offender and could also have collective implications. Of course, corporal and collective punishments were not exclusive. These could intersect in a single context and arise from a singular event. There were a variety of ways in which a household or responsible party could face negative consequences for the actions of another.

Collective labour coercion can be seen through the accounting practices of the Ur III period. Accounts could end up with a surplus (diri) but often resulted in a deficit (la$_2$-ia$_3$ and si-i$_3$-tum) owed to the "state".[66] While these debts were often allowed to accumulate without any discernible consequence, at least in the preserved record, the overseer lived with the possibility of debt repayment being required by the palace. In such instances, the overseer could be imprisoned for being in debt.[67] Further, there are instances in which outstanding debts were collected from the household.[68] For example, lines obverse 1 to reverse 8 of MVN 10, 155, note the following:[69]

142 litres of clarified butter, 180 litres of kašk cheese, the year, "Simurum was destroyed for the third time"; deficit of UrKAnara, the cattle herder.

---

[66]The "merchant" accounts in the Ur III period have been studied in detail by, among others, Daniel C. Snell, *Ledgers and Prices: Early Mesopotamian Merchant Accounts* (New Haven, CT, 1982); Piotr Steinkeller, "The Organisation of Crafts in Third Millennium Babylonia: The Case of the Potters", *Altorientalische Forschungen*, 23 (1996), pp. 232–253; Robert K. Englund, "Administrative Timekeeping in Ancient Mesopotamia", *Journal of the Economic and Social History of the Orient*, 31 (1988), pp. 121–185; Robert K. Englund, *Organisation und Verwaltung der Ur III-Fischerei* (Berlin, 1990); Jacob L. Dahl, "The Ruling Family of Ur III Umma: A Prosopographical Analysis of a Provincial Elite Family in Southern Iraq ca. 2100–2000 BC" (Ph.D., University of California Los Angeles, 2003); Dahl, "A Babylonian Gang of Potters"; Steven J. Garfinkle, "Was the Ur III State Bureaucratic? Patrimonialism and Bureaucracy in the Ur III Period", in *idem* and Johnson, *Growth of an Early State*, pp. 55–61; Steven J. Garfinkle, "What Work Did the Damgars Do?: Towards a Definition of Ur III Labour", in Kogan *et al.*, *City Administration in the Ancient Near East*, pp. 307–316; Steven J. Garfinkle, *Entrepreneurs and Enterprise in Early Mesopotamia: A Study of Three Archives from the Third Dynasty of Ur*, Cornell University Studies in Assyriology and Sumerology (CUSAS) 22 (Bethesda, MD, 2012); J. Nicholas Reid, "Cuneiform Tablets of the University of Mississippi Museum", *Akkadica*, 138 (2017), pp. 153–180.

[67]See discussion in Reid, "Birth of the Prison", pp. 91–93.

[68]See Dahl, "The Ruling Family of Ur III Umma", p. 39.

[69]MVN 10, 155, clay tablet, c.2100–2000 BCE, Bibliothèque de Versailles, Versailles, France, BV 20 (= Jean Pierre Grégoire, *Inscriptions et archives administratives cunéiformes*, Part I (Rome, 1981)). See also Englund, *Organisation und Verwaltung*, pp. 42–48; Englund, "Hard Work", p. 268.

UrKAnara died; Baba, his child, Ba'aba ..., Er-..., Agati, Zala'a, female slaves, as estate instead of the deficit, of the deliveries their deficit is removed (from his account).

This is an example of a deficit owed by a cattle herder. Since he has died owing a debt, his entire household is seized.

In another example, members of the native population are seized and forced to work in the stead of family members who have fled. Lines 4 to 16 of HLC 374, plate 141, reverse column 1 state:[70]

Geme-Nungal, full output (worker receiving) 30 litres instead of Lu-Ninšubur, her husband, who ran away. Baba-Ninam, full output (worker receiving) 30 litres instead of Nig-Baba, her brother, who ran away. Nin-inimgina, full output (worker receiving) 30 litres instead of Lugal-x, her brother, who ran away. Geme-Agimu, full output (worker receiving) 30 litres instead of Ur-Ebabbar, her husband, who ran away. Geme-eškuga, full output (worker receiving) 30 litres instead of Elak-s'uqir, her husband, who ran away. Work taken from the tablet(?) Wives of runaway workers (erin₂). To the millers. Reverse column 2, line 6: [x x] and males and females who have been seized [with weapons].[71]

In this instance, female relatives are seized to replace runaway husbands and brothers.[72] There is no indication that these runaways were slaves. Instead, they appear to be state dependents obligated to perform work. While, according to the records for this period, runaways would have been likely pursued,[73] the practice of

---

[70]HLC 374, pl. 141, clay tablet, c.2100–2000 BCE, provenance Girsu (mod. Tello), dated Šulgi Year 48 Month 5 Day 15, Oriental Institute, University of Chicago, IL, OIM A32029 (= George A. Barton, *Haverford Library Collection of Cuneiform Tablets or Documents from the Temple Archives of Telloh*, Part III (Philadelphia, PA, 1914)); see also K. Maekawa, "Ur III Girsu Records of Labor Forces in the British Museum (I)", *Acta Sumerologica*, 20 (1998), pp. 63–110, 86; Reid, "Runaways and Fugitive-Catchers", pp. 597–598.

[71]HLC 374, pl. 141. Maekawa, "Ur III Girsu Records, p. 86: reverse column 1, lines 4–16: 1(aš) 3(ban₂) geme₂-^{d}nun-gal / mu lu₂-^{d}nin-šubur dam-ni ba-zaḫ₃-še₃ / 1(aš) 3(ban₂) ^{d}ba-ba₆-nin-am₃ / mu nig₂-^{d}ba-ba₆ šeš-a-ni ba-zaḫ₃-še₃ / 1(aš) 3(ban₂) nin-inim-gi-na mu lugal-x dam-ni ba-zaḫ₃-še₃ / 1(aš) 3(ban₂) geme₂-^{d}a-gi-mu₂ / mu ur-e₂-babbar₂ dam-ni ba-zaḫ₃-še₃ / 1(aš) 3(ban₂) geme₂-eš₃-ku₃-ga / mu e-la-ak-šu-qir dam-ni ba-zaḫ₃-še₃ / a₂ im-ta / 1 line blank / dam erin₂ zaḫ₃-me / uš-bar-še₃ / [blank space] / column 2, line 6: [...] u₃ geme₂ guruš geš-e dab₅-ba-me. a₂ im-ta appears to be a *hapax legomenon* for the published Ur III record. Maekawa (at p. 86) proposes the reconstruction of ḫe₂-dab₅, which he interprets to mean "newcomers". This reconstruction and interpretation are reasonable since the tablet deals with people entering the workforce and those who have been seized because of their familial relationship to runaways. The reading "seized with weapons" is a reconstruction based on a related text. A similar text with a similar context (CT 10, pl. 24; see next footnote) suggests we can emend the text here from u₃ geme₂ guruš geš-e dab₅-ba-me ("and males and females who have been seized") to u₃ geme₂ guruš geš-tukal-e dab₅-ba-me ("and males and females who have been seized with weapons").

[72]Note related texts such as CT 10, pl. 24, clay tablet, c.2100–2000 BCE, British Museum, London, UK, BM 014313 (= Leonard W. King, *Cuneiform Texts from Babylonian Tablets in the British Museum* (London, 1900)) and BE 3/1, 1, clay tablet, c.2100–2000 BCE, University of Pennsylvania Museum of Archaeology and Anthropology, Philadelphia, Pennsylvania, United States, CBS 11176 (= Myhrman, *Babylonian Expedition* III/I).

[73]See discussion in Reid, "Runaways and Fugitive-Catchers".

seizing relatives would have served as an additional coercive measure to make workers report for work rather than attempting flight. Further, in the absence of these runaway male relatives, the negative consequences were directed towards their female relatives.

Collective punishments for labour control serve as powerful motivators. When one's family members could be seized because of flight or outstanding debt, this would serve as a motivating factor towards adopting approved actions and behaviour. It could also serve as a deterrent that extends beyond any negative personal consequences one might face.

Conclusion

There were benefits and threats attached to being involved in labour projects during the Ur III period. Working for the "state" provided access to rations and clothing.[74] Even when forced to work on "state" and community projects, much of the work performed related to meaningful community projects such as irrigation. Moreover, performing work for the temple might have had some positive benefits, at least notionally. Others working for the "state" were given opportunities to gain access to resources that could lead to personal advancement. So, while many often seemed to run a negative balance, the opportunity to benefit from the relationship as an "agent of the state" was present. As for slaves, they could be entrusted with business for their master and hope that faithful service could result in release, often with the death of the owner.

Although slave and non-slave workers in Mesopotamia were likely subjected to various forms of corporal punishment relating to labour coercion in all periods, the record indicates that differences were present in the punishment of slaves and other lower-stratum workers. It seems that while physical abuse likely occurred for persons of different statuses, the more extreme threats of physical punishment such as the death penalty or mutilation appear reserved for "criminals", prisoners of war (for mobility control and labour creation),[75] and slaves (for labour coercion).

---

[74]Richardson, "Building Larsa". For evidence of slaves having positions of influence and wealth for the later period in Mesopotamia, see Dandamaev's discussion of the slave Dayān-bēl-uṣur, of whom Dandamaev ("The Economic and Legal Character of the Slaves' Peculium in the Neo-Babylonian and Achaemenid Periods", in Edzard, *Gesellschaftsklassen im Alten Zweistromland*, pp. 35–39, 39) writes: "He was one of those slaves who possessed houses and were influential persons, usurers on a large scale, who lent out money and produce to freemen and to other slaves. Despite his wealth and influence, however, Dayān-bēl-uṣur was completely dependent upon the whim of his master, and in the course of 48 years he, together with his family, was six times sold or bestowed as a gift or put up as security for a debt." For the Ur III period, see Hans Neumann, "Slavery in Private Households Toward the End of the Third Millennium B.C.", in Culbertson, *Slaves and Households*, pp. 21–32, 24–26, and for the Garšana evidence: Heimpel, *Workers and Construction Work*, pp. 45–122. Further, in later periods, slaves could train as apprentices (see Heather Baker, "Degrees of Freedom: Slavery in Mid-First Millennium BC Babylonia", in "The Archaeology of Slavery", Special Issue, *World Archaeology*, 33:1 (2001), pp. 18–26).

[75]On the blinding of prisoners of war in early Mesopotamia, see Piotr Steinkeller, "An Archaic 'Prisoner Plaque' From Kiš", *Revue d'assyriologie et d'archéologie orientale*, 107 (2013), pp. 131–157, see 143–144, n. 38; Heimpel, "Blind Workers in the Ur III Texts", pp. 43–44; Jerrold S. Cooper, "Blind Workmen, Weaving Women and Prostitutes in Third Millennium Babylonia", *Cuneiform Digital Library Notes*, 5 (2010).

Although the difference between mutilation for mobility control and mutilation for labour control is fine, it is worth highlighting. Yet, as argued above, even these more extreme examples of punishment were the exception and not the norm. Most slaves were simply returned to their positions and detained.

In conclusion, slavery seems to have made up a limited portion of the labour force needed to maintain and perform the various projects of the Ur III period. Slaves were worked alongside persons of different statuses who owed service to and were dependent upon the "state". While outliers in treatment are attested, the most common response to flight appears to have been detention. State officials used existing structures, such as overseers and guards, to detain and coerce labour. Detention provided one of the means by which fluctuating labour needs were addressed by maintaining a more stable pool of human resources.

The study of punishment, as such, provides insight into the labour coercion of persons of different statuses, both in how their lives intersected and how they sometimes diverged. An area for future research will be to consider how overseers of individual and discreet projects during particular periods acquired and maintained access to the human resources necessary to meet changing labour needs, as well as how the terminology related to slaves might be elaborated upon and understood on a case-by-case basis.

Cite this article: J. Nicholas Reid. Punishment for the Coercion of Labour during the Ur III Period. *International Review of Social History*, 68:S31 (2023), pp. 15–32. https://doi.org/10.1017/S0020859022000864

International Review of Social History, 68:S31 (2023), pp. 33–52
doi:10.1017/S0020859022000852

RESEARCH ARTICLE

Regulating Labour through Foreign Punishment? Codification and Sanction at Work in New Kingdom Egypt

Alexandre A. Loktionov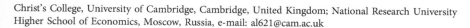

Christ's College, University of Cambridge, Cambridge, United Kingdom; National Research University Higher School of Economics, Moscow, Russia, e-mail: al621@cam.ac.uk

Abstract

This paper investigates two New Kingdom Egyptian texts pertaining to labour regulation: the Karnak Decree of Horemheb and the Nauri Decree of Seti I. They focus on combating the unauthorized diverting of manpower and represent the oldest Egyptian texts (fourteenth–thirteenth century BCE) explicitly concerned with the legal dimension of managing the workforce. After a brief historical overview, the paper outlines each text's key content and stylistic features. It shows that while some of these are likely native to Egypt, others may have been imported from Mesopotamia. More specifically, it appears that the sentence structure is native Egyptian, but the sanctions deployed are likely of foreign origin, aligning more closely to the contemporary punitive tradition of Mesopotamia. This is probably no coincidence, given the close contact between Egypt and the broader Near East at that time. This uptake of foreign ideas may have achieved more efficient labour regulation by enforcing stricter rules for non-compliance while simultaneously maintaining a veneer of Egyptian authenticity in line with official state ideology.

Introduction

This paper looks at two texts of the Egyptian New Kingdom (c.1550–1069 BCE, Figure 1),[1] both concerned with questions of good government and, more specifically, labour regulation, including combating the unauthorized diverting of manpower and resources from state-sanctioned projects. These texts are two royal decree stelae: the Karnak Decree of Horemheb (c.1323–1295 BCE)[2] and the Nauri Decree of Seti I

---

[1] Throughout this paper, dates follow the chronology in Ian Shaw (ed.), *The Oxford History of Ancient Egypt* (Oxford, 2000), pp. 479–483.

[2] For the original edition and commentary in French, see Jean-Marie Kruchten, *Le Décret d'Horemheb. Traduction, commentaire épigraphique, philologique et institutionnel* (Brussels, 1981). For a more recent English translation, see William J. Murnane, *Texts from the Amarna Period in Egypt* (Atlanta, GA, 1995), pp. 235–240. Note that the inscribed date of the text has not survived, so it could have been written at any time in Horemheb's reign, although a relatively early promulgation coinciding with a new accession seems likely.

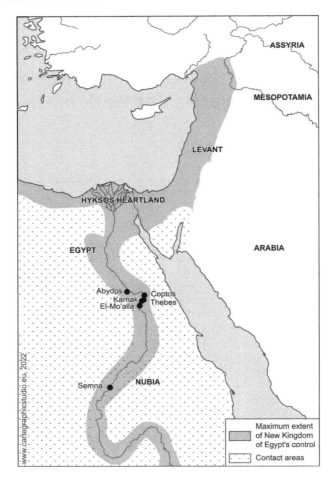

Figure 1. Map showing all ancient Egyptian sites mentioned in the text.

(c.1290 BCE),[3] which together represent the oldest Egyptian texts explicitly concerned with the legal dimension of managing the workforce. After providing a summary of the historical context, this paper will outline each text's key content and stylistic features before investigating their possible origins. As will be demonstrated, the predominant sentence structure in each text has Egyptian precursors of

---

[3]For the original edition, with photographs, transcription, and a drawing of the stela, see Francis Llewellyn Griffith, "The Abydos Decree of Seti I at Nauri", *Journal of Egyptian Archaeology*, 13 (1927), pp. 193–208. A more recent hieroglyphic transcription is available in Kenneth A. Kitchen, *Ramesside Inscriptions: Historical and Biographical* (Oxford, 1975), I, pp. 45–58, with accompanying translation in Kenneth A. Kitchen, *Ramesside Inscriptions Translated and Annotated* (Wallasey, 2017), I, pp. 29–37. For an alternative translation and legal commentary, see William F. Edgerton, "The Nauri Decree of Seti I: A Translation and Analysis of the Legal Portion", *Journal of Near Eastern Studies*, 6 (1947), pp. 219–230. The text has an inscribed date in year four of Seti I, which would place it in 1290 BCE according to the chronology in Shaw, *Oxford History of Ancient Egypt*.

significantly greater age. The same cannot be said of the sanctions specified in the content. Instead, these align more closely with the contemporary punitive tradition of Mesopotamia, and such an alignment is unlikely to be coincidental given the close contact between Egypt and the broader Near East at that time. Hence, it will be shown that the texts imbue a native Egyptian structure – reflecting a broader underlying intellectual tradition – with meanings and regulations imported from elsewhere. In turn, this was likely central to their purpose of achieving more efficient labour regulation by enforcing stricter rules for non-compliance while simultaneously maintaining a veneer of Egyptian authenticity in line with official state ideology.

Historical Context: Socio-Political Turbulence Against a Backdrop of Imperial Expansion

The four decades preceding the reigns of Horemheb and his successor, Seti I, were characterized by political, religious, and dynastic tumult. The upheavals began with Egypt witnessing the abolition of its traditional pantheon under the rule of Akhenaten (r. 1352–1336 BCE), who introduced an exclusive focus on worshipping the sun disc instead and also saw the royal court relocated to a new capital city built at vast expense on a previously uninhabited desert site.[4] This new religion and capital both promptly collapsed during the subsequent reign of Tutankhamun (r. 1336–1327 BCE), who was throughout his reign a child king suffering from severe ill health and physical deformities, and whose pharaonic power was almost certainly wielded by others on his behalf.[5] Furthermore, he died childless, with the throne passing to an elderly royal advisor, Ay (r. 1327–1323 BCE). Ay himself was unable to secure the succession for his designated heir, Nakhtmin, and was instead succeeded by another leading courtier, Horemheb (r. 1323–1295 BCE), with whom Ay had endured a fractious relationship.[6] Under Horemheb's rule, the Egyptian government again altered its course, with Akhenaten, Tutankhamun, and Ay denounced as heretical for not breaking with the past in sufficiently radical fashion. To complicate matters further, all this political instability appears to have been exacerbated by malaria and plague outbreaks,[7]

---

[4]The literature on Akhenaten and his reign is extensive. See for instance Nicholas Reeves, *Akhenaten: Egypt's False Prophet* (London, 2001); Dimitri Laboury, *Akhénaton* (Paris, 2010); Barry J. Kemp, *The City of Akhenaten and Nefertiti* (London, 2012).

[5]For more on the restoration of Egypt's traditional religion, see David P. Silverman, Jennifer H. Wegner, and Josef W. Wegner, *Akhenaten and Tutankhamun: Revolution and Restoration* (Philadelphia, PA, 2006); Aidan Dodson, *Amarna Sunset: Nefertiti, Tutankhamun, Ay, Horemheb and the Egyptian Counter-Reformation* (Cairo, 2018). For a recent detailed study of key events and policies under Tutankhamun, see Marianne Eaton-Krauss, *The Unknown Tutankhamun* (London, 2015).

[6]For a study of the struggle between Ay and Horemheb, see Nozomu Kawai, "Ay versus Horemheb: The Political Situation in the Late Eighteenth Dynasty Revisited", *Journal of Egyptian History*, 3 (2010), pp. 261–292.

[7]For more on diseases at this time, see Eva Panagiotakopulu, "Pharaonic Egypt and the Origins of Plague", *Journal of Biogeography*, 31 (2004), pp. 269–275; Lisa Sabbahy, "Did Akhenaten's Founding of Akhetaten Cause a Malaria Epidemic?", *Journal of the American Research Center in Egypt*, 56 (2021), pp. 175–179.

as well as famine.[8] All of this would almost certainly have negatively impacted the prestige of successive Egyptian kings, who faced an acute crisis of legitimacy.

At the same time, while individual kings struggled to assert themselves, Egypt as a polity was arguably "wealthier and more powerful than it had ever been before".[9] Despite the internal chaos, the country was nearing its maximum territorial extent, comprising both a military and trading empire stretching from various vassal states in the Levant to south Sudan.[10] This presented rulers with both a challenge and an opportunity: on the one hand, internecine strife had made the monarchy weak; on the other hand, a king who could successfully restore stability and royal power had the prospect of ruling over what was at the time one of the world's largest and wealthiest states, while also complying with Egypt's long-standing ideological trope of a new monarch restoring order.[11] Effective regulation of labour and control of the workforce would inevitably have to be part of this.

Karnak Decree of Horemheb

The Karnak Decree of Horemheb is the older of the two texts addressed here and was found carved on a large stela at the Karnak temple complex in Thebes, Upper Egypt. After the upheavals described above, the reign of Horemheb represented a return to relative political and religious stability.[12] Thus, it is likely that – especially given his lack of royal descent and difficult relationship with the previous pharaoh, Ay – one of Horemheb's most pressing priorities upon acceding to the throne was to reassert the primacy of his royal authority. The Karnak decree was, therefore, most probably designed to shore up the legitimacy of both the royal office as an institution and of Horemheb specifically as its rightful holder.[13]

The decree text provides a symbolic affirmation of the pharaoh's commitment to maintaining order in Egypt while also laying down practical rules for how this was to be done. It begins with a relatively short preamble describing how Horemheb possesses divine favour, and how he will use his royal status to establish justice in the land. This is followed by the main decree, consisting of provisions condemning

---

[8]For more on poor nutrition during this period, see for instance Jerome C. Rose and Melissa Zabecki, "The Commoners of Tell el-Amarna", in Salima Ikram and Aidan Dodson (eds), *Beyond the Horizon: Studies in Egyptian Art, Archaeology and History in Honour of Barry Kemp* (Cairo, 2010), pp. 408–422; Gretchen R. Dabbs, Jerome C. Rose, and Melissa Zabecki, "The Bioarchaeology of Akhetaten: Unexpected Results from a Capital City", in Salima Ikram, Jessica Kaiser, and Roxie Walker (eds), *Egyptian Bioarchaeology: Humans, Animals and the Environment* (Leiden, 2015), pp. 31–40.

[9]Jacobus van Dijk, "The Amarna Period and the Later New Kingdom", in Shaw, *Oxford History of Ancient Egypt*, pp. 272–313.

[10]For more on the extensive territorial claims of imperial Egypt at this time, see most recently Ellen Morris, *Ancient Egyptian Imperialism* (Hoboken, NJ, 2018), pp. 117–252.

[11]Texts praising kings for establishing order by various means, including defeating enemies, launching building works, and resolving disputes, are prevalent across all phases of Egyptian history. For a representative range of New Kingdom examples and further references, see Miriam Lichtheim, *Ancient Egyptian Literature, Volume II: The New Kingdom* (Berkeley, CA, 2006), pp. 41–86.

[12]For a biography of Horemheb, see Charlotte Booth, *Horemheb: The Forgotten Pharaoh* (Stroud, 2009).

[13]For more detailed discussion of the nature and purpose of the decree, see Andrea Gnirs, "Haremhab. Ein Staatsreformator? Neue Betrachtungen zum Haremhab-Dekret", *Studien zur Altägyptischen Kultur*, 16 (1989), pp. 83–110.

a range of illegal practices perpetrated by royal officials abusing their power. Offences include seizing boats and wood belonging to private individuals (i.e. non-state property), seizing labourers working on private projects, seizing animal skins from the rural population, demanding unjustifiably high tax payments, and taking grain, fruit, vegetables, and linen from private estates. A key concern of the text is thus the protection of private wealth and property, and one form of such wealth is privately owned labour. The following passage illustrates the nature of the labour concerns raised in the decree:[14]

n3 n sḏm.(w)-ꜥš iṯ p3 ḥm t3 ḥm.t n nmḥy mtw n3 n sḏm.(w)-ꜥš h3b.w m wp.wt r
t3 kṯ ḥr hrw-6 hrw-7 iw bw rḫ.tw šm.t m-di=sn m wsṯn r-nty ḥn pw n h3w p3y m
rdi ir.tw m-mit.t grw

The attendants[15] grab the male and female servant(s) of the private party, and the attendants send them on assignments (*wp.wt*)[16] to gather saffron for six days or seven days, without them having permission to go freely. Thus, this is a matter of excess. Do not allow such action anymore.

Judging from content earlier in the decree, it is apparent that the "attendants" in question are state officials who have – at least in Horemheb's eyes – become overmighty and are threatening to strip the non-state sector of the Egyptian economy of its labour capacity. The provision of the decree, therefore, effectively amounts to a regulation of conscription. To counter the apparent threat of non-state actors carrying out such conscription for labour projects, the text decrees that these offenders should be dealt with as follows:[17]

ir sḏm.(w) nb n ꜥt ḥnkt pr-ꜥ3 ꜥnḫ.(w) wḏ3.(w) snb.(w) nty iw.tw r sḏm r-ḏd st ḥr
kfꜥ r t3 kṯ grw ḥnꜥ nty ky ii.t r smi r-ḏd iṯ.(w) p3y=i ḥm t3y=i ḥm.t in=f ir.tw hp
r=f m sw3 fnḏ=f di.w r T3rw ḥnꜥ šd.(t) p3 b3k n p3 ḥm t3 ḥm.t m hrw nb irr=f
m-di=f

As for every attendant of the chamber of offerings of Pharaoh (l. p. h.)[18] about whom one will hear that they are requisitioning (people) to gather saffron, moreover with somebody coming to report: "my male servant and/or my female servant have been seized by him", the *hp*-law[19] will be enforced against him in

---

[14]Kruchten, *Le Décret d'Horemheb*, p. 58 (ll. 21–22), p. 60 (E–H). This and all subsequent translations into English are mine.

[15]This refers to *sḏm.(w)-ꜥš* – officials in state service, as opposed to private parties (*nmḥy*). The accusation seems to be of abuse of (originally legitimate) power.

[16]For the full range of meanings associated with this term, see Adolf Erman and Hermann Grapow, *Wörterbuch der Ägyptischen Sprache* (Berlin, 1926), I, pp. 302–304. Based on context, a generic translation of "assignment" seems most appropriate here.

[17]Kruchten, *Le Décret d'Horemheb*, p. 58 (ll. 22–23), pp. 60–61.

[18]Conventional blessing formula after mention of the pharaoh: "may he live, prosper, and be healthy".

[19]In contexts such as these, *hp*-law appears to denote legal provision of a tightly codified nature. For the most recent discussion of the topic, see Alexandre A. Loktionov, "The First 'Lawyers'? Judicial Offices, Administration and Legal Pluralism in Ancient Egypt, c.2500–1800BCE", in Edward Cavanagh (ed.),

severing his nose, deporting him to Tjaru,[20] and confiscating the (fruits of) the work done by the male servant and/or female servant on every day that he worked for him.

The decree also deals with a series of related offences that are not strictly concerned with regulating the provision of manpower but do directly address the abuse of state-sanctioned authority and the misappropriation of resources associated with the labour regime. For instance, in the section on the extortion of animal skins, the following provision is made:[21]

ir ꜥnḫ nb n mšꜥ ntw iw.tw r sḏm r-ḏd sw ḥr šm.t ḥr nḥm dḥr.w grw š3ꜥ m p3 hrw ir.tw ḥp r=f m ḥw.(t)=f m sḫ-100 wbn.w-sd-5 ḥnꜥ šd.(t) p3 dḥr it.n=f m-di=f m-t3.w

As for any soldier about whom one will hear that he is still coming to seize animal skins up to this day, the *ḥp*-law will be enforced against him in striking him with 100 stick blows and five open wounds, and confiscating the animal skin which he seized for himself through theft.

The final part of the text is a self-laudatory royal narrative reinforcing the themes set out in the introduction, wherein Horemheb recapitulates how he established justice in Egypt, appointed fair officials to judge cases, mercilessly crushed corruption, and ultimately caused the land to flourish. The king pledges to maintain good order and rule in accordance with the established custom in the future and sets out various ceremonial and administrative duties, which he intends to assign to his subordinates. The text ends with an affirmation of the king's divinity, likening his radiance to that of the sun and stressing the importance of his instructions being followed. The individual judicial provisions of the decree are therefore shown to effectively be a case study demonstrating the wide-ranging justice dispensed by the king – and labour regulation is part of that precept.

Nauri Decree of Seti I

Seti I promulgated his decree, carved into a monumental clifftop stela at the site of Nauri in Egyptian-occupied Nubia (Figure 2), perhaps only two decades after the Horemheb decree and almost certainly at a time when the release of the earlier text was still in living memory. The circumstances of his accession were also not dissimilar: while, unlike Horemheb, Seti I was the son of a king, his father,

---

Empire and Legal Thought: Ideas and Institutions from Antiquity to Modernity (Leiden and Boston, MA, 2020), pp. 36–68, 50–53. Specific periodic contexts of *ḥp*-law are also discussed in depth in Charles F. Nims, "The Term *ḥp*, 'Law, Right' in Demotic", *Journal of Near Eastern Studies*, 7 (1948), pp. 243–260; Adeline Bats, "La loi-*ḥp* dans la pensée et la société du Moyen Empire", *Nehet*, 1 (2014), pp. 95–113.

[20] A fortress on Egypt's north-eastern border in the Levant, representing banishment to the very edge of the country. For the latest research on this site, see El Aguizy, "The *Khetem* of Tjaru: New Evidence", *Nehet*, 6 (2018), pp. 1–7.

[21] Kruchten, *Le Décret d'Horemheb*, p. 80 (l. 27), p. 83 (O–P).

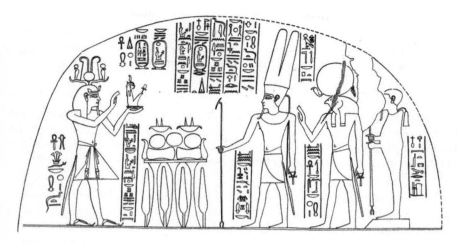

Figure 2. Upper register of the Nauri decree stela, depicting Seti I offering to the gods an effigy symbolizing justice.

Ramesses I, had enjoyed an exceptionally brief reign of only one year and was not of royal blood. Therefore, Horemheb's concerns about royal legitimacy probably applied, to some extent, to Seti I's motives, too, even if he was inheriting a country after a period of rather more stable government compared to the environment that Horemheb had faced. Even so, given its overall temporal proximity to the Horemheb text, it is perhaps unsurprising that the Nauri decree is generally similar in content to the Horemheb decree, with the difference that it relates specifically to actions in and around the king's temple foundation (termed "Menmaatre, heart content in Abydos"). Like the Horemheb text, the Nauri decree begins with a preamble – this time of somewhat greater length – emphasizing the credentials of the king as the defender of the realm and pious servant of the gods. In particular, it stresses how these good qualities are brought out through the king's devotion to the temple he has constructed at Abydos. The text then moves to the main body of the decree, condemning a wide variety of practices, including the seizing of labourers working on the royal temple estate for unrelated purposes, the arbitrary detaining of boats, tampering with fields of the royal temple estate, seizing cattle and other animals belonging to the estate, and unspecified wrongful conduct against hunters, fishermen, and tenants of the estate.

Its concerns about people – or, more specifically, workers with duties on the estate – being unfairly forced into unrelated labour are phrased in a similar way to the Horemheb decree. For instance, among the stated aims of the decree is:[22]

r tm rdi.t it3.tw rmṯ nb n pr pn m kf ͨ.w m w n w m bryt m bḥw n sk3 m bḥw n
ͨw3y in s3-nsw nb ḥry-pḏ.t nb ḥ3.ty- ͨ nb rwḏ.w nb rmṯ nb h3b.w m wp.t r K3š

---

[22]Kitchen, *Ramesside Inscriptions*, p. 51 (ll. 5–8).

To prevent any person of this estate being taken as a captive from district to district, by obligatory service (*bryt*)[23] or by forced labour (*bḥw*)[24] of ploughing, or by forced labour (*bḥw*) of reaping by any King's Son (i.e. viceroy), any troop-commander, any count, any agent or any person sent on an assignment (*wp.t*) to Kush.

When describing specific offences and punishments relating to illegal appropriation of labour, the Nauri decree goes into more detail than the Horemheb decree. The main block of text about this is as follows, characterized by lengthy clauses and a high degree of specificity in setting out the punishments due:[25]

ir^{SIC} s3-nsw n K3š nb ḥry-pḏ.t nb ḥ3.ty-ᶜ nb rwḏ.w nb rmṯ nb nty iw=f r iṯ3 rmṯ nb n t3 ḥw.t Mn-M3ᶜ.t-Rᶜ ib hr.w m 3bḏt m kfᶜ.w m w n w m bryt m bḥw n sk3 m bḥw n ᶜw3y m m-mit.t p3 nty iw=f r iṯ3 s.(t)-ḥm.t nb n rmṯ nb n t3 ḥw.t Mn-M3ᶜ.t-Rᶜ ib hr.w m 3bḏt m-mit.t n3y=sn ḥm.w m kfᶜ.w r ir.t wp.t nb nty m t3 r ḏr=f m-mit.t kḏn nb ḥry-iḥ.w nb rmṯ nb n pr-nsw h3b.(w) m wp.t nb n pr-ᶜ3 ᶜnḥ.(w) wḏ3.(w) snb.(w) nty iw=f r iṯ3 rmṯ nb n t3 ḥw.t Mn-M3ᶜ.t-Rᶜ ib hr.w m 3bḏt m w n w m bryt m bḥw n sk3 m bḥw n ᶜw3y m-mit.t r ir.t wp.t nb ir.tw ḥp r=f m ḥw.t=f m sḫ-200 wbn.w-sd-5 ḥnᶜ šd.(t) b3k.w n p3 rmṯ n t3 ḥw.t Mn-M3ᶜ.t-Rᶜ ib hr.w m 3bḏt m-ᶜ=f m hrw nb nty iw=f r ir.(t)=f m-ᶜ=f dd.(w) r t3 ḥw.t Mn-M3ᶜ.t-Rᶜ ib hr.w m 3bḏt

As for any King's Son (i.e. viceroy), any troop-commander, any count, any agent or any person who will take any person of the Foundation[26] as a captive from district to district by obligatory service (*bryt*) or by forced labour (*bḥw*) of ploughing, or by forced labour (*bḥw*) of reaping, likewise the one who will take any wife of any person of the Foundation, and likewise their dependents, as captives to do any assignment (*wp.t*) which is in the entire land, and likewise any charioteer, any overseer of herds, or any person of the royal estate sent on any assignment (*wp.t*) of Pharaoh (l. p. h) who will take any person of the Foundation from district to district by obligatory service (*bryt*) or by forced labour (*bḥw*) of ploughing, or by forced labour (*bḥw*) of reaping, and likewise to do any assignment (*wp.t*), the *ḥp*-law shall be done (i.e. enforced) against him by beating him with 200 blows and five inflicted wounds, together with confiscating the (fruits of) the work of the people of the Foundation, from him with regards to every day which he will spend with him, it being given to the Foundation.

---

[23]For this word, see Erman and Grapow, *Wörterbuch der Ägyptischen Sprache*, p. 30. It is very rare and appears to denote obligatory service of some form, but attestations are too few to provide a more specific definition.

[24]For this word, see Erman and Grapow, *Wörterbuch der Ägyptischen Sprache*, p. 468. Much like *bryt*, its rarity means that, beyond a general connection to forced labour, a specific definition is impossible. It is near certain that *bḥw* and *bryt* differed, but it is unclear how.

[25]Kitchen, *Ramesside Inscriptions*, pp. 52 (l. 13)–53 (1.10).

[26]In the original text, the name of the foundation is invariably written in full: "Menmaatre, heart content in Abydos".

Other punishments prescribed in the decree include severing the ears and nose, impalement, and compulsory labour for both convicts and their families.[27] While not all of these are strictly related to violations related to the provision of human labour, all are in some way associated with resource management or the logistics thereof, and are thus directly related to the work environment. At the end of the decree, just as with the Horemheb text, there is a short epilogue stressing that the royal instructions provided earlier reflect the divine will and that they, therefore, evince the responsible nature of the king's rule.

Overall, the Horemheb and Nauri decrees are very similar, both in style and content. Stylistically, both have a tripartite structure, with the main body of the text – the decree proper, including the discussion of labour regulation – illustrating the justice, wisdom, and divine favour of the monarch, which is extolled explicitly in the prologue and re-emphasized by the ring composition achieved through these same themes being highlighted once more at the end. In terms of content, they share both a common set of behaviours, which they seek to curtail, namely, abuses in and around labour misappropriation, and similar sets of punishments marked by a violent, highly physical nature – although the later decree is more detailed and seemingly more brutal in its provisions.

Differences can also be observed with regard to the type of labour being regulated: in the Horemheb text, emphasis is placed on curbing abuse of authority by royal officials appropriating private labour and the fruits thereof, while the Nauri text protects labour that is itself tied to a royal foundation, although the offenders are still royal officials. Given the slightly later date of the Nauri text, one might speculate that the shift in focus towards specifically protecting royal labour is linked to the crown having, by that point, accrued additional estates and resources that previously did not need protecting because they were not there. Horemheb inherited a crown weakened by decades of political chaos, and it would have been logical for him to rely on private labour as part of his rebuilding mission. Seti I may not have had to rely on the private sector as much, as he would have benefited from the relative stability of what had come before him. Nonetheless, such a hypothesis must not be overstated: first, the comparison is imperfect since neither text is perfectly preserved, with the Horemheb decree, in particular, missing many fragments, and second, the existing labour management differences might be down to the specific functions of the individual decrees rather than any broader socio-economic phenomenon: the function of the Nauri text was to protect a particular royal foundation and its workers, whereas the Horemheb text was more concerned with remedying labour management ills at large. The fact that these texts had different goals might suggest a change in the situation, but it cannot prove it. On the other hand, the similarities between the texts, as revealed by their common structure, the offences targeted, and the punishments deployed, cannot be subjected to similar doubt. Nor can the promulgation of such decrees so close to one another chronologically be convincingly attributed to coincidence, especially bearing in mind that no comparable text of labour regulation had ever been produced before.

---

[27]Edgerton, "The Nauri Decree of Seti I", pp. 221–227.

Precursors: How Did These Forms of Labour Management Come About?

The Horemheb and Nauri decrees can be considered among the oldest records of tightly defined legislation relating to labour management in ancient Egypt. However, while they are certainly innovative – and, indeed, unique – in this regard, they contain numerous traits that are also evident in earlier documents. Of great significance here is the grammatical structure employed in setting out the legal provisions in the decrees: it is the protasis-apodosis conditional sentence, wherein the execution of the punishment laid out in the second clause (the apodosis) is dependent on the offence specified in the first clause (the protasis) on both a broader conceptual and a narrower syntactic level. Thus, the two texts are related not only in law but also in grammar.

The roots of the protasis-apodosis formulation can be traced to as early as the Old Kingdom, over an entire millennium earlier. We already see something stylistically and conceptually similar in a decree on a stela of King Neferirkare (r. 2475–2455 BCE), although – as will be discussed – the level of detail and legal sophistication provided is not quite comparable. The text, which is unfortunately not fully preserved, gives instructions about how certain classes of delinquent are to be treated, and its shorter clauses make the individual provisions easy to break down into their constituent protasis-apodosis components:[28]

ìr s nb n š.t ìt.ty=fy ḥm.w-ntr nb nty.w ḥr 3ḥ.t ntrì w‘b.t=sn ḥr=s m š.t tw r r3-‘.wy ḥn‘ k3.t nb.t n.t š.t m3‘=k sw r ḥw.t-wr.t dì r k3.t... m3t sk3 ìt bd.t

As for any man of the district who will take any *ḥm-ntr*-priests who are upon the sacred land upon which religious service is conducted in this district for corvée labour (*r3-‘.wy*) together with any work of the district,	Protasis: offenders/offences committed
you shall lead him to the great enclosure (*ḥw.t-wr.t*) and put (him) to work [...] granite and harvesting barley and emmer.	Apodosis: envisaged sanction

ìr s nb n š.t ìt.ty=fy mr.t nt.t ḥr 3ḥ.t ntrì n.t š.t r r3-‘.wy ḥn‘ k3.t nb.t n.t š.t m3‘=k sw r ḥw.t-wr.t dì r k3.t...m3t sk3 ìt bd.t

As for any man of the district who will take *mr.t*-people [tenants?] who are upon the sacred land of the district for corvée labour (*r3-‘.wy*) together with any work of the district,	Protasis: offenders/offences

---

[28]Hratch Papazian, *Domain of Pharaoh: The Structure and Components of the Economy of Old Kingdom Egypt* (Hildesheim, 2012), p. 130. Modifications highlighting the protasis-apodosis clauses have been added by the present writer. For a study of the full decree, see Hans Goedicke, *Königliche Dokumente aus dem Alten Reich* (Wiesbaden, 1967), pp. 22–36, while a convenient English translation is available in Nigel C. Strudwick, *Texts from the Pyramid Age* (Atlanta, GA, 2005), pp. 98–101. A transcription can be found in Kurt Sethe, *Urkunden des Alten Reichs* (Leipzig, 1933), I, pp. 170–172.

you shall lead him to the great enclosure
(*ḥw.t-wr.t*) and put [him] to work [...]
granite and harvesting barley and emmer.

Apodosis:
envisaged sanction

The Neferirkare text, while perhaps the most explicitly connected to labour management, appears to have been part of a broader tradition of Old Kingdom rulers issuing decrees of this sort, intending to set out punitive consequences for various offenders operating on royal estates. Other examples, all dating to the twenty-third and twenty-second centuries BCE, include the Edicts of Pepi II (Coptos B), Neferkauhor (Coptos I), and Demedjibtawy (Coptos R).[29] However, in these much older attestations, the legal framework associated with the New Kingdom stelae has yet to develop. Instead of alluding to a concrete concept of *ḥp*-law as justification for punishment, the Neferirkare text and other decrees in its tradition make far more generic claims, such as that seizing parts of the workforce has consequences for the perpetrator, who is himself reduced to unfree labour. Instead of being framed as legislation – a set of provisions governed by law – these Old Kingdom clauses are royal instructions, probably not part of any wider corpus and designed for ad hoc use but nonetheless serving as important reminders of the significance of labour regulation even at this early time. It is, however, noteworthy that the New Kingdom decrees prescribe harsh corporal punishments alongside forced labour – providing a level of detail comprehensive enough to count individual blows and wounds – whereas the Old Kingdom text makes no mention of corporal punishments whatsoever and may indicate a more flexible approach to determining sanctions, which would be in keeping with an ad hoc style. On the other hand, the structure characteristic of the New Kingdom decrees is already fully formed, with clauses beginning with the same conditional construction (beginning with the introductory *ir*).

It should also be emphasized that while the Old Kingdom decrees are comparatively rare examples of early protasis-apodosis texts that discuss labour regulation in some form, more generally, the protasis-apodosis style of formulation was common across multiple avenues of Egyptian thought. Prominent examples of its use are found in threats to potential tomb desecrators, as illustrated, for instance, in the tomb of the prominent local governor Ankhtifi at El-Mo'alla, dating to the First Intermediate Period (c.2100 BCE):[30]

ir ḥḳꜣ nb ḥḳꜣ.t(y)=f(y) m Ḥfꜣt ir.t(y)=fy ꜥ ḏw bin r di tn r mn.w nb.w n.w pr pn sḫ.t ḥpš=f n Ḥmn

As for any ruler who will rule in Mo'alla and who will carry out a bad and evil

[29]Goedicke, *Königliche Dokumente*, pp. 87–116, 172–177, 214–225. For convenient English translations, see Strudwick, *Texts from the Pyramid Age*, pp. 107–109, 117–118, 123–124. Transcriptions of the Edicts of Pepi II and Demedjibtawy are available in Sethe, *Urkunden*, pp. 280–283, 304–306. For further discussion of Old Kingdom decrees in a wider legal context, see also David Lorton, "The Treatment of Criminals in Ancient Egypt: Through the New Kingdom", *Journal of the Economic and Social History of the Orient*, 20 (1977), pp. 2–64, 6–12.

[30]Jacques Vandier, *La Tombe d'Ankhtifi et la Tombe de Sébekhotep* (Cairo, 1950), pp. 206–207 (ll. II. 03–III. 1).

act against this coffin and any monument of this tomb, his arm will be cut off for Hemen.

It is profoundly unclear whether the wrongdoer was actually expected to be punished by physical severance of the arm, as opposed to the sanction being an allusion to a divine curse.[31] Still, this is another illustration of cause and consequence being framed in protasis-apodosis terms as early as the third millennium BCE, and numerous curses of a similar structure persisted throughout the second millennium BCE.[32] These did not have to prescribe violent punishments. For instance, a famous example is the exhortation made by Middle Kingdom ruler Senusret III (r. 1870–1831 BCE) to his children on his Second Semna Stela demarcating the Egyptian border with Nubia, where unsatisfactory children face the threat of being disowned:[33]

ir gr.t s3=i nb srwḏ.t(y)=fy t3š pn ir.n Ḥm=i s3=i pw ms.tw=f n Ḥm=i tw.t s3 nḏ.ty it=f ir gr.t fḫ.t(y)=fy sw tm.ty=fy ꜥḥ3 ḥr=f n s3=i is n ms.tw=f is n=i

Now, as for any son of mine who will strengthen this border which my Majesty made, he is my son; he was born to my Majesty. It is proper for a son to be an avenger of his father. Now, as for him who will lose it and will not fight over it, he is not my son; he was not born to me.

Curses of the protasis-apodosis variety also extended into the explicitly religious literature concerned with the afterlife, where even supernatural beings could be threatened. A representative example can be found in Coffin Text Spell 277 (c.2100 BCE), which offers protection to the deceased by singling out various potential wrongdoers for punishment:[34]

ir nṯr nb ir nṯr.t nb.(t) ir 3ḫ nb ir mt nb mt.t nb.(t) ns.wt r3=f ḫft=i ḥr=f n šꜥ.t ḥk3 imy n ḫt=i

As for any god, as for any goddess, as for any spirit, as for any dead man or any

---

[31]For this alternative view, see Harco Willems, "Crime, Cult and Capital Punishment (Mo'alla Inscription 8)", *Journal of Egyptian Archaeology*, 76 (1990), pp. 27–54, 46–47. For more on the possibility of "supra-practical" punishments in ancient Egypt, where mutilation referred to a divine curse, see also Alexandre A. Loktionov, "May My Nose and Ears Be Cut Off: Practical and 'Supra-Practical' Aspects of Mutilation in the Egyptian New Kingdom", *Journal of the Economic and Social History of the Orient*, 60 (2017), pp. 263–291.

[32]For a selection of examples, see Willems, "Crime, Cult and Capital Punishment", pp. 34–41.

[33]Kurt Sethe, *Aegyptische Inschriften aus den Königlichen Museen zu Berlin* (Leipzig, 1913), I, p. 258 (ll. 17–20). For a more recent discussion of the stela and its significance, see Stephan J. Seidlmayer, "Zu Fundort und Aufstellungskontext der großen Semna-Stele Sesostris' III", *Studien zur Altägyptischen Kultur*, 28 (2000), pp. 233–242.

[34]Adriaan de Buck, *The Egyptian Coffin Texts IV: Texts of Spells 268–354* (Chicago, 1951), p. 19. For additional context and further relevant examples, see Robert K. Ritner, *The Mechanics of Ancient Egyptian Magical Practice* (Chicago, 1993), p. 98.

dead woman, who will lick off his spell against me today, he shall fall to the execution blocks and the magic that is in my belly.

On the other hand, the same structural formula, albeit translated a little differently in English, could also be deployed just as effectively in healing contexts as those of punishment. It is standard in medical texts, as illustrated by this example from Papyrus Ebers (c.1550 BCE):[35]

ir gm=k ḏbᶜ s3ḥ r-pw mr=sn pḫr mw ḥ3=sn ḏw sty=sn ḳm3=sn s3 ḏd.ḥr=k r=s mr iry=i

If you find [lit. as for your finding] a finger or a toe and they are painful, and fluid circulates around them, and they smell bad and emit a worm, you should say: "a disease I must treat".

The protasis-apodosis structure also entered the realm of Egyptian magical practice, enabling scribes to write down what the consequences caused by certain spells might be. A basic example is:[36]

ir šnw.t r3 pn r ḫfty nb n... ḫpr ḏw im=f r hrw-7

If this conjuration of the mouth [is deployed] against any enemy of [name of whoever was being protected], badness will come to pass concerning him for seven days.

Thus, one can trace the protasis-apodosis structure across all manner of contexts. Such varied examples indicate that the stylistic aspect of regulating labour in the Horemheb and Nauri decrees of the New Kingdom is by no means novel: on the contrary, it is highly conventional, and fits into the broader Egyptian intellectual tradition of forming conditional clauses in settings ranging from justice and law enforcement to chthonic curses, protective magic, and medicine. Nevertheless, alongside the new concept of *hp*-law, there is one other highly significant modification: the deployment of harsh corporal punishment, the origin of which warrants additional investigation.

Corporal Punishment in the Horemheb and Nauri Decrees: Influence from Mesopotamia?

For the period before the Horemheb and Nauri decrees, there is no firm evidence of Egyptian labour being regulated by the threat of legally mandated corporal punishment. Indeed, while beatings were a common method of the ad hoc disciplining of

---

[35]Alan H. Gardiner, *Egyptian Grammar* (Oxford, [1927] 1957), p. 349. For many more examples, see for instance Gonzalo M. Sanchez and Edmund S. Meltzer, *The Edwin Smith Papyrus: Updated Translation of the Trauma Treatise and Modern Medical Commentaries* (Atlanta, GA, 2012).

[36]Siegfried Schott, *Urkunden Mythologischen Inhalts. Erstes Heft: Bücher und Sprüche gegen den Gott Seth* (Leipzig, 1929), p. 61 (ll. 17–18). For this spell in context, see Ritner, *The Mechanics of Ancient Egyptian Magical Practice*, p. 190.

subordinates by superiors as early as the Old Kingdom,[37] corporal punishment as a legal sanction is not even conclusively attested in any Egyptian context before the New Kingdom.[38] While such absence of evidence cannot be deemed conclusive evidence of absence, it is nonetheless striking given that there is no shortage whatsoever of evidence for corporal punishment in the period immediately following. Corporal punishment, in various forms, appears to have become prominent after the Hyksos occupation of the Egyptian delta (c.1650–1550 BCE), which is unlikely to be coincidental. Based on an analysis of personal names, it seems highly likely that the Hyksos were a Semitic-speaking people.[39] This is consistent with material culture finds that suggest an origin in the southern Levant.[40] If so, it is logical to postulate that their legal tradition was not dissimilar to that of other Semitic-speaking peoples, most notably that of Akkadian speakers. While it is important to note that the geographic distance between the original Hyksos heartland and the core of the Akkadian world, Mesopotamia, was considerable, it is widely accepted that the Akkadian influence on the scribal traditions, schools, and intellectual culture of territories to the west of Mesopotamia was significant.[41] In the Akkadian legal tradition, we find many instances of corporal punishment strikingly similar to those in the Nauri and Horemheb decrees. For example, in arguably the most famous Akkadian legal text, the Laws of Hammurabi (c.1810–1750 BCE), one may find the following clause (§282) providing a legal mandate for facial mutilation:[42]

šumma wardum ana bēlišu ul bēlī atta iqtabi kīma warassu ukânšuma bēlšu uzunšu inakkis

If a slave has said to his lord: "you are not my lord", when he has substantiated that he is his slave, his lord will sever his ear.

This is highly representative of the Hammurabi legal corpus as a whole, with other clauses granting similar legal justification for putting out eyes (§193, §196), breaking

---

[37]For examples, generally in the form of beating scenes on tomb walls, see e.g. Dows Dunham and William Kelly Simpson, *The Mastaba of Queen Mersyankh III* (Boston, MA, 1974), fig. 9; Ann Macy Roth, *A Cemetery of Palace Attendants* (Boston, MA, 1995), fig. 185. See also the article by Adam Fagbore in the present volume.

[38]See e.g. Renate Müller-Wollermann, *Vergehen und Strafen. Zur Sanktionierung abweichenden Verhaltens im alten Ägypten* (Leiden, 2004); Loktionov, "May My Nose and Ears Be Cut Off".

[39]Manfred Bietak, "The Egyptian Community in Avaris during the Hyksos Period", *Ägypten und Levante*, 26 (2016), pp. 263–274, 267–268.

[40]Anna-Latifa Mourad, *Rise of the Hyksos: Egypt and the Levant from the Middle Kingdom to the Early Second Intermediate Period* (Oxford, 2015), p. 10.

[41]For the most recent discussion on this, including plentiful further references, see Juan Pablo Vita, "Akkadian as a *Lingua Franca*", in Rebecca Hasselbach-Andee (ed.), *A Companion to Ancient Near Eastern Languages* (Hoboken, NJ, 2020), pp. 357–372, 360–362. More specifically on the comparative legal history of ancient Egypt and Mesopotamia in this period, see Raymond Westbrook (ed.), *A History of Ancient Near Eastern Law* (Leiden, 2003).

[42]Normalization based on Martha T. Roth, *Law Collections from Mesopotamia and Asia Minor* (Atlanta, GA, 1995), p. 132 (§282).

bones (§197), severing tongues (§192), breasts (§194), and hands (§195, §218, §226, §253), knocking out teeth (§200), whipping (§202), and impaling (§153).[43] This mutilatory tradition displayed considerable staying power, as Assyrian kings set out similar punitive provisions seven centuries later. For example, in Middle Assyrian Laws Tablet A (*c.*1100 BCE), the following provision is made:[44]

A §4 *šumma lu urdu lu amtu ina qāt aššat a'īle mimma imtaḫru ša urde u amte appēšunu uznēšunu unakkusu šurqa umallû a'īlu ša aššiti[šu] uznēša unakkas u šumma aššassu uššer [uz]nēša la unakkis ša urde u amte la unakkusuma šurqa la umallû*

If either a male or female slave has received anything from the wife of a man, they will sever the nose and ears of the male or female slave. They will restore the stolen goods. The man [whose] wife it is shall sever her ears, and if he spares his wife (and) does not sever her [e]ars, they will not sever those of the male or female slave, (and) they will not restore the stolen goods.

There are many other examples of this sort in the text, including severing ears (§5, §24, §40, §44, §59), noses (§5, §15), fingers (§8, §9), genitalia (§15) and possibly breasts (§8), as well as various forms of beating (§57, §59), whipping (§44) and impalement (§53).[45] These sanctions are predominantly associated with theft and matters of domestic insubordination, and – both in the Assyrian examples above and in earlier legal documents from the Old Babylonian and Ur-III periods – it is striking that corporal punishment is generally reserved for slaves and other classes of unfree labourer.[46] Clearly, the topic of the Egyptian Horemheb and Nauri decrees is overall rather different, with these texts often being concerned with regulating and, if necessary, punishing relatively or even very senior officials. Still, the punishments themselves are nonetheless markedly similar and, in many cases, identical to their Mesopotamian counterparts. Bearing in mind that these decrees were published after the Hyksos period, when elements of Semitic law could conceivably have been imported into Egypt, a case can be made for influence from the Semitic legal tradition being directly present in the Egyptian decrees. This influence was clearly not a wholesale uptake, as the offenders targeted were a different social group. Instead, it appears that the Egyptians sought to mix and match, bringing in punishments from abroad to help regulate labour in line with the demands of their own socio-economic reality.

The case for such influence is strengthened further by the appearance of a substantial number of Semitic loanwords related to judicial administration, crime, and punishment in the Egyptian language, all of which date to the period after the Hyksos ascendancy. While many of these words occur only rarely or are only firmly

---

[43]For the full set of laws in Akkadian and English, see Roth, *Law Collections*, pp. 71–142. For more on sanctions in Hammurabi's laws in the context of labour regulation, see the article by Nicholas Reid in the present volume.

[44]Roth, *Law Collections*, p. 156 (§4).

[45]For the full set of laws in Akkadian and English, including comparanda from other contemporary Assyrian legal corpora, see Roth 1995, *Law Collections*, pp. 153–209.

[46]For more on this, see the article by Nicholas Reid in the present volume.

Table 1. Semitic loanwords connected to justice and related concepts appearing in the Egyptian language after Hyksos Rule (post-1550 BCE) and broadly coinciding with the rise of corporal punishment as a means of labour regulation in Egypt.

Egyptian word	Likely Semitic root/cognate	Reference[47]	Likely translation
ꜥnḏꜣr (n)	root ḥsr	73–74 (n. 82)	enclosure; court
ꜥꜣšꜣḳ (n, v)	Syriac ꜥšaq	79–81 (nn. 92–94)	to extort; defraud; oppress; acts of oppression
ꜥꜣdwti (n)	Akkadian adû	86 (n. 105)	conspiracy
bꜣryt (n)	Akkadian birītu	99–100 (n. 124), 108–109 (n. 135)	obligation to work the land
bꜣḏꜣyr (n)	root slp (by metathesis via psl?) Even if not, the spelling is non-native for Egyptian, indicating a Semitic origin	116–117 (nn. 147–149)	stick; rod; cudgel
mstꜣyr (n)	root šṭr (nominal derivative); Akkadian šaṭāru	154–155 (n. 202)	office; place of writing
mꜥšꜣkꜣbw (n)	Akkadian miksu	160–163 (n. 209)	(import?) tax official
nꜥšiw (v)	Akkadian nišu or nēšu	184 (n. 247)	to oppress
nꜣṯꜣꜥꜣ (v)	Akkadian nešû or nasāḫu; Hebrew dnḥ/dnḫ also suggested	196–198 (n. 265)	to desert, divorce
swmꜣꜥny (n)	root šmꜥ	260 (n. 368)	hearing
sꜣdbti (n)	the word looks Semitic, although no root has so far been located	271 (n. 386)	hall; court
šꜣꜥꜣr (n)	root tgr	273–274 (n. 390)	gate; holding pen
šꜣwꜣšꜣti (n)	root sws	275 (n. 394)	administration
šꜣpwti (v)	root tpt/špṭ; Akkadian šapāṭu	278 (n. 398)	to judge
šꜣmꜥ (v)	root šmꜥ	279 (n. 400)	to hear

[47] All references are to James E. Hoch, *Semitic Words in Egyptian Texts of the New Kingdom and Third Intermediate Period* (Princeton, NJ, 1994).

ḳbꜥꜣ (v)	root qbꜣ; Akkadian qabû	292–293 (n. 424)	to tease; mock
k̠ꜣrwꜣꜣ (n)	Ugaritic gr; Syriac giyurā	295–296 (n. 429)	vagabond; one in a state of not having possessions
k̠ꜣrwiwt (n)	Akkadian kalû, perhaps linked conceptually to bit kili (prison)	328 (n. 474)	prison
k̠ꜣyriati (v)	root klꜣ; Akkadian kalû	328 (n. 475)	to be restrained; caged
gꜣwꜣšꜣ (n, v)	root qwš	347–348 (nn. 509–510)	to be crooked; crookedness
gꜣnysꜣ (n)	root ngs (by metathesis)	349–350 (n. 512)	violence; injustice
t̠wpꜣyr (n)	root spr/špr	364 (n. 540)	scribe
t̠ꜣhyr (v)	Aramaic saḥira	370–371 (n. 553)	to be offensive

attested after the New Kingdom, the number of items is nonetheless too large to ignore. Thus, this is, at the very least, explicit evidence of the uptake of judicial terminology, which – while it does not constitute categorical proof of an accompanying shift in legal practice – does make it appear highly likely. A summary of the key terms in question is given above (Table 1).

This table cannot be deemed satisfactory proof of post-Hyksos Egyptian justice evolving along Semitic lines, and even less that the administration of labour was evolving under an imported influence. However, what it does show is that – at least to a certain extent – the language of penal administration was becoming permeated with a Semitic lexicon, which may point to a degree of intellectual closeness which, in turn, manifests itself in the growing tendency towards corporal punishment as a judicial sanction. As has been shown, the latter is of considerable importance to Egyptian labour management specifically.

It should also be noted that such emerging intellectual proximity between Semitic and Egyptian traditions of the later second millennium BCE already has known parallels in other fields of written culture. For instance, in the domain of divination, it has been illustrated that lecanomancy – a highly technical mantic practice originating in the Mesopotamian Old Babylonian Period (2000–1600 BCE), which generated omens by observing oil patterns on water – was adopted by the Egyptians in the New Kingdom.[48] Similarly, the typically Mesopotamian genre of disputation literature – stories involving verbal superiority contests between various living things or inanimate objects, attested there from the third millennium BCE – appears in Egypt for the first time and in multiple attestations during the New Kingdom.[49] Meanwhile, Semitic religious traditions from the Levant also percolated into Egypt, with quintessentially Levantine deities such as Anat, Ba'al, Qudshu, Astarte, and Reshep all appearing in the Egyptian written record at a time roughly contemporaneous to the Nauri and Horemheb decrees.[50] The evidence for such a wide range of influences from the Semitic world is further enhanced by archaeological findings of cuneiform Akkadian texts at New Kingdom sites, most notably the famous Tell el-Amarna cuneiform archive, which contains documents ranging from royal letters to mythological compositions.[51] In such a context, a degree of Semitic influence –

---

[48]For more on Mesopotamian oil divination, see most recently Alexandre A. Loktionov and Christoph Schmidhuber, "Luminous Oils and Waters of Wisdom: Shedding New Light on Oil Divination", in Katrien De Graef and Anne Goddeeris (eds), *Law and (Dis)Order in the Ancient Near East: Proceedings of the Rencontre Assyriologique Internationale Held at Ghent, Belgium, 15–19 July 2013* (University Park, PA, 2021), pp. 169–176. For more on the tradition appearing in Egypt, see Sara Demichelis, "La divination par l'huile à l'époque ramesside", in Yvan Koenig (ed.), *La magie en Égypte. À la recherche d'une définition* (Paris, 2002).

[49]For a summary of the examples and further references, see Enrique Jiménez, *The Babylonian Disputation Poems: With Editions of the Series of the Poplar, Palm and Vine, the Series of the Spider, and the Story of the poor, forlorn Wren* (Leiden and Boston, MA, 2017), pp. 128–130.

[50]See for instance Adhémar Massart, *The Leiden Magical Papyrus; I 342 + I 345* (Leiden, 1954) for a papyrus of this period mentioning all these Semitic gods. For a comprehensive listing of deities from the Levant in New Kingdom Egyptian texts, see Keiko Tazawa, *Syro-Palestinian Deities in New Kingdom Egypt: The Hermeneutics of their Existence* (Oxford, 2009).

[51]For accessible English translations of key Amarna documents, see William L. Moran, *The Amarna Letters* (Baltimore, MD, 1992). For a comprehensive (albeit dated) edition, see Jörgen A. Knudtzon, *Die*

emanating from Mesopotamia and its surrounding polities – seems entirely logical in the field of punitive and labour administration within New Kingdom Egypt. Indeed, it would be somewhat strange for such an influence to be absent, given its prominence in so many other textual genres of the period.

Conclusion

Labour regulation in the Nauri and Horemheb decrees relies on a mixture of native Egyptian and imported Semitic features, most likely associated with the Hyksos presence in Egypt and the continued links with Levantine and Mesopotamian intellectual culture thereafter. The phrasing of the decrees is characteristically Egyptian, and there is precedent for pharaohs issuing decrees in this style going back to the Old Kingdom an entire millennium earlier. However, the allusions to a broader concept of law (*hp*) – as opposed to just ad hoc provisions – and the provision of tough corporal punishments are new, both for Egyptian justice in general and for Egyptian labour regulation more specifically. While the new conceptualization of law (*hp*) might conceivably be an Egyptian innovation, the new punishments almost certainly point to some degree of foreign influence, especially given the extent of contact with the linguistic, religious, and broader intellectual traditions of Mesopotamia and the Levant at the time. However, it is interesting to note that the way these punishments are deployed is distinctly Egyptian. Unlike the Mesopotamian setting, they are not limited to slaves and other unfree labourers but can instead target high officials.

The underlying reasons for these changes most likely cannot be limited solely to an organic phenomenon of cultural assimilation based on the historical reality of contact between Egypt and the Semitic world. While such an unplanned diffusion of concepts may have played a part, with the fluid transmission of intellectual culture contributing to the hybrid nature of the legal changes, it is nonetheless probable that the uptake of foreign ideas into the sphere of Egyptian law and labour regulation was largely a deliberate decision. Such a choice would have been linked to efforts to further cement royal power at a crucial time: on the one hand, this was a phase when New Kingdom Egypt was nearing its greatest territorial extent, and a period when the crown of Egypt as an institution was arguably politically and militarily stronger than at any other point in its entire ancient history; on the other hand, this time also saw dynastic weakness and legitimacy crises, which could cast doubt on any given holder of the crown. By regulating labour through *hp* – imposed top-down from the pharaonic government – agency in interpreting vague regulations (and hence potential for abuse of power) was being stripped away from provincial officials (whom the royal decrees see as their main adversaries). The crown was saying *exactly* what had to be done, thereby transferring agency to itself, and it now had a specific term for it. Brutal penalties, borrowed from a foreign tradition that had assimilated into Egyptian legal culture, reinforced the point even further, presumably in the hope of attaining higher productivity as a result, and possibly with the additional aim of

---

El-Amarna-Tafeln, mit Einleitung und Erläuterungen (Leipzig, 1915). For a key text of cuneiform mythology from Amarna, see Shlomo Izre'el, *Adapa and the South Wind: Language Has the Power of Life and Death* (Winona Lake, IN, 2001).

scaring other would-be offenders, including relatively high-ranking ones, into compliance. Given the vast infrastructural outputs of the New Kingdom, as evidenced
by the many flamboyant and vastly labour-intensive pharaonic building projects
emblematic of the period, it appears that, at least for several centuries, this strategy
was not without success. In turn, these infrastructural outputs allowed the crown
to materialize its power further, presenting itself as a force capable of dominating
the land through monumentalism. Thus, the pharaoh could take physical action to
shape both his country and the bodies of those who worked in it – or, rather,
those who did not work to a required standard and therefore deserved mutilation
or beating.

Acknowledgements. The author would like to thank the Master and Fellows of Christ's College,
Cambridge, for generously providing financial backing for this work through the Lady Wallis Budge
Fund. Funding was also gratefully received from the Arts and Humanities Research Council (project reference AH/V006711/1). Additional thanks are due to the McDonald Institute for Archaeological
Research, Cambridge, and the HSE University Institute for Oriental and Classical Studies, Moscow, for providing supportive research environments during the unprecedented challenges of the global Covid-19
pandemic.

Cite this article: Alexandre A. Loktionov. Regulating Labour through Foreign Punishment? Codification
and Sanction at Work in New Kingdom Egypt. *International Review of Social History*, 68:S31 (2023),
pp. 33–52. https://doi.org/10.1017/S0020859022000852

International Review of Social History, 68:S31 (2023), pp. 53–71
doi:10.1017/S0020859023000032

RESEARCH ARTICLE

Punishment, Patronage, and the Revenue Extraction Process in Pharaonic Egypt*

Adam Simon Fagbore [ID]

Bonn Center for Dependency and Slavery Studies, University of Bonn, Bonn, Germany,
e-mail: afagbore@uni-bonn.de

Abstract

The processes of control and collection are prominent themes throughout pharaonic history. However, the extent that the central regime attempted to administer agricultural fields to collect revenues directly from the farmer who actually worked the land is unclear during the pharaonic period (c.2686–1069). Relations between those involved in agricultural cultivation and local headships of extended families and wider kinship groups were deeply embedded within a broad range of interpersonal discourses, behaviours, and practices. Village headmen and officials at all levels of an impersonalized "state" hierarchy were themselves landholders who drew income from the land and were held responsible for collecting revenues from their fields. It is therefore necessary to define, with a focus on the imperatives of a subsistence economy, who was working the land and what the relationship was between them, the headmen, and those from within outside power structures (in the context of direct intervention against specific groups of the population). To address these points, I will focus on revenue extraction as a "state" process, how it was connected to the role of punishment, and its impact on local hierarchies (the targets of revenue extraction).

Estimations of the total size of the rural population are typically based on locally restricted data from distinct periods of pharaonic history. Still, most of those living in rural villages were likely occupied in the farm cultivation of the inundated land.[1] Relations between

---

*I would like to thank the Bonn Center for Dependency and Slavery Studies and the German Research Foundation (Deutsche Forschungsgemeinschaft) for funding my research during the period this article was written. I would also like to thank Chris Eyre, Ludwig Morenz, Christian De Vito, and the peer reviewers for reading earlier drafts of this article and for making suggestions for improvement.

[1] For population sizes in pharaonic Egypt, see Christopher J. Eyre, "Economy and Society in Pharaonic Egypt", in Panagiotis Kousoulis and Nikolaos Lazaridis (eds), *Proceedings of the Tenth International Congress of Egyptologists: University of the Aegean, Rhodes. 22–29 May 2008* (Leuven, 2015), I, pp. 707–725, 721–723; Harco Willems, "Zur Kulturgeschichte einer Region. Al-Jabalayn während der Ersten Zwischenzeit", *Orientalistische Literaturzeitung*, 109:2 (2014), pp. 87–103, 88–89; Ludwig Morenz, *Die Zeit der Regionen im Spiegel der Gebelein-Region* (Leiden, 2010), pp. 67–72. For a general overview of agriculture and the pharaonic countryside, see Juan Carlos Moreno García, "Introduction. Nouvelles recherches sur l'agriculture institutionnelle et domestique en Égypte ancienne dans le contexte des sociétés antiques", in Juan Carlos Moreno García (ed.), *L'agriculture institutionnelle en Égypte ancienne. État de la question et perspectives interdisciplinaires* (Villeneuve, 2005), pp. 11–78. For pharaonic agricultural productivity

those involved in agricultural cultivation and local headships of extended families and kinship groups were embedded within a broad range of behaviours and practices. Village headmen and local authorities appointed as agents of provincial institutions – who themselves were landholders that controlled local access to cultivable fields – would have delegated them the difficult task of balancing the collection of grain revenues from rural revenue payers (that actually cultivated their holdings) with the demands made by non-local revenue agents of outside power structures (temple estates and private landholders).[2] As there were no forms of commoditized land ownership in pharaonic Egypt,[3] it is necessary to define the relationship between those that actually worked the land, the village headmen, higher-level magnates, and those from outside power structures, with a focus on the peasant imperatives of a subsistence economy against those claiming revenues. I will assess the role of punishment as a mode of managing rural producers, the degree to which "state" power penetrated local hierarchies, and how these overlapped with the role of patronage (i.e. client obligation, service, and handing over production to a profiting lord). My focus is not on the role of punishment as it occurred *in the production process* but its role *in the context of revenue extraction* (i.e. in the control of production outcomes). In this context, the punishment of revenue defaulters was not about organizing labour but penalizing defaulters for failing to pay grain revenues from worked lands. This article analyses how the central regime delegated revenue extraction processes to local authorities, the role of punishment in managing (enforcing) the collection of revenues from rural producers, and its impact on local hierarchies.

Patronage and the Revenue Extraction Process

The relationship between the role of the headmen, how the peasantry gained access to land during the inundation each year,[4] and the extent to which temple estates and

---

based on a theoretical model of population size, see David A. Warburton, "Ancient Egypt: A Monolithic State in a Polytheistic Market Economy", in Martin Fitzenreiter (ed.), *Das Heilige und die Ware. Eigentum, Austausch und Kapitalisierung im Spannungsfeld von Ökonomie und Religion* (London, 2007), pp. 79–97, 85; David A. Warburton, "Un(der)employment in Bronze Age Egypt: Anachronism or Insight?", *Journal of Egyptian History*, 12:2 (2019), pp. 137–258.

[2] For recent studies of taxation in pharaonic Egypt, see Juan Carlos Moreno García, "Changes and Limits of Royal Taxation in Pharaonic Egypt (2300–2000 BCE)", in Jonathan Valk and Irene Soto Marín (eds), *Ancient Taxation: The Mechanics of Extraction in Comparative Perspective* (New York, 2021), pp. 290–324; Lesley Anne Warden, "Centralized Taxation during the Old Kingdom", in Peter der Manuelian and Thomas Schneider (eds), *Towards a New History for the Egyptian Old Kingdom. Perspectives on the Pyramid Age* (Leiden, 2016), pp. 470–495; Chris Eyre, *The Use of Documents in Pharaonic Egypt* (Oxford, 2013), pp. 1–15, 179–201. For an overview of the historical debate, see Sally L.D. Katary, "Taxation (until the End of the Third Intermediate Period)", in Juan Carlos Moreno García and Willeke Wendrich (eds), *UCLA Encyclopaedia of Egyptology* (Los Angeles, 2011), pp. 1–25.

[3] For a non-Eurocentric model of land ownership in pharaonic Egypt, see Eyre, "Economy and Society", pp. 710–711; Christopher Eyre, "How Relevant Was Personal Status to the Functioning of the Rural Economy in Pharaonic Egypt?", in Bernadette Menu (ed.), *La Dépendance Rurale dans l'antiquité Égyptienne et Proche-orientale* (Cairo, 2004), pp. 157–186, 157–158; Christopher J. Eyre, "Peasants and 'Modern' Leasing Strategies in Ancient Egypt", *Journal of Economic and Social History of the Orient*, 40:4 (1997), pp. 367–390. For the broader historical context, see Jack Goody, *The Theft of History* (Cambridge, 2003), pp. 42–60.

[4] Thomas Park has argued that ecological and ethnographic comparisons can be made between the ecological regime documented for the Senegal river basin and that for the premodern system used in the

major private landholders attempted to collect grain revenues directly from the farmer that cultivated the land is not entirely clear during the pharaonic period (c.2686–1069 BCE; Figure 1).[5] The most important pharaonic source for low-level agricultural social relations is the Heqanakht Letters from the early Twelfth Dynasty (c.1961–1917 BCE).[6] The papyri deal with the domestic and financial matters of a *ka*-priest and village headman called Heqanakht, who completely controlled a kin-based undertaking on temple endowment lands.[7] The household was made up of Heqanakht's immediate family – his mother, second wife, three children, and youngest brother – and the foreman, who had authority over non-family members employed in short-term work (three subordinates, three cultivators, and three female servants). Each family unit worked its own plots of land, held grain reserve for seed, and made its own judgements about the planting of crops according to the local condition of the floods. In return for their service, payments of unprocessed grain were made to each individual nuclear family of the kinship-based group – based partly on the seniority of each member – who then processed their grain into food.[8]

Heqanakht had access to cultivatable land in different villages and geographical regions of Egypt, allowing him to cultivate a variety of crops (emmer, barley, and flax), each suited to local environmental conditions when the level of the flood was known.[9] His letters do not refer to other crops, which he presumably grew on the side, but the usage of different seed varieties, different plots of land for different

---

ancient Nile Valley. Once the quality of the flood was known, the productive manning of the watered lands was directed by extended families or kinship groups that held land in common property (holdings were held in different locations that were separated geographically), and reallocated land to dependents annually when the pattern of the inundation became clear. See Thomas K. Park, "Early Trends towards Class Stratification: Chaos, Common Property, and Flood Recession Agriculture", *American Anthropologist*, 94:1 (1992), pp. 90–117. For the application of Park's model (standard risk management involving "communal" land holdings, with annual redistribution of cultivable land based on the quality of the flood) tested against the surviving data for the fiscal regime and the status of the rural population in pharaonic Egypt, see Eyre, "How Relevant Was Personal Status", pp. 164–170.

[5] Christopher Eyre, "Feudal Tenure and Absentee Landlords", in Schafik Allam (ed.), *Grund und Boden in Altägypten (Rechtliche und Sozio-ökonomische Verhältnisse). Akten des Internationalen Symposions, Tübingen 18.-20. Juni 1990* (Tübingen, 1994), pp. 107–133; Eyre, "Peasants and 'Modern' Leasing Strategies", pp. 374–376; Christopher J. Eyre, "The Village Economy in Pharaonic Egypt", in Alan K. Bowman and Eugen Rogan (eds), *Agriculture in Egypt: From Pharaonic to Modern Times*, (Oxford, 1999), pp. 33–60; Eyre, *Use of Documents*, p. 164; Moreno García, "Changes and Limits of Royal Taxation", pp. 313–318; Warden, "Centralized Taxation", pp. 488–490.

[6] James P. Allen, *The Heqanakht Papyri*, Publications of the Metropolitan Museum of Art, Egyptian Expedition 27 (New York, 2002) [hereafter, *HP*]. See also Ben Haring, "Access to Land by Institutions and Individuals in Ramesside Egypt (Nineteenth and Twentieth Dynasties; 1294–1070 BC)", in Ben Haring and Remco de Maaijer (eds), *Landless and Hungry? Access to Land in Early and Traditional Societies: Proceedings of a Seminar held in Leiden, 20 and 21 June, 1996* (Leiden, 1998), pp. 74–89, 77; Eyre, "Feudal Tenure", pp. 111, 115; Barry J. Kemp, *Ancient Egypt: Anatomy of a Civilization* (London, 2006), p. 323; Rainer Nutz, *Ägyptens wirtschaftliche Grundlagen in der Mittleren Bronzezeit*, Archaeopress Egyptology 4 (Oxford, 2014), pp. 132–134.

[7] A family paid a *ka*-priest to perform the daily offerings at the tomb of the deceased and they likely had access to private endowment land connected with the deceased's cult. See *HP*, pp. 179–180.

[8] Heqanakht Letter II, Metropolitan Museum of Art [hereafter, MMA] 22.3.517, rt. 7 (= *HP*, pl. 30).

[9] Mark Lehner, "Fractal House of Pharaoh: Ancient Egypt as a Complex Adaptive System", in Timothy A. Kohler and George J. Gumerman (eds), *Dynamics in Human and Primate Societies: Agent-Based Modelling of Social and Spatial Processes* (New York; Oxford, 2000), pp. 275–353, 316–317.

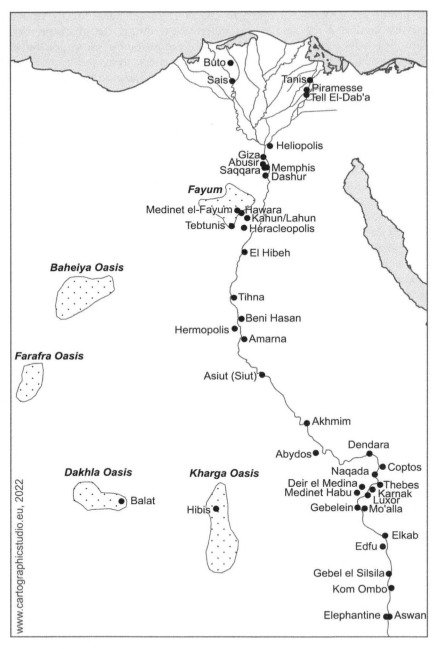

Figure 1 Map of pharaonic Egypt with reference to some of the major sites discussed in this article.

crops, and the timing of its planting reflected concern to have access to suitable land fit for the harvest. As the amount of food produced was completely dependent on the basis of the inundation, the lack of specificity in the location of the plots implies that the individual right of access to a suitable area of inundated land and the right to profit from its exploitation was Heqanakht's immediate concern. This is reflected in his use of intermediaries (i.e. the Overseer of the Delta, Herunefer), who supported him in locating suitable land that could be leased and cultivated.[10] Cultivating several plots rather than a consolidated holding was familiar enough in subsistence farming, where the amount produced in any given year depended on the availability of family labour, and plots with even slight ecological variation were a strategy for mitigating the risk of variations in the annual inundation from one year to the next.[11]

On the other hand, it is unclear whether the revenue expected from a plot was adapted based on the quality of the flood that year. Annual leases at inundation imply that failure to pay grain revenues would result in the default of the farmer,[12] but the issue of getting some crop off land that was not fully inundated is a practice that must have been normal in years of poor harvest. As a generalization, this was probably one of the main contexts where punishment was inflicted upon the representatives of field labourers since the only possible adjustment based on a defective flood was a reduction of their share. This is the context in which the headman of Elephantine argues in a letter (P. Valençay I) to the Chief Taxing Master of the Temple of Amun that he cannot pay full revenues for a field in the region of Edfu because it had only partly flooded during the annual inundation (c.1099–1069 BCE).[13] He further argues that he had productively ensured that the land was occupied to the extent that it was possible to cultivate under local conditions, that he had paid the dues owed for that small area of land, and that no further repayment was outstanding. This demonstrates that there was no a priori flexibility of the land revenue since the responsible headman that failed to deliver what was expected from him was compelled to develop an extended argument to explain his failure to his superior. Still, there seems to be some basis – or perhaps just fierce resistance at the local level – to paying full rent or revenues to external authorities when the land was left partly un-inundated after the annual flood. Although the letter does not document the outcome of the dispute, tomb scenes from the New Kingdom that depict the

---

[10]Heqanakht Letter I, MMA 22.3.516, rt. 9 (= *HP*, pl. 28). For lease arrangements in the Heqanakht texts, see *HP*, pp. 117, 149–159; Bernadette Menu, "La gestion du 'patrimoine' foncier d'Hekanakhte", *Revue d'égyptologie*, 22 (1970), pp. 111–129, 118–124; Danielle Bonneau, *Le fisc et le Nil. Incidences des irrégularités de la crue du Nil sur la fiscalité foncière dans l'Égypte grecque et romaine* (Paris, 1971), pp. 126–130; Eyre, "Peasants and 'Modern' Leasing Strategies", pp. 164–169; Eyre, *Use of Documents*, pp. 187–190.

[11]Dorothy J. Crawford, *Kerkeosiris: An Egyptian Village in the Ptolemaic Period* (Cambridge, 1971), p. 80; Eyre, "Peasants and 'Modern' Leasing Strategies", pp. 382–384; Eyre, "How Relevant Was Personal Status", pp. 164–169.

[12]For private leases that may imply a change of terms based on the level of the inundation, see Eyre, "Village Economy", pp. 47–53; Stephan J. Seidlmayer, *Historische und Moderne Nilstände. Untersuchungen an den Pegelablesungen des Nils von der Frühzeit bis in die Gegenwart* (Berlin, 2001), pp. 69–70. For examples from the Demotic period, see Heinz Felber, *Demotische Ackerpachtverträge der Ptolemäerzeit. Untersuchungen zu Aufbau, Entwicklung und Inhaltlichen Aspekten einer Gruppe von Demotischen Urkunden*, Ägyptologische Abhandlungen 58 (Wiesbaden, 1997), pp. 164–167.

[13]P. Valençay I, letter, private collection of Jean Morel in the Château de Fins, Dun-le-Poëlier (= Alan H. Gardiner, *Ramesside Administrative Documents* (Oxford, 1948), pp. 72–73 [hereafter, *RAD*]; Edward F. Wente, *Letters from Ancient Egypt* (Atlanta, GA, 1990), pp. 130–131). See also Bonneau, *Le Fisc et le Nil*, pp. 126–130; Seidlmayer, *Historische und Moderne Nilstände*, pp. 33–37, 59–61.

measurement of standing grain may imply that the process was sometimes used to judge what was taxable, with the implication being that only the standing crop was counted.[14] This scenario of resisting villages attempting to remain disengaged from institutional and private estates that wanted to enforce an intrusive revenue extraction process was likely the norm for the majority of Egyptian history.

The situation can be compared with demands for additional payments of grain rations made in Heqanakht Letter II but at the private level this time. It appears that Heqanakht's dependents had previously written to their lord to complain of hunger after he had placed them on half rations while he was absent from home.[15] The rations were reduced from the standard calculation of 1.5 *khar* of grain a month. As a figure, that probably reflects the absolute minimum immediate consumption that Heqanakht felt his dependents needed to survive.[16] In other words, the working dependents of Heqanakht's household still expected to receive the higher level of subsistence that the poor harvest that year made impossible, leading the headman to justify his position in writing. Heqanakht advises that he is the lord (*nb*) and reminds the sender that he is solely responsible for the organization of his holdings and that all decisions concerning subsistence provisioning are made based on the size of the inundation.[17] It is implied that all parties understood that local conditions during the annual flood could have a detrimental effect on what could be provided in productive social relationships at the village level.[18] The broader implication is that claims on the subsistence farmer's income by a landlord were sometimes judged in times of difficulty simply on what the landlord defined as what was necessary to survive. This is a point that was used not only to justify the reductions but presumably also the share of the product of the land to be claimed by Heqanakht. The issue was how much was left, rather than how much had been claimed by the landlord, and demands for revenue of the produce of the land do not appear in the letters. Thus, it is clear that Heqanakht was responsible for managing the collection and payment of revenues for rented land that his family or their subordinate labourers had

---

[14]For standing crops as revenue assessments, see Eyre, *Use of Documents*, p. 191. For the tomb scenes, see Suzanne Berger, "A Note on Some Scenes of Land-measurement", *Journal of Egyptian Archaeology*, 20 (1934), pp. 54–56. For Demotic Egypt, see Ursula Kaplony-Heckel, "Zur Landwirtschaft in Oberägypten. Demotische Akten und Urkunden aus Gebelein (II. Jhr. v. Chr.) und der arabische Leitfaden des Mahzumi († 1189 n. Chr.)", in Irene Shirun-Grumach (ed.), *Jerusalem Studies in Egyptology*, Ägypten und Altes Testament 40 (Wiesbaden, 1998), pp. 57–66, 58–62, 64. For Ptolemaic Egypt, see Manning, *Land and Power in Ptolemaic Egypt: The Structure of Land Tenure* (Cambridge, 2003), pp. 152–154. For Islamic Egypt, see Gladys Frantz-Murphy, *The Agrarian Administration of Egypt from the Arabs to the Ottomans* (Cairo, 1986), pp. 12, 36–37, 47; Gladys Frantz-Murphy, "Land Tenure in Egypt in the First Five Centuries of Islamic Rule (Seventh-Twelfth Centuries AD)", in Alan K. Bowman and Eugen Rogan (eds), *Agriculture in Egypt: From Pharaonic to Modern Times* (Oxford, 1999), pp. 237–266, 249–250.

[15]A point underlined by wage adjustments in the wage table in Letter II. See Heqanakht Letter II (= *HP*, pl. 30). See also Eyre, "The Village Economy", pp. 48–51; Eyre, "How Relevant Was Personal Status", pp. 171–172.

[16]For the problem of calorific values of different Egyptian grains, see W. Paul van Pelt and Frits Heinrich, "Emmer Wheat and Barley Prices in the Late New Kingdom: A Ramessid Price Paradox Resolved", *Journal of Egyptian Archaeology*, 104:1 (2018), pp. 103–107.

[17]Heqanakht Letter II, rt. 3–5 (= *HP*, pl. 30).

[18]Heqanakht Letter II, rt. 25–27 (= *HP*, pl. 30).

cultivated and then the redistribution of grain rations to working family members or field labourers.

The Heqanakht Letters represent the best evidence in pharaonic Egypt of the relationship between the subsistence farmer that worked the land, the headman and representative of an outside power structure that managed the collection of revenues (here, Heqanakht), and the powerful magnates (here, the Overseer of the Delta) that facilitated access to watered fields. The letters make no specific reference to outside institutions making a claim against the revenues collected from Heqanakht's lands. However, we must be careful in assuming that our sources give a full account of events. Any suitable land that high-level magnates allocated to village authorities as the inundation progressed each year likely meant the responsible village headman (and not the dependent or subsistence farmer actually working the plot of land) would be held accountable for the management, collection, and payment of revenues by the magnate that arranged for the land to be leased. This is again the context in P. Valençay I.[19] The collecting scribe made a revenue demand of grain for holdings that were asserted to be worked under the authority of the village headman (Elephantine) on behalf of the responsible institution (the House of the Divine Adoratrice of Amun) but under the overarching authority of the Temple of Amun. The collecting scribe does not go to the plot that was actually worked to seek payment from the tenant or the farmer;[20] he goes directly to the headman (Meriunu), who was assumed to be responsible for the collection of revenues and who was known to have access to a central storage point where processed grain was known to be held. According to Meriunu, he was not responsible for one of the revenue claims (100 *khar* from a worked field in the "Island of Ombos") because it had actually been cultivated by *nmḥw* "free men" – someone whose household is not socially and economically dependent on another household – who had already paid gold (*nbw*) to the royal treasury.

The description of the delivery of revenues in P. Valençay I can be compared with the collection of harvest in the Turin Taxation Papyrus (*c.*1099–1069 BCE).[21] The viceroy of Kush and Overseer of the Granary, Panehesy, sent the Scribe of the Tomb Dhutmose to collect grain revenues from royal lands for other state institutions, including those intended to cover the wages of the workforce of the royal tomb at Deir el-Medina. Although the grain originally came from the fields, the collecting scribe did not retrieve it from the fields themselves; it was brought from the

---

[19]P. Valençay I (= *RAD*, pp. 72–73; Wente, *Letters from Ancient Egypt*, pp. 130–131). See also Alan H. Gardiner, "A Protest against Unjustified Tax-Demands", *Revue d'égyptologie*, 6 (1951), pp. 115–133, 128–133; Alan H. Gardiner, *The Wilbour Papyrus* (London, 1948), II, pp. 205–206; Sally L.D. Katary, *Land Tenure in the Ramesside Period* (London; New York, 1989), pp. 207–216; Eyre, "Feudal Tenure", p. 183.

[20]P. Valençay I (= *RAD*, pp. 72–73; Wente, *Letters from Ancient Egypt*, pp. 130–131).

[21]P. Turin 1895 + 2006, Turin Taxation Papyrus, Museo Egizio, Turin, rt. 1.3–1.7 (= *RAD*, pp. 35–44). See treatments in Christopher J. Eyre, "Pouvoir Central et Pouvoirs Locaux. Problèmes Historiographiques et Méthodologiques", *Méditerranées*, 24 (2000), pp. 15–39, 35; Kemp, *Ancient Egypt*, p. 256; Jac J. Janssen, *Commodity Prices from the Ramessid Period: An Economic Study of the Village of Necropolis Workmen at Thebes* (Leiden, 1975), pp. 455–459; Alan H. Gardiner, "Ramesside Texts Relating to the Taxation and Transport of Corn", *Journal of Egyptian Archaeology*, 27 (1941), pp. 19–73, 22–37.

threshing floor of various temple granaries throughout Upper Egypt.[22] The revenues gathered by the collecting scribe came mostly from royal *khato* lands under the management of local temple officials (*ḥm-nṯr*), but some came directly from local "cultivators" (*iḥwty*). Iosif Stuchevskii has argued that those with the title "cultivator" were, in effect, local headmen responsible for collecting and paying revenues.[23] Still, there seems to be a difference between "cultivators", who were held accountable for the payment of revenues for land that they held in some sense, and "cultivators", who acted as headmen responsible for cultivation but were not necessarily the actual field worker who worked the land. This explains why the harvest received by the collecting scribe is often broken down into the amounts that the tenant or cultivator delivered but at a level of separation from the management of the fields.[24] In other revenue documents of the Ramesside period (P. Baldwin-Amiens), the collection of grain under the authority of the headman responsible for delivering revenues was also typically made at the threshing floor before it was loaded onto a fleet of cargo ships belonging to the Temple of Amun.[25] The verso of this text does not mention the threshing floor. Instead, it focuses on the collection of grain that was collected from the "house of the cultivator" by boat from various collection points under the authority of local headmen at the riverbank for river transportation to a central storage point.[26] The text is clear that grain from the worked land was actually brought from the cultivator's household where the grain was presumably threshed.[27] This took place during the winter growing season when the height of the Nile was presumably convenient for transportation (and not during periods of low water or inundation).

My broader point is that the village headmen responsible for collecting revenues, who could consolidate those resources at central collection points under their authority, were frequently targeted by non-local agents of external authority. The threshing floor provided the primary point of contact with external hierarchies, but outside claims for revenues were collected by boat at local riverbank quaysides under the authority of local headmen. The processes described here are pretty logical since the grain must be threshed before it can be stored, and the straw and chaff are used locally, which meant there was no reason to collect from the worked fields but from the place where the removal of straw from the delivered grain took place. The surviving data does not record how physical violence was applied against the

---

[22]Eyre, "The Village Economy", p. 44; Gardiner, "Ramesside Texts", pp. 47–48, 59–64; Jac J. Janssen, *Grain Transport in the Ramesside Period: Papyrus Baldwin (BM EA 10061) and Papyrus Amiens*, Hieratic Papyri in the British Museum 8 (London, 2004), pp. 36–37.

[23]Jac J. Janssen and Inge Hofmann, *Annual Egyptological Bibliography / Bibliographie Égyptologique Annulle: 1975* (Leiden, 1979), p. 217; Iosif A. Stuchevskii, "Псевдоземледельцы древнего Египта. 'агенты' фиска", in Isidor S. Katsnel'son (ed.), *Древний Восток. Сборник 1. к семидесятипятилетию академика М. А. Коростовцева* (Moscow, 1975), pp. 141–153.

[24]Eyre, *Use of Documents*, p. 200.

[25]P. Amiens, grain accounts, British Museum, rt. 1, lines 1–12; P. Baldwin, grain accounts, British Museum, rt. 1, lines 1–12 (= Janssen, *Grain Transport in the Ramesside Period* [hereafter, *GT*], pp. 12–15). See also Gardiner, "Ramesside Texts", pp. 37–56; Katary, *Land Tenure in the Ramesside Period*, pp. 184–192.

[26]P. Amiens, vs. II, lines 1–13 (= *GT*, pp. 47–48).

[27]P. Baldwin, vs. II, line 4: "brought from the house of the cultivator Hori of the House of Amon, from the farmland which he tilled" (= *GT*, pp. 43).

vast number of landholders listed in the Ramesside documentation. However, it is the figure of the village headman, who was in total control of the management of labour and the distribution of wealth and resources to the rural peasantry, that is consistently held responsible in earlier pharaonic sources for the non-payment of grain revenues by the outside functionaries that came to inspect and collect their revenues from the threshing floor.

Punishment and the Threshing Floor

The threshing floor was the primary contact between the official responsible for collection and the outside authority expecting to receive revenues from the worked lands. In the Old and Middle Kingdoms (c.2686–1773 BCE), the collection of the harvest at the threshing floor was consistently associated with the flogging of farmers and responsible village (*ḥḳ3 niwt*) and estate headmen (*ḥḳ3 ḥwt*) before the scribes of the *ḏ3ḏ3t*-court of private mortuary estates (*pr-ḏt*). For instance, a Fifth Dynasty scene from the Saqqara chapel of the "Overseer of the Great House" Akhethotep (c.2494–2345 BCE) depicts the beating of revenue defaulters that owed grain revenues to Akhethotep's estate.[28] In a scene captioned "the counting of the rulers (of villages) by the assessors of the House of Eternity", revenue payers are led by muscular men with sticks, some of which are shaped like a hand, into the presence of the scribal assessors, before being held to account during the "bringing of the count" (*int ḥsb*) by a local tribunal of the private funerary endowment. Other scenes are more explicit in content. In the Sixth Dynasty tomb of Khentika at Saqqara (c.2345–2181 BCE),[29] the deceased tomb owner oversees the flogging of five chiefs of estates who are either tied to a post or lie prostrate on the ground while two "scribes of the House of Eternity" busily review accounts (see Figure 2). Likewise, a Sixth Dynasty scene from the tomb chapel of the nomarch Ibi at Deir el Gebrâwi is captioned "bringing the overseers of cattle to the count" and "the beating with the *ḳt3yt*-stick" (c.2278–2184 BCE).[30] The scene depicts scribes writing accounts while two men lead another man towards them, as another man drags him to the ground. It seems that the scribal assessors of the private estates, which provided for the deceased's cult and its dependents,[31] were also responsible for collecting its revenues. As in the Ramesside temple revenue documents, it is the headmen who are responsible for collecting revenues from the estates and towns they manage, which are targeted by the agents of external authority.[32]

---

[28]Christiane Ziegler, *Le mastaba d'Akhethetep*, Fouilles du Louvre à Saqqara 1 (Paris, 2007), pp. 74–75, 136–137.

[29]Thomas G.H. James, *The Mastaba of Khentika called Ikhekhi* (London, 1953), p. 45, pl. ix.

[30]Norman de G. Davies, *The Rock Tombs of Deir el Gebrâwi* (London, 1902), pl. 8; Naguib Kanawati, *Deir el-Gebrawi, Volume II: The Southern Cliff: The Tombs of Ibi and Others*, Australian Centre for Egyptology 25 (Oxford, 2007), pp. 36–37, pls. 17, 50.

[31]For the provisioning of the estates, see Kurt Sethe, *Urkunden des Alten Reiches* (Leipzig, 1903–1933), I, p. 14, line 16; p. 15, line 7; p. 144, lines 11–15 [hereafter, *Urk.* I]. For the provisioning of dependents, see *Urk.* I, p. 174, line 8; p. 254, line 16. See also Elmar Edel, "Inschriften des Alten Reichs (6. Folge)", *Zeitschrift für ägyptische Sprache und Altertumskunde*, 83 (1958), pp. 3–18.

[32]Eyre, "Village Economy", pp. 45–47.

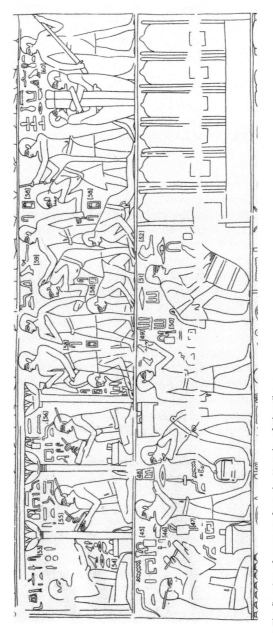

Figure 2 The flogging of peasants from the Mastaba of Khentika.
After James, The Mastaba of Khentika called Ikhekhi, IX; courtesy of Egypt Exploration Society.

The management of large New Kingdom temple estates (made up of extensive collections of small plots in practice) also relied on outside officials to inspect and hold local hierarchies to account. However, there is a shift from earlier tomb scenes that depict scribes from private estates recording the delivery of revenues from local headmen but not the supervision of agricultural work itself.[33] By the New Kingdom (c.1550–1069 BCE), we begin to see a clear situation where local, low-level functionaries are now directly involved in both agricultural production and the collection of revenues. In Eighteenth Dynasty scenes from the Theban tomb of the Overseer of Fields of the Lord of the Two Lands Menna (c.1400–1350 BCE), the tomb owner is depicted personally supervising activities related to planting, growing, and harvesting by subordinates, and the measuring and collection of grain. The revenue collection scene depicts the tomb owner dealing with a local defaulter,[34] who is shown lying face down in front of him, possibly accused of non-payment, revenue abuse, or perhaps some other misdeed. As in the Old and Middle Kingdom examples, the form and function of the scene are based on a vision of an external hierarchy (the agents of temple or private landowners) performing an idealizing objective intended to emphasize their authority over rural taxpayers – who were responsible for ensuring the land was occupied, worked, and revenues collected – in contexts where enforcement may be required to overcome resistance to external demands.

This is also the case in a fragmentary administrative document from the late Eighteenth Dynasty (c.1400–1390 BCE). The document details a hearing held to determine whether a landholding of a soldier (w^cw) named Mery was subject to a revenue claim ($b3k$) from the Overseer of Sealings, Sobekhotep.[35] Sobekhotep, as the outside representative of the Temple of Hathor,[36] was responsible for collecting revenues from local hierarchies that managed field holdings under the temple's authority.[37] It appears Sobekhotep, or perhaps his agents, had notified Mery of the outstanding revenue claim, but that Mery had referred the claim to a local hearing ($knbt$ sdm) consisting of the viziers Ptahhotep and Hapu and several other minor local functionaries.[38] The fragmentary passage explicitly mentions that the taxes of the "goddess" (from the time of Thutmose III) have been examined. The specific reason why Mery contested the claim is not given, but the tribunal decided that the soldier's challenge of Sobekhotep's rightful ($m3^c$) claim was wrong ($^cd3$) and he was sentenced to a "beating with 100 blows" (hw m $šh$ 100).[39] The punishment of beating

---

[33]See the examples collected in Eyre, *Use of Documents*, pp. 194–195.

[34]Colin Campbell, *Two Theban Princes, Kha-em-Uast & Amen-khepeshf, Sons of Rameses III., Menna, a Land Steward, and Their Tombs* (Edinburgh, 1910), p. 89.

[35]P. Munich 809, Staatliche Sammlung Ägyptischer Kunst [hereafter, SSAK] (Papyrus Mook) (= Wilhelm Spiegelberg, "Ein Gerichtsprotokoll aus der Zeit Thutmosis' IV", *Zeitschrift für ägyptische Sprache und Altertumskunde*, 63 (1929), pp. 105–115).

[36]The Temple of Hathor, known as "mistress of the Two Rocks", was probably located in the Gebelein region. See Spiegelberg, "Ein Gerichtsprotokoll", p. 109.

[37]P. Munich 809, SSAK (P. Mook), 1–9 (= Spiegelberg, "Ein Gerichtsprotokoll", p. 106). See also Schafik Allam, *Hieratische Ostraka und Papyri aus der Ramessidenzeit* (Tübingen, 1973), pls. 102–103; Jin Shoufu, "Bemerkungen zum pMünchen 809: zum Verständnis des Begriffes hp", *Discussions in Egyptology*, 48 (2000), pp. 89–94.

[38]Spiegelberg, "Ein Gerichtsprotokoll", p. 108.

[39]P. Munich 809, SSAK (P. Mook), 4–5 (= Spiegelberg, "Ein Gerichtsprotokoll", p. 106).

with one hundred blows is also known from administrative documents from Middle Kingdom Lahun.[40] It is also familiar in Ramesside legal oaths as punishment for lying or non-payment, and extensive flogging as a mode of enforcement becomes more frequently documented in royal decrees and provincial documentation of the Ramesside period. For instance, the decree of Seti I, which aims to protect the endowment of his Abydene temple, states that officials that exploited labour for personal gain were to be physically punished with "two hundred lashes, and [to receive] five open wounds".[41] The threat of flogging as part of the interrogation process is most evident in the tomb robbery papyri, where individuals suspected of being involved in looting royal tombs were made to swear oaths to the king (which imply that beatings and mutilation would precede impalement[42]), before being repeatedly beaten during interrogation.[43] Although the historical contexts are completely different, they provide evidence for the broader use of flogging to enforce several other pharaonic social processes not directly related to revenue extraction.

There are clear ideological continuities in the reproduction of political power in the iconographical scenes and textual evidence from the Old to the New Kingdom despite the shifting fates of specific regimes and lineages. The function of the threat of punishment is the same in all these cases: to demonstrate the power of the central regime or its representative and enforce compliance among the targeted group within a particular social process. This inclination towards an idealized form of causality seeks to consolidate the perpetuation of political order to help ensure the revenue extraction process will progress in a relatively predictable manner (i.e. the expected order of events: to ensure the delivery of revenues to the threshing floor, to chill the spine of the headman, to recall him to his duties, and to enforce collection from the peasantry). The impression that later periods of pharaonic history were more violent may be due to an increase in the scale of royal monuments or the more abundant documentation that has survived from the Ramesside period.[44] A

---

[40]University College London, Petrie Museum of Egyptian Archaeology, UC 32133 E, vs. 2 (= Mark Collier and Stephen Quirke, *The UCL Lahun Papyri: Accounts* (Oxford, 2006), pp. 234–235).

[41]Nauri Decree, *c*.1290 BCE, ll. 46–47 (= Kenneth A. Kitchen, *Ramesside Inscriptions: Historical and Biographical* (Oxford, 1975), I, p. 53 [hereafter, *KRI* I]). See also the contribution by Alex Loktionov to this Special Issue.

[42]P. Abbott, Tomb-robbery Fragments, British Museum, London [hereafter, BM], EA10221,1, 5.5–7 (= Kenneth A. Kitchen, *Ramesside Inscriptions: Historical and Biographical* (Oxford, 1983), VI, p. 468 [hereafter, *KRI* VI]).

[43]P. Abbott, "Tomb Robbery Fragments", BM EA10052,1, 9.3–6 (= *KRI* VI, pp. 767–803).

[44]See the discussion in Chris Eyre, "Calculated Frightfulness and the Display of Violence", in Tamas A. Bács and Horst Beinlich (eds), *Constructing Authority: Prestige, Reputation and the Perception of Power in Egyptian Kingship, Budapest, May 12–14, 2016*, 8. Symposion zur ägyptischen Königsideologie (Wiesbaden, 2017), pp. 89–122, 108. For (real or symbolic) violence during the Old and Middle Kingdoms, see Laurel Bestock, *Violence and Power in Ancient Egypt: Image and Ideology before the New Kingdom* (London and New York, 2018); Richard Bussmann, "Krieg und Zwangsarbeit im pharaonischen Ägypten", in Kerstin von Lingen and Klaus Gestwa (eds), *Zwangsarbeit als Kriegsressource in Europa und Asien* (Paderborn, 2014), pp. 57–72; Kerry Muhlestein, *Violence in the Service of Order: The Religious Framework for Sanctioned Killing in Ancient Egypt* (Oxford, 2011), pp. 16–44. For violence and torture throughout the pharaonic period, see Uroš Matić, *Violence and Gender in Ancient Egypt* (London and New York, 2021), pp. 26–44; Harco Willems, "Crime, Cult and Capital Punishment (Mo'alla Inscription 8)", *Journal of Egyptian Archaeology*, 76 (1990), pp. 27–54; David Lorton, "The Treatment of Criminals

recent investigation of human remains from the Old Kingdom settlement at Elephantine discovered clear evidence of spiteful violence: one man had suffered thirty-one fractures in fourteen different parts of his body.[45] The authors identified some well-healed fractures in combination with newer non-healed fracture lines, which implies the man had suffered "physical punishment with fracture consequence" on at least two separate occasions. It remains unclear why the man was so severely beaten. Specific textual examples that characterize the violent mistreatment of rural revenue payers at the hands of village headmen, as opposed to the headmen at the hands of the agents of local magnates, during the production process and the collection of revenues (*b3k*) is found in the Sixth Dynasty autobiography of Nekhebu (*c.*2345–2181 BCE).[46] Nekhebu, who had replaced his unnamed brother as ruler of the village (*ḥḳ3 niwt*) after his sibling had been appointed to the post of Overseer of Works, claims:[47]

> Never did I beat any man there, until it happened that he had [fell] under my fingers. Never did I (put to) work (*b3k = i*) any people there. As for the people whom were arguing with me there. I was the one who used to make them content. Never did I spend the night angry with any people. I am one who used to give clothing, bread, and beer to every naked and hungry man there.

Depending on the context, *b3k* "work", in the sense of production, can also be translated as "taxation", "end product", or "revenue".[48] The term essentially defines social relationships between subordinate and lord and, perhaps more importantly, what is

---

in Ancient Egypt through the New Kingdom", *Journal of the Economic and Social History of the Orient* 20:1 (1977), pp. 2–64.

[45] Julia Gresky, Nikolas Roumelic, Alexandra Kozak, and Michael Schultz, "'Folter' im Alten Reich? Untersuchungen zu den Ursachen und der Häufigkeit von Traumata bei der altägyptischen Population von Elephantine", in Dietrich Raue, Stephan P. Seidlmayer, and Phillipp Speiser (eds), *The First Cataract of the Nile: One Region – Various Perspectives* (Cairo, 2013), pp. 77–89.

[46] Among people for whom the term *b3k* is used is the well-documented community of workmen of Deir el-Medina in charge of the construction of the royal tomb under the New Kingdom. The mistreatment of the royal workmen and their families is best exhibited in a series of accusations made against the chief workman Paneb during the Nineteenth Dynasty. Paneb was accused of theft, physically abusing his subordinates, sexually assaulting their dependents, and the wrongful appropriation of labour. The distinction, however, is that Paneb was using his authority as village headman to casually abuse other members of the village who had only limited involvement in agriculture and *not* to enforce a particular revenue process. See P. BM EA10055 (= Jaroslav Černý, "Papyrus Salt 124 (Brit. Mus. 10055)", *Journal of Egyptian Archaeology*, 15:3/4 (1929), pp. 243–258). For further analysis, see Pascal Vernus, *Affairs and Scandals in Ancient Egypt*, trans. David Lorton (Ithaca, NY, 2003), pp. 70–94. To the best of my knowledge, the extensive documentation known from the workers' village never mentions physical violence as a retaliation by the authorities for a default in their work. For instance, one individual example records a sanction that was applied to a man for cursing the king's name (Turin Strike Papyrus, rt 2, 8–10), and when the tomb workmen are collectively sanctioned by the authorities (without mentioning physical violence) this is for a severe misconduct such as suspected involvement in the theft of royal property from the royal tombs.

[47] *Urk.* I, p. 217, lines 4–9; English translation derives from Nigel C. Strudwick, *Texts from the Pyramid Age* (Atlanta, GA, 2005), pp. 266–269.

[48] Jac J. Janssen, "*b3kw*: From Work to Product", *Studien zur Altägyptischen Kultur*, 20 (1993), pp. 81–94; Tobias Hofmann, *Zur Sozialen Bedeutung zweier Begriffe für 'Diener': b3k und ḥm. Untersucht an Quellen vom Alten Reich bis zur Ramessidenzeit*, Aegyptiaca Helvetica 18 (Basel, 2005).

produced within these social relationships. The sense here is that Nekhebu, as the acting authority within the village, is in total control of the distribution of wealth and resources to the peasantry and can abuse those dependent on his patronage to maintain local hierarchies. Nekhebu does not deny beating the subordinates but merely that those unable to work any further were justifiably beaten and that those who handed over production to the lord were treated fairly. This implies that Nekhebu not only intervened indirectly in the management of labour (at the moment of revenue collection), but also directly during the actual production process. The legitimation of punishment is socially constructed, based on the exercise of strength as a demonstration of authority and the practice of hierarchical behaviour as a statement of reality. As such, the headman's denial that exploitative practices were used to intimidate *bȝk*-paying dependents functioned to hide the realities of violence and coercion at the village level.

The Impact of Enforcement and the Flight of Rural Revenue Payers

As enforcement was structural to revenue extraction processes, there was a difficult balance between outside pressures for income and potential problems caused by non-payment or flight. Indeed, the sources give the impression that a peasant farmer will generally not pay tax unless compelled to do so by the visit of a tax collector. The central issue is how the visiting official uses that power to the unreasonable disadvantage of the farmer in practice. Any attempt to violently draw full income from wholly or partly inundated lands could lead to the depopulation of the land.[49] In Papyrus Lansing, the arrival of the revenue-collecting scribe as the exploitative representative of external authority has dire and immediate consequences for the cultivator and his entire household:[50]

> The scribe has moored at the riverbank. He reckons the harvest with assistants with *šȝbd*-staffs and Nubians with *bdn*-rods. Them: "Give the grain"! "There is none". They beat [him] furiously. He is bound, thrown in the well, beaten and drowned, as his wife was being bound in front of him. His children are in fetters. His neighbours have abandoned them and fled.

As in the Heqanakht Letters, the Lansing farmer appears to be an independent cultivator, working within a rural community that provided subsistence for dependents,[51] when an external authority turns up to assess and collect his revenues. The scribe arrives with assistants (*iry-ʿȝ*) carrying *šȝbd*-sticks and Nubians carrying the same *bdn*-clubs that were used as interrogation tools to cause various forms of disfigurement of the hands and feet in the royal tomb robbery investigations.[52] The *iry-ʿȝ* "gatekeepers" are also known from other pharaonic contexts where revenue

---

[49]Eyre, *Use of Documents*, p. 186.

[50]P. Lansing, scribal manuscript, BM EA9994, 7.1–7.5 (= Alan H. Gardiner, *Late-Egyptian Miscellanies* [hereafter, *LEM*], Bibliotheca Aegyptiaca 7 (Brussels, 1937), p. 105, line 11–p. 106, line 1; Mariam Lichtheim, *Ancient Egyptian Literature: Volume II: The New Kingdom* (Berkeley, CA, 1976), pp. 170–171).

[51]Eyre, "Feudal Tenure", p. 110.

[52]See P. Leopold II (orig. Amherst P. VI), Koninklijke Musea voor Kunst en Geschiedenis / Royal Museums of Art and History, Brussels, E.6857, 3.6; Thomas. E. Peet, *The Great Tomb Robberies of the*

extraction is handed over. For instance, Dhutmose, from the Turin Taxation Papyrus discussed earlier, was sometimes accompanied by his *iryw-ꜥ3* when visiting the threshing floors of various sites to collect grain revenues.[53] The presence of the armed men implies that the village members did not receive well attempts by outsiders to survey the land during the survey processes. Likewise, the Lansing scribe arrives with his henchmen with an external demand for payment of grain. The farmer is unable to pay. Beatings and torture follow for the farmer, his family are imprisoned, and his dependents (*s3ḥw*) flee in panic. The result leaves the farmer unable to cultivate the land and ill-equipped to provide for dependents who must seek work elsewhere. In practical terms, targeting the farmer or village headman and his immediate family – rather than their dependents – is logical in the sense that they would be expected to manage and control what was produced on his lands.

Abusing women in front of other family members was intended to put extreme pressure on the farmer. In a Middle Kingdom scene from the tomb of the nomarch Baqet III at Beni Hassan, captioned "I was put before the mayors", the scribe of the house and others oversee the interrogation of men and women brought before them.[54] A man with a stick orders the herder, "Come you!", and the herdsman replies, "I was being put on the ground", presumably before being beaten. In the next register, a young woman holding a child is on her knees as a man strikes her with a stick telling her to stand up, with the implication that they are vulnerable because they do not have male protection. The reason for her treatment is unclear. Another girl on the ground is held by an older woman who demands to know "the full (number of) donkeys born"; the girl turns towards her and says "woe" (*iꜥnw*). This last example does not concern the collection of grain revenues but the counting of cattle as a revenue demand. The sources imply that the punishment of revenue defaulters (i.e. some manner of beating with sticks or substitution) was not differentiated according to the gender, age, or social status of the punished. The seizing of families held captive until the outstanding obligations were fulfilled is frequent enough in the source material to infer that the tactic was used to put psychological pressure on individuals to return and perform their duties. This is clear in administrative documentation from the Middle Kingdom. For instance, P. Berlin 10021 declares that if any of its listed workers cannot be found, substitutes should be brought in as replacements.[55] This practice is also evident in a Lahun letter that describes the seizing of the temple doorkeeper by district officers as a substitute for his son who had failed to turn up for *h3w*-duties.[56] The local village must be seen in a context in which local hierarchies were reinforced

---

Twentieth Egyptian Dynasty: Being a Critical Study, with Translations and Commentaries, of the Papyri in Which These are Recorded (Oxford, 1930), pl. v.

[53]Turin Taxation Papyrus, rt. 3,1–3,8; rt. 3,9–4,5 (= *RAD*, pp. 35–44). Translation in Miriam Lichtheim, *Ancient Egyptian Literature, Vol II: The New Kingdom* (Berkeley, CA, 1976), pp. 168–172.

[54]Percy E. Newberry, *Beni Hasan* (London, 1893), II, pl. 7; Naguib Kanawati, and Linda Evans, *Beni Hassan, Volume IV: The Tomb of Baqet III*, Australian Centre for Egyptology 42 (Oxford, 2018), pp. 41–42, pls. 49a, 62.

[55]P. Berlin 10021, letter, Staatliche Museen zu Berlin, lines 1–6, (= Ulrich Luft, *Urkunden zur Chronologie der Späten 12 Dynastie: Briefe aus Illahun* (Vienna, 2006), pp. 44–45).

[56]P. Berlin 10023A, letter, lines 1–3, Staatliche Museen zu Berlin (= Ulrich Luft, *Das Archiv von Illahun* (Berlin, 1992, P. Berlin 10023A, pp. 1–2).

by the uncertain intervention of the central regime during the harvest.[57] The relation-ship between the flight of the peasantry and the unfair enforcement of agricultural revenues (*b3k*) from cultivators (*iḥwty*) is explored in *The Loyalist Teaching*, where it is framed as the antithesis to productive leadership:[58]

> Do not deprive the cultivator (*iḥwty*) over his work (*b3k*); he thrives, and he will find you next year. If he lives, you are in his hands. You deprive him and he deci-des to be a wanderer. The one who appoints work-production in proportion to the grain [...] is in the heart of god, but the wealth of the evil-doer does not survive.

Within this context, the point of social hierarchy was to control and exploit what is productive within any given social-economic relationship (control over *b3k*). Nevertheless, there is a clear emphasis that economic power and political authority would collapse if dependents received unfair rewards for service. The end result is the flight of the peasantry from the fields. The theme of non-payment or flight in contexts where pressure from the outside becomes intolerable to the farmer is fre-quent enough in the source material to imply that it was pretty commonplace. A model letter from the Ramesside period describes a situation where the cultivators (*iḥwty*) of a royal plot of land flee after being beaten by the stable master.[59] The scribe responsible for the land has to find someone else to man the fields but has no choice but to advise his lord that the lands have been abandoned because of the actions of the stable master. The theme is best summed up later in the literary text known as *The Eloquent Peasant*. High Steward Rensi is informed that one of his minor functionaries has beaten and robbed a peasant travelling into the Nile Valley from the countryside:[60]

> Surely, it's a peasant of his, who has come to another at his side. Look, it's what they do to their peasants who come to others beside them. Look, it's what they do. This is a case to punish this Nemtinakht for a little natron and a little salt.

His entourage determine that the peasant has just fled his master and that they should reimburse the value of his goods. From their perspective, punishment is not only given to those that deserve to be punished but is something that the local hierarchy

---

[57]Eyre, "How Relevant Was Personal Status", p. 167.

[58]*Loyalist Instructions*, lines 11–12. *The Loyalist Teaching*, or *The Loyalist Instructions*, is the name given to a didactic work surviving as an imperfectly preserved Middle Kingdom literary composition in Middle Egyptian. See Georges Posener, *L'enseignement Loyaliste. Sagesse égyptienne du Moyen Empire* (Geneva, 1976), pp. 125–129. The English translation given here is from Richard B. Parkinson, *Voices from Ancient Egypt: An Anthology of Middle Kingdom Writings* (London, 2008), p. 71.

[59]The reason why the men are beaten is not specified. See P. Bologna 1094, Museo Civico Archeologico, Bologna, lines 2,8–6,5 (*LEM*, pp. 1–12, 3). English translation in Ricardo A. Caminos, *Late-Egyptian Miscellanies*, Brown Egyptological Studies 1 (London, 1954), pp. 11–12.

[60]Peasant B1, lines 75–79 (= Richard B. Parkinson, *The Tale of the Eloquent Peasant* (Oxford, 1991)). The translation follows Richard B. Parkinson, *Tale of Sinuhe and Other Ancient Egyptian Poems 1940–1640 B.C.* (Oxford, 2009), see pp. 60–61.

does to control their people fleeing to a patron other than their lord.[61] The concern of provincial administrations in restricting the mobility of rural populations attached to specific workforces in the countryside is found in Middle Kingdom administrative documents such as P. Brooklyn 35.1446 (c.1985–1773 BCE). This administrative text is concerned with the institution known as the "Great Enclosure" (*ḫnrt wr*), the "Office of Assigning People" (*ḫʒ n dd rmṯ*), and with the peopling of *ḥbsw*-lands.[62] Although the exact function of the "Great Enclosure" and its relation-ship with the "Office of Assigning People" is uncertain, it might be related to the management of labour, the manning of agricultural lands, and, in the case of the enclosure, a place of confinement for agricultural defaulters.[63] The recto of P. Brooklyn 35.1446 contains a series of punishments given to agricultural defaulters (mostly men but some women) that are dealt with according to the law (*hp*) concern-ing individuals who were missing (*tš*) or had fled (*wꜥr*).[64]

The punishment of offenders is varied. One passage describes how a ship's captain was stripped of his position and his family assigned to a labour camp because he had helped a defaulter escape.[65] In another example, the daughter of the Scribe of the Fields is judged according to the law concerning one who flees but is later released after completing her service.[66] As in the case of the discussed tomb scenes depicting the punishment of revenue defaulters, those suspected of flight were sometimes also sentenced by a local tribunal (*dʒdʒt*). For instance, one example describes how an unnamed male and his entire family were sentenced by a tribunal to work *ḥbsw*-lands for all time (*dt*).[67] The threat and application of punishments that emphasize the dan-ger of losing one's individual social status and privilege (i.e. compulsory fieldwork) mark an interesting contrast with the role of rightful substitution of family members or village dependents as reflecting the standard hierarchical rights of the landholder. These practices (removal of office, forced labour, and collective punishment) can be compared with the threat found in the Abydene decree of Neferirkare that individuals who fail to comply with royal commands would be stripped (*sdʒ*) of their households (*pr*), fields (*ʒḥt*), and dependents (*mrt*) before being made to do fieldwork.[68] They can also be compared with the clauses in the Ramesside Nauri decree of Seti I that

---

[61]Eyre, "How Relevant Was Personal Status", p. 180.

[62]William C. Hayes, *Papyrus of the Late Middle Kingdom in the Brooklyn Museum* (New York, 1955), pp. 16, 36–42, 65–66; Bernadette Menu, "Considérations sur le droit pénal au Moyen Empire égyptien dans le p. Brooklyn 35.1446 (Texte Principal du Recto). Responsables et Dépendants", *Le Bulletin de l'Institut français d'archéologie orientale*, 81 (1981), pp. 57–76; Stephen Quirke, *Titles and Bureaux of Egypt, 1850–1700 BC* (London, 2004), pp. 127–154; Eyre, *Use of Documents*, pp. 71–73; Micòl Di Teodoro, *Labour Organisation in Middle Kingdom Egypt*, Middle Kingdom Studies 7 (London, 2018), pp. 62–73. For *ḥbsw*-lands, see Bernadette Menu, "Fondations et concessions royales de terres en Égypte ancienne", in *idem*, *Recherches sur l'histoire juridique, économique et sociale de l'ancienne Égypte* (Cairo, 1998), II, pp. 130–131.

[63]Hayes, *Papyrus of the Late Middle Kingdom*, p. 16, 54–56; Quirke, *Titles and Bureaux*, pp. 94–95.

[64]Hayes, *Papyrus of the Late Middle Kingdom*, pp. 34–35, 47–52.

[65]*Ibid.*, p. 53.

[66]P. Brooklyn, Brooklyn Museum, 35.1446 (= William C. Hayes, *A Papyrus of the Late Middle Kingdom*, pp. 64–65, pls. v–vii).

[67]P. Brooklyn 35.1446, 57 (= Hayes, *Papyrus of the Late Middle Kingdom*, pl. vi).

[68]Decree of Neferirkere, c.2446–2438 BCE, Museum of Fine Arts, Boston, MFA 03.1896, lines 20–28 (= Hans Goedicke, *Königliche Dokumente aus dem Alten Reich* (Wiesbaden, 1967), p. 23).

punish corruption with beatings, disfigurements, or fieldwork as a temple cultiva-tor.[69] The punishments handed out by the local tribunal provide extra contextual information about how village councils dealt with those suspected of flight after fail-ing to pay grain revenues on delegated plots (as opposed to the interrogation and tor-ture of those resisting external demands on grain revenues) and how newer government institutions from later periods of pharaonic history such as the "Great Enclosure" were used alongside more traditional forms of enforcement such as the $ḏ3ḏ3t$-tribunal during the enforcement of revenue collection processes.

The Role of Punishment and Its Impact on the Control of the Outcome of Production ($b3k$)

A major aim of this article has been to analyse how the role of punishment intersects with the management of labour to demonstrate how the imposition of diversified forms of punishment contributed to creating and maintaining existing labour distinc-tions. Its focus on a specific field of activity in pharaonic Egypt (agriculture and the collection of grain revenue by the central regime) is justified by the fact that the pri-mary source material implies that the use of physical violence for tax extraction was a historical process that specifically targeted cultivators or headmen involved in agricul-tural production.[70] Agricultural labour management was based on a hierarchy of patron-client relations and relations with the crown through the village headmen as the representative of his rural community, with scribes who acted as agents of the temple and provincial authorities. Based on the surviving sources, the central regime did not attempt to directly administer or collect revenues from farmers who worked inundated land during the pharaonic period. It may be the case that the docu-mentation has not survived. Still, the norm appears to have been that revenue collec-tion was delegated to those who had personal knowledge of local conditions during the inundation and had the resources to collect and transport revenues. For practical reasons, periodic surveys, revenue estimates, and attempts to physically enforce com-munal responsibility through the responsible headmen or local intermediary, who might well be a prosperous farmer, were probably the norm throughout the pharaonic period. It was simply more efficient for local notables to collect revenues from the countryside and for agents of institutional or private estates to collect from the local authority than it was to run an efficient centralized taxation system.

---

[69]Nauri Decree, lines 50–52 (= *KRI* I, p. 53, line 16–p. 54, line 4). Marcella Trapani, "Un édit de Séthi II Réprimant la Corruption des Prêtres de Karnak", in Christine Gallois, Pierre Grandet, and Laure Pantalacci (eds), *Mélanges offerts à François Neveu. Par ses amis, elèves et collègues à l'occasion de son soixante-quinzième anniversaire* (Cairo, 2008), pp. 179–287, 282–287.

[70]The surviving data is not concerned with other professions such as craftsmen or other people involved in food production, such as fishermen or gardeners who were also expected to hand over production ($b3k$) to a lord related to an amount of work, most probably the amount of the produce of this work requested to these professions by the institution which employed them (magnates, temples, or the crown). Literary texts satirizing the trades and caricaturing these professions do not mention the systematic use of physical vio-lence for tax extraction, unlike those involved in agricultural production, as if this were a kind of occupa-tional cliché.

In the case of a collective default, the village headmen and other intermediate local hierarchies were held responsible by the agents of external authority because they were responsible for collecting grain from the villages and towns they managed. Different punishments were used to demote officials and headmen to lower levels of status and the harsher forms of agricultural labour that came with a loss of privilege: peasant farmers and headmen were beaten, officials put to work, some lost their office and property, and revenue defaulters were consigned to holding camps until obligations had been settled. The punishment of defaulters and the violent enforcement of outside revenue claims, which were, naturally, heavily resisted at the local level, should be seen as structural to pharaonic revenue extraction processes (rather than as a form of punishment that enforced the production process). It is also relevant to note that the textual and iconographic evidence discussed in this article certainly applies to what can be called institutional estates – including land belonging to a temple, the crown, or the large estate a magnate received from the king for his funerary endowment. By the New Kingdom period (and probably for part of the land held by Heqanakht in the early Middle Kingdom), a system of almost privately held fields had developed on smaller and independent land tenures. How tax collection occurred and physical violence was applied against the large number of landholders (headmen, women, soldiers, and servants) listed in Ramesside documents like the Wilbour Papyrus remains almost unknown.

Cite this article: Adam Simon Fagbore. Punishment, Patronage, and the Revenue Extraction Process in Pharaonic Egypt. *International Review of Social History*, 68:S31 (2023), pp. 53–71. https://doi.org/10.1017/S0020859023000032

International Review of Social History, 68:S31 (2023), pp. 73–92
doi:10.1017/S0020859023000019

RESEARCH ARTICLE

Corporal Punishment at Work in the Early Middle Ages: The Frankish Kingdoms (Sixth through Tenth Centuries)*

Alice Rio

King's College London, United Kingdom, e-mail: alice.rio@kcl.ac.uk

Abstract

This article deals with a paradox. Evidence for the punishment of workers during the early Middle Ages is richer in the earlier period (sixth and seventh centuries), when rural workers are generally thought to have been the least oppressed; by contrast, direct discussion of the subject largely drops out of the record in the Carolingian era (eighth to tenth centuries), despite clear evidence for renewed intensification of economic exploitation by both lay and religious lordships over the same period. Whereas the punishment of slaves had once provided a richly productive metaphor for thinking through issues of moral authority and legitimate leadership, Carolingian moralists and commentators no longer took the punishment of workers as a meaningful model for other, more morally or religiously motivated practices of punishment. Despite interest in punishment in other, non-exploitative contexts, lords' practices of punishment of their workers were no longer taken as productive of meaning, whether positive or negative. The relationship of lords with their lowest-ranking dependents no longer defined or illustrated their power in the way that it had for the earlier Roman and late antique paterfamilias. One reason for this was the increasing tension perceived between profit-seeking and the correct, justified exercise of punishment: the two were kept at arms' length by Carolingian writers to a surprising extent.

Within the context of Western European history, the early Middle Ages are regarded as a period of relatively low levels of oppression of peasants – the vast majority of workers at that time.[1] For the Frankish kingdoms (which in time grew to cover an area corresponding to modern-day France, Belgium, the Netherlands, Switzerland, Germany, and Austria), this seems to have been especially true during the sixth and seventh centuries, during the Merovingian period, when most lords enjoyed

---

*I would like to thank the Leverhulme Trust for funding the period of research leave during which this article was written. I also thank Alice Taylor for commenting on a draft version, and the two anonymous reviewers for their helpful comments.
[1]Chris Wickham, *Framing the Early Middle Ages* (Oxford, 2006), pp. 519–588.

only limited (for lords) social, economic, and political domination over rural populations. It is not that they were any less keen to punish their workers and dependents than those who came either before or after them. The extraction of labour, whether in the form of "productive" or "care" work, very likely continued to involve a great deal of day-to-day violence. The basic punishment toolkit was all there; the only thing lords lacked to turn it into more productive control and higher revenue extraction was the ability to extend such methods of coercion systematically.

Towards the latter end of our period (roughly corresponding to the Carolingian period, eighth and ninth centuries), lords did gradually manage to intensify their political and economic control over peasants, and one would naturally expect punishment and the threat of violence to have featured prominently as part of their arsenal of coercion. In practice, it is virtually certain that these did play a significant role.[2] Oddly, though, it is precisely around the same time that references to the punishment of workers start to fade from the record. If anything, sources become ever coyer about lords' punishment of their dependents, yielding fewer concrete examples and less direct reflection on the subject. Their engagement with the issue also becomes more generic and superficial.

One way to account for this chronological contrast might be the greater practical distance that then separated lord and worker, which went hand in hand with the intensification of exploitation. Merovingian lords had typically sought to control just a small force of directly exploited workers and mostly left their tenants alone. By contrast, the larger-scale estate management practised by some lords in the Carolingian period, including important ecclesiastical and monastic lordships, involved coordinating the work of tenants, which, in turn, placed more emphasis on layers of delegation through estate managers. Delegated punishment of workers by estate managers is more elusive in the record, essentially because it did not reflect upon the moral character of anybody worth talking about. But this cannot be the whole story behind the change in the nature of the discussion across the period: Carolingian lords continued to have domestic servants as well, and many of these were, in fact, drawn from the very tenant families that were being brought increasingly under their control.[3] The issue of how to deal with subordinates who were meant to work for them was therefore as relevant to them as it had been to earlier or later elites. But it does seem to have led to remarkably little contemporary discussion.

This is all the more surprising as, besides being a period of intensification in rural exploitation, the eighth and ninth centuries were also a time in which strong emphasis was increasingly being laid on the duty of correction, which became seen as a crucial element in the mission handed down by God to kings, and, in turn, by kings to royal officials, bishops, abbots, and heads of households.[4] Punishment and

---

[2] Jean-Pierre Devroey, *Puissants et misérables* (Brussels, 2006), pp. 295–304.

[3] *Idem*, "Femmes au miroir des polyptyques", in Stéphane Lebecq, Alain Dierkens, Régine Le Jan, and Jean-Marie Sansterre (eds), *Femmes et pouvoirs des femmes. Byzance et en Occident (VIe-XIe siècles)* (Lille, 1999), pp. 227–249; also Alice Rio, *Slavery After Rome, 500–1100* (Oxford, 2017), pp. 161–165.

[4] *Correctio* defies footnoting, but a good starting point is still Rosamond McKitterick, *Carolingian Culture: Emulation and Innovation* (Cambridge, 1994).

its legitimacy were certainly a matter for discussion in political and religious life.[5] Yet this confluence of greater economic exploitation of peasants and more robust moral backup for correcting subordinates did not lead to greater engagement with the question of how or when to punish workers; it anything, it led to less. It is worth asking why it should have been precisely at this time that the punishment of workers fell from its earlier position as a key analogy for thinking through such fundamental themes as moral leadership, mutual ties, discipline and responsibility, to turn into something at once more distasteful and more anodyne, that no-one much liked to write about.

Most sources under consideration here are ecclesiastical and monastic, which greatly impacts the overall profile of punishment that emerges from them. This perspective looms large not just because of the natural slant in the surviving source material, but also because religious institutions were at a fruitful intersection of multiple regimes and disciplines of labour, people, and jurisdictions, all of which makes them useful for thinking through the themes of this Special Issue. They were establishing their authority over large numbers of rural workers and experimenting with new models of work management while at the same time self-consciously elaborating a distinctive and explicit punishment regime through monastic rules, canon law, and penitentials. They were lords of labouring people themselves, but they also claimed a duty and right to judge the correctness of other people's practices of punishment of their own labour force, for instance, by imposing penance or giving sanctuary. It is, therefore, worth paying attention to when and why they made, or failed to make, the connection between punishment and work.

I refer here to both "masters" and "lords", but this is not to imply a strong or clearly datable chronological rift between Roman masters and medieval lords. The distinction between the two for the early medieval period is really a matter of emphasis. Most lords were also masters, in the sense that they had unfree dependents, both domestic and rural, but not all masters were lords (for instance, merchants like the one from the *Miracles of Saint Goar* whom we will meet below, or Jews, or, indeed, well-to-do peasants). Non-lordly masters, though, are even less well documented and played no part in shaping the elite discourse of punishment. So, in practice, I will mostly stick here to masters who were also lords and use the terms fairly interchangeably. Peasants, rural workers, could be either free or unfree; those I discuss here were mainly tenants who held farms from their lords in exchange for rent, and later also for regular dues in kind and in labour. "Unfree" and "slave" are legally equivalent, but the first term takes in the whole – very broad – spectrum of who could be claimed under that status, whereas "slave" denotes only the most closely supervised and heavily subjected end of that spectrum.

The Rise and Fall of the Paradigm of Slavery

The diminishing interest in punishment in surviving written sources closely tracks a simultaneous decline in engagement with slavery as a symbolic and moral theme.

---

[5] For a recent treatment of punishment in the Carolingian period, see Maximilian P. McComb, "Strategies of Correction: Corporal Punishment in the Carolingian Empire 742–900" (unpublished Ph.D., Cornell University, 2017).

This left an important gap in the discussion of labour in general, because the entire framework for discussion of the punishment of workers had been heavily overdetermined by the model of slavery, which dominated all discourse about it, even though it almost certainly did not dominate in terms of actual labour relations in either antiquity or the early Middle Ages.[6]

Slavery had taken on this importance not because it was the main form of labour relationship but because it helped to put things in the starkest possible terms. Late antique patristic writers had engaged with it quite intensively because the complex ethical problems involved in one individual holding virtually unrestricted power over another turned it into a productive source of analogies through which to discuss power more generally, both worldly and divine.[7] When, in the mid-fifth century, Salvian, a priest in Marseille, wrote his *De gubernatione Dei*, in which he argued that late antique Gallic elites fully deserved the harsh treatment that God had recently been meting out to them, he used punishment and slavery as the key to understanding both his own times and man's relationship to God. He first berated the elites as bad slaves who failed to obey their master: although they deserved death, God had sent them only lighter punishments to make them mend their ways. He continued the servile analogy (which doubtless would have been very shocking to those he was addressing), observing: "our very nature and wickedness are of a servile sort: we wish to do wrong and not be beaten for it" (IV, 2). He then drew up a standard and highly stereotypical list of the common faults of slaves, including thieving, lying, greediness, and running away, and presented them as, first, driven largely by circumstances of their masters' own making, and second, as less harmful and wrong than what masters did themselves. Key among these masters' failures were their bad practices of punishing their slaves, which Salvian contrasted with God's own just punishment of humanity. For him, the punishment of slaves was clearly absolutely necessary and something that good masters knew how to do fairly and productively. These masters' punishments were wrong because they were hypocritical (in that they were punishing their slaves' sins harshly, despite being guilty of worse ones themselves, for which they nonetheless expected God to forgive them) and because they were cruel, leading slaves to further sin and dissimulation instead of correction and obedience.[8]

Salvian's work represents a high point in the level of symbolic importance attached to the punishment of slaves, but this remained an important and fruitful theme throughout the patristic era. The *Life* of the bishop Caesarius of Arles, written about a century later than Salvian and also in the south of Gaul, sought to establish its subject's ability to correct appropriately by saying that he never condemned anyone, "whether one of his slaves or the freeborn men subjected to him" (*sive de servis sive de ingenuis obsequentibus sibi*), to more than the "legitimate discipline" of thirty-

---

[6]Wickham, *Framing the Early Middle Ages*, pp. 570–588.

[7]The works of John Chrysostom alone yield over 5,000 references to slavery: Kyle Harper, *Slavery in the Late Roman World, AD 275–425* (Cambridge, 2011), p. 18; Chris de Wet, *Preaching Bondage: John Chrysostom and the Discourse of Slavery in Early Christianity* (Oakland, CA, 2015).

[8]Georges Lagarrigue (ed.), *Salvien de Marseille. Oeuvres*, vol. 2, Sources chrétiennes, 220 (Paris, 1975); Salvian, *On the Government of God*, transl. Eva M. Sanford (New York, 1930). On this passage, see C. de Wet, "The Great Christian Failure of Mastery", *Religion and Theology*, 25:3–4 (2018), pp. 394–417.

nine lashes. This odd number matches the maximum allowable number of lashes to which a judge could condemn a fellow Jew according to Jewish law. Beyond this number, the punishment was presented as a humiliation and a denial of brotherhood: "Forty stripes he may give him, and not exceed: lest, if he should exceed, and beat him above these with many stripes, then thy brother should seem vile unto thee" (Deuteronomy 25:3, King James Version). Forty had later been amended to thirty-nine in the Mishna: there, the judge, after consulting a doctor regarding the highest number of lashes the condemned person could withstand without risk, had to prescribe the next highest number that was divisible by three (one third to be administered on the chest, two thirds on the back), resulting in an absolute maximum figure of thirty-nine.[9] Other elements in the same chapter of the *Life* of Caesarius offer an intriguingly close match with provisions found in the same section of the Mishna (tractate Makkot 3), so this does seem to be the result of direct influence, whether on Caesarius's actual policies or in the writing of the *Life*.[10] Arles had a large Jewish community (albeit one with which Caesarius had a terrible relationship), so direct borrowing is far from implausible, even if it only came out of an unwillingness to concede religious and moral high ground – though it is also somewhat ironic given Caesarius's insistence in other contexts that Christians should not adopt Jewish customs. In any case, the reference to thirty-nine lashes was intended to show that Caesarius ignored worldly status distinctions altogether and treated all his workers as his "brothers" in religion – albeit in a rather harsh sense.[11]

This denial of worldly status distinctions was obviously rather double-edged. While the message the reader was meant to take away from this story was clearly that Caesarius treated his slaves no more harshly than his free people (that is, there were limits to how far they could be punished), it is also a little surprising to see him subject his free workers to flogging in the first place. According to Roman law and older Roman ideas of household governance, a paterfamilias, in principle, had the legal authority to inflict punishment on his children and his slaves, but not on anyone else.[12] Perhaps Caesarius's position as a bishop, which gave him

---

[9]*Vita Caesarii*, I.25, ed. Bruno Krusch, MGH *Scriptores rerum Merovingicarum*, 3 (Hannover, 1896), p. 466; William Klingshirn (transl.), *Caesarius of Arles: Life, Testament, Letters* (Liverpool, 1994), p. 21. Mishna, Makkot 3.10–11. "Forty lashes less one" also features as a standard Jewish legal penalty in Paul, 2 Corinthians 11:24, which could also be where Caesarius had got that number, but in Paul it has none of the same connotations of restraint.

[10]Other direct parallels: an overseer of the church who went beyond thirty-nine lashes, if this resulted in death, was held guilty of murder; for very serious or compounded crimes, the lashing could resume after a few days of healing (both provisions in Mishna Makkot 3.14). Contributors to Book I of the *Vita*, composed shortly after Caesarius's death, included Cyprianus, bishop of Toulon, a close associate of his, and Firminus of Uzès (Klingshirn, *Caesarius of Arles*, p. 1); both were bishops in Southern Gaul where Jewish communities were at the time much more prominent than elsewhere. The early diffusion of the Mishna in the Latin West is very difficult to ascertain, but the reference seems clear enough here.

[11]As noted by Mary Sommar, *Slaves of the Churches: A History* (Oxford, 2020), p. 115, though without noting the reference to Jewish law. Sommar takes this at face value as evidence that Caesarius treated his slaves "relatively well", but in the Mishna, thirty-nine lashes are certainly seen as sufficient to risk killing someone.

[12]The classic article is by Richard Saller, "Corporal Punishment, Authority and Obedience in the Roman Household", in Beryl Rawson (ed.), *Marriage, Divorce and Children in Ancient Rome* (Oxford, 1991), pp. 144–165. Saller argued that there would have been a much greater reluctance to punish adult offspring

some judicial authority and discretion, at least for legal cases involving church business, contributed to muddying the waters: free people could certainly be condemned to corporal punishment as a result of a judicial process, even if this applied only to *humiliores*, "the more humble" or the socially weak. Caesarius's action is framed in the text as correcting a sin (*quisquis peccans*) rather than in the light of labour coercion. However, since the same chapter mentions overseers (*ordinator*, *praepositus*) as the ones inflicting the punishment and needing to be warned against exceeding its limits, labour exploitation certainly seems to be the context for it. The blithe unconcern of the authors of the *Life* on this score suggests they did not expect anyone to be shocked by it. At the same time, Caesarius, in warning that overzealous punishers who killed someone in the process of punishing them would be charged with homicide, was also ignoring Roman law in a more benign sense: epitomes of Roman law circulating at this time and later continued to emphasize that a master who killed his slave while punishing him for doing something wrong (*culpa*) was not guilty of homicide unless there had been a clear intention to kill, *nam emendatio non uocatur ad crimen*, "for correction should not be reckoned a crime".[13] The message was that Caesarius, through his regime of punishment, sought to go above the social divisions of Roman law by appealing instead to Old Testament law's basic assumption of equality among God's people.

Towards the end of the sixth century and further north, in the Loire valley, the theme of the punishment of slaves was still richly productive of meaning for Gregory of Tours, though mainly in order to criticize abuses of power rather than as a metaphor for God's power. His *Histories* contain two especially striking "bad master" examples. Sichar, as he ordered one of his slaves to work, beat him so savagely, striking him repeatedly with a rod, that the slave drew his master's sword and wounded him with it; Sichar's "friends" (his *amici*, which is to say, his military retinue) ran up, beat the slave "cruelly", cut off his hands and feet, then hanged him from a gibbet. In the same work, the *dux* Rauching forced his slaves to hold lit candles between their legs, under threat of death, while he sat at dinner; he also punished two of them, who had run away together to a church in the hope of getting married, by burying them alive together in the same coffin, having promised the priest he would not separate them.[14] In the case of both Sichar and Rauching, the reason why these stories were included at all was to offer a negative gloss on the other, more meaningful violence in which they were otherwise engaged, namely, that against their peers. Their behaviour towards their slaves was worth recording, *en passant*, to fill in a generally

---

since the punishment of adults was so strongly associated with slavery and therefore humiliating. On the afterlife of such ideas in a monastic context, see Julia Hillner, "Monks and Children: Corporal Punishment in Late Antiquity", *European Review of History / Revue européenne d'histoire*, 16:6 (2009), pp. 773–791.

[13]*Lex Romana Visigothorum*, IX, 12 (slaves) and 13 (children). Unless otherwise stated, all translations are mine. The clause was taken up by Regino of Prüm, *De synodalibus causis et disciplinis ecclesiasticis*, ed. Friedrich Wilhelm H. Wasserschleben (Graz, 1840, repr. 1964), II, 59, p. 237. Stefan Jurasinski, "The Old English Penitentials and the Law of Slavery", in Stefan Jurasinski, Lisi Oliver, and Andrew Rabin (eds), *English Law Before Magna Carta: Felix Liebermann and "Die Gesetze der Angelsachsen"* (Leiden, 2010), pp. 97–118, 108–109.

[14]Gregory of Tours, *Libri historiarum X*, eds. Bruno Krusch and Wilhelm Levison, MGH Scriptores rerum Merovingicarum, I, 1 (Hannover, 1951): VII, 47 (Sichar); V, 3 (Rauching).

disreputable picture. In this, Gregory represents more a return to an older and not especially Christian tradition, according to which the excessively harsh or cruel treatment of slaves was an important signal of bad moral character that cast severe doubt on suitability for holding authority over others. In Gregory of Tours, it is much harder than in Salvian or the Life of Caesarius to see the positive version of the punishment of slaves: instances of punishment related by him tend to be excessive and gruesome, whereas, in the case of "good" masters, punishment or correction are not discussed.[15]

Throughout the sixth century, then, the punishment of slaves was used to express all kinds of meaningful things about the proper exercise of authority: it was fruitful both as a general metaphor and as a moral and spiritual test of powerful people. This is very much in contrast with the use of the theme in Carolingian-era writings, in which it is both rarer and somewhat vacuous. How good or bad someone was at punishing their slaves, for instance, disappears entirely from assessments of character. Although Carolingian-era writers were just as keen as their predecessors on character assassination, they never discussed this aspect of people's behaviour. If anything, rather the reverse: one of the most notable character assassinations of the Carolingian era, that of the ex-slave archbishop Ebbo of Reims by the historian Thegan, decried the fact that a slave had been treated too *well*.[16]

Punitive violence against slaves did still turn up sporadically in church councils, penitentials, saints' lives, or manuals of good conduct. The most evocative reference, by Jonas, bishop of Orléans, in a manual of good conduct written in the 820s for a lay magnate at the Frankish court, pictured lay lords who, despite being themselves "slaves of God" (*servi Dei*), "with wild indignation, enraged with the fury of an agitated mind by the mistakes of their slaves, beat them to excess, killing them with savage blows or maiming them by amputating limbs", and warned that God, for whom all men are equal, would hold such men accountable (the implication, naturally, being that no one else would).[17] His aim here, though, was to stimulate a general feeling of brotherhood in a pastoral sense rather than encourage a more appropriate punishment regime. Most of the passage does not focus on punishment nor on how to manage direct power over someone, but rather on not despising those lower down in the social hierarchy. It puts at least as much emphasis on *pauperes*, generically "poor" or socially vulnerable people, as on slave dependents.

Carolingian-era conciliar legislation did very occasionally deal with the excessive punishment of slaves. Still, it was exclusively via late antique citations rather than contemporary case material when it did so. One woman whose case had been considered at the Council of Elvira in 306 was thus immortalized as *the* quintessential enraged mistress who beat her slave woman to death, standing in for all later and future cases: the clause about what her penance should be was cited in Carolingian-era councils and penitentials, which both suggests that her case was

---

[15]For instance, in the story of Attalus, which shows only collaboration and camaraderie between master and slave: Gregory of Tours, *Libri historiarum X*, III, 15.

[16]Thegan, *Gesta Hludowici imperatoris*, c. 20 and 44.

[17]Jonas of Orléans, *De institutione laicali*, II, 22, ed. Odile Dubreucq, *Jonas d'Orléans. Instruction des laïcs*, 2 vols, Sources chrétiennes, 549–550 (Paris, 2012–2013).

still seen as relevant and simultaneously shields from our view anyone else who ever behaved like her afterwards.[18]

Both slavery and the punishment of slaves seem to have become, by the Carolingian era, less powerful tools for writers and intellectuals to think with. For this period, we therefore mostly lack the richly textured reading of master–slave relations that it is possible to gain from reading patristic authors or Gregory of Tours – even as, paradoxically, practical processes of exploitation by lords suddenly become far better documented through estate surveys ("polyptychs") produced by great monastic and ecclesiastical lordships, on the basis of which the social and economic history of the peasantry has been written for this later period.[19]

This change can no longer really be ascribed to the disappearance of slavery, which was for so long a mainstay of the historiography of this period, since it is clear that this disappearance has been largely overstated.[20] While the commercial slavery most iconically associated with Roman antecedents seems by then to have mostly fed overseas markets in the Muslim world, people within the Frankish kingdoms continued to be actively claimed as unfree for a wide variety of purposes, including some new ones, in both rural and domestic settings. Sometimes, the outcomes of such claims were relatively benign, but they were, above all, unpredictable and might change very significantly through the generations: a male tenant head of household might agree to be labelled as unfree to shut down a dispute with his lord and experience little immediate change as a result, but later down the line his daughter might well be claimed as a textile worker or domestic servant at the estate centre, or his sons arbitrarily reassigned as farmhands on other tenancies. Conversely, someone might be enslaved for being unable to pay a fine, or even for selling themselves, but end up with a tenancy and relatively little to tell them apart from their free neighbours – at least until new sources of conflict or local stress came into play. The fading out of interest in the punishment of slaves, then, does not link as straightforwardly to changes on the ground as might once have been thought.

Corporal Correction and the Denial of Self-Interest

One mid-ninth-century text makes it especially clear that the correct punishment of slaves was no longer a meaningful way of representing authority over a well-ordered household. In his commentary on the Benedictine Rule written in the mid-ninth century, Hildemar of Civate insisted strongly on distinguishing the physical disciplining of monks (children or, more rarely, adults) from that reserved for slaves (*servi*).

---

[18]The case was cited, for instance, in the Council of Mainz (847): MGH *Concilia*, III, no. 14, c. 22, pp. 172–173 (also citing the 506 Council of Agde on the killing of *servi* "without the knowledge of a judge"); and also by Regino of Prüm, *De synodalibus causis*, II, 58, p. 237.

[19]The literature is vast, but for great classics of the social history of this period based largely or mainly on polyptychs, see Devroey, *Puissants et misérables*; Ludolf Kuchenbuch, *Bäuerliche Gesellschaft und Klosterherrschaft im 9. Jahrhundert* (Wiesbaden, 1978).

[20]Rio, *Slavery After Rome*. As I argued there, the fact that there was slavery should not be considered per se to imply continuity from the Roman era, as assumed by the so-called feudal mutationist school that pushed most significant social changes down to the year 1000 (Pierre Bonnassie, *From Slavery to Feudalism in South-Western Europe*, transl. Jean Birrell (Cambridge, 1991), ch. 1).

Unlike for slaves, he wrote, the punishment of monks should be carefully measured so that it did not create a strong sense of fear. Acting out of fear of punishment, he said, was the mark of the slave, not the monk; monks should obey out of loyalty, more like *vassalli*, free dependents (though, as we shall see below, this may have been viewing the lives of the latter through rose-tinted glasses).[21] This section of the commentary is only distantly connected to the original text of the Rule, where the corresponding chapter was actually only about doing things "without delay", so it very much represents Hildemar's own input. By the mid-ninth century, then, even some monks – in contrast with Jonas of Orléans – seem to have become reluctant to think of themselves as "slaves of God". By then, the phrase had become such a cliché that Hildemar was likely being deliberately provocative in arguing against it.

The monastic life was the context in which the ends and means of punishment, and especially of corporal punishment, were discussed most explicitly and at the greatest length, all the way from late antiquity, with the writing of the first monastic rules, through the Carolingian era, with commentaries on the Rule of Saint Benedict once the latter had become adopted as standard. Monks make the best-documented lords and masters in this era for the same reasons that they are also the best-documented parental figures: that is, not because they were typical, but because they were so distinctive. It is precisely because monasteries amounted to a bizarre, experimental, reinvented version of both lordship and household that they presented a need to articulate and make self-conscious choices about things that in more "normal" contexts simply went without saying.

Julia Hillner has shown that monastic rules in late antiquity were not strongly committed to corporal punishment and mostly tried to limit it to certain ends and certain people. Early monastic rules in the West fairly consistently limited corporal punishment to those under fifteen.[22] Below that age, children were thought to be too young to understand the gravity of excommunication, the usual punishment for serious wrongdoing by adult monks, so correcting them required more physical methods, such as fasting or flogging.[23] Monastic rules, however, also left open the possibility that adult monks who, for reasons other than age, proved equally impervious to the threat of excommunication might benefit from corporal punishment, too. The corporal punishment of adult monks, though, remained a sensitive, difficult issue and created uneasiness: witnessing a brother being beaten was clearly expected to be traumatic for the community.[24] All this is also what one finds in later, Carolingian-era commentaries on the Rule of Benedict. Benedict of Aniane envisaged corporal punishment for adults only to deal with very serious sins, such as fornication, adultery, or persistent drunkenness. Hildemar of Civate also stipulated that punishment, whether

---

[21]Slaves vs *vassalli*: Hildemar of Civate, *Expositio regulae ab Hildemaro tradita et nunc primum typis mandata*, ed. Rupert Mittermüller (Regensburg, NY, and Cincinnati, OH, 1880), c. 5, p. 188. The text, along with an in-progress English translation, is available at The Hildemar Project: http://hildemar.org; last accessed 21 July 2022.

[22]Hillner, "Monks and Children", p. 781.

[23]Rule of Benedict, c. 30: "let them be punished by severe fasting or sharp stripes, in order that they may be cured".

[24]"[T]he victim of physical assault clearly loses status": Lynda Coon, *Dark Age Bodies: Gender and Monastic Practice in the Early Medieval West* (Philadelphia, PA, 2011), p. 85.

through beating or excommunication, could only be inflicted through a transparent hierarchy: no one other than the abbot was allowed to punish.[25] If one monk struck or excommunicated another in response to a serious fault (Hildemar takes as his example the uncontrollable outrage one might feel at witnessing someone mishandling a library book) without having received any special authority to do so from the abbot, this was treated as a lesser offence than simple brawling, but it was an offence nevertheless.[26] Everyone, however, could punish the children, as long as it was with moderation and without anger.

Notably, none of this discussion involved failure to do manual work. This is, in a way, surprising since manual work was, like disciplining and punishment, central to the conceptualization of the monastic life. The two, however, were left unconnected and had been so since the fifth century. John Cassian, c.420, went further than most writers of monastic rules in allowing for the corporal punishment of adult monks. Still, he did not prescribe it in any contexts that involved failure to do work: laziness, or preferring reading to working, were deserving of a public rebuke, but not of corporal punishment or expulsion from the monastery, which were reserved for much more serious sins like breaking discipline, having female friends, eating between meals, or desiring and acquiring things that other monks did not have.[27]

Hildemar's commentary similarly lacks any discussion of punishment in relation to manual labour, though it has plenty to say about both punishment and labour independently of each other. Even when it was productive, work by monks was not about profit or gain but about combating idleness (as well as, in some cases, sheer survival of the community). Hildemar, in fact, cites Augustine on the problem of acquisitiveness and "the anxiety of getting" as sources of worry at the other end of the scale from laziness.[28] He warns, for instance, that monks who were also craftsmen should not be too proud of their skill and that their goods should be sold for less than market price. In relation to work, Hildemar seemed to expect to find the greatest resistance when it came to kitchen duty. Even there, though, he recommended that the abbot, faced with a monk's refusal to take his turn, should take pains to explain the usefulness and charity of the task until everyone consented to serve. For the most obdurate, the punishment for not taking part was simply not being served oneself.[29]

Hildemar has much to say about child monks and is comfortable with the idea that children should be beaten – though much more than any other writer or commentator of a monastic rule, he insisted that this was intended only as "medicine" where preventative measures had proved insufficient, and therefore, in some sense, amounted to an admission of failure.[30] Hildemar also discusses children being put to manual work in the abbey, cleaning, cutting wood, or preparing vegetables. But

---

[25]Hildemar, *Expositio regulae*, c. 70, p. 621.

[26]*Ibid.*, p. 622.

[27]Hillner, "Monks and Children", p. 779. Cassian, *Institutes*, 4, 16.

[28]Hildemar, *Expositio regulae*, c. 48, pp. 476–477, referring to Augustine, *De Opera monachorum*, c. 15, Corpus Scriptorum Ecclesiasticorum Latinorum 41, p. 557. If anything, Hildemar envisages punishment more in connection with those who refused to read: pp. 485–486.

[29]Hildemar, *Expositio regulae*, c. 35, p. 398.

[30]Mayke de Jong, "Growing Up in a Carolingian Monastery: Magister Hildemar and His Oblates", *Journal of Medieval History*, 9:3 (1983), pp. 99–128, 107, citing *Expositio regulae*, p. 337. A reading of

even in their case, he does not put the two together and does not discuss punishment for doing this work badly or not at all: the only point where he mentions corporal punishment in relation to the performance of tasks was in an exclusively educational setting, when children made the same mistakes repeatedly while singing or reading.

Therefore, punishment and work were kept in different conceptual spheres to such a degree that this seems a very deliberate and self-conscious choice. High-minded punishment was not focused on petty material outcomes but on disciplining mind and body. The kind of punishment that was being discussed in monastic texts was linked to the goal of shaping the recipient into a better Christian or a better monk; it was never explicitly linked to obtaining labour, nor as part of a productive process, nor ever as a means to any other, more practical end. When framed as a means of obtaining any sort of advantage, including work, punishment seems to have been regarded as morally dangerous or, at best, uninteresting. If anything, punishment was linked most to care: the labour, the work, was seen as done by the punisher for the punished.

Everywhere a contrast was drawn, implicitly or (in the case of Hildemar) explicitly, between the work of monks and the work of anyone whose main role was productive rather spiritual. Monastic writers did not have much to say about the latter. There is no discussion regarding the moral danger of falling into excess while punishing servants: Hildemar had no problem with *slaves* living in fear of punishment. The punishment of servants or peasants was simply not, it seems, meaningful in any sense that made it worth discussing. Monasteries in the time of Hildemar were at the forefront of new experiments in the management of their tenant workforce (notably with the "bipartite estate", through which they obtained both dues and workdays from their tenants). Still, monks themselves would, generally, probably not have been directly involved in disciplining: this was done by agents or estate managers, who were not included among those the Rule was meant to guide. Lists of dues and workdays owed by tenants in monastic polyptychs show unquestionably that tenants were increasingly being squeezed; the big question begged and left unanswered by these lists was, "Or what?" It is easy, and almost certainly correct, to fill this gap with the threat of corporal punishment; it is nevertheless a notable absence in discourse.

Other People's Peasants Versus a Church's Own

On the other hand, the issue of when and how to punish peasants was discussed much more intensively in the area of jurisdiction, where it featured as an important symbolic weapon. Religious authorities presented themselves as ready to pick up the pieces whenever lay lords did punishment wrong. This kind of intervention could go either way: they might intervene to protect workers against their own lords' punishment but also to punish where lords were deemed to have failed to do so.

The first was the more traditional of the two types of intervention and linked back to practices of sanctuary that had begun to develop in the late Roman empire. The protection of the weakest and most vulnerable among Christians was a responsibility

---

corporal punishment as medicine was in itself fairly common and also features outside the Latin context in the rule of Basil of Caesarea: Hillner, "Monks and Children", p. 776.

that churches had taken on from the very early days. When discussed in councils, this involved essentially slaves: other types of workers were not mentioned since sanctuary was reserved for people who would otherwise have had no right to evade corporal punishment – a category that included slaves and criminals but not free people running in fear of their lives. Priestly intercession was about convincing masters to forgo a right to which they were entitled, not about offering a haven against violence in general. Fugitive Christian slaves had featured very prominently in laws relating to sanctuary in the Theodosian code, the main source for Roman law in Western Europe, still circulating throughout the early medieval period in the abbreviated form of the *Lex Romana Visigothorum* and its various epitomes. The basic tenor was that slaves should not be ejected from a church unless its clerics could obtain an undertaking from the slave's master that they would not be punished.[31] Priests' role of intercession between slaves and the masters seeking to reclaim them continued in Frankish-era secular and ecclesiastical legislation. The Council of Orléans (511) specified that the slave could not refuse to come back once the master had promised not to punish him and also that if the master then went against his promise, he was to be excommunicated.[32] No attempt was made to extend a fundamental challenge to lay lords' or masters' rights of punishment: canon law and penitentials prescribed excommunication and penance for those who killed their slaves (which is admittedly more than secular laws did), but they did not comment on punishment short of death.[33]

Miracle stories sometimes include narratives that played out some of these sanctuary scenarios, for instance, by showing masters being themselves subject to divine punishment after punishing their slaves despite their seeking sanctuary.[34] These stories were no longer widespread by the Carolingian period: the *Miracles of Saint Goar* by Wandalbert of Prüm, from the ninth century, are relatively unusual in including the stories of two slaves who ran to a church to escape their masters' punishment. Both were in fear of *supplicium* for making unspecified mistakes. The first was killed before the altar by his enraged lay master, a merchant, who died horribly as a divine punishment. The other was owned by a cleric of the church, and his anticipated punishment was also presented as much more thought-out, process-driven, and less fundamentally impulsive (his arms were already bound in preparation for punishment, implying it was not a spur-of-the-moment thing): he was saved through a miracle,

---

[31] *Codex Theodosianus*, IX.45.5 (from 432). Karl Shoemaker, *Sanctuary and Crime in the Middle Ages, 400–1500* (New York, 2011), p. 52.

[32] *Concilium Aurelianense* (511), c. 3. For a review of the evidence for slaves fleeing to churches in Francia: Shoemaker, *Sanctuary and Crime*, pp. 63–67.

[33] See above, n. 13. Later Old English versions of Continental penitentials were even easier on masters since even if the slave did die, penance only had to be done if s/he had not been guilty of a fault and had only been killed out of anger (which, in the absence of any enquiry, means it would really have been up to the master or mistress whether they thought they had acted wrongly). Jurasinski, "Slavery", pp. 106–108.

[34] For a discussion of sixth-century examples, see Edward James, "*Beati pacifici*: Bishops and the Law in Sixth-Century Gaul", in John Bossy (ed.), *Disputes and Settlements: Law and Human Relations in the West* (Cambridge, 1983), pp. 25–46, 36–40.

which released him from his bonds, and his owner wisely knew better than to claim him back for punishment.[35]

The second strand of intervention ought to dispel any emerging sense of Christian religious leadership being somehow intrinsically "soft" on punishment: churchmen could take the initiative to punish as much as to protect.[36] The Carolingian period was a time when corporal punishment, particularly flogging, became a standard part of the coercive toolkit for ecclesiastical authorities dealing with "lowly and useless little people" (*viles et nequam homunculi*, as Amolo of Lyon once put it).[37] Sometimes, this was in tension with lay lords' labour needs and their sense of their own rights and jurisdiction. The Council of Soissons of 853 ruled against lords who tried to prevent bishops or their representatives, apparently in the course of dealing out ecclesiastical justice, from beating their peasants (*coloni*), as well as against lords who took vengeance against them once they had done so.[38] In this context, we are also dealing with a much broader category of "peasants" and "lowly people" rather than just slaves.

All this attention to the punishment of such people, however, was very much centred on religious correction, not work. The one element explicitly related to labour documented in this material involved the prohibition of work on Sundays – which means, ironically, that the clearest connection made between righteous punishment and work in this period actually involves peasants being punished *for working*, rather than to coerce them into it.[39]

Ecclesiastical writers and thinkers in general, then, had plenty to say about punishing other people's workforce and how to go about it. By contrast, their punishment of their own workforce remained very undertheorized, much as we saw earlier in the case of monks. The highly developed Christian discourse of punishment as an inherently selfless act was not easily adapted to discussing churches' own practices of labour management. Disobeying a saint (and by extension his community) by refusing to perform tasks or performing them poorly might easily, of course, have been held to be a sin in itself and a good enough reason to punish – as clearly it had seemed to Caesarius of Arles. But this proved to be a dead end, and it is extremely

---

[35]Wandalbert of Prüm, *Miracula Sancti Goaris*, c. 24 and 25. The *Life* of Swithun contains striking English examples of a saint protecting slaves – though, in England, the pairing of slavery and punishment made up a very different sort of cocktail, paying much greater respect to masters' right to discipline their slaves, as noted by Jurasinski, "Slavery".

[36]Punishment in ecclesiastical legislation in general could be extremely harsh and also include corporal punishment: see, for instance, the *Capitula Remedii*, ed. Elisabeth Meyer-Marthaler, *Lex Romana Curiensis*, Sammlung schweizerischer Rechtsquellen 15.1.1, 2nd edn (Aarau, 1966), pp. 645–649. For a discussion, see McComb, "Strategies of Correction", pp. 78–85.

[37]Amolo of Lyon, *Epistolae* no. 1, c. 4, ed. Ernst Dümmler, *Epistolae Aevi Karolini* (Berlin, 1899), III, p. 365; on this particular case, see Shane Bobrycki, "The Flailing Women of Dijon: Crowds in Ninth-Century Europe", *Past & Present*, 240 (2018), pp. 3–46; Charles West, "Unauthorized Miracles in Mid-Ninth-Century Dijon and the Carolingian Church Reforms", *Journal of Medieval History*, 36 (2010), pp. 295–311.

[38]Council of Soissons (April 853): Wilfried Hartmann (ed.), *Die Konzilien der Karolingischen Teilreiche 843–859*, MGH *Concilia*, III (Hannover, 1984), no. 27, c. 9, pp. 288–289. The clause was later taken up by Regino of Prüm; McComb, "Strategies of Correction", pp. 77–78.

[39]On the prohibition of Sunday work throughout this period, see Dorothy Haines, *Sunday Observance and the Sunday Letter in Anglo-Saxon England* (Cambridge, 2010), pp. 1–16.

rare in later Lives to find a saint being depicted engaged in direct violence against his own workforce. That scenario is virtually absent from Carolingian-era sources, presumably to avoid mixing up saints' deployment of violence with base motivations of self-interest. If anything, one finds the opposite. In a famous passage from the *Life* of Gerald of Aurillac by Odo of Cluny, from the tenth century, Gerald, a layman secretly committed to living the life of a monk, sees some of his peasants (*coloni*) moving away from his lands: his attendants urge him to beat them and force them back to their farms, but he lets them go.[40] Laymen punished their workers to force them to work, but by this time saints – unlike in Caesarius's day – apparently no longer approved of punishment for labour and surplus extraction purposes.

This sense of unease about extractive violence extended to the work of church overseers, who were often decried as villains by the very religious authorities they served. The abuses of overseers are a common theme running through the religious literature of the entire period, including Salvian and the *Life* of Caesarius, though there it had been to accuse them of excessive, disproportionate violence.[41] In one story from a Carolingian-era miracle collection associated with Saint Germanus of Auxerre, by contrast, *any* amount of violence is made to look excessive: an estate manager of a monastery, when assigning daily tasks to peasants, met with resistance and had one of them beaten; Germanus responded by breaking his leg. The point is brought home even more forcefully when a character in the same story voices a dissenting opinion: one well-to-do lady, a *matrona*, commented that the saint had gone too far and that the manager had only been within his rights, and she, too, was punished by becoming crippled in her right leg.[42] That this attitude had more to do with punishing violent acquisitiveness and profit-seeking among representatives of churches and monasteries, rather than inherently with being nice to peasants or disliking violence, comes through in another miracle story in which a future saint shook a peasant violently by the head for persisting in ploughing over and across the public highway: punishment might be visited on peasants or overseers alike for having the wrong priorities and privileging material interests.[43]

The only direct discussion of a religious institution's violent coercion of its peasants in its own material interest comes from Alcuin, in a brief poem advising what to do when workers caused trouble out of fear of being oppressed by the monastery of Saint Amand. His message was: flog their backs, spare their souls.[44] This does, as in the *Life* of Caesarius, close the distance between peasants shirking work and committing a sin. Still, it is doubtful whether Alcuin would have been so open

---

[40]Odo of Cluny, *Vita Sancti Geraldi Auriliacensis Comitis*, I, 24.

[41]Salvian, *De gubernatione Dei*, IV, 3; *Vita Caesarii*, I, 25.

[42]Heiric of Auxerre, *Miracula Germani*, ed. Jacques-Paul Migne, *Patrologia Latina*, vol. 124, c. 75, col. 1242, cited in Matthew Innes and Charles West, "Saints and Demons in the Carolingian Countryside", in Thomas Kohl, Steffen Patzold, and Bernhard Zeller (eds), *Kleine Welten. Ländliche Gesellschaften im Karolingerreich* (Ostfildern, 2019), pp. 67–97, 76.

[43]Flodoard of Reims, *Historia remensis ecclesiae*, I, 25, ed. Martina Stratmann, *Die Geschichte der Reimser Kirche*, MGH Scriptores 36 (Hanover, 1998), p. 129.

[44]Alcuin, *Carmina* CVIII.2: *Rumpantur dorsa flagellis / Sit rea ruricolis tantum substantia salva*, ed. Ernst Dümmler, MGH *Poetae Aevi Carolini*, I (Berlin, 1881), p. 334; McComb, "Strategies of Correction", p. 76.

about it if the peasants had belonged to one of his own abbeys: Saint Amand was a monastery with which he had a friendly relationship, but out of whose dealings with peasants he did not stand to gain anything personally. Even the most vociferous among other ecclesiastics of this period somehow never liked to portray themselves punishing peasants in their own self-interest or even that of their community. While the pastoral model of punishment here, as in a monastic context, gave scope for subjecting a wider range of people to beatings, including free adults, it simultaneously seems to have become ever more difficult to reconcile with a profit motive – at least at the level of discourse.

Perspectives on Lay Lordship

One would not expect the corporal punishment of workers and subordinates to have presented the same problems of self-presentation for lay lords. The punishment of workers for the express purpose of extraction of labour was necessarily the type of punishment most central to the elite household – as opposed to ecclesiastical, monastic, or royal punishment, which, of course, included this aim but also had more diverse applications and purposes, many of which could be presented as having nothing to do with self-gain.

It is not that being lay was in any way in itself a bar to wielding the power of "correction" in a spiritual sense: doing God's work was very much part of laypeople's remit and responsibility as well, and several capitularies urged lay heads of households to correct those under their authority (their *familia*).[45] There is a fleeting sign of a cross-over impact of monastic models on at least one member of the lay elite's way of thinking about the punishment of those under their authority. In the early 840s, Dhuoda, a mother writing a manual of good conduct for her son William, followed the monastic ethos closely by urging him to correct, "with beatings or with words", the people under his command, as an act of charity and mercy.[46] Here, too, punishment could only be made legitimate and meaningful by eliminating any direct connection between punishment and anything William might have wanted his people to *do* for him. The more lay punishment fitted the model of righteous, spiritually motivated punishment, the less it could have to do with obtaining anything specific from subordinates. It is unlikely that more than a few exceptionally plugged-in laypeople like Dhuoda ever tried to involve themselves in this model or to align themselves to this kind of understanding of their own powers of punishment. Carolingian lords' punishment of their own workers is nonetheless just as elusive as religious institutions' punishment, though for different reasons.

The correct deployment of corporal punishment over subordinates seems to have become less relevant to lords' cultivation of their image and the construction of their legitimacy. In the time of Gregory of Tours, elite males had been discussed and

---

[45]*Capitularia regum Francorum* I, ed. Alfred Boretius, MGH *Leges* II, 2 vols (Hannover, 1883–1897), no. 65, c. 5.

[46]Dhuoda, *Liber manualis*, IV.30, ed. Pierre Riché, *Dhuoda. Manuel pour mon fils*, Sources chrétiennes, 225 (Paris, 1975); for English translations: Marcelle Thiébaux, *Dhuoda, Handbook for her Warrior Son: Liber manualis* (Cambridge, 1998); Carol Neel, *Handbook for William: A Carolingian Woman's Counsel for Her Son* (Lincoln, NE, 1991). Compare Rule of Benedict, e.g. cc. 23, 28.

judged chiefly as good (or bad) masters and as good (or bad) friends. The most mean-ingful tests at the time were polarized around what were conceived as either extreme vertical relationships (slaves) or basically horizontal ones ("friends", *amici* – masking the fact that the latter term by then also covered what were very clearly hierarchical relationships, as we saw earlier in the case of Sichar).[47] By the Carolingian era, this had clearly changed: I know of no author from this period who seems to have con-ceived of the punishment of workers in lords' households or on their estates as an effective theatre of power, whether in positive or negative terms. Unlike the Roman-style paterfamilias, for whom what mattered was the appearance of complete control of his household and everyone within it, Carolingian lords were judged more on their ability to operate as the nexus of a political network of military dependents, rooted in a much less absolute kind of authority. For them, the real test was how they dealt with this level of dependent, not the lowest vertical rung of slaves and peasants. For this purpose, skill and fairness in deploying and managing gifts – when to give them, when to withdraw them – was more important than when and how to apply corporal punishment. For that type of dependent, taking away landed benefices, not flogging, was the ultimate punishment. This is where most conflict and negative judgements about lords' wielding of their power became concentrated.[48]

The only extended, explicit discussions of corporal punishment by lords, accord-ingly, involve attempts to impose boundaries in more doubtful cases regarding people who were placed right on the edge between the lowest level of dependent, behaviour towards whom, one way or another, was becoming ever less relevant to the construc-tion of authority, and the higher-level type, who were to be won over and kept in line using only charisma, largesse, and the odd opportunity for plunder. For example, Charlemagne once ruled that beating with a stick (*baculum*) should count as one of the very few reasons why a lower-ranking retainer (*vassus*) could leave his lord. A *vassus* was a lowly kind of retainer at the time: this was the kind of dependence that Hildemar said monks' service to God should be like, as opposed to slavery, but in saying this, he was not referring to anything very elevated. Other valid reasons for a *vassus* to leave his lord included if the lord tried to kill him, defile his wife or daughter, or take away his inheritance – though he said nothing about other forms of corporal punishment, such as beating with fists, for instance.[49] Beating with a stick, out of all forms of punishment, was the one most iconically associated with slaves, so this may have been why it was being singled out as an unacceptably low-status form of violence, especially harmful for someone whose social position was not the strongest in the first place. Charlemagne clearly thought it important to make sure lords did not abuse their powers here while at the same time interfering in lord-retainer relations only in a very light-touch way.

---

[47] For an important discussion of these terms and relationships: Gerd Althoff, *Family, Friends and Followers: Political and Social Bonds in Early Medieval Europe*, transl. Christopher Carroll (Cambridge, 2004).

[48] A fascinating example of a lord dealing with his dependents is that of Hincmar of Laon (admittedly a bishop, but in relationships with this type of dependent the distinction was not so crucial): see Charles West, "Lordship in Ninth-Century Francia: The Case of Bishop Hincmar of Laon and His Followers", *Past & Present*, 226 (2015), 3–40.

[49] *Capitularia regum Francorum*, vol. 1, no. 77, c. 16, p. 172.

Perhaps more unexpectedly, priests were apparently regarded as another such marginal category. By the ninth century, priests were increasingly being brought into the charmed circle of those immune in principle from corporal punishment. Still, this bodily and ritual inviolability was evidently hard-won, and kings and bishops had difficulty convincing lay lords that they could not physically discipline the priests officiating within their households.[50] The problem was perhaps compounded by the fact that some household priests were also slaves, but clearly, they were not the only ones at risk.[51]

Being disciplined by someone else without recourse remained, conceptually at least, profoundly connected with slave status and slave connotations. In Carolingian legislation, as earlier in Roman law and in Salic and Ripuarian laws (all of which were still regarded as valid reference points), the legitimate imposition of corporal punishment by a head of household, as a practice of internal discipline entirely subsumed within a hierarchy over which he presided without the need to consult anyone else, was in principle limited to slaves.[52] Documents of self-sale or other forms of entry into unfree service explicitly transferred the right to the new master to "inflict the same discipline upon my back as upon that of your other servants".[53] In practice, though, a lot more people than this were vulnerable to violence. The concentration in Salic law and other "barbarian" law codes on slaves as the legitimate victims of corporal punishment, while free people were treated as if they all lived in a world of honour price, vengeance, and retaliation, left an immense gap in dealing with violence and punishment from a hierarchical superior *outside* a slave–master relationship. While written laws, read at face value, suggest a zero-tolerance approach to any kind of interference with free people's bodies, it was the claimant who had to make this zero-tolerance approach stick, and only a few could do so. While slaves could definitely be beaten, then, and high-status males definitely could not be, between these two poles of clarity, everyone had to find out for themselves where they fitted in over the course of events through the action they were able to take and how it was received. Many people would have found themselves in an ambiguous position, especially those who, regardless of their status, were placed in a hierarchical relationship with the person who might wish to subject them to physical coercion, for whom there was obviously very little practical recourse.

It is telling that in the case of the two kinds of people (priests and *vassi*) we have just seen teetering on this boundary, it was the rather special nature of the work, spiritual or military, which spoke in favour of their being elevated to a higher,

---

[50]McComb, "Strategies of Correction", pp. 39–42.

[51]Louis the Pious's *servus* Atto was an unfree priest who complained he had been subjected to corporal punishment: Ernst Dümmler (ed.), *Epistolae variorum* no. 25, MGH *Epistolae Karolini aevi* III, pp. 339–340. Susan Wood, *The Proprietary Church in the Medieval West* (Oxford, 2006), pp. 526–527; Marie-Céline Isaïa, "La justice des hommes, celle de l'empereur et celle de Dieu. Expérience et espérances du prêtre Atto", in Maïté Billoré and Johan Picot (eds), *Dans le secret des archives. Justice, ville et culture au Moyen Âge* (Rennes, 2014), pp. 29–46; McComb, "Strategies of Correction", pp. 43–45.

[52]E.g. *Capitularia regum Francorum*, vol. 1, no. 102, c. 16; also vol. 1, no. 82, c. 9 – both envisage only disputes or crimes, that is, cases that might have made it to a public court otherwise.

[53]*Formulae Marculfi*, ed. Karolus Zeumer, *Formulae Merowingici et Karolini Aevi* (Hannover, 1886), II, 27; see also II, 28. For an English translation: Alice Rio, *The Formularies of Angers and Marculf* (Liverpool, 2008).

flogging-free level. Clearly, though, many lords did think that corporal punishment was appropriate in their cases. All this implies that corporal punishment remained as central as ever to the practice of lordship, but at the same time, the sparse treatment of this issue also suggests that it had become less central to its conceptualization. Corporal punishment had lost none of its practical relevance: what it had lost was its meaningfulness, at least in the eyes of contemporary and mostly clerical commentators.

Royal Justice and Royal Estates

This is in marked contrast with the discussion of corporal punishment by officials representing the power of the king, who *were* very much represented as wielding awesome punitive power and whose performance in this area was important to establishing their legitimacy or otherwise. For them, as in the case of bishops or other people in a pastoral role, the deployment of violence remained central and meaningful, regardless of whether it was being presented negatively (as in Theodulf of Orléans's poem *Address to Judges*, in which he criticizes violent punishment and the use of torture) or more positively (as in the anonymous *Poem of Count Timo*, where a count is praised – though possibly ironically – for imposing a range of violent punishments, including judicial mutilation).[54]

As far as punishment in a labour context on fiscal lands was concerned, though, the picture is left just as blank as on ecclesiastical estates. Royal legislation might restate and reinforce the duties of peasants living on fiscal or ecclesiastical lands, much as monasteries did in their polyptychs. But, in either case, the punitive regime backing up these expectations was left very vague. Charles the Bald, for instance, when confronted with situations where some rural tenants (*coloni*) of either the fisc or the church declared themselves unwilling to transport marl, said they had to do it anyway. Still, he did not say what overseers might do to make his ruling stick.[55]

One unusual document is a bit more forthcoming on the punishment of workers on royal estates: the *Capitulare de villis*, issued under the reign of Charlemagne, which contains an idealized description of royal estate management framed as a set of instructions for royal *iudices* (stewards or managers). The impression given in this document is very much that punishment on royal estates should be organized as a mini-version of the kingdom, as a microcosm of correct governance and accountability, including opportunities for complaints and accusations by subordinates and supposedly strict maintenance of the free/unfree divide for purposes of punishment – but

---

[54]Both discussed by Patrick Geary, "Judicial Violence and Torture in the Carolingian Empire", in Ruth Mazo Karras, Joel Kaye, and E. Ann Matter (eds), *Law and the Illicit in Medieval Europe* (Philadelphia, PA, 2008), pp. 79–88.

[55]*Capitularia regum Francorum*, vol. 2, no. 273B, c. 29. In discussing labour management, royal legislation ranged beyond the fisc's own lands only very exceptionally and with unknown success. When it did, it mostly did so to back up lords after being asked to intervene, at which point it might confirm the imposition of duties, though without specifying what lords could do to enforce them. For an example (atypical in its ambitions), see Charles West, "Carolingian Kingship and the Peasants of Le Mans: The *Capitulum in Cenomannico pago datum*", in Rolf Grosse and Michel Sot (eds), *Charlemagne. Les temps, les espaces, les hommes: Construction et déconstruction d'un règne* (Turnhout, 2018), pp. 227–244.

even then with the expectation that both free and unfree should be governed by a judicial or quasi-judicial process led by the stewards.[56] The way in which this royal document handled punishment for self-gain, and found a place for it within an idealized framework, was, then, to bring it as close as possible to more public-facing models.

The desire to keep any appearance of profit-seeking as a motive for violence in favour of a more pastoral conception extended even to some cases of judicial punishment, especially if the punishment had to do with protecting royal interests through the imposition of large fines: Charles the Bald, in the Edict of Pîtres (864), stipulated that those who had refused good silver coins but could not afford to pay compensation should not be "weighed down unduly or beyond measure; for, as Scripture says, 'we do not require the amount, but the fruit'; that is, we do not demand dishonest profit, but only what is given to the kingdom for punishment".[57]

Conclusion

Corporal punishment in the Carolingian period remained crucial to how everyone, from the fisc to the churches to the monasteries to the lay lords, extracted work from people. At the same time, it was made ever less *meaningful* compared to the place reserved for it by earlier punishment regimes. Various factors contributed to this. One was the increasing tension perceived between profit-seeking and the correct exercise of punishment in a pastoral context. From monastic rules to the *Capitulare de villis* and Dhuoda, corporal punishment had the potential to increase symbolic authority only insofar as it resembled forms of justice where the punisher could come across as an accountable mini-ruler marshalling a quasi-judicial process not primarily geared towards self-gain. By contrast, punishing peasants at all in a way that was connected primarily to material gain was beginning to be cited as a sign of abuse in itself, for instance, in saints' lives. This was obviously not a realistic way of holding lords to account since all of them, including monastic lordships, obviously did rely on violence for such ends. This conceptual shift is reminiscent of, and likely later fed into, the representation and critique by ecclesiastical sources of eleventh-century "bad customs" and bad lordship, unrestrained by public concerns and selfishly bent on securing its own material advantages.

At the same time, models of "good" lordship no longer really hinged on applying more positive models of corporal punishment either. The relationship of lords with the lowest-ranking of their dependents no longer defined nor illustrated their power, as it had done for the head of household in an earlier Roman context, for whom the enjoyment of near-absolute power over children and slaves had been a significant element in the representation of authority. The correct distribution of gifts and resources at much higher levels of dependence, not the correct application of corporal punishment at lower levels, had become the litmus test of good lordship.

---

[56] *Capitulare de villis*, c. 4 (on the punishment of free vs unfree workers); see also c. 16 (on negligent middle management) and 57 (on accusations from subordinates): *Capitularia regum Francorum*, vol. 1, no. 32; for the Latin text with English translation: https://www.le.ac.uk/hi/polyptyques/capitulare/latin2english.html; last accessed 23 April 2022.

[57] *Capitularia regum Francorum*, vol. 2, no. 273B, c. 22.

The Carolingian period, then, draws something very near a blank when it comes to investigating moral regimes of labour exploitation. Lords' practices of punishment of their workers, however real and present in lived experience they must have been, were no longer being taken by leading cultural and political authorities as productive of meaning, whether positive or negative. The ability to exploit, crucial as it was in practical terms, was no longer as important or valued an element in the construction of authority – in fact, it was placed in tension with the more moral and pastoral ends towards which the construction of authority was moving. This explains why the increasing exploitation of peasants went with a decreased interest in sources discussing methods of coercing them and why there is almost no discussion of any economy of punishment as a management tool for this period: in this, the early medieval evidence is very unlike, say, Roman treatises on managing agricultural estates. This adds up to a source base where punishment linked to exploitation was hardly discussed and where the increased coercion and violence that must necessarily have gone hand in hand with the intensification of economic exploitation remains shielded from view.

Cite this article: Alice Rio. Corporal Punishment at Work in the Early Middle Ages: The Frankish Kingdoms (Sixth through Tenth Centuries). *International Review of Social History*, 68:S31 (2023), pp. 73–92. https://doi.org/10.1017/S0020859023000019

International Review of Social History, 68:S31 (2023), pp. 93–108
doi:10.1017/S0020859022000888

RESEARCH ARTICLE

Moving to Your Place: Labour Coercion and Punitive Violence against Minors under Guardianship (Charcas, Sixteenth through Eighteenth Centuries)*

Paola A. Revilla Orías [ID]

Universidad Católica Boliviana, San Pablo in La Paz, Bolivia and Institut d'Études Avancées de Nantes, France, e-mail: p.revillao@gmail.com

Abstract
This article examines the experience of minors at the intersection of guardianship, domestic servitude (free and unfree labour), and punitive violence in Charcas (Bolivia) in the sixteenth through eighteenth centuries. The author proposes that the study of the role of punishment in the lives of working children and adolescents allows us to question how practices that occurred under the legal cloak of guardianship – in which many members of colonial society participated – were used as a hidden practice of domination that sought to reproduce servitude based on certain origins from an early age. In this context, punitive violence exercised by masters and lords would have been at the core of prevailing prejudices about ethnic and racial difference.

Introduction

Child labour is a long-standing regional problem in Latin America and the Caribbean. The practice not only relates to financial difficulties seen in recent decades, but also to forms of labour relationships dating back several centuries. In these pages, I propose a view of the experience of minors at the intersection of guardianship, labour coercion, and punishment. I focus on children and adolescents in domestic service – understood in the broadest sense of the concept, in activities both inside and outside the home – and any kind of service position that operated under the jurisdiction of Charcas (Bolivia) (Figure 1) in colonial South America, from its administrative headquarters in the city of La Plata, between the sixteenth and eighteenth centuries. I argue that some mechanisms of discipline and control,

---

*A preliminary version of this text was presented at the Fourth Conference of the European Labour History Network on 31 August 2021 in Vienna, and as a lecture at the Bonn Center for Dependency and Slavery Studies on 15 September 2021, where the author was a postdoctoral researcher. Special thanks to Christian G. De Vito, Adam Fagbore, and to the peer reviewers for their comments on the final draft of this text.

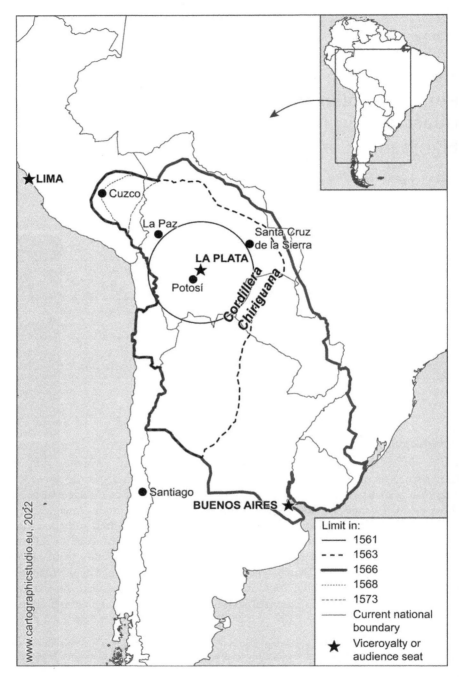

Figure 1. Map of the Real Audiencia de Charcas (with changes during the sixteenth century) and location of the Cordillera Chiriguana. Based on the work of Joseph Barnadas (1973) and cartographer Federico García Blaya (2021).

exercised by the masters and authorities over child labourers, within the logic of paternalistic guardianship, played a key role in ensuring the reproduction of labour of certain origins from a tender age.

First, I focus on workers who lived in or passed through the farm (*chacra* or *chácara*), the workshop, or the colonial settlement in the city, where there were hundreds of male and female children of different ethnic origin. I am interested in highlighting the multiplicity of work systems and situations that led to child labourers being employed under the service of master or lord at these worksites, whom they supported in various tasks. Second, I study the relationship between the application of the legal figure of guardianship and coercive work (free and unfree labour) in which minors, mainly indigenous and Afrodescendants, were compelled to participate. I focus specifically on minors who did not have *patria potestad* (parental authority) due to a lack of knowledge, orphanhood, illegitimacy, or kidnapping, among other reasons. Finally, I assess both physical and psychological forms of violence inherent in the nature of guardianship of minors and "rescued", "deposited", or "settled" minors who were placed under the protection of a guardian. For this purpose, I analyse how *señores* and *señoras* (lords and ladies) subjected child labourers to various forms of punishment and intimidation, but also how local authorities intervened on behalf of the Crown in certain situations.

The proposed methodology of a broad view and concrete cases enters into dialogue with recent studies on the history of socio-labour practices and power relations in America under the colonial regime. It stops at considerations of labour differentiation according to gender – formed, stereotyped, and practical – and does not disassociate the history of minors from that of the adults around them. Constructed in fuzzy boundary categories, the analysis is the result of an inter-ethereal relational approach, in the sense that is does not seek to artificially separate a history of "adults" from one of legal minors, but rather it aims to glimpse the complexity of the relationship between the two within certain historical phenomena.

Immersion in the Servile Experience

In Latin American colonial societies, having a populated house in the city and on the farm was synonymous with economic prosperity and status. This was clearly the case for the residents of La Plata (Figure 2).[1] Its status as the seat of the court (since 1560) and archbishop (since 1609), as well as the resources it administered from the nearby Potosí mines (87 km away) and from the more than 60,000 Indians who were tributaries in its twenty-nine divisions, led its inhabitants to consolidate the idea that they were residing in a privileged place within the group of "overseas provinces".[2]

In the early seventeenth century, La Plata's population – some 14,000 inhabitants, originating from diverse cultures of different origins, together with temporary

---

[1] Settlement in the Andean mesothermal valleys populated by the Yampara *señorío* (lordship), incorporated into the Inca State in the mid-fifteenth century and called Villa de (La) Plata in the Province of Charcas by the Spaniards from the sixteenth century onwards. Cf. Josep M. Barnadas, *Charcas, orígenes de una sociedad colonial 1535–1565* (La Paz, 1973).

[2] Fray Antonio de la Calancha, *Crónica Moralizada del Orden de San Agustín en el Perú, con sucesos ejemplares en esta Monarquía* (Barcelona, 1638), vol. 3, bk. 2, ch. 40, p. 298.

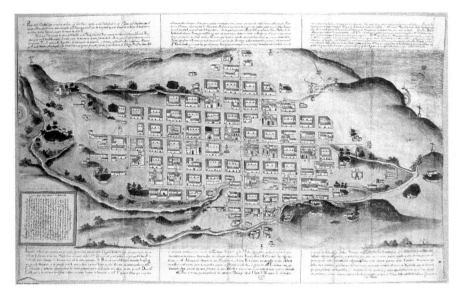

Figure 2. Plan of the city of La Plata (Sucre or Chuquisaca) by Ildefonso de Luján (1777). *Archivo General de Indias MP, Buenos Aires, 244.*

workers from the surrounding area and merchants and people passing through on their way to other regions – gave shape to a particularly pluralistic scenario of the daily life of *tratos y contratos* (dealings and contracts).[3] According to Antonio de Herrera y Toledo, "The Spanish neighbourhood had just over 650 reasonable dwelling houses and, together with those of the Indians, which were smaller, [the number of houses in Plata] amounted to 1300".[4] Most of them had small and medium-sized farms in the surrounding areas, where they frequently came and went with their goods and dependents along roads that linked them with each other and the city.

Servitude was essential to demonstrating wealth. Whether slave, free, or belonging to the ambiguous categories of freedman or pacified, hundreds of people of different origins and life paths made up La Plata's households and resided or spent a large part of the day in them.[5] Although not all family nuclei achieved this form, the Catholic monarchy sought to consolidate an archetype that reflected its own relationship, with the figure of the king (and his delegated authorities) as the father of a large and hierarchical family. Some of the domestic servants in these spaces were children and young people under the age of twenty-five, minors within the legal parameters of

[3]Pedro Ramírez del Águila, *Noticias políticas de Indias y relación descriptiva de la ciudad de La Plata, metrópoli de la provincia de los Charcas* (Bloomington, IN, [1639] 1963), p. 74.

[4]Antonio de Herrera y Toledo, *Relación eclesiástica de la Santa Iglesia Metropolitana de los Charcas*, ed. Josep M. Barnadas (Sucre, [1639] 1996), pp. 43–44. Unless otherwise stated, all translations are mine.

[5]The term "pacified" refers to the indigenous people of the lowlands of Charcas, who were considered rebellious and taken captive in the cities and farms of the colonial jurisdiction. Isabelle Combès and Thierry Saignes, *Alter Ego. Naissance de l'identité chiriguano* (Paris, 1991).

the time.[6] The diversity of origins, experiences, and paths that led them to the homes of third parties make it necessary to exercise caution when historicizing their reality, and to avoid arbitrary homogenizations of this group of dependents.[7] First, there were the sons of service *mitayos* who came from the surrounding areas.[8] They entered the homes accompanying and helping their mothers to fulfil different tasks that they had been assigned, while their fathers complied with their own work schedule in the city or on the farms, performing agricultural labour, handicraft, general labour, and construction, among other forms of work. As prescribed, they were supposed to work for the public benefit but, in reality, they were regularly assigned to personal service, albeit this was presented as being voluntary.[9] The length of their stay varied and although it was stipulated that they could not stay indefinitely, on occasion they did. If a *mitayo* arranged with his *cacique* to stay longer than initially planned, he could then try to get his daughters work in domestic service or urban commerce and his sons a position in a workshop where they could learn a trade.[10]

In these spaces they met other children of indigenous, mestizo, Afrodescendant, and European origin who had to work in manual trades to support themselves. Among them, children of urban *yanaconas* – whose parents were specialized in various arts and crafts – were trained as specialist workers like their parents.[11] Vázquez de Espinoza claimed that, by 1610, there were sixty-four *tiendas* (artisan workshops) in La Plata, most of them employing *indios oficiales* (official Indians) of all trades.[12] These workshops were both a place of work and a residence for the settled minors, to whom the artisan had to offer food, clothing, and sometimes a certain amount of pesos in exchange for their service and for the duration of their stay, which, according

---

[6]"Domestic" servant is understood as a concept that denotes a servant's relationship with the master's house but whose activities are not limited to those performed in it.

[7]Childhood, a broad stage between birth and adolescence up to about fourteen years of age, was differentiated from infancy, the period before the child learned to speak. Cristina V. Masferrer, "Hijos de esclavos. Niños libres y esclavos en España novohispana durante la primera mitad del siglo XVII", *Ulúa*, 19 (2012), pp. 81–99. However, it is not accurate to say that children and adolescents were limited to certain activities because of their age and that there were designated adult tasks. It all depended on the capabilities that the child had developed as he or she grew up in his or her immediate environment. In this sense, age was merely referential.

[8]From the Quechua *mit'a*, meaning "shift or period of service", this system of compulsory and rotating work in the Tawantinsuyu (the name of the Inca Empire among its subjects) was adopted by the Spaniards, who gave it its own characteristics. It implied the performance of a series of tasks to be carried out by a male population between the ages of eighteen and fifty. The worker was known as a *mitayo*.

[9]Juan de Matienzo, *Gobierno del Perú con todas las cosas pertenecientes a él y a su historia* (Paris, [1566] 1967), pp. 18–20; Herrera y Toledo, *Relación eclesiástica*, p. 296.

[10]A *cacique* or *curaca* is understood to be the highest authority of the community or colonial settlement.

[11]In the era of the late Tawantinsuyu, the *yanakuna* were those who, having been separated from their community of origin, were not obliged to participate in the usual rotation of servants. They had been distributed by the Inca into the service of a lord for whom they worked as perpetual servants, bequeathing their condition to their descendants. The practice was adopted and became institutionalized as *yanaconazgo* in the colonial period.

[12]Antonio Vázquez de Espinosa, *Compendio y Descripción de las Indias Occidentales* (Washington, DC, 1628–1629] 1948), p. 602. Around 103 *yanaconas* residing in the city towards the end of the sixteenth century were counted by Juan de Matienzo to elaborate the "Tasa de los yanaconas de la ciudad de La Plata" dated 1575. Most of them were from Cuzco. Archivo Histórico de Potosí (Historical Archives of Potosí [hereafter, AHP]): *Cajas Reales*, 18.

to the archives, could last from a few months to several years. Some children of *yana-conas* also served for an indefinite period in public institutions, together with their parents. Others worked with traders, in a fluid dynamic between the farms and the city, and even beyond La Plata's jurisdiction. Unlike the children of *mitayos*, the *yanaconas* did not have to return to the *pueblos de indios* (Indian villages) with their parents, so their immersion in activities and prolonged apprenticeships was more feasible.[13]

We also find them with their parents on the farms around La Plata, in small houses near the lord's hacienda, cultivating the land on whose usufruct they lived for generations. Legally, minors under taxable age should not be compelled to work.[14] They could, however, voluntarily participate in domestic service and, with their parents' authorization, they could be compelled to perform certain occupations for which they had to be paid. The law stated: "[I]f, of his own free will and with that of his parents, a boy wants to be a shepherd, he shall be given two and a half reales every week [...] plus food and clothing."[15] Nevertheless, minors participated in different agricultural activities on the farms.

The sons and daughters of Africans and Afrodescendants (whether of African descent, Bozales, or Creoles, slaves or manumitted) were also present in all of the aforementioned labour spaces. Enslaved children arrived in the markets of Charcas quite early during the conquest process and some were even born in the homes of their parents' masters. We see them accompanying their enslaved parents in their daily chores. However, not all slaves resided in their masters' house, nor can we say that all freedmen always resided in their own house. In fact, it is not surprising that many remained for a period or, indeed, indefinitely in their former masters' homes due to a lack of resources, out of gratitude, or because of preconditions placed on the manumission and their children with them.

Both enslaved and freedmen sought to place their children in the domestic service of others, in agricultural and livestock activities on farms or as apprentices in artisan workshops.[16] Minors could achieve better living conditions and generate resources that, in some circumstances, would allow them to obtain the manumission of one of their relatives. The masters did not usually object. Having slaves with skills was beneficial, because it increased their price in the local market and the slaves themselves could benefit from a higher *jornal* (daily wage).[17] The freedmen proceeded in the same way with their children.[18] They usually stayed two to three years in the workshop, after which they took a "skill and ability" test and became journeymen, receiving tools. It is important to emphasize that this was

---

[13]The concept of *pueblo de indios* should be understood as a space differentiated from the Spanish cities, within the social separation measures established by Viceroy Toledo in the second half of the sixteenth century, in the period between the so-called two republics.

[14]*Recopilación de Leyes de Indias* [hereafter, *RLI*] (Madrid, 1681), bk. 6, tit. 13, law 9.

[15]"Que las mujeres e hijos de indios de estancias que no estén en edad de tributar no sean obligados a ningún trabajo", *RLI*, bk. 6, tit. 13, law 9.

[16]Archivo y Biblioteca Nacionales de Bolivia (National Archives and Library of Bolivia [hereafter, ABNB]), Escrituras Públicas (Public Deeds [hereafter, EP]) 1575, García de Esquivel, vol. 19, fo. 645. ABNB: EP, Luis Guisado de Umanes, 14 March 1595, fos 679–680.

[17]ABNB, EP 1593, Luis Guisado de Umanes, vol. 40, fos 549v–550v.

[18]ABNB, EP, Luis Guisado de Umanes, 18 January 1594, fo. 616; Jerónimo de Porres, 18 September 1589, fo. 696.

not only a learning experience for the minors, but also a work experience and service to the artisan. The process mirrors that of the *mozos para todo* (boys for everything) in exchange for lodging, food, some clothes, and care in case of illness, as was performed in Spain.[19] The formal boundary between apprenticeship and domestic service is blurred. No less important is the presence of the children of indigenous Chiriguano captives from the lowlands of Charcas, who had been kidnapped from their place of origin and traded as service *piezas* (pieces) to work in domestic spaces, workshops, and farms in La Plata. They were devalued, barbarized, infantilized, and even demonized because of their ethnicity. Something similar happened with the inhabitants of southern Chile.[20] Even after their trade and enslavement was prohibited, its practice continued and was legitimized by custom. Their children grew up in the places where their parents worked, whose status as "pacified Gentiles" plunged them into an ambiguous limbo between slavery and legal freedom.

The differentiation of jobs by gender was assimilated and naturalized from a very early age.[21] The multiple tasks performed by girls and young women in the houses and streets of La Plata were usually described as "service" in reference to domestic work, which was not considered a trade.[22] Unlike their male counterparts, there are no data on girls with artisan or agricultural occupations, which certainly does not mean that they did not participate in work activities together with their relatives.

After performing temporary service, these children were placed in either the home, workshop, or farm of the lord their family served, before returning to their communities, in the case of service *mitayos*, under servitude but detached from *yanaconazgo*, captivity, or inherited slavery. Some were even born in these spaces, immersed from an early age in the mechanisms of servile labour, and can be linked to different labour systems. The more fortunate could pursue apprenticeships and develop skills that allowed them to live with a greater degree of autonomy within a strongly hierarchical and racialized setting. Most were of indigenous and African descent. Not all kept their inherited affiliations; on the contrary, frequently, they were hinges between systems. It is not surprising to find children of *mitayos* (pacified or freed Afroindigenous *yanaconized*) in the city and the farms, temporarily or indefinitely, both the lord and the worker profiting from the opportunity. Regardless of their place of residence, these children maintained links with their relatives and places of origin where, with the exception of Africans and first-generation captive Chiriguanos, they used to come and go, creating bridges that transcended the limits of the social separation order

---

[19]Antonio Muñoz Buendía, "La infancia robada. Niños esclavos, criados y aprendices en la Almería Del Antiguo", in María D. Martínez San Pedro (ed.), *Los marginados en el mundo medieval y moderno* (Almería, 2000), pp. 65–78, 68.

[20]Jaime Valenzuela, "Esclavos mapuches. Para una historia del secuestro y deportación de indígenas en la colonia", in Rafael Gaune and Martín Lara (eds), *Historias de racismo y discriminación en Chile* (Santiago de Chile, 2009), pp. 225–260; Catherine Julian, "Colonial Perspectives on the Chiriguaná (1528–1574)", in María Susana Cipolleti (ed.), *Resistencia y adaptación nativas en las tierras bajas latinoamericanas* (Quito, 1997), pp. 17–76.

[21]There were also many boys in domestic service in the households of Charcas, although there was always a differentiation with their female counterparts, who were assigned tasks considered appropriate to their sex.

[22]ABNB, Expedientes Coloniales (Colonial Files [hereafter, EC]) 1623, no. 10, fo. 7.

that Viceroy Francisco de Toledo tried, unsuccessfully, to impose on them. However, not all of them had parents or relatives to take care of them. This is a sensitive issue that deserves further study in relation to the work situations to which they were exposed.

Guardianship and the Labour Coercion of Minors

There were a number of reasons why working children may have had absent parents. If they were slaves, this could be due to the master's decision to sell the child to another family. Similarly, the descendants of captive Indians from the lowlands of Charcas had an ambiguous legal status, which meant that their lords acted as their de facto masters. The sons of *yanaconas* and *mitayos* were able to work in different spaces for the same lord, some in farms, others in the city house, depending on the delegated activity. Indigenous and Afrodescendant children, whether *horros* or free, settled in urban workshops while their relatives could live in the surrounding *repartimientos*, or they could work on the farms while their parents lived in the city.[23]

These diverse situations of coerced or voluntary family distancing, for work-related reasons, led to increased dependence not only materially but also affectively on the figure of the master whom the minor served and from whom he learned his craft. The sociability of minors was thus moulded beyond their nucleus of origin in spaces where they coexisted with peers from other cultures with whom they had in common the occupation and the authority under which they were organized. Sharing a roof and daily life with a family was, in this sense, the privilege of some.

The family strategies that mediated these separations not only obeyed material imperatives, but were also influenced by the idea that by linking them to urban activities in the homes of neighbours in La Plata, the children could receive a better education, indoctrination, and protection. Thus, when thirteen-year-old Domingo went to serve in the house of Manuel de Orías for three years in 1579, it was requested that, in exchange for the work, he be taught to live *en policía*, that is to say, in accordance with good customs.[24] Parents of different origins placed their children in temporary *depósito* (deposit) in the house of others to whose authority they were obliged to submit. As Ramírez del Águila mentions: "The *caciques* give their children to Spaniards, to serve them, because they teach them to speak Spanish, read and write, which they are very fond of", and he adds that one reason for establishing *compadrazgo* between Spaniards and Indians was precisely to have the possibility of leaving their godchildren with their godparents in the city to serve them in exchange for protection and education.[25] Some celebrated a written agreement before a notary as a guarantee for these minors *mandados a criar* (sent to be raised), but most were satisfied with a verbal arrangement. The Crown and the Church did not oppose this practice.[26] This "tutored servitude" of minors thus led to the coexistence of boys

---

[23]See ABNB, EP, Luis Guisado de Umanes, 14 March 1595, fos 679–680.

[24]ABNB, EP 1579, Juan García Torrico, vol. 26, fos 14v–15v. All the information quoted comes from the quill feather of notaries. It is interesting to highlight the labour relationship that the writing draws, according to the formulas of the time, to justify certain practices.

[25]Ramírez del Águila, *Noticias Políticas*, p. 268.

[26]*Siete Partidas de Alfonso X* (Valladolid, [1256–1265], 1988), *Partida* 4, law 1, tit. 20.

and girls of different origins within the same houses, satisfying the needs of families, the desire of others to become servants, and the dynamics of the colonial market.[27] It should be noted that in Charcas, as in Chile, when parents had debts or faced economic difficulty, the service of their children was sometimes ceded to third parties for a period.[28]

There is also data relating to indigenous children forced to leave their *repartimientos* to work in the homes of neighbours in the city.[29] Something similar was happening in Quito, for which the Crown issued a document dated 1577, which states that "although it is understood that they take them so that they may learn and have *policía* and be better trained and taught, the purpose for which they do so is only to keep them as slaves and serve them and then leave them lost".[30] Kidnappings of minors from the so-called unredeemed lowlands of Charcas occurred with particular frequency and crudeness throughout the colonial period under the legal formula of *ventas a la usanza* (sales in the style) and of *rescate* (ransom).[31] Once taken captive, they were (re)sold in the colonial cities and farms at prices two to three times lower than those of enslaved Africans.[32]

Traces of such violent captivity and uprooting can be found in the documentary evidence.[33] These practices with minors, which had been expressly prohibited by the Crown, were not viewed widely with opprobrium; on the contrary, they were socially accepted.[34] These minors were often baptized by their captors, others by the men or women who bought or even ordered them. Thus, in 1593, Juan Bravo de Castro, a priest in Tomina, commissioned Miguel Gutiérrez Bonilla, an inhabitant

---

[27]Nara Milanich, "Degrees of Bondage: Children's Tutelary Servitude in Modern Latin America", in Gwyn Campbell, Suzanne Miers, and Joseph C. Miller (eds), *Child Slaves in the Modern World* (Athens, OH, 2011), ch. 5, pp. 104–123, 106.

[28]In this regard, the Archbishop of Charcas wrote to the king in 1639 that some *mitayos* "sell their wives and children to different houses and persons". Archivo y Biblioteca Arzobispal de Sucre (Archbishop's Archives and Library of Sucre [hereafter, ABAS]), Capitular, RC (1619–1700), 1693. See also Milanich, "Degrees of Bondage", p. 110; Valenzuela, "Esclavos mapuches", p. 240.

[29]See ABNB, EC 1705, 35, fo. 3.

[30]Richard Konetzke, *Colección de documentos para la historia de la formación social de Hispanoamérica (1943–1810)* (Madrid, 1953), p. 503.

[31]Jaime Valenzuela (ed.), *América en diásporas. Esclavitudes y migraciones forzadas en Chile y otras regiones americanas (siglos XVI–XIX)* (Santiago de Chile, 2017); Hugo Contreras, "Siendo mozetón o güeñi salió de su tierra a vivir entre los españoles. Migración y asentamiento mapuche en Chile central durante el siglo XVIII, 1700–1750", *Historia Indígena*, 9 (2005), pp. 7–32; Ignacio Chuecas Saldías, "Venta es dar una cosa cierta por precio cierto. Cultura jurídica y esclavitud infantil en pleitos fronterizos chilenos (1673–1775)", in Macarena Cordero, Rafael Gaune, and Rodrigo Moreno (eds), *Cultura legal y espacios de justicia en América, siglos XVI–XIX* (Santiago de Chile, 2017), pp. 167–194; Daniel Villar and Juan Francisco Jiménez, "Para servirse de ellos. Cautiverio, ventas a la usanza del país y rescate de indios en las pampas y araucanía (siglos XVII–XIX)", *Relaciones de la Sociedad Argentina de Antropología*, 26 (2011), pp. 31–55.

[32]Paola Revilla Orías, *Coerciones intrincadas. Trabajo africano e indígena en Charcas. Siglos XVI y XVII* (Cochabamba, 2020), p. 64.

[33]See: ABNB, EP, Francisco Pliego, 26 October 1589, fos 469–470; 1587, Gerónimo de Porres, vol. 51, fos 491–491v.

[34]Prohibido por cédula real de 1553 y 1563. See *RLI*, bk. 6, tit. 2, law 13. José María Ots Capdequí, *Manual de Historia del Derecho español en las Indias y del derecho propiamente indiano* (Buenos Aires, 1945), p. 140.

of Lima passing through La Plata, and Antonio Gutiérrez Barreto, a resident of La Plata, to deliver two unbaptized boys of sixteen and eighteen years of age and a Chiriguana of eight years of age, whom he had "rescued" from the Cordillera Chiriguana region, to the edge of the tropical forest.[35] Sometimes, the kidnapping and its purpose were undisguised, and the priest who baptized the child registered the child as a servant, pointing out that the parents were "on their land".[36]

Local authorities did not contemplate the possibility of returning them. Despite having censured the captivity and notorious trade, they preferred to place the minor in temporary custody by assigning him a guardian who might instruct him in life *en policía*. This may have seemed more convenient in a scenario in which the *encomienda* system had entered into crisis and where obtaining labour grants was more complicated than gaining access to it by force.[37] Guardianship was thus a means of covering up the coercion and labour exploitation of minors who could hardly refuse to live this reality.

Those in a position to acquire slaves, regardless of their origin, did so, within or outside the norm, and there were certainly those who preferred to acquire them as children to educate them in servitude. In 1597, Don Juan de Aymoro, *cacique* of the Yampara, bought for 500 pesos a ten-year-old enslaved boy named Francisco Moreno, born in the house of Pedro Serrudo.[38] The freedman Agustín Mensia, a dance teacher, bought a Bozal child named Felipe in 1598, whom he would later sell to the freedwoman Gracia García.[39] Children were thus passed from house to house, and could be exchanged, mortgaged, or donated several times.[40] The prices paid for them by the inhabitants of La Plata were significant.[41]

Among the most vulnerable minors under servitude were orphans. When, for various reasons, the children had no one to exercise parental authority over them, the competent authority placed them in custody and under the temporary guardianship of a neighbour, who was responsible for them, in exchange for their service. Given the strong patriarchal bias of colonial society, there were children who, even though they had a mother, were treated as orphans since legal parental authority rested with

---

[35] ABNB, EP, Juan de Saldaña, 25 August and 10 October 1593. Legally speaking, the *rescate* meant that the Indians had been taken from their land during the battle or bought to prevent them from being subdued and violated by others. This never applied legally to minors.

[36] ABAS, Archivo Parroquial (Parish Archives [hereafter, AP]), Santo Domingo, baptisms, vol. 1, 9 December 1571, fo. 53.

[37] The *encomienda* institution comprised the lands and the services of indigenous people granted by the Crown to those who had made merits for the conquest. See Ana María Presta, "Encomienda, familia y redes en Charcas colonial. Los Almendras 1540–1600", *Revista de Indias*, 57:209 (1997), pp. 21–53.

[38] ABNB, EP, Agustín de Herrera, 3 December 1597, fos 36–37.

[39] ABNB, EP 1598, Agustín de Herrera, 10 August 1598, fos 105–107.

[40] See: ABNB, EC 1642, no. 8, 1680, no. 17, 1674, no. 35, 1695, no. 4; EP, Gaspar Núñez, 12 October 1613, fos 11–19v; EP, Luis Guisado de Umanes, 13 June 1594, fos 463–465; EP, Jerónimo de Porres, 4 July 1587, fo. 491.

[41] From a sample of 1545 cases studied, among which, in addition to the unit price, there is information on the sex and the estimated age of the enslaved traded in La Plata between 1560 and 1630, 19 per cent were between twelve and eighteen years old and their price was between 468 and 700 pesos; 38 per cent were between nineteen and twenty-five years old and their price was around 623 pesos on average; and only 3 per cent were children between three and eleven years old whose price ranged between 250 and 300 pesos. Girls were in all cases more expensive than boys.

men.[42] Others were considered ignorant or "morally unfit" to be educated *en policía* because their parents were poor. By soliciting, kidnapping, and receiving "orphans" in their homes, colonial society guaranteed the reproduction of uprooted domestic servitude.[43]

It could happen that the orphan minors themselves asked for a guardian in order to be able to gain a position in the service of third persons and secure a livelihood. Thus, Polo de Ondegardo, mayor of La Plata around 1593, appointed a tutor for the young Francisco, son of the deceased mulatto Francisco del Solar, who wanted to learn the carpenter's trade.[44]

Among those considered orphans there may also have been some illegitimate children, whom a lord refused to publicly acknowledge because they were the product of a spurious, adulterous, incestuous, or sacrilegious encounter. Without recognizing their origin or indicating another, they kept them in their homes, under their authority.[45] Sometimes, the lords made a certain affective effort with them, treating them the same as their other children; other times they did not, with the illegitimate children growing up receiving very different treatment from their siblings and often working as servants.

In spite of the fact that Viceroy Toledo, adopting the determination of Carlos I of 1571, had ordered that "free black men and women or slaves should not serve Indians", the assets detailed in the will of the freed black woman Esperanza de Robles, dated 1589, included an orphaned indigenous girl named Yulsita, left to her by her mother before her death.[46] Christian affection and charity may have mediated in this type of spontaneous *depósitos* in which the local royal authority did not intervene; this does not mean, however, that the weight of the servitude to which the minor was obliged was less.

In addition to the high degree of dependence all these minors had on their guardians, the vulnerability with which they lived the day-to-day life of imposed servitude exposed them to all kinds of abuses that were part of a certain legitimized logic of disciplining the dependents.

The Punitive Violence of Civilizing Paternalism

While it is true that minors who entered servitude under guardianship in scenarios like those described above could generate bonds of friendship with and deep affection for their masters, it is no less true that the exercise of tutelage could also prove to be very violent. This is despite the implicit agreement of protection that the guardian owed to all dependents in his household as paterfamilias. To understand this reality, we must consider that, in colonial society, the ideology of paternalism was mixed with notions of *limpieza de sangre* (blood cleansing), transferred from the European

---

[42]Bianca Premo, *Children of The Father King. Youth, Authority and Legal Minority in Colonial Lima* (Chapel Hill, NC, 2005), p. 28.

[43]Luis Miguel Glave, "Mujer indígena, trabajo doméstico y cambio social en el virreinato peruano del siglo XVII. La ciudad de La Paz y el Sur Andino en 1684", *Bulletin de l'Institut Français d'Etudes Andines*, 16:3–4 (1987), pp. 39–69.

[44]ABNB, EP 1593, Luis Guisado de Umanes, vol. 40, fos 549v–550v; EP 1599.

[45]The father was not obligated to his upbringing. *Siete Partidas*, Partida 4, tit. 14, law 3.

[46]*RLI*, bk. 7, tit. 5, law 7. ABNB, EP, Francisco Pliego, 26 October 1589, fos 469–470.

imaginary and recreated anew.[47] These notions nurtured strong discrimination and racialization in relations between subjects.[48] The exercise of patriarchal tutelar authority over minors, mostly indigenous and Afrodescendants in the service of houses, farms, and workshops in Charcas, reflected this civilizing paternalism.

In the already asymmetrical relationship of dependence between lords and minors at their service or in apprenticeship, it was believed that part of the educating, "civilizing" role of the former was the correction of the conduct of the latter. Physical and verbal violence and punishments were, in this sense, considered a sign of the proper exercise of authority, responsibility, and love towards the dependent in the execution of his tasks.[49] In this context, prejudice triggered actions that went far beyond what could be legally justified as corrective punishment, and which was nothing more than abuse, revealing the power of control and discipline over servitude.

Without seeking to generalize, and assuming the diversity of relationships between lords, ladies, and minors, we can imagine that the orphans were exposed to significant arbitrariness and (bad) treatment. This does not contradict another reality, which is that due to the prevailing power relations, the authority of the parents in servitude over their children was notably diminished compared to that of the lords in whose service and under whose tutelage they were, making it very difficult for them to avoid outrages against them.

From an early age, the enslaved had to suffer the intervention of the master's will on their bodies, who considered the gesture a property right. The skin of thousands of Africans, but also sometimes of lowland Indians, was burned with red-hot iron on different parts of the body.[50] However, it was not only a matter of making clear the ownership over their persons, but also of punishing behaviour. Another highly infamous (because of its link to slavery) punishment was whipping, used when the master considered it necessary to correct the behaviour of not only his enslaved but his free dependents.[51] It could be that the worker had not complied with an order, that he had performed a task badly, that he was suspected of having stolen or broken an object in the house, that he had tried to run away, or that he had disrespected his master; there were many reasons that "justified" corrective flagellation. It should not be believed that free workers were not subject to this type of punishment. In urban workshops it was usual for the craftsman in charge to use the whip when he

---

[47]That is to say, the mechanism of discrimination against those who, because of their filiation, birth, or beliefs, were seen as "contaminated". Paternalism is understood as the application of the notion of paternal authority towards children to other spheres, in this case labour, leading to the loss of autonomy and freedom of the worker under the justification of their protection.

[48]Max S. Hering Torres, "La limpieza de sangre. Problemas de interpretación: acercamientos históricos y metodológicos", *Historia Crítica*, 45 (2011), pp. 32–55.

[49]Mónica Ghirardi, "Familia y maltrato doméstico Audiencia episcopal de Córdoba, Argentina. 1700–1850", *Revista Historia Unisios*, 12:1 (2008), pp. 18–24, 19; Natalie Guerra Araya, "Representaciones del cuerpo-niño: desprotección y violencia en Chile colonial", in Susana Sosensky and Elena Jackson (eds), *Nuevas miradas a la historia de la infancia en América Latina. Entre prácticas y representaciones* (México D.F., 2013), pp. 63–87, 79.

[50]See the case of María, a Chiriguaná whose face was shaved: ABNB, EP, Diego Sánchez, 14 October 1595, fos 305–306.

[51]See Patricia Zambrana, "Rasgos generales de la evolución histórica de la tipología de las penas corporales". *Revista de Estudios Histórico-Jurídicos*, 27 (2005), pp. 197–229.

considered it necessary, in a similar way to how the father used it at home with his children. Wives or widows who assumed the administration of the household and its dependents also took the reins of punishment.[52]

Punishments could be given in different spaces, with varying degrees of intensity, by different people and levels of authority, according to the degree of the offence and the intention of the lords to make it public or not. Legal parameters were followed, but local customs and habits were also influenced by the imagination and temperament of those who deemed them necessary to inflict punishment. A case-by-case analysis of the exercise of punitive violence and its justification leads to the conclusion that the criteria for its application was manifold. Minor offences were usually corrected in the privacy of homes in the city and on the farms. Punishment was meted out by the lord or, failing that, by his delegated servants.[53] When it was supposed to be exemplary, it was given in front of other servants, in the common courtyards. Hair cutting – particularly in the case of women – and temporary confinement might complement the whipping. There was no lack of minors whose hands and feet were immobilized by stocks and punished with iron shackles. Some houses, workshops, and institutions had these instruments of torture permanently available, and they were not only used with adults. Depending on the fault and those affected, the punishment could be decided and defined by the local authority in agreement with the *señor* or *señora*, in open spaces that allowed punishment and humiliation to serve as a warning to other workers. Hence towns and cities like La Plata used to have a *rollo* in the main square, to act as a space of exemplary torment. In these cases, the punishment was inflicted by the delegates of the mayor, the *corregidor*, among other local secular and ecclesiastical authorities.

But how far did corrective punishment go and what justified its application in either private or public spaces? A lot depended on the specific relationship between master and servant, on their ways of being, on the situations in which they found themselves. There were, however, some punishments that masters and lords could not give without authorization from the local authorities. This was the case with the tearing of ankles and wrists, legitimized by Viceroy Toledo, when the enslaved tried to flee or steal.[54] By way of reference, the code of the *Siete Partidas of Alfonzo X* (1256–1265), the *Ordenanzas* of Viceroy Toledo (1575–1580), and multiple laws gathered in the *Recopilación de Leyes de Indias* (1681) prescribe specific punishments that lords and justice administrators should impose for certain offences and according to the condition, *calidad* (quality), gender, and age of the subjects – but these were far from being systematically applied. On the other hand, intensity was not always well measured. Sometimes, the force of punishment was such that it ended with mutilation. The enslaved twenty-year-old Juan, accused of stealing money, was condemned to such torment that he ended up losing an arm.[55] The

---

[52]This denotes a certain plasticity in the exercise of patriarchal authority, which tends to be understood as exclusively masculine, although parental authority was always ultimately vested in men.

[53]For more information on people who had private prisons in their homes despite it being forbidden, see ABNB, EC 1678, no. 40, fo. 6.

[54]*Siete Partidas de Alfonso X, Partida* 4, tit. 21, law 6. If the runaway had lasted more than ten days, the slave could be taken to the public *rollo* to be punished. ABNB Dir., no. 9, fos 54–55.

[55]ABNB, EC 1675, no. 21.

number of floggings permitted had some age considerations but also fell into excess.[56] Since the enslaved were valuable assets to their masters, the punishments aimed, at least in theory, to avoid mortal wounds and bloodshed. Part of this ritual of physical punishment of subordinates, whether the local authorities intervened or not, involved the master paying for treatment at home or at the Santa Bárbara hospital.

In addition to the actual punishment carried out, the threat of punishment had an important effect on the relationship between master and dependent. Lucía, an enslaved woman born in Lima and living in the house of Francisca Bustos in La Plata, said, in 1666, before the court, that "every day she threatens me that she wants to sell them to me", in reference to her mistress and her sons José and Francisco.[57] Hers is not an isolated case. Fearing that the threat of removing their children would be carried out, when they had the opportunity and were emboldened to confront the intimidation of their masters, the enslaved initiated processes whose outcome could prove vital for their descendants. Cases of unusual violence have been reported, against which the authorities acted. One such case was that of María, no more than seven years old, whose mother, Isabel Mansilla, asked justice administrators from the Royal Audiencia de La Plata, to remove the child from the power of Doña Antonia Delgadillo since, rather than the Christian education and good treatment the lady had promised to give her, she had instead prostituted her.[58] In addition, she had caused the little girl to lose an eye and had broken her arm with the blows she had given her.

The legal difference between punishment considered legitimate and *sevicia* prohibited as inhumane lay in the intensity of correction.[59] The *señores* and *señoras* knew this, and to avoid difficulties with the justice system, they made formal and explicit requests to the authorities to infer certain mistreatments and punishments that were not customary. These could be accepted or rejected as excessive, as was the case with Diego Verasmendi's request to brand his slave for being a maroon.[60] Archival records make it possible to identify situations in which, in addition to the intention to discipline, a violent lack of control and abuse of power by the master is evident. In 1665, the case of Francisco de Perález, who had cruelly whipped the son of his slave Inés, in addition to having *carimbado* both of them in their faces, a forbidden practice, was heard before the court of La Plata.[61] Such cases of excessive cruelty reveal the extremes to which the control and exercise of discipline over the bodies and lives of those in servitude, often from a very tender age, could reach.

---

[56]In terms of what has been documented for Charcas in the sixteenth and seventeenth centuries, between twenty-five and fifty lashes for adults was considered light punishment, 100 unbearable, and more than 200 placing the person's life at risk.

[57]ABNB, EC 1666, no. 32.

[58]ABNB, EC 1780, no. 64.

[59]*Sevicia* should be understood as the most common term used at the time to refer to treatment with excessive cruelty.

[60]Archivo de la Casa de Moneda de Potosí (Potosí Mint Archives), Cabildo, Gobierno e Intendencia (Cabildo, Government and Quartermaster's Office) 1666, no. 1136, fo. 4v.

[61]ABNB, Acuerdos del Cabildo de La Plata (Agreements of the Cabildo of La Plata), 19 November 1665, no. 63, vol. 6, fo. 51. *Carimbar* was the act of marking parts of the body of enslaved persons with red-hot iron.

The royal authorities intervened in notorious cases of excessively violent punishment or if someone (possibly the minor themselves via a concerned jurist) had filed a complaint. In 1697, the Audiencia de La Plata received the case of several minors between four and fifteen years old, free mulattoes, who had been placed under the guardianship of Lieutenant Juan Perafán, a neighbour of Córdoba in Tucumán, so that "they would not be idle".[62] The eldest of them, Gabriel, accused his guardian of treating them as slaves of the *encomienda* where his father worked as a slave, without paying them wages and without taking care of their subsistence: "[W]henever he wants or has wanted to, he has given me enough [money to buy] underwear and an old *ongarina* to suppose that if it were not for my mother we would be walking around naked, me and my other siblings." The court decided to place him in custody in the public jail, where he was assisted by the defence attorney José Menacho. Disgruntled, Perafán sought to intimidate him by preventing his mother from assisting him with food. To escape prison, the young man agreed to return to serve the ensign if the authorities ordered him to do so, "even if they recognize the bad treatment that he will give me and that he will not pay me for my service and personal work [...]. [B]eing as I am imprisoned and locked up in this jail, I will not be able to go in search of the witnesses that I could give". The Audiencia ordered his release, after which Gabriel fled. Perafán, enervated, asked that Gabriel be given an exemplary punishment once found, "for being so shameless [...] with the justices and Spaniards".[63] The ensign did not assume when making these statements that he was talking about a recognized free Indo-African minor, master of his own will and one who did not owe him gratuitous service.

There is further evidence of minors addressing the courts with the support of assigned lawyers. Another case is that of the enslaved eighteen-year-old Miguel Baluín. His deceased mistress had left him in the service of Don Martín Arroyo in Potosí. In 1696, Miguel went before the court of La Plata, stating that Arroyo had "treated him with such rigour in word and deed that it was not possible to tolerate him".[64] He asked not to return under his roof because he knew he would be punished in retaliation and, as he was ill, feared it would cost him his life. When it was not possible to file a complaint as a minor, some did so later, demanding fairer treatment by the family with whom they had grown up and of which they were often blood relatives.[65] Thanks to testimonies such as those discussed here, we now know that violence against minors in the service of others, under the auspices of disciplining and teaching them to live *en policía*, poorly hid the desire to ensure control of their labour.

Conclusions

As we have seen, there is a direct relationship between the practice of guardianship of minors and the reproduction of servitude from an early age in colonial Charcas. This

---

[62]ABNB, EC 1697, no. 14, fos 17–18.

[63]ABNB, EC 1697, no. 14, fo. 21.

[64]ABNB, EC 1696, no. 8, fo. 1.

[65]See the case of Marcela Velázquez in 1630, who defended herself against being treated as a slave by her brothers: ABNB, EC 1630, no. 11. See also ABNB, EC 1677, no. 2; ABNB, EC 1684, no. 3.

was due not only to a different view of childhood and early youth, but also to the prevailing model of socio-labour relations and the desire of some to be served by others, to take advantage of their efforts, and to achieve greater status in their "populated house".

Minors, especially Afrodescendant and indigenous children, were immersed alongside their parents in a variety of coercive labour systems performing multiple assigned tasks. Some slaves, others recognized as free, found themselves in the homes, farms, and workshops of the *señor* or *señora* and thus grew up in servitude. What the masters wanted to pass off as activities in the public interest were, in fact, personal service, which, in theory, was forbidden for the king's free subjects.

Minors' vulnerability increased in the absence of their parents due to death, temporary surrender, or kidnapping, and their age became a control mechanism. I have given special attention to the justification of guardianship for raising *en policía*, which revealed itself as a disguised form of reproduction of servitude of certain origins that were strongly racialized and discriminated against through the generations. Even in the artisan workshops where minors were settled as apprentices, the price of labour training was often exploitation.

This case analysis of the corrective and exemplary punishments documented by the archival records doesn't just reveal the abuses experienced by minors. The practical and symbolic mechanisms of punitive, physical, and psychological violence bring out the desire to remind the minor of his subordinate role as a worker and as an ethnic and racialized subject. Apart from considerations about the legal status of people when inflicting punishments, it is perceptible how violence deepens prejudices that recreate differentiations that are strongly anchored in colonial society and perpetuated at different levels. The exercise of abusive power did not occur without the reaction of the minors who, when they could, made themselves heard before the courts to defend their violated rights. Regrettably, however, the dynamics of the relationship to which we have referred would remain in force for a long time to come.

Cite this article: Paola A. Revilla Orías. Moving to Your Place: Labour Coercion and Punitive Violence against Minors under Guardianship (Charcas, Sixteenth through Eighteenth Centuries). *International Review of Social History*, 68:S31 (2023), pp. 93–108. https://doi.org/10.1017/S0020859022000888

International Review of Social History, 68:S31 (2023), pp. 109–134
doi:10.1017/S002085902200089X

RESEARCH ARTICLE

Status, Power, and Punishments: "Household Workers" in Late Imperial China

Claude Chevaleyre ⓘ

Centre national de la recherche scientifique, Institut d'Asie orientale, Lyon, France, e-mail:
claude.chevaleyre@cnrs.fr

Abstract
In the past four decades or so, China scholars have shone a new light on the history of labour in late imperial China, particularly on the role of the household as a unit of production and on the contribution of women to commercial production and family income. Beyond members of the kin group itself, attention is seldom paid to the individuals brought into the Chinese households solely to provide additional manpower. To "break the carapace" of the late imperial Chinese household, this article focuses on the often-omitted "household workers", that is, on its enslaved (*nubi*) and hired (*gugong*) constituents. It approaches the topic from the angle of the vulnerability of these non-kin "workers" to punishments and violence. To evaluate their vulnerability to punishment and gauge the disciplinary powers of the household heads, it examines the relationship between punishments and "household workers" in Ming law. It then explores lineage regulations, before moving closer to the ground by mobilizing a wider variety of day-to-day sources, such as contracts and narrative sources produced in the context of the late Ming and early Qing crisis.

Whenever she bought female slaves (*nünu*), after contracts were established and [the slaves] had walked through the door, she would make them kneel and bend down. First, she admonished them with hundreds of words. She called it "to instruct" (*jiaodao*). Once instructed, she undressed them, tied their hands behind their back, and whipped them a hundred times. She called it 'to experiment punishment' (*shixing*). Would one move or wail, she struck harder, until they became silent and still as if she were flogging trees and rocks. She called it "to know fear" (*zhiwei*). Then she gave them orders and assignments. [...] Her male and female slaves (*tongpu bi'ao*) came and went in rows. Even soldiers trained by great generals are not that disciplined.[1]

The above excerpt is from a late eighteenth-century anecdote recorded by Ji Yun (1724–1805) in his popular *Jottings from the Hut of Subtle Perception* (*Yuewei caotang*

---

[1]Ji Yun, *Huaixi zaji* (1792), in *Quanben Yuewei caotang biji* (Chengdu, 1995), p. 272. Unless otherwise stated, all translations are mine.

biji).[2] Often quoted as evidence of the physical abuses endured by the enslaved in late imperial China, this passage should be taken with a grain of salt.[3] A tireless collector of "tales of the strange", Ji Yun probably recorded this anecdote less for its representativeness than for its unusual display of "severity" (*yan*). And one might reasonably assume that he was first attracted by the supernatural events surrounding the burial of the cruel mistress (wife to an anonymous assistant minister), such as the inexplicable combustion of her coffin.

Its dubious value as historical evidence notwithstanding, Ji Yun's anecdote suggests that buying people to "give them orders and assignments" (*qushi*) was still common practice in the late eighteenth century. It also shows that the household was a site of labour management and that corporal punishments were part of the portfolio of labour control methods.

Labour in late imperial China is hardly a new topic of historical research. In the past four decades, China scholars have greatly expanded the scope of our knowledge of labour relations and labour mobilization. The most salient achievements have come from gender historians. In the process of "break[ing] open the carapace of the Chinese household",[4] they have underlined the centrality of the household in the organization of work and production. They have also reassessed the substantial contribution of women's work to commercial production and family income.[5] Historians have also shone new light on "tributary labour relations" within the Manchu Banner system, the organization of work inside the imperial palace, and the strategies of labour mobilization at work in polygenic and polyandric marriages.[6]

Beyond the members of the kin group itself, the outsiders brought into the households to provide additional work nonetheless rarely surface in recent scholarship on late imperial China.[7] The relative lack of source documents is an insufficient

---

[2]On Ji Yun and his work, see Sing-chen Lydia Chiang, *Collecting the Self: Body and Identity in Strange Tale Collections of Late Imperial China* (Leiden, 2005), pp. 197–243.

[3]Hsieh Bao Hua, *Concubinage and Servitude in Late Imperial China* (Lanham, MD [etc.], 2014), p. 127.

[4]Francesca Bray, *Technology and Gender: Fabrics of Power in Late Imperial China* (Berkeley, CA [etc.], 1997), p. 180. For an overview of the contribution of gender studies to Chinese labour history, see Susan Mann, "Work and Household in Chinese Culture: Historical Perspectives", in Barbara Entwisle and Gail E. Henderson (eds), *Re-Drawing Boundaries: Work, Households, and Gender in China* (Berkeley, CA [etc.], 2000), pp. 15–32.

[5]Bray, *Technology and Gender*, pp. 175–178, 206–236; Susan Mann, *Precious Records: Women in China's Long Eighteenth Century* (Stanford, CA, 1997), pp. 143–177; Bozhong Li, *Agricultural Development in Jiangnan, 1620–1850* (Houndmills [etc.], 1998), pp. 12, 24, 92–93, 141–151; Bryna Goodman and Wendy Larson (eds), *Gender in Motion: Divisions of Labor and Cultural Change in Late Imperial and Modern China* (Lanham, MD, 2005); Guotong Li, "The Control of Female Energies: Gender and Ethnicity on China's Southeast Coast", in Beverly Bossler (ed.), *Gender and Chinese History: Transformative Encounters* (Seattle, WA [etc.], 2015), pp. 41–57.

[6]Christine Moll-Murata, "Tributary Labour Relations in China During the Ming-Qing Transition (Seventeenth to Eighteenth Centuries)", *International Review of Social History*, 61 (2016), pp. 27–48; idem, "Working the Qing Palace Machine: The Servant's Perspective", in Martina Siebert, Kai Jun Chen, and Dorothy Ko (eds), *Making the Palace Machine Work* (Amsterdam, 2021), pp. 47–72; Hsieh, *Concubinage and Servitude*, pp. 141–304; Matthew H. Sommer, *Polyandry and Wife-Selling in Qing Dynasty China: Survival Strategies and Judicial Interventions* (Oakland, CA, 2015).

[7]Exceptions include Hsieh, *Concubinage and Servitude*, pp. 95–139; Moll-Murata, "Tributary Labour Relations", pp. 43–48; Joseph P. McDermott, *The Making of a New Rural Order in South China, Volume 2: Merchants, Markets, and Lineages, 1500–1700* (Cambridge, 2020), ch. 6.

explanation (the topic used to be widely studied by Chinese and Japanese historians).[8] A better explanation might be the lack of even approximate figures and lack of consensus about the numerical importance of servile labour and its evolution. Some historians have estimated that servile labour decreased from the Ming (1368–1644) and finally disappeared during the eighteenth century.[9] Evidence nonetheless points to an increase in the enslaved population during the Ming (up to a few per cent of the whole population in the 1640s, according to my estimates).[10] It also points to a hardly measurable decrease from the eighteenth century onwards (not a complete disappearance).[11]

This article intends to "break the carapace" of the late imperial Chinese household a little more by shining light on the often-omitted slaves and other "household workers". I approach the topic from the angle of the vulnerability of non-kin "workers" to punishments and violence. The term "household workers" is not a contextual (emic) category. I use it to refer to two distinct legal groups: *nubi* (enslaved) and *gugong* (hirelings). Everyone worked (or was expected to work) in the Chinese household, including women whose domestic *and* productive labour ideally took place "inside" (*nei*), while men worked "outside" (*wai*).[12] Although everyone worked, not every outsider was brought into a household as a worker. Wives (*qi*), concubines (*qie*), uxorilocal husbands (*zhuixu*), and adoptees (*yinan*) were undoubtedly incorporated into the kin group for their ability to work. Still, their primary function was to ensure the perpetuation of the agnatic descent line. *Nubi* and *gugong*, on the contrary, were brought into the household to provide labour, not to integrate the kin group.

Gender certainly affected the lived experiences of household workers in various ways. As disposable and marketable assets, women may have been more numerous among the enslaved than among hirelings (considering that the latter worked "outside" their own households). The fact that household heads had both a moral duty to give female slaves into marriage when coming of age and, until the eighteenth century, legitimate access to their bodies for sex and reproduction also led to differentiated life and work cycles.[13] Yet, the gender dimension seldom surfaces in the sources used in this article, where *nubi* and *gugong* are mainly considered as uniform social and legal groups.

To evaluate their vulnerability to punishments and to gauge the disciplinary powers of the household-heads, I first examine the relationship between punishments

---

[8]Besides numerous articles and book chapters published since the 1920s, two major reference works were published in the last decades of the twentieth century: Wei Qingyuan, Wu Qiyan, and Lu Su, *Qingdai nubi zhidu* (Beijing, 1982); Jing Junjian, *Qingdai shehui de jianmin dengji* (Hangzhou, 1993).

[9]Mark Elvin, *The Pattern of the Chinese Past* (Stanford, CA, 1973), p. 235; Sommer, *Polyandry and Wife-Selling*, p. 8.

[10]Claude Chevaleyre, "The Abolition of Slavery and the Status of Slaves in Late Imperial China", in Alessandro Stanziani and Gwyn Campbell (eds), *The Palgrave Handbook of Bondage and Human Rights in Africa and Asia* (New York, 2019), pp. 57–82, 60. See also Wei, Wu, and Lu, *Qingdai nubi zhidu*, p. 5.

[11]For instance, Johanna S. Ransmeier, *Sold People: Traffickers and Family Life in North China* (Cambridge, MA, 2017), p. 241 passim.

[12]For example, Huo Wanjie, "Taiyuan Huoshi zhongfang zupu jiazhen" (1481), in *Taiyuan Huoshi Chongbentang zupu*, 9 vols (Nanhai, 1722), III, p. 86. Available at: http://www.foshanmuseum.com/gjdzs/as/117/mobile/index.html; last accessed 2 August 2022. See also Susan L. Mann, *Gender and Sexuality in Modern Chinese History* (Cambridge, 2011), p. 6.

[13]Matthew H. Sommer, "Making Sex Work: Polyandry as a Survival Strategy in Qing Dynasty China", in Goodman and Larson, *Gender in Motion*, pp. 29–54, 33; Wei, Wu, and Lu, *Qingdai nubi zhidu*, pp. 129–133.

and "household workers" in Ming law. Then, I explore its transposition into lineage regulations. Finally, I move closer to the ground by mobilizing a wider variety of day-to-day sources, such as contracts and narrative sources produced during the late Ming and early Qing (1644–1911) crisis.

Although I focus on the late Ming to early Qing period (when the enslaved population was at its highest and before the eighteenth-century reconfiguration of status laws), the sources I use cover the whole late imperial period (i.e. the Ming and Qing dynasties).[14] The *Great Ming Code* (my main source in the first section) was promulgated in the last decade of the fourteenth century, but it was still very much in use in the seventeenth century. Similarly, many of the genealogical records used in the second section were printed during the Qing era but contain regulations written in the Ming. Although the sources do not always allow term-to-term comparisons of the two groups, they open different windows on their relations to punishments.

The State's Perspective: Enforcing Status and Empowering Masters

The *Great Ming Code* (*Da Ming lü*) was promulgated in its final version in 1397. Since the first Ming emperor (Hongwu, r. 1368–1398) had prohibited the alteration of dynastic laws, by the end of the dynasty the *Code* was out of step with social and economic realities.[15] Although it merely unveils an ideal(ized) vision of the late Ming social order, it nonetheless gives us a sense of the state ideology of the time. It also allows us to outline the contours of always implicit legal statuses and social categories, to seize the state-promoted conceptions of social dynamics of power, and to highlight the role of punishments in the control of "household workers".

Recruitment and Punishments

At the state's level, punishment(s) played various roles in relation to "household workers". First, punishment was, in theory, the only legitimate path towards enslavement, alongside capture in war, despite the well-documented proliferation of private enslavement through (self-)sales and abductions. Relatively silent about enslavement, early Ming official sources suggest that, as a group, *nubi* were to remain numerically marginal. They also show that the state legally recognized enslavement and intended to maintain a firm monopoly on the production of *nubi* through punishment.[16] Two centuries after the fall of the dynasty, the author of the *Essentials of the Ming Institutions* (*Ming huiyao*) still presented enslavement in Ming times as the result of punishments meted out to the relatives of major criminals: "In the Ming system, the children of war captives (*fuhuo*) and the persons seized (*chaomo*) as [relatives of] criminals were awarded as *nubi* to the families of meritorious officials (*gongchen*)."[17]

---

[14]For discussions on the periodization of "late imperial China", see Bossler, *Gender and Chinese History*, p. 12; Hsieh, *Concubinage and Servitude*, p. xvii; Bray, *Technology and Gender*, pp. 2–3.

[15]Jiang Yonglin, *The Great Ming Code / Da Ming lü* (Seattle, WA, 2005), p. 59.

[16]Claude Chevaleyre, "Asservir pour punir. La nature pénale du statut d'esclave dans la Chine des Ming (1368–1644)", *Extrême-Orient, Extrême-Occident*, 41 (2017), pp. 93–117, 97–98.

[17]Long Wenbin, *Ming huiyao* (Beijing, [1887] 1956), p. 970. See also Wang Kentang, *Da Ming lü fuli jianzhi* (pref. 1612), 20:15b.

Besides containing tax evasion, prohibiting private enslavement was meant to preserve the agrarian and self-sufficient social order envisioned by the founder of the Ming in which the population was hereditarily bound to their land and occupations and laboured for and by themselves.[18] As expounded by jurist Gao Ju in the early seventeenth century, the people "must fundamentally work hard and to the best of their ability. They must not own *nubi*. Only meritorious officials can. Commoners who harbour and raise [*nubi*] transgress their condition".[19] If enslavement was, in theory, a monopoly of the state, *nubi* ownership was, also in theory, a privilege of the state's most prominent servants. And it was the state's duty to protect the population from enslavement.[20] From a conceptual standpoint, enslavement was thus, first and foremost, a punitive regime for criminals by association, not a labour regime.

Unlike *nubi*, which emerged as a legal category at the dawn of the imperial era,[21] the *gugong* category was a legal innovation of Ming law.[22] *Gugong* were not criminals at all. Unlike "raising" (*xuyang*) *nubi*, hiring people on a daily, monthly, or annual basis was not objectionable, except in cases of hiring others to perform one's state-imposed labour duties.[23] In the Ming legal context, *gugong* thus mainly referred to commoners hired to perform work for others on a time-limited and contractual basis in exchange for food and monetary compensation.[24] Punishments had nothing to do with the mobilization of hirelings.

To us, who are accustomed to regarding contractual labour relations mediated through money as the epitome of "free" and autonomous work, the difference between *nubi* and *gugong* seems as radical as the opposition between slavery and freedom. The twist, however, is that *nubi* and *gugong* were not so radically opposed in Ming law. Despite entirely different recruitment processes and degrees of social autonomy, within the boundaries of their relations with their master/employer, *nubi* and *gugong* were treated as cognates. They appeared in the same legal statutes. They were governed by the same legal regime of punishments derived from the parent–child relationship by analogy, placing them in a similar relation of subordination to the authority of the household head.

Nubi and the Analogy with Children

The punishments prescribed by the *Great Ming Code* were not solely designed to punish the crimes and offences committed by *nubi* and *gugong*. They were also tailored to redress status transgressions. Punishments can thus be analysed to evaluate

---

[18]On tax evasion, see Cheng Minzheng, *Huang Ming wenheng* (Shanghai, [1510] 1936), 27:7a. On the prohibition against private enslavement, see Gao Ju, *Ming lü jijie fuli* (Beijing, [1610] 1908), 4:9b.

[19]Gao, *Ming lü jijie fuli*, 4:11a.

[20]Chevaleyre, "Asservir pour punir", pp. 100–105.

[21]Robin D.S. Yates, "Des hommes sans honneur et sans nom", in Paulin Ismard, Benedetta Rossi, and Cécile Vidal (eds), *Les mondes de l'esclavage. Une histoire comparée* (Paris, 2021), pp. 53–59, 55.

[22]Fu Zhongyao, "Zhongguo gudai guyong qiyue zhidu yanjiu" (Master's thesis, Jilin University, 2006), pp. 3, 10.

[23]See Hai Rui's (1514–1587) proposal to replace enslaved workers with hirelings in Chen Yizhong (ed.), *Hai Rui ji*, 2 vols (Beijing, 1962), I, p. 73. See also Gao, *Ming lü jijie fuli*, 13:14b.

[24]Claude Chevaleyre, "Serving and Working for Others: Negotiating Legal Status and Social Relations of Household Laborers in Late Imperial China", *Journal of Global Slavery*, 5 (2020), pp. 170–203, 174–176.

the level of power conferred upon masters and employers by the state, as well as the protection afforded to that power.

In its most basic expression, the *Great Ming Code* is an elaborate grid of correspondence between incriminations and punishments. Each incrimination corresponds to a reference punishment. Each punishment could then be modulated in aggravating or extenuating circumstances. As an example, "assaulting" (*ou*) others "with hands and feet" without causing injuries was liable to ten blows of a *chi* (light stick), whereas assaulting others "with other tools" (aggravating factor) was liable to thirty blows.[25]

In addition, punishments were further modulated according to the relative position of the offender and the victim. Relational asymmetries shifted from one person to the next and derived from status and/or relative position within the family and household hierarchy. Status was the main mitigating factor when the offender and the victim were unrelated (i.e. when they belonged to different households, families, and lineages). Several social groups (like officials and members of the imperial clan) enjoyed legal privileges in the Ming system, but "debased people" (*jianmin*, of which *nubi* were the main component) were systematically discriminated against in relation to commoners (*liangmin*, or "honourable" people). A commoner who physically assaulted an unrelated *nubi* was sentenced to the reference punishment for "assaulting others" minus one degree. In contrast, a *nubi* who struck an unrelated commoner was sentenced to the same reference punishment increased by one degree.[26]

When the offender and the victim were relatives or lived in the same household, the criteria of gender, age, rank of birth, generation, and ritual proximity combined to produce context-specific relational asymmetries. Expressed in degrees of mourning, ritual proximity acted as a catalyst of pre-existing hierarchies based on inferiority/juniority (*beiyou*) and superiority/seniority (*zunzhang*).[27] Assaulting one's father or mother (seniors of the first degree of mourning) or one's paternal grandparents (seniors of the second degree of mourning) was a far more serious offence (punished with death by decapitation) than assaulting outsiders to the household. Striking one's children (juniors of the second degree of mourning), on the contrary, was without legal consequences so long as it did not cause death.[28]

As the closest, most vertical and asymmetric of all family bonds, the parent–child relationship also served as a major reference point to frame *nubi* status and to enforce their subordination to the household head (*jiazhang*). The *nubi*-children analogy is ubiquitous throughout Ming normative and moral sources. Its ubiquity does not mean that *nubi* were socially equal to their master's children. Framing the master–*nubi* relationship in such paternalistic terms nonetheless permitted borrowing from the most asymmetric relation of all. A few moralists, especially in the late Ming period, took this analogy at face value to outline the contours of a genuinely reciprocal, "benevolent", and "humane" relationship – even sometimes to question the legitimacy of enslaving one's fellow human beings. To many others, however, the fatherly

---

[25]Gao, *Ming lü jijie fuli*, 20:1a.
[26]*Ibid.*, 20:22a.
[27]Hsieh, *Concubinage and Servitude*, pp. 46–47.
[28]Gao, *Ming lü jijie fuli*, 20:38b.

"benevolence" expected from masters was no more than a way to legitimize enslavement in Confucian terms.[29]

Principles of reciprocity and benevolence are barely mentioned in dynastic law. The analogy with children is nonetheless constantly and selectively mobilized to narrow the range of identities that *nubi* could assume vis-à-vis others. It was used to frame a specific regime of punishments that, in all circumstances, placed *nubi* under the direct control and exclusive authority of the household head and his closest kin. For instance, like other household members, *nubi* were required to provide asylum to and conceal the crimes of those who "lived together" (*tongju*) without fear of prosecution. However, they were denied such privilege themselves. In the same manner, whereas junior and inferior members of the household could not be accused of "theft" (*dao*) in a legal sense (all personal belongings were considered part of the collective property), *nubi* who stole from household members were prosecuted for theft.[30]

Ming law thus conveniently excluded *nubi* from genuine household membership when access to privileges and property was at stake. At the same time, it assimilated them with children in imposing the specificities of the most asymmetric hierarchical relation.[31] As an example, according to the statute on the desecration of graves, children and *nubi* were the only ones to face the death penalty for damaging the corpse of a deceased parent or master when "smoking out foxes" (*xun huli*) on their graveyard.[32] According to Ying Jia (1494–1554), the severity of the law reflected the specificity of the relationship between (grand)children and (grand)parents, which, by extension, applied to *nubi*.[33]

Similar examples of the analogical use of the parent–child relationship are found in the three statutes dealing specifically with the offences and crimes committed by *nubi* against the household head and his close relatives (statutes on fornication, insults, and assaults).[34] When comparing the punishments meted out to *nubi* and children, we observe that for serious offences, *nubi* were treated like children. For striking, causing death, or intentionally killing one's parent, grandparent, or master, all were sentenced to the same forms of the death penalty. However, for lesser crimes, like injuring or killing "by mistake", *nubi* were sentenced to slightly more severe punishments. Those differences were usually explained by the difference in nature inherent in the master–*nubi* and parent–child bonds: children were considered as naturally more inclined to be "respectful and cautious", whereas *nubi* were perceived as being of a different "kind" (*lei*) and more "neglectful" by nature.[35]

A close comparison between the regimes of punishments of children and *nubi* also shows that the analogy reaches a limit when we move away from the direct master–

---

[29]Claude Chevaleyre, "Acting as Master and Bondservant: Considerations on Status, Identities and the Nature of 'Bond-Servitude' in Late Ming China", in Alessandro Stanziani (ed.), *Labour, Coercion, and Economic Growth in Eurasia, 17th–20th Centuries* (Leiden, 2013), pp. 237–272, 254–260.

[30]Gao, *Ming lü jijie fuli*, 18:1b, 1:64b, 4:26b–27b.

[31]For merely "disobeying orders", children were liable to 100 strokes: Gao, *Ming lü jijie fuli*, 22:37a.

[32]Gao, *Ming lü jijie fuli*, 18:63a.

[33]Ying Jia, *Da Ming lü shiyi* (1552), in *Xuxiu siku quanshu* edn (Shanghai, 1995–2002), DCCCLXIII, 18:29b.

[34]Gao, *Ming lü jijie fuli*, 21:3b, 25:8b, 20:25a.

[35]Feng Zi, *Da Ming lü jishuo fuli* (pref. 1592), 8:25a. See also Wang, *Da Ming lü fuli jianzhi*, 20:17a.

nubi relation. With very few exceptions, children were always liable to lesser penalties than *nubi* when the victim was a more distant relative. For instance, children who injured *their* relative of the second degree of mourning were sentenced to three years of penal servitude. In contrast, *nubi* who injured *their master's* relative of the second degree of mourning were sentenced to death by decapitation.[36] Thus, unlike children whose relative identity changed according to their direct relation to others in the family, *nubi*'s relations to others in the household were always indirect and mediated through the fatherlike figure of their master (leading to generally harsher punishments).

The analogy between *nubi* and children was thus a malleable and utilitarian legal fiction. It extended to *nubi* the almost absolute authority that parents exercised over their children so that *nubi* were permanently relegated to the lowest levels of the household hierarchy (in addition to being relegated to the lowest levels of society as "debased people"). The punishment matrix so created was also a powerful institutional machinery that empowered masters and protected their paternalistic authority against the transgressions and challenges of the enslaved. By threat or by actual referral to the judicial authorities, masters could at all times reassert their authority over enslaved people who, like children, could not appeal to the courts against them.[37]

Disciplining Nubi and Gugong

The pending question is that of the extent of power vested in masters/employers by the state. Although not clearly outlined, its contours can be inferred from the content of the three above-mentioned statutes on crimes committed by *nubi* against the household head and his close relatives, which also extended to *gugong*.

As seen above, the statute on assaults ("Slaves striking the household head", no. 337) was ruthless against *nubi* and *gugong*.[38] Its ruthlessness was nonetheless perceived by jurists as central to the defence of hierarchies, as it not only "addresse[d] affrays between masters and *nubi*" but also "[kept] the world running by distinguishing between statuses and by correcting denominations".[39] In other words, its centrality lay in the defence of the authority of the household head since "correcting denominations" (*zhengming*) meant, in Confucian terms, ensuring the proper correspondence between "the names" and "the substance" of social roles.[40]

After enumerating the punishments prescribed against disobedient and renegade *nubi* and *gugong*, statute no. 337 addresses situations where masters and employers (and their relatives of the first two degrees of mourning, who shared their disciplinary power) struck and killed their subordinates. With regard to *nubi*, the law only considered cases of homicide. It distinguished between accidental death in the process of legitimate disciplining, the intentional killing of "guilty" *nubi*, and the arbitrary killing of "innocent" *nubi*. The intentional killing of "guilty" (*youzui*) *nubi* was liable to a moderate sentence of 100 strokes. The issue was not that masters could beat their

---

[36]Gao, *Ming lü jijie fuli*, 20:25a.
[37]*Ibid.*, 22:30a, 31a.
[38]*Ibid.*, 20:25a–26a.
[39]Feng, *Da Ming lü jishuo fuli*, 8:24a.
[40]Michael Nylan, *The Five Confucian Classics* (New Haven, CT, 2001), p. 274.

nubi, but that in the process they "arrogate[d] the right to beat and kill" (*shanzi sizi ousha*), which was a monopoly of the state.[41] The "arbitrary" (*feili*) killing of innocent *nubi* was liable to a more severe sentence of one year of penal servitude (plus the emancipation of the family of the deceased enslaved).[42] "Accidental" or "unexpected" (*xiehou*) death resulting from "legitimate disciplining" (*yifa juefa*) of "disobedient" (*weifan jiaoling*) *nubi*, however, was not liable to prosecution. According to Gao Ju, "legitimate disciplining" meant beating on the buttocks.[43] In other words, although the law had a whole arsenal of provisions tailored to address crimes and offences committed by *nubi* (from insulting to killing one's master), the state granted masters almost unlimited disciplinary powers against disobedient and unruly behaviours, so long as they did not cause death.

As to *gugong*, the law neither considered homicides nor distinguished between innocent and guilty *gugong*. The principal line of demarcation was that which separated legitimate discipline from damages to the body. Like masters, employers could not be prosecuted for killing *gugong* "accidentally" or "unexpectedly" in the process of legitimate discipline. Nor could they be punished for simply "beating" *gugong*. However, they faced severe punishment if they beat and caused "fractures or worse" (*zheshang yishang*). For instance, death resulting from a beating was liable to three years of penal servitude, whereas "deliberate" killing was liable to death by strangulation.[44]

The different levels of protection granted by the state to *gugong* and *nubi* show that, despite being legally akin and subjected to analogous regimes of punishments, there was a major legal difference between the two categories. Unlike *nubi*, *gugong* were not permanently "debased" and cast out of the society of "honourable" people. Their absence from the statutes addressing crimes and offences between unrelated "mean" and "honourable" people shows that the socially demeaning bearing on *nubi* applied to *gugong* only within the boundaries of their employer's household and for the duration of their employment.[45]

Inside their employer's household, *gugong* were considered "inferiors and juniors". Like *nubi*, they could be prosecuted for "theft" and were required to conceal crimes committed by "seniors and superiors" without benefiting from the reciprocal privilege. In some cases, they were liable to slightly lesser sentences than *nubi*. But when subordination to the authority of the household head had to be emphasized (as in cases of crimes with strong ritual significance like the desecration of their employer's buried body, premeditated murder, and illicit sexual relations), they received the same punishments as *nubi* and children.[46] As underlined by Zhang Kai (1398–1460), inside the household, "*gugong* do not compare to *nubi*, [...] yet, both are mean dependents" (*jianli zhi tu*).[47]

---

[41]Feng, *Da Ming lü jishuo fuli*, 8:23b. According to the same author, "guilty" meant committing a crime punishable under the law.

[42]Gao, *Ming lü jijie fuli*, 20:28a.

[43]*Ibid.*, 20:28b.

[44]*Ibid.*, 20:26a.

[45]Chevaleyre, "Serving and Working for Others", p. 179.

[46]Gao, *Ming lü jijie fuli*, 18:61b–63b, 19:5b, 25:11b.

[47]Zhang Kai, *Lütiao shuyi* (1467), in Yang Yifan (ed.), *Zhongguo lüxue wenxian*, ser. 1, 4 vols (Harbin, 2004), III, p. 371.

To summarize, modalities of entry into a "labour" relation, duration, and conditions of remuneration were not prominent factors in determining the level of power that "employers" were entitled to exercise over "workers". The key factor that made *gugong* akin to enslaved people was that they worked for others, not themselves. To benefit from others' "benevolence and solidarity" (*enyi*, in the form of "wages"), they were called upon to "serve and be commanded" (*yishi*).[48] Legal commentators of the Ming and Qing era all recognized that to receive "a [money] price" (*guzhi*) in exchange for performing "service" (*yi*) was socially different from being enslaved and serving for a lifetime (*zhongshen*).[49] However, to "serve" (which in practice meant to obey orders) was the starting point of a process of entrenched hierarchical differentiation that required complete obedience and subordination. To ensure that social hierarchies, roles, and order were preserved, the state placed serving people (hirelings as much as enslaved) under the indisputable and exclusive authority of the household heads, granted them extended disciplinary powers, and protected their paternalistic power with an arsenal of highly asymmetric legal punishments.

The Lineage Perspective: Paternalism and Discipline

In addition to "universal" dynastic law, the corporate lineages that flourished in the Ming also drafted their own regulations "to govern their houses" (*zhijia*).[50] Ordering one's house was not simply a matter of family organization. It was a political duty that contributed to maintaining the broader social order. But it was also a vital means for patrilineal descent groups to ensure their self-governance, protect their assets, and curtail state interferences with their affairs.

Included in registers (*jiapu, zupu*) that lineages printed at great cost and kept secret, these regulations touched upon many aspects of lineage activity (such as the management of collective assets, the education of the younger generations, the allocation of lineage subsidies, the organization of rituals and solidarity, hierarchies, and the observance of proper behaviours).[51] As tools of labour and social management, these regulations also shine a light on household-level control mechanisms, on the perceptions that lineage authorities had of their power, and on the anxieties that disciplinary methods were meant to address.

Lineage Regulations

Chinese lineage registers are usually composed of a wide variety of documents (genealogic tables, prefaces, deeds, maps, etc.), some of which had a significant normative value. "Admonitions" (*jiaxun*) and "regulations" (*zugui, zonggui, jiafa*, etc.), in particular, were designed to prescribe and correct individual behaviours and thereby

---

[48]Bao Shuyun (ed.) and Zhu Qingqi (comp.), *Xing'an huilan* (1834), in Yang Yifan *et al.* (eds), *Xing'an huilan quanbian* (Beijing, 2008), pp. 2035–2036.

[49]Shen Zhiqi, *Da Qing lü jizhu* (Beijing, [1715] 2000), p. 747.

[50]Huo, "Taiyuan Huoshi zhongfang zupu jiazhen", p. 86.

[51]On Chinese lineages, see Maurice Freedman, *Lineage Organisation in South-Eastern China* (London, 1958); David Faure and Xi He, "Family and Lineage in Late Imperial China", *Oxford Research Encyclopedia of Asian History*, 2020. Available at: https://doi.org/10.1093/acrefore/9780190277727.013.394; last accessed 29 July 2022.

preserve harmony.[52] If the two genres conflate somewhat in content and purpose, admonitions generally consist of didactic texts written by illustrious ancestors, whereas regulations usually take the form of structured lists of rules and prohibitions (sometimes modelled after the penal code) to be used in the administration of lineage justice.

Not all Chinese families could afford to structure themselves in elaborate ways. Compiling documents, writing one's lineage history, and engraving woodblocks were resource-consuming tasks. Printing registers was thus a marker of social standing and an expression of adherence to state-sponsored Confucian values. The standards and norms that these texts unveil are thus mainly those of the propertied Confucian elite.

As their authors often underscored, lineage regulations had a function like that of dynastic law: "The realm has legal statutes (*falü*). Families have admonitions and regulations (*xungui*). Both are the same. How can the realm be governed when statutes are not enforced? How can households be ordered when regulations are not enforced?"[53] Lineage justice was thus not a mere substitute for imperial justice, but an internal and lower-level body of dispute resolution designed to maintain order and prevent, as much as possible, the involvement of the imperial administration. As stressed in the previous section, the state protected the authority of the lineage- and household heads and invested them with powers to control and discipline their kin and non-kin subordinates. On occasion, lineage regulations were also granted binding power when stamped by the administration or endorsed by the emperor.[54]

Like dynastic normative sources, lineage admonitions and regulations seldom provide details about concrete and potentially unflattering daily practices. "Household workers" are far from being present in every lineage register and are far less present than members of the kin group, particularly children whose education was their principal concern.[55]

A first observation can nonetheless be made from the relative frequency of "household workers" in those texts. *Gugong* are seldom mentioned and mainly surface in texts dealing with activities that required additional labour input and generated costs to be paid by the lineage (in food and money allocations), like agriculture, construction works, and ritual activities.[56] Thus, it seems that despite the ambiguous status of *gugong* as temporary and partial insiders to the household, their presence and management were not a significant concern for the lineages.

Nubi are slightly more present in lineage registers. They are the subject of more detailed and varied prescriptions. Like the state, lineages strictly restricted the acquisition of *nubi* to only one supply source. To them, *nubi* were not criminals condemned by justice but outsiders who voluntarily sold themselves or their offspring

---

[52]Thousands of volumes of registers have been preserved: Yuan Meilin, "Ming Qing jiazu sifa tanxi", *Faxue yanjiu*, 3 (2012), pp. 181–194, 182. Most of those available in print were compiled in the Qing period, often based on pre-existing documents. Some of the texts used in this article date back to the Ming dynasty, but the majority cannot be dated with precision.

[53]Zhang Rizuo, *Qinghe Zhangshi zongpu* (1752), in Zhang Haiying, Wu Xinli, and Li Wanqing (eds), *Zhonghua zupu jicheng*, 100 vols, (Chengdu, 1995), Zhang ser., VIII, 13:12b.

[54]Hui-chen Wang Liu, *The Traditional Chinese Clan Rules* (New York, 1959), p. 24.

[55]Huo, "Taiyuan Huoshi zhongfang zupu jiazhen", p. 86.

[56]Huo Huaiting, "Taiyuan Huoshi zhongfang bashi zu Huaiting weng jiazhen fulu" (1534), in *Taiyuan Huoshi Chongbentang zupu*, III, pp. 115–116. Taga Akigoro (ed.), *Sōfu no kenkyū. Shiryō hen* (Tokyo, 1960), pp. 519, 545, 554, 562–564, 571.

"because of cold and hunger" (*jihan*).[57] In keeping with the tenets of dynastic law and the legal ban on trafficking,[58] they prohibited practices such as buying people of "unclear origin" and from traffickers;[59] or profiteering from indebtedness to enslave others.[60] If lineage authorities wished above all to avoid (shameful and costly) prosecutions, their prescriptions illustrate the gap between state norms and social practices of enslavement.

Lineage authorities similarly regarded the use of *nubi* as a privilege and made the management and allocation of enslaved manpower a prerogative of their appointed managers, not of individual members. Huo Tao (1487–1540)'s influential *Family Admonitions* (*Jiaxun*), for instance, allocated the patriarch and the estate managers a handful of *nubi* for such tasks as guarding the main gates, receiving visitors, measuring the grains, and so forth. Aside from that, only members who enjoyed academic prestige (like officials returning home on sick leave) could receive *nubi* from the lineage for their personal service.[61] Huo Tao barely mentions the possession of *nubi* by individual members, suggesting that acquiring and owning *nubi* was a monopoly of the corporate lineage. Huo nonetheless alludes to privately owned *nubi*, suggesting that the practice was at least tolerated.[62] More generally, the example of Huo Tao's *Admonitions* unveils a picture of the lineage order that is similar in many respects to the Ming founder's ideal agrarian society. Lineage members were expected to have honourable occupations and to work for and by themselves, not to rely on the work of others.[63] Enslaving outsiders for the collective use of the lineage was unquestionably legitimate and even necessary, but it had to remain limited in numbers and to specific tasks.

Paternalistic Control

The most salient feature of lineage admonitions and regulations, however, is their display of a pervasive tension between paternalistic principles and anxieties caused by the presence of *nubi*. As seen from their tables of contents, sections dealing with the "use" and "control" of *nubi* are usually paired with sections on "commiseration" and "magnanimity".[64] No similar example can be found for *gugong*, but both categories are sometimes caught together in the nets of paternalistic discourses. We can read in Pang Shangpeng's (1524–1580) *Family Admonitions* (*Pangshi jiaxun*) the following:

> With regard to hirelings and enslaved: Except for those who are cunning, ignorant, and lazy and who should be expelled, for those who are fit for use

---

[57]Huo, "Taiyuan Huoshi zhongfang zupu jiazhen", p. 90.

[58]Claude Chevaleyre, "Human Trafficking in Late Imperial China", in Richard B. Allen (ed.), *Slavery and Bonded Labor in Asia, 1250–1900* (Leiden, 2021), pp. 160–175.

[59]Huo, "Taiyuan Huoshi zhongfang bashi zu Huaiting weng jiazhen fulu", p. 114.

[60]Guan Weihuang, *Nanhai Jili xiaqiao Guan Shude tang jiapu* (1889), in Zhang Zhiqing and Xu Shu (eds), *Beijing tushuguan cang jiapu congkan–Min-Yue (qiaoxiang) juan*, 50 vols (Beijing, 2000), XXIX, 1:10b. Miu Yuanwen, "Lanling jiaxun" (1610), in Taga, *Sōfu no kenkyū*, p. 607.

[61]Huo Tao, *Huo Weiya Jiaxun* (1529), in Sun Yuxiu (ed.), *Hanfenlou miji*, 80 vols (Shanghai, 1916–1921), XII, 4a, 7a.

[62]Huo, *Huo Weiya Jiaxun*, 3b–4a.

[63]*Ibid.*, 19a, 28b–29a. Taga, *Sōfu no kenkyū*, p. 606.

[64]Taga, *Sōfu no kenkyū*, pp. 623, 632–33, 637, 753–54.

(*kanyong*), [one shall ensure that] they are timely provided with food and beverages, that they are neither hungry nor thirsty, and that their work (*lao*) and rest (*yi*) are balanced. Tao Yuanming said: "They are also children of human beings. You shall treat them well." If you expect [them] to provide their best efforts (*sili*), you shall first gain their compliance (*huanxin*). As to those who are loyal (*zhong*) and diligent (*qin*) and that can be relied on, you must extend special generosity (*zhouxu*) in order to show stimulation.[65]

An influential text (reprinted in various registers until the Republican era),[66] Pang's *Admonitions* show that *gugong* were indeed perceived as akin to *nubi*, although the majority of lineage regulations seldom elaborate on their management as they do about *nubi*. If some authors seemed to genuinely acknowledge the contribution of "household workers" (first of all *nubi*) to the survival and wealth of their lineage and sometimes even express authentic commiseration,[67] many other authors saw treating subordinates well merely as a utilitarian means to instil gratitude and obedience.

As exemplified by Pang's *Admonitions*, "magnanimity" barely amounted to ensuring that *nubi* did not suffer from cold and hunger or that discipline and indulgence, rest and labour, were properly balanced.[68] As frequently noted, enslaved people "listen to hunger and cold before listening to orders" (*xian ting jihan, hou ting shihuan*).[69] Whereas dynastic law mobilized the parent–child analogy to create the conditions of a stringent and unchallengeable relationship of subordination, lineages resorted to paternalistic rhetoric in a pragmatic way: to defuse insubordination, contain resistance, and promote an ideal vision of a pacific relation of domination.

Of course, *nubi* were not all "satisfied with their lot" (*anfen*), obedient, and sensitive to paternalistic discourses. Discipline was thus the necessary corollary to commiseration, benevolence, and reciprocity. That provisions on discipline and control always outnumber discourses on commiseration demonstrates that control and discipline were the primary concerns of household heads and lineage authorities. As mentioned in a lineage register printed in the late nineteenth century:

Enslaved people (*tongpu*) are the same to their masters (*zhuren*) as the minister (*chen*) is to his sovereign (*jun*). Although the situations (*shi*) differ, the relative positions (*fen*) are analogous. With regard to the enslaved, a master must treat them with benevolence (*en*) but also needs means of control (*yu*).[70]

Discipline, however, did not mean tyranny. Household heads were frequently reminded to "cherish" (*aixi*) the "enslaved they bought and those who came to provide labour and services" (*suomai nubi ji laitou gongyi*), to refrain from "abuses"

---

[65]Pang Shangpeng, *Pangshi jiaxun* (Shanghai, [1571] 1935–1937), p. 9. Taga, *Sōfu no kenkyū*, p. 696.
[66]Taga, *Sōfu no kenkyū*, p. 607.
[67]*Xinan Jiangshi jiapu* (c.1600), in Taga, *Sōfu no kenkyū*, p. 788.
[68]Chevaleyre, "Acting as Master and Bondservant", pp. 257–260.
[69]*Gushi zupu* (1779), in Taga, *Sōfu no kenkyū*, p. 620.
[70]Lan Xing, *Lanshi xuxiu zupu* (1881), in Zhang and Xu, *Beijing tushuguan cang jiapu congkan*, XXV, p. 106.

(*lingnüe*),[71] to closely monitor work, and to explain assignments clearly to avoid mistakes and unnecessary punishments. As underlined by Huo Wanjie in the late fifteenth century, "commanding [*nubi*]" (*shi*) required "technique" (*fang*). But when it proved insufficient, "beating and scolding" (*dama*) became necessary.[72]

Punishments, Obedience, and Anxieties

Lineage punishments were generally much less violent than those prescribed by the *Code*. This applied not only to *nubi*, but also to everyone in the lineage. Lighter and more incremental (even in cases of serious offences like cursing or assaulting one's parents or master),[73] the lineage punishments amounted to warnings, injunctions to reform oneself, partial or total suspension of lineage subsidies, fines, beating with various instruments (first among which "planks" [*ze*]), expulsion from the lineage, and, in last resort, referral to the administration for processing under the law.

For instance, article 12 of the *Family Regulations* (*Jiagui*) of the Zhang lineage from Qinghe (Anhui, printed 1752) provides a rare example of the tension between paternalism and anxieties, as well as of the disciplinary methods used by the lineages. Entitled "Employing *nubi*" (*bipu yishi*), the article comprises twenty-four short rules.[74] Only the first one elaborates on the reciprocal and benevolent nature of the master–*nubi* relationship. It states: "Although [*nubi*] are said to be inferior and debased (*beijian*), they are children of human beings (*jie renzi ye*). Since they serve the household (*gongyi wujia*), they must be raised with benevolence (*enyang*). Only then can we benefit from their manpower (*de renli*)."[75]

The following three rules expound on the risks related to the presence of *nubi* in the lineage, the first among which is theft and sexual relations with lineage women. The remaining twenty rules follow the model of the *Code*: they enumerate offences and prescribe corresponding punishments. The crimes covered by this text range from disobedience to conspiracy against one's master. They include theft, illicit sexual relations, arguments, insults, and assaults against lineage members, but also avoiding service, laziness, and lack of dedication when performing a task.

The punishments listed in this text mainly consist in administering flogging with the "light" and "heavy" sticks (the *chi* and *zhang* used by the imperial authorities), but also with "planks" depending on the gravity of the crime, sometimes supplemented with "demotion" (*geyi*) or "expulsion" (*gechu*) of the culprit *nubi*.[76] For instance, laziness and protestations were punished with twenty blows of the *chi*, and sexual intercourse with outsiders with thirty blows of the *zhang* (and with expulsion, should the culprits refuse to reform their behaviour). "Disobedience" (*juming*) and sharing

---

[71]*Xinan Jiangshi jiapu* (c.1600), in Taga, *Sōfu no kenkyū*, p. 788.

[72]Huo, "Taiyuan Huoshi zhongfang zupu jiazhen", p. 89.

[73]Wang Zhong, *Wangshi Sansha quanpu* (Wuxi, 1879), in Zhang, Wu, and Li, *Zhonghua zupu jicheng*, Wang ser., IX, p. 655. Zhu Zhongwen, *Kaoting Zhushi wenxian quanpu* (1620), in Taga, *Sōfu no kenkyū*, pp. 609–610.

[74]*Qinghe Zhangshi zongpu* (1752), in Zhang, Wu, and Li, *Zhonghua zupu jicheng*, Zhang ser., VIII, 13:9a–19a.

[75]*Qinghe Zhangshi zongpu*, 17b–18a.

[76]The implications of "demotion" and "expulsion" are unclear, but it seems that masters sometimes preferred to get rid of the unruliest *nubi*.

"intelligence with one's master's enemies" (*sijiao zhuchou*) were liable to the heaviest penalties (sixty blows of the *zhang* and one hundred blows of the *zhang* supplemented with expulsion, respectively). Only one case required outside intervention: "plotting rebellion against one's master" (*mouni qinzhu*), which was to be "referred to the local magistrate so that [the culprit can] be sentenced to death". Thus, except in cases of very serious crimes and homicides (which were not covered but were undoubtedly referred to the authorities), lineage regulations were far more indulgent with *nubi* than dynastic law (most of the crimes enumerated being liable to heavier sentences under the law).

Such "leniency" was typical neither of the Zhang lineage nor of the treatment of *nubi* in general. However, one specificity of the Zhang lineage regulations is that, unlike other lineages that prescribed physical punishments for crimes committed by their constituents, the article on *nubi* is the only one to systematically prescribe physical punishments.[77] This text thus encapsulates most of the concerns shared by owners of *nubi* and exemplifies the prevalence of punishment over benevolence.

The range of behaviours targeted by lineage regulations first shows that discipline and punishments were less designed to manage *nubi* labour per se (in terms of regulating work or increasing productivity) than to ensure complete obedience and subordination. Lineages undoubtedly expected to extract labour in exchange for their "benevolence", as suggested by references to getting their "strength" (*renli*) and by prescriptions against "laziness".[78] However, "dedication" (*qin*) and "hard work" (*lao*) were required not only from *nubi*, they were also required from every lineage constituent whose work contributed to safeguarding and expanding the collective heritage.[79] Like everyone else, *nubi* were enjoined to work hard, yet their presence in the lineage was seldom framed in the language of work. Their function in the lineage was, first and foremost, to "serve" (*yi*).[80]

To "serve" essentially meant to obey in all circumstances with diligence and loyalty. This opened the way to labour extraction with little limitation, but discipline was primarily designed to contain the dangers posed by the presence of *nubi* to lineage order. Perceived as a permanent "source of trouble" (*sheng tudu*),[81] *nubi* were often depicted as deceitful, prone to theft, violence, resistance, and laziness, and inclined to abuse their master's influence for profit (which undermined the reputation of the whole family and could bring charges against its members).[82] Yet, the primary anxiety expressed in lineage registers regarding *nubi* was bloodline pollution.

---

[77]For crimes committed by other members of the lineage, the Zhang *Household Regulations* usually formulate prohibitions, all introduced by the negative adverb "don't…" (*wu*) and calling to lineage solidarity, respect of moral prescriptions, hierarchies, and self-preservation. Even for younger and inferior lineage members, infringement only led to reprimands and demanded repentance (*hui*).

[78]Huo, "Taiyuan Huoshi zhongfang zupu jiazhen", p. 89.

[79]Pang, *Pangshi jiaxun*, p. 11; Huo, "Taiyuan Huoshi zhongfang bashi zu Huaiting weng jiazhen fulu", p. 107. Taga, *Sōfu no kenkyū*, pp. 789, 612, 789, 822; Bray, *Technology and Gender*, pp. 243–247.

[80]Chevaleyre, "Serving and Working for Others", p. 181.

[81]Pang, *Pangshi jiaxun*, p. 12.

[82]Wang Yan'gan, *Jingjiang Wangshi zongpu* (1935), in Taga, *Sōfu no kenkyū*, p. 672. Lan, *Lanshi xuxiu zupu*, p. 106; Huo, "Taiyuan Huoshi zhongfang zupu jiazhen", p. 89.

Incorporating outsiders into the lineage (as wives, concubines, adoptees, etc.) was a constant source of anxiety.[83] Lineage regulations were, in this regard, often stricter than the dynastic law. Whereas the latter did not prohibit marriages between enslaved females and ordinary men,[84] lineages condemned unions between lineage members and *nubi* of any sex in the strongest terms.[85] Such alliances were an offence to one's ancestors (*shang ru zuzong*), a burden on one's descendants (*xialei zisun*), and a shame to the whole clan (*hezu xiuyu shijian*), to the point that infringement of the rule was sometimes liable to elimination from the genealogical tables.[86]

This fear of "pollution" is also exemplified by various prohibitions against male *nubi* coming into contact with the women of the household.[87] Lineages required male and female *nubi* to strictly abide by gender separation. For instance, in the fifteenth century's Huo lineage from Nanhai (Guangdong province), female *nubi* were forbidden to "go outside" (*chuwai*) upon reaching fourteen *sui* old (circa thirteen years old), while male *nubi* were forbidden to "go inside" (*jinnei*) upon reaching sixteen.[88]

From the lineage perspective, *nubi* (and, to a lesser extent, *gugong*) only existed through the two opposite dimensions of paternalistic discourses and disciplinary prescriptions. Framing the exercise of mastery in terms of benevolence, magnanimity, and reciprocity was an absolute prerequisite because the enslaved present in the households of the late Ming and early Qing period were not criminals but were ordinary people who had abdicated their relative autonomy "willingly". However, as outsiders incorporated to "serve", their mere presence (albeit necessary) posed multiple dangers calling for constant checks and strict methods of control. Although they should know "fear" and be promptly punished when causing trouble,[89] discipline could not amount to "abuses" and be "excessive", since excessive violence resulted in "severing the feelings" (*qingshu*) that were supposed to cement the master–*nubi* relationship.[90]

The parameters of *nubi* discipline did not differ much from those applied to other lineage members. However, what distinguishes them from other lineage constituents is that discipline outweighed all other considerations. *Nubi* were persons to be controlled, not simply a labour force to be managed, even less genuine lineage members to be educated, taken care of through lineage solidarity, and included in ritual activities. As noted in the *Family Rules* (*Jiazheng*) of the Zhu lineage from Kaoting (Fujian, 1620): "As to *nubi*, one [only] wishes to have them in good order" (*bipu yu qi zhengqi*).[91]

---

[83]Chen Ruilan, *Pucheng Chenshi jiapu*, in Zhang and Xu, *Beijing tushuguan cang jiapu congkan*, XVI, pp. 43–44; see also Chen Rui, "Ming Qing shiqi Huizhou zongzu neibu de xueyuan zhixu kongzhi", *Zhongguo shehui lishi pinglun*, 8 (2007), pp. 264–276.

[84]Gao, *Ming lü jijie fuli*, 6:33b–35a.

[85]Tao Licun, *Ningxiang Taoshi jiapu* (1892), in Taga, *Sōfu no kenkyū*, p. 744.

[86]Zu Guojun, *Lianhu Zushi zupu* (1899), in Zhang and Xu, *Beijing tushuguan cang jiapu congkan*, XXXI, 1:7b–8a.

[87]Pang, *Pangshi jiaxun*, p. 8.

[88]Huo, "Taiyuan Huoshi zhongfang zupu jiazhen", p. 86.

[89]See the Huang lineage pact written to "handle with force" (*lichu*) what seems to have been massive desertion among the enslaved of Qimen district (Anhui) in 1728. Quoted in Wei, Wu, and Lu, *Qingdai nubi zhidu*, p. 126.

[90]*Gushi zupu* (1705), in Taga, *Sōfu no kenkyū*, p. 620.

[91]Zhu, *Kaoting Zhushi wenxian quanpu*, p. 610.

Although closer to the ground, lineage sources cannot be taken as true reflections of the everyday disciplining of "household workers". Lineage authorities could certainly be mobilized when situations escalated, or to make an example of (just like imperial justice could be mobilized to the same effect). However, considering the threats of prosecution repeatedly made against masters who failed to "control" their *nubi*,[92] it is more than likely that everyday discipline was seldom delegated to lineage authorities and remained in the hands of individual masters. Bringing to life the day-to-day management of enslaved and hirelings, however, is a more difficult task than exploring normative prescriptions like the *Code* and lineage rules.

Punishment(s) in Practice

Unearthing actual practices related to "household workers" is indeed challenging. When sources are available, the voices that we hear are overwhelmingly those of the (male) educated elites, who usually considered private affairs too trivial to be worth writing about, and who mostly reported on practices that, in one way or another, came out of the ordinary.

The previous sections have underlined both proximity and distance between *nubi* and *gugong*. In law, *nubi* was the matrix from which the parameters of the legal treatment of *gugong* were framed. Domestic regulations reaffirmed this affinity in principle, but they did not demonstrate the same level of concern about controlling *gugong* as they did about *nubi*. Sources reporting on everyday practices like contracts, management treatises, and narratives of things "seen and heard" hardly help remove these ambiguities, especially in the late Ming period when the numbers of *nubi* grew significantly and when "labour" relations seem to have been widely contaminated by the axiom of the master–*nubi* relation.

Contracts

Contracts show both differences and commonalities between the two categories. *Nubi* contracts standardly open with the exposition of the "poverty" of the contracting party. This served to legitimize the self-sale of a person (alone or with their family) or the sale of a child.[93] *Nubi* contracts seldom describe work obligations, and they usually remain vague as to what enslaved people received in return (food and clothes at a minimum, sometimes a house to inhabit, the promise of marriage, or a lump sum of silver upon entering the relationship).[94] However, they often insist on the commitment to "obey orders" (*tingcong shihuan*), to "serve" (*yishi, yingyi, fuyi*), and sometimes to "work with diligence" (*qinli yiye*). And they always contain clauses absolving buyers from responsibility if something "unexpected" happened to the enslaved, including untimely and accidental death.[95]

Nubi contracts also frequently end with a formal acceptance by the contracting party of their "punishment" (*fa, zui*) should they disobey, run away, or cause trouble.

[92]*Liangjin Sunshi jiasheng* (1919), in Taga, *Sōfu no kenkyū*, p. 789.

[93]For example, *Ming Qing Huizhou shehui jingji ziliao congbian*, 2 vols (Beijing, 1988), I, p. 553.

[94]Contracts including specific clauses nonetheless exist, like the contract of one Hong Sanyuan, established in Huizhou, 1609. Zhang Chuanxi, *Zhongguo lidai qiyue huibian kaoshi* (Beijing, 1995), p. 929.

[95]Yang Guozhen, *Ming Qing tudi qiyue wenshu yanjiu* (Beijing, [1988] 2009), p. 42.

Not always specifying who had the authority to punish, some contracts clearly provide for referral to the judicial authorities (*jinfa jiuzhi, chengguan zhongjiu*, etc.).[96] Others include provisions for fines and corporal punishments by the master himself, as was the case in the late Ming "enslaved-tenant" (*dianpu*) contract from Huizhou prefecture:

> In case of mistake or negligence (*shiwu*), I will accept to [pay] a fine of five piculs of polished rice to the [master's] ancestral hall. I will buy a pig and a goat to sacrifice to the [master's] ancestral graves, and I will willingly receive 80 [blows of the] plank (*ze*).[97]

Guaranteed in law and framed in lineage regulations, punishments also took on a contractual dimension in the late Ming, when *nubi* were mainly commoners who sold themselves or their children "willingly" and when people increasingly tended to consider (self-) enslavement as a temporary lifeline to cope with economic hazards. Formal recognition (in the presence of witnesses) of the disciplinary powers of the buyer thus reinforced subordination. It served to manifest a sold person's acceptance of their new social and legal identity as genuine *nubi*.

Gugong contracts show significant differences from *nubi* contracts. A typical *gugong* contract would specify the duration of the employment as well as the amount and frequency of the wages. Instead of an exposition of the poverty of the contracting party, they simply underline that people were previously "out of work" (*jin wei wuhuo*). They sometimes specify tasks to be performed contractually (like "till the land and the gardens"),[98] and include a commitment not to steal, damage, or lose the tools provided by the employer, but no explicit threat of punishment.[99]

However, in addition to their systematic reference to the employer as a "master" (*zhuren, zhujia*), *gugong* contracts also emphasize the duty to "serve" and to "obey", to work from dawn to dusk "without dawdling" (*bu landuo*), and sometimes provide for wages deduction in cases of "bad work" (*wugong*).[100] In a mid-fifteenth-century model contract for "willingly hiring out and pawning sons" (*qingyuan jiang nan diangu*) as "little servants" (*xiaosi*), we not only read similar justifications (i.e. poverty), but also duties similar to those enumerated in *nubi* contracts: "Once hired out through pawning, [the child] will serve conscientiously (*xiaoxin fushi*). He will stand by to receiving orders (*tinghou shiling*) and will

---

[96]See the self-sale contracts established by one Zheng Hei'er and one Jiang Guanda in Huizhou (1589 and 1645), in *Ming Qing Huizhou shehui jingji ziliao congbian*, I, pp. 553–554, and the contract of sale of a boy (1551) in Zhang, *Zhongguo lidai qiyue huibian kaoshi*, p. 823. On contracts in general, see Wang Shuaiyi, *Mingyue Qingfeng. Ming Qing shidai de ren, qiyue yu guojia* (Beijing, 2018), pp. 93–94.

[97]Ye Xian'en, *Ming Qing Huizhou nongcun shehui yu dianpuzhi* (Hefei, 1983), fig. 6. Historians still do not agree about the *nubi* status of "enslaved tenants". See Chevaleyre, "Une révolte d'esclaves ou de tenanciers?", in Ismard, Rossi, and Vidal, *Les Mondes de l'esclavage*, pp. 192–194.

[98]See the model contract reproduced in Zhang, *Zhongguo lidai qiyue huibian kaoshi*, p. 1069.

[99]Chi Xinzi (comp.), *Xinjuan Chizi huibian simin liguan hanfu jinnang* (1585), in *Mingdai tongsu riyong leishu jikan*, 16 vols (Chongqing [etc.], 2011), IV, p. 510.

[100]Xiong Xuanji (ed.), *Xinjuan zengbu jiaozheng Xuanji Xiong xiansheng chidu shuangyu* (late Ming), in *Mingdai tongsu riyong leishu jikan*, XVI, p. 579.

dare neither to discuss [orders] nor dawdle (*weiman*), desert (*paoli*) or run away (*tao*)."[101] Such a "pawning" contract is not a typical *gugong* contract, as it does not set a clear end to the employment and only mentions the payment of a lump sum to the parents upon signing the contract. The situation was thus more that of a child used as collateral for a loan and risking permanent enslavement in case of a payment default. However, it demonstrates that situations close to (or preceding) enslavement could be framed in the language of "hiring out" (*chugu*).

Management Prescriptions

Sources alluding to the management of household workers are quite rare in the literary landscape of the late Ming and early Qing period. The few examples available convey a somewhat mixed picture. Treatises of agronomy and estate management sometimes include prescriptions about the management of *nubi* and *gugong*, but they seldom insist on discipline and punishment.

As to *gugong*, they usually focus on incentives and "benevolence" as means to ensure efficient labour and to curtail laziness. The often-quoted *Agricultural Treatise of Master Shen* (*Shenshi nongshu*, Zhejiang province, c.1639) essentially prescribes "generous" food allocations and their adjustment to seasonal variations to ensure compliance to work and to prevent defection. In this text, the emphasis is placed on compliance and generosity as preconditions to "reprimand" (*jie*) hirelings when necessary.[102] Defection, taken very seriously in the case of *nubi*, is merely mentioned as something to be prevented, not as a crime to be corrected by capture and prosecution.

Prescriptions for *nubi* management are found in Zhang Lüxiang's *Supplement to [Master Shen's] Agricultural Treatise* (*Bu nongshu*, published 1658). Zhang simply reproduces prescriptions formulated centuries earlier in Sima Guang's (1019–1086) *Miscellaneous Etiquette for Family Life* (*Jujia zayi*) that neither mention discipline nor refer to benevolence and generosity. The text describes a typical workday, during which *nubi* would get up at dawn, clean the house, and prepare food before the masters wake up, perform a "hundred services" (*gong baiyi*), "obey their master's orders" (*wei zhuren zhi ming*), and "accomplish their tasks" (*ge cong qi shi*) until dusk.[103] Here, the emphasis is placed on nothing else but "service" and continuous and absolute obedience.

Punishments and discipline thus do not appear central in texts alluding to labour management. The differences between the management of *nubi* and *gugong* seem rather tenuous, despite a greater emphasis placed on gaining the compliance of hirelings rather than immobilizing them by force.

---

[101]*Xinbian shiwen leiju qizha qingqian* (1455), quoted in Yang, *Ming Qing tudi qiyue wenshu yanjiu*, p. 46.

[102]*Shenshi nongshu*, in Tao Yue (ed.) and Cao Rong (comp.), *Xuehai leibian*, 120 vols (Shanghai, [1831] 1920), CIV, 19a.

[103]Zhang Lüxiang, *Yangyuan xiansheng quanji* (Beijing, [1704] 2002), p. 978. On *Shenshi nongshu* and *Bu nongshu*, see Francesca Bray and Georges Métailié, "Who Was the Author of the *Nongzhen Quanshu*?", in Catherine Jami, Peter Engelfriet, and Gregory Blue (eds), *Statecraft and Intellectual Renewal in Late Ming China: The Cross-Cultural Synthesis of Xu Guangxi (1562–1633)* (Leiden [etc.], 2001), pp. 330–331.

The Tenuous Line Between Discipline and Violence

Discipline and violence appear in a different light in the sources produced during or in the aftermath of the late Ming social, economic, and military crisis. In the urban strikes and riots initiated by skilled hired workers at the turn of the seventeenth century, discipline is never mentioned as a trigger. For instance, the so-called "weaver workers revolt" (*zhiyong zhi bian*) that broke out in Suzhou in 1601 was essentially caused by an increase in the costs of raw materials and by the aggressive methods of tax collection by imperial envoys.[104] On the contrary, punishments and high levels of brutality were apparently decisive in the numerous murders of masters recorded in the sixteenth and seventeenth centuries, as well as in the *nubi* revolts (*nubian*) that sporadically broke out between the 1630s and the 1650s.

Faced with the growing presence of *nubi* within families and society,[105] from the mid-sixteenth century onwards, the literati increasingly voiced concerns over the laissez-faire attitude of masters, the influence of powerful *nubi*, and the visible excesses of slaving practices. Retrospectively, an excessively laissez-faire approach and brutality were pointed out as hallmarks of the social decay of the late Ming, which led to *nubi* unrest and the ultimate fall of the dynasty in 1644. Calling for the more rigorous control of *nubi*, promoting the ideal figures of benevolent "master–father" (*zhufu*)[106] and loyal enslaved (*yipu*), and even sometimes questioning the social relevance of enslavement, diaries, letters, anecdotes, and jottings all offer valuable glimpses of the extensive disciplinary powers that masters exercised.

The emphasis that the literati put on punishing *nubi* more "humanely"[107] where necessary shows that discipline was consubstantial with enslavement and suggests, as many observers have underlined, that *nubi* were frequently "less well treated than dogs and swines" (*zhi quanzhi zhi buruo*).[108] Examples of brutality abound in the sources produced before the outbreak of *nubi* revolts. Caning (*zhang*), "cruel beatings" (*kuda*),[109] and the like were disciplinary methods of choice and became the epitome of the master's cruelty. As one revolt leader declared: "Why should our enslaved lives be satisfied with receiving caning and being lectured?"[110] Dong Chuance (1530–1579), who was murdered in Huating (Jiangsu) by a group of *nubi* on 31 May 1579, is said to have abused many with the cane: "Vice-Minister Dong Youhai [i.e. Chuance] was an inflexible and severe person who treated household slaves (*jianu*) with excessive rigour. When they committed a fault, they immediately received caning. When using the cane, [Dong] counted to one hundred [blows].

---

[104]Wu Jen-shu, "Mingmo Qingchu chengshi shougongye gongren de jiti kangyi xingdong", *Zhongyang yanjiuyuan jindaishi yanjiusuo jikan*, 28 (1997), pp. 47–88, 59–60.

[105]This (hardly quantifiable) increase is often mentioned in late Ming and early Qing sources. It was already noted in 1430 by Zhou Chen (1381–1453): Cheng, *Huang Ming wenheng*, 27:7a.

[106]Zhang, *Yangyuan xiansheng quanji*, pp. 977–978.

[107]*Ibid.*, p. 1287.

[108]Xie Zhaozhe, *Wuzazu* (Shanghai, [1608] 2012), p. 143.

[109]Mao Yilu, *Yunjian yanlüe* (Wanli era), in Yang Yifan and Xu Lizhi (eds), *Lidai panli pandu*, 12 vols (Beijing, 2005), III, pp. 582–583.

[110]Chen Qinian, *Jialing wenji* (postf. 1687), in Zhang Yuanji *et al.* (comp.), *Sibu congkan*, 3112 vols (Shanghai, 1919–1936), CCI, 1:15a.

Many died from it."[111] Like many others, Dong is also said to have employed a wide variety of disciplinary and punitive methods. Upon discovering that one of his retainers had exchanged words with a concubine, he had him locked up. When the retainer finally ran away, he had him tracked down and executed with impunity.[112]

Late Ming and early Qing observers widely testify to the many forms and few limitations that punishments and brutality could take. *Nubi* could be victims of extortion from their masters when they managed to accumulate some wealth for their own. They were frequently said to suffer from cold, hunger, and lack of decent clothes. They also experienced physical and psychological violence, sexual abuse,[113] and even mutilation.[114] Sources also provide numerous cases where masters denied *nubi* the right to mourn their parents or "killed [them] and burned [their bodies] without anyone daring to denounce them",[115] or with minimal consequences.[116]

Revolts

Although the extent and frequency of violence against *nubi* cannot be evaluated with any level of precision, it is best exemplified by the violence that *nubi* unleashed against their masters during the late Ming revolts. *Nubi* revolts hardly formed a consistent "emancipation movement" (as is often claimed),[117] but they systematically targeted masters and aimed to destroy enslavement contracts. When masters and their families were not killed on the spot, they were put on trial for mistreatment and submitted to rituals of role inversion, being forced to serve others and taste their own disciplinary methods. The Baoshan district revolt (Jiangsu province, 1644) provides a typical example:

> Unleashing great violence, thousands and hundreds gathered to burn the houses and reclaim contracts by force. Clouds of ashes obscured the sky. While the enslaved sat down, masters stood still and served them meals. At the slightest sign of discontent, they [the masters] were thrown on the ground and beaten with *zhang* [the cane]. This was a catastrophe like no other in a thousand years.[118]

Everywhere the revolts were triggered by excessive brutality. On the front line of the repression in 1644, Qi Biaojia (1603–1645) notes that retaliation against masters

---

[111]Li Shaowen, *Yunjian zashi* (Shanghai, 1936), 1:9b–10a.

[112]Xu Zhongyuan, *Sanyi bitan* (1828), *Biji xiaoshuo daguan* edn (Shanghai, 1912[?]), 4:1b–2a.

[113]Male and female *nubi* could all be victims of sexual abuses. Matthew H. Sommer, *Sex, Law and Society* (Stanford, CA, 2000), pp. 45–54, 128–129.

[114]Zhang Mingbi, *Yingzhi quanji*, quoted in Fu Yiling, "Mingmo nanfang de dianbian, nubian", *Lishi yanjiu*, 5 (1975), pp. 61–67, 66; Gu Cheng, *Mingmo nongmin zhanzheng shi* (Beijing, 1984), p. 341. See also Fu Yiling, "Mingji nubian shiliao shebu", *Fujian xieda xuebao*, 1 (1949), pp. 163–169, 164; *Jinhua fuzhi* (1578), 5:6b; Li Yu, *Zizhi xinshu* (1663), in *Ming Qing fazhi shiliao jikan*, 37 vols (Beijing, 2008), I, p. 460.

[115]Zhang, *Yangyuan xiansheng quanji*, p. 575.

[116]Huang Zhangjian (ed.), *Ming Shenzong shilu* (Taipei, 1962–1968), 286:5b.

[117]Wu Zhenhan, "Mingdai nupu zhi yanjiu" (Ph.D., National Taiwan University, 1980), p. 240; Fu Yiling, *Ming Qing nongcun shehui jingji* (Beijing, 1961), p. 131.

[118]*Baoshan xianzhi* (Qianlong era), quoted in Fu, *Ming Qing nongcun shehui jingji*, p. 95.

"beating *nubi* cruelly" (*kao nu ku*) was the insurgents' first motivation.[119] A year later, in Taicang (Jiangsu), several masters were judged and humiliated for systematically beating their enslaved for trifles, like coming back late from picking up tea leaves or lousy cooking.[120] Zhang Mingbi (1584–1653) extensively recounts how such trials were carried out in Jintan (Jiangsu) in 1645. Masters were made to get a taste of the instruments they had used in the past to punish *nubi*. While beating their masters with "sticks" (*bang*) or pricking them with "awls" (*zhui*), after each blow and after each cry of pain, *nubi* first asked, "does it hurt?" and then asked why they used physical violence when they knew how painful it was.[121]

For challenging the social order, *nubi* insurgents were nonetheless punished with exemplary severity. All the revolt leaders ended up executed with their heads exposed on pikes. Their followers were beaten and sent back to their former masters, whom the local authorities left to decide how to punish them.[122] In a way, the resolution of the *nubi* revolts illustrates how disciplinary and punitive powers were distributed between the state and the heads of lineages and households: the state had no say and no interest in the matter as long as things remained under control and did not impact broader society.

Of course, counterexamples of loyal, rich, and influential enslaved (as well as models of benevolent masters) can be found in the sources at our disposal.[123] And in the context of an increasing and multifaceted crisis, the protection offered by voluntary enslavement was valued and preferred by many to the precariousness of autonomy and economic uncertainty.[124] The information that we can extract from the sources nonetheless leads to three conclusions.

First, the actual condition of *nubi* almost entirely depended on the will of one's master. The specific parameters of the relation with a master, whose extensive power was safeguarded by the whole sociopolitical order (from the state down to the local community and the lineage structures), were crucial in determining the degree of autonomy that each *nubi* could enjoy in practice (or could conquer by "manipulating" their masters, as many sources also underline).

Second, in a sociolegal environment designed to protect the fatherlike figure of the household head and to uphold the indisputability of his authority, discipline and violence overlapped and can barely be distinguished. Both were consubstantial with enslavement and knew very few limitations. *Nubi* were permanently vulnerable to violence and punishments. At any time, even the most autonomous and powerful ones remained powerless against discipline and violence unless a third party decided to stand up for them (be it a magistrate, a sympathetic neighbour, an enemy of their master, or a more influential master offering protection).

---

[119]Wang Siren *et al.* (eds), *Qi Zhongmin gong nianpu* (pref. 1837), in *Taiwan wenxian shiliao congkan*, 190 vols (Taipei, 1987), CVII, p. 150.

[120]Yu Yong, *Jinsha xituo*, in *Qingshi ziliao*, 2 (1981), pp. 153–170, 160.

[121]Zhang, *Yingzhi quanji*, quoted in Fu, "Mingmo nanfang de dianbian, nubian", pp. 62–63.

[122]*Zidicun xiaozhi* (1718), in Shanghaishi difangzhi bangongshi (ed.), *Shanghai xiangzhen jiuzhi congshu*, 15 vols, (Shanghai, 2004), XIII, 72–73.

[123]Chen Hongmou, *Xunsu yigui* (1742), *Siku quanshu cunmu congshu* edn (Jinan, 1994–1997), *zi* ser., LVIII, 2:20a; Hsieh, *Concubinage and Servitude*, p. 98.

[124]Wang Shixing, *Guangzhi yi*, *Siku quanshu cunmu congshu* edn, *shi* ser., CCLI, 3:11a.

The case of one *nubi* named Gu Liang can be taken as the epitome of the potential for unbridled violence and the powerlessness of *nubi*. Gu had voluntarily offered himself (*tou*) and his wife as *nubi* (*weipu*) in the service of one Zhuang Ying from Shanghai district in exchange for being housed and fed. Zhuang, however, coveted Gu's wife. One day, in 1607, he voluntarily blinded Gu and sold his wife after Gu had repeatedly objected to Zhuang having sexual intercourse with her. The prefectural judge in charge of the case, Mao Yilu (?–1629), sentenced Zhuang to penal servitude and to pay Gu ten taels of silver and a piece of land so that he could effectively "leave the household" and make a living of his own. In so doing, Mao Yilu applied the law protecting *gugong* from brutality (see the first section above) in the application of a sub-statute (dated 1588) stipulating that *nubi* owned by commoners (rather than by officials) shall be judged like *gugong*.[125] This can be taken as proof that the little protection offered in law to *nubi* and *gugong* was enforced by late Ming magistrates. Yet, the case was not brought to court by Gu Liang himself. It was unveiled during an investigation of theft against Gu and his relatives. One thus wonders what would have happened had Gu referred to the judge himself and thus broken the law prohibiting *nubi* from accusing their master.

Finally, although the sources at our disposal seem to suggest that punishments were less central to the management of *gugong*, due to their proximity to *nubi*, the importance of role performance in the assessment of statuses, and the power that was vested in household heads, *gugong* could easily be assimilated to *nubi* and subjected to similar forms of control and discipline. The late Ming period is characterized by a widespread extension of *nubi* status to other relations and a blurring of social and labour identities. This extension sometimes took the form of subtle contamination, as in the case of one Tang Yuan, also adjudicated by Mao Yilu. For reasons that remain unclear, Tang had moved with his aunt and her husband, two *nubi* in the service of the Han family in Huating district. According to Mao, Tang was of commoner status. However, for sharing the roof of his relatives' master for years and for accepting money to help him marry, he was reported as a runaway *nubi* after he left their household to settle on his own. Although Tang ultimately committed suicide, the magistrate concluded that he had benefited from the Han family's "benevolence". This fact alone had created a bond similar to signing a bondage contract. In the magistrate's terms, it had created a "difference between master and *nubi*" (*zhupu mingfen*), which gave ground to the Han family's claims.[126]

The practice of labelling *gugong* as *nubi* and forcing them into permanent enslavement by the threat of prosecution as runaways is also widely evidenced. In a memorial written in the aftermath of the last serious revolt in Guangshan (Henan, 1658), prefect Jin Zhen (1622–1685) listed the existence of "enslaved hired workers" (*yonggong zhi pu*) as one major cause of the revolt. The practice he describes was a mix of hired work and uxorilocal marriage, by which men agreed to work for a fixed period in exchange for an enslaved woman to marry (one such contract set the term to

[125]Mao, *Yunjian yanlüe*, pp. 417–418.
[126]Mao, *Yunjian yanlüe*, p. 574.

twenty-two years).[127] Once the term was over, employers threatened to report *gugong* as "runaway slaves" and retained them permanently.[128]

Epilogue

As a cornerstone of the late imperial social order, the authority of the father/household head was indisputable in late imperial China. Benefiting from high protection in law, it extended not only to children, but also to all those, kin and non-kin, who "lived together" and were part of the household. The parameters of subordination to the power of the household head nonetheless varied slightly depending on whether a person descended from the patriline, was incorporated to ensure reproduction, or was brought in (permanently or temporarily) to "serve". In the last case, of which *nubi* are the epitome, the analogical reference to the figure of the father was central in elaborating a fictitious filiation devoid of the prerogatives of actual membership of the family, to which only the duty of absolute obedience and subordination remained.

As "serving" outsiders, *nubi* and *gugong* were similarly placed under the direct and exclusive authority of the household head, which was protected by an asymmetric regime of legal punishments and guaranteed by the conferment of extensive disciplinary powers. The legal framework elaborated by the founder of the Ming dynasty had thus created the conditions for an almost absolute and potentially violent domination of "household workers" who, for their part, benefited from minimal legal protection and could hardly challenge the household head's power by appealing to justice. In everyday practices, the paternalistic requirement for "benevolence", reciprocity, and mutual affection prescribed by moralists and by lineage admonitions certainly played a role in mitigating violence and abuses of all sorts. However, as the *nubi* revolts of the mid-seventeenth century demonstrate, such requirements did not weigh much against the indisputability of the household-head's authority.

At the end of this overview of the many dimensions of punishment in the relationship between "household workers" and their masters/employers in late Ming and early Qing China, we are nonetheless left with ambiguities, uncertainties, and pending questions, in particular regarding the actual differences in vulnerability to punishments, discipline, and violence between the two legal categories of "household workers" examined in this article. Although treated like cognates in law, we have seen that in the sources alluding to lineage organization and day-to-day practices, controlling, disciplining, and immobilizing *gugong* by force seemed a far lesser concern than in the case of *nubi*. This apparent difference can be explained by the fact that hirelings entered their employer's household on different terms. They were neither owned by their employers nor "debased" beyond the boundaries of their employer's household and the time frame of their employment. As one commentator of the *Great Qing Code* noted in 1715:

---

[127]Zhang, *Zhongguo lidai qiyue huibian kaoshi*, p. 1063.

[128]Jin Zhen, "Tiaochen Guangshan panpu xiangyi" (*c.*1659), in *Guangshan Xianzhi* (Guangshan, [1786] 1889), 19:16a–18b.

[*Gugong*] only perform services for others (*weiren zhiyi*) in exchange for wages (*guzhi*). Their activity (*shi*) is demeaned, not their person (*shen*). Once their employment and wages are over, the head of the household is like an ordinary person [to them] (*tong fanren*). They are thus different from those who, as persons, are *nubi* (*shen wei nubi*).[129]

The temporary and lesser incorporation of *gugong* into the household might thus be the sign of a significantly different labour regime (control of "activities" versus domination of "persons"), of an evolution of labour relations in the late Ming period, and maybe of an "emancipation" of hirelings from the paternalistic power of the household head, as various historians have already argued.[130]

This leads us to make several concluding remarks. Although cross-examining normative sources with documents like contracts and court cases is methodologically more relevant than focusing on one single dimension, taking "China" in a centuries-long perspective as a research object presents serious limitations that can only be overcome by narrowing the focus on multiple local micro-social histories of work. Such studies already exist at the scale of specific prefectures and provinces, but they usually remain limited, in great part due to an overwhelming focus on labels and "labour" categories.[131]

Legal and "customary" categories are, indeed, far too limiting to understand the dynamics of labour relations in practice. Labels reflect practices and norms, but those two dimensions never perfectly align, while "labelling" can be as much a legal as a social practice. Exploring the contextual plurality of punitive practices might thus be a more relevant method to overcome the bias of label-centred approaches in the study of social practices of labour and coercion (and to overcome the classical question of the "free"/ "unfree" nature of hired work in late imperial China).[132]

Finally, we are also left with the lingering question of the relationship between the domination of people and work. Historians of slavery would probably agree that the exercise of "mastery" cannot be reduced to the single dimension of the exploitation of the workforce of other human beings, even with a broad and encompassing definition of work in mind. In this respect, the sources used in this article remain ambiguous because the labour dimension is never the most salient, to the point that the relation between punishments and the management of work remains tenuous. In the case of *nubi*, labour is undoubtedly never too far away in the prohibitions against "laziness",[133] in the statements demanding constant "diligence" (*qinjin*),[134] in those promoting reciprocity as a means to benefit from their "strength" to "develop one's household",[135] and in those explaining that *nubi* were brought in "to work in one's

---

[129]Shen, *Da Qing lü jizhu*, p. 747.

[130]Chevaleyre, "Serving and Working for Others", p. 171.

[131]Ye Xian'en, *Ming Qing Huizhou nongcun shehui yu dianpuzhi* (Hefei, 1983); Huang Shuping, *Guangdong shipuzhi yanjiu* (Guangzhou, 2001).

[132]Liu Yongcheng, *Qingdai qianqi zibenzhuyi mengya chutan* (Fuzhou, 1982), p. 79.

[133]Wang Jiazhzen, *Yantang jianwen zaji* (1911), in *Taiwan wenxian shiliao congkan* (Taipei, 1984), V, p. 30.

[134]Zhang, *Zhongguo lidai qiyue huibian kaoshi*, p. 1011.

[135]Chen Hongmou, *Jiaonü yigui* (1742), *Sibu beiyao* edn (Shanghai, 1936), ser. 267, VI, 1b.

place" (*dailao*).[136] However, in the control of outsiders made into permanent or temporary insiders to the household, what mattered to lineages and families was to keep "household workers" in their place, to maintain hierarchies, and to avoid "disturbance" (*luan*). Instead of work and labour, the ubiquitous keyword in late imperial Chinese sources is "service", which could encompass any productive, non-productive, and reproductive task.[137] In a court case of the nineteenth century, we read the following remark: "*Gugong* simply make a living by being hired as workers (*shougu yonggong*). Since they are serving and ordered (*yishi*), a difference between superior and inferior must [nonetheless] be demonstrated (*shi yi shangxia zhi fen*)."[138] The meaning of "service" thus went beyond simply performing labour (even in the case of *gugong* whose main functions were more closely related to work).[139] It was far more saturated in the language of obedience and anxieties than in the language of work and management. What "pluralization" and contextualization could bring to the study of labour, coercion, and punishments should thus be a broader reflection on the categories that we use as entry points to the history of social practices.

---

[136]Xiangjian Buxiang Zi, *[Xinjuan] Fajia tou danhan* (pref. 1618), p. 161. Digital edition by Sun Jiahong and Gong Rufu. Available at: http://lsc.chineselegalculture.org/Documents/E-Library/Magistrates_handbooks_pettifoggers?ID=241; last accessed 2 March 2022.

[137]Hsieh, *Concubinage and Servitude*, p. 96ff.; Mann, *Precious Records*, pp. 37–38; Wei, Wu, and Lu, *Qingdai nubi zhidu*, p. 77–105.

[138]He Changling (comp.), *Huangchao jingshi wenxian* (Beijing, [1826] 1992), 92:39a–40a.

[139]The notion of "service" should not be conflated with "domestic work" before the nineteenth century, as is often the case. See Susan Mann, "Women's Work in the Ningbo Area, 1900–1936", in Thomas G. Rawski and Lilian M. Li (eds), *Chinese History in Economic Perspective* (Berkeley, CA [etc.], 1992), pp. 243–270, 255.

Cite this article: Claude Chevaleyre. Status, Power, and Punishments: "Household Workers" in Late Imperial China. *International Review of Social History*, 68:S31 (2023), pp. 109–134. https://doi.org/10.1017/S002085902200089X

International Review of Social History, 68:S31 (2023), pp. 135–155
doi:10.1017/S002085902200092X

"They Have No Property to Lose": The Impasse of Free Labour in Lombard Silk Manufactures (1760–1810)

Lorenzo Avellino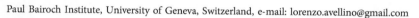

Paul Bairoch Institute, University of Geneva, Switzerland, e-mail: lorenzo.avellino@gmail.com

Abstract
With the abolition of the guild system and the rise of a new legal regime based on free contract, a central dilemma emerged in Europe: how to enforce labour control in this new era of individual economic freedom. This article examines how this issue was addressed in the State of Milan, where ideas about freedom of contract championed by state reformers such as Pietro Verri and Cesare Beccaria were met with continued requests from merchant-manufacturers to apply corporal punishment and threat of imprisonment to ensure workers' attendance. Analysing the new regulations, the ideological credos of the new regime, and the effectiveness of the reforms as they played out on the ground in the silk industry, this article shows that the chance that labour relations could be managed within a civil law regime appeared to be in direct contrast with the dominant conception of workers' conditions, in particular their lack of propriety and good faith. As credit-debt bonds and limitations to weavers' mobility stood as the most effective means to ensure labour coercion, a closer look at the daily interactions in the workshop allows us to shed new light on the rationality of workers' practices like Saint Monday, cast by contemporary commentators in merely moralistic terms.

The form of a document can sometimes reveal more than its content. That is certainly the case for a report sent in 1784 to the government of Milan by Gaetano De Magistris, the decan (*abate*) of the silk weavers' guild. In his letter asking for a reward for his zealous work, the decan offers a detailed account of his interventions to maintain order in the city's textile workshops. The report was received by Pietro Verri (1728–1797), the most prominent Italian political economist of the eighteenth century, employed at the time as a councillor in the government. Even if the demise of the guild system in Milan had begun nine years before, Verri seems astonished at the prolific activity the document revealed and suggested, writing in the margins of a page, that perhaps it would be necessary to discuss the "usefulness and necessity of such an inspector even after the abolition of the guilds in order to preserve discipline and good order in the factories" (Figure 1).[1]

---

[1] Handwritten note on Gaetano De Magistris report, 5 June 1784, State Archive, Milan [hereafter, SAMi], Commercio, p.a., c. 240. Unless otherwise stated, all translations are mine.

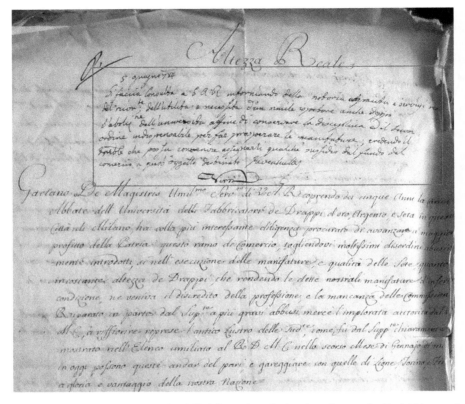

Figure 1. Pietro Verri's note on workers' discipline written by hand on Gaetano De Magistris's report. Photograph by the author.
Courtesy of Ministero dei Beni e le Attività Culturali N. 5070.

The abolition of the guild system in Italy followed the trend across eighteenth-century Europe. Decrees abolishing craft associations were enacted in France (1791), Spain (1840), and Austria and Germany (1859–1860), as the growth of science, technology, and industrialization, the development of the factory system, and changing ideas about the economy and the rights of common people led to a decline of the merchant and craft guild system that had flourished between the eleventh and sixteenth centuries. As a new contractual view of society spread across Europe, the need to enforce the obedience of workers under a new legal paradigm emerged as a common dilemma: how to express the apologia of regulations using the new language of economic individualism?[2] This article examines how this issue was

---

[2]Jean-Pierre Hirsch, *Les deux rêves du commerce. Entreprise et institution dans la région lilloise, 1780–1860* (Paris, 1991). See Dorte Kook Lyngholm's contribution to this Special Issue. Italy faced these discussions very early, see Corinne Maitte, "Le réformisme éclairé et les corporations. L'abolition des Arts en Toscane", *Revue d'histoire moderne contemporaine*, 491 (2002), pp. 56–88. For a general overview, see Alessandro Stanziani, *Les métamorphoses du travail contraint. Une histoire globale (XVIIIe–XIXe siècles)* (Paris, 2020), pp. 89–131.

addressed in the Duchy of Milan, where ideas about freedom of contract fostered by Lombard Enlightenment reformers such as Pietro Verri and Cesare Beccaria were challenged by continued requests to enforce corporal punishment and imprisonment to ensure attendance at work.

The article begins by describing the demise of the guild system as a result of a royal decree in 1764 that created parallel legislation to the guild statutes. Inspired by the model of domestic service, this edict became the only legal basis for punishing workers who took advantage of their new margin of freedom after the abolition of the guilds. The article then retraces the ideological background of the new regime of freedom of work and trade that was supposed to govern economic life after the abolition of the guilds' privileges. Finally, in discussing the effectiveness of these reforms, I investigate the daily workshop interactions in the main Lombard industrial sector, silk fabric production, by looking at some examples of conflict at work and punishments used by the authorities.

Free Contracts and Good Faith in the Age of Reform

The discussion about the role of guilds in the pre-industrial economy has always fascinated historians. The last decade was marked by the fierce debate between Sheilagh Ogilvie and S.R. Epstein concerning the guilds' ability to guarantee quality, skills, and innovation. Ogilvie argued that corporations were essentially a rent-seeking coalition blocking economic development.[3] They prevented outsiders (foreigners, women) from accessing the trade, avoided innovation, and could not guarantee the quality of products while artificially raising prices. Epstein, on the contrary, stressed that the guild successfully responded to information asymmetries in times when markets had high transaction costs, fulfilled an important role in protecting innovation, and helped to transmit technical knowledge through apprenticeship.[4]

Until recently, in Italy, historiography has mostly posited the pernicious role of the guilds, especially in the early modern period, with judgements oscillating between their uselessness and harmfulness to economic growth.[5] However, an extensive quantitative analysis of the sectoral distribution of the guilds has recently shown that their expansion was often located in fast-growing industries with a strong outbound

---

[3]Sheilagh Ogilvie, "Guilds, Efficiency, and Social Capital: Evidence from German Proto-industry", *Economic History Review*, 57 (2004), pp. 286–333; *idem*, "'Whatever Is, Is Right'? Economic Institutions in Pre-industrial Europe", *Economic History Review*, 60 (2007), pp. 649–684; *idem*, "Rehabilitating the Guilds: A Reply", *Economic History Review*, 61 (2008), pp. 175–182; *idem*, *The European Guilds: An Economic Analysis*, (Princeton, NJ, 2019).

[4]S.R. Epstein, "Craft Guilds, Apprenticeship, and Technological Change in Preindustrial Europe", *Journal of Economic History*, 58 (1998), pp. 684–713; *idem*, "Property Rights to Technical Knowledge in Premodern Europe, 1300–1800", *American Economic Review*, 94 (2004), pp. 382–387; *idem*, "Craft Guilds in the Pre-Modern Economy: A Discussion", *Economic History Review*, 61 (2008), pp. 155–174. Concerning the porosity of guild's entrance barriers, new evidence is presented in Maarten Prak *et al.*, "Access to the Trade: Monopoly and Mobility in European Craft Guilds in the Seventeenth and Eighteenth Centuries", *Journal of Social History*, 54 (2020), pp. 421–452.

[5]Carlo M. Cipolla, "The Decline of Italy: The Case of a Fully Matured Economy", *Economic History Review*, 5 (1952), pp. 178–187; Luigi Dal Pane, *Storia del lavoro in Italia dagli inizi del secolo XVIII al 1815*, (Milan, 1958), pp. 253–284; Amintore Fanfani, *Storia del lavoro in Italia. Dalla fine del secolo XV agli inizi del XVIII* (Milan, 1959), pp. 192–194.

orientation.[6] That evidence undermines the widespread belief that guilds represented the last bastions behind which backward sectors hid to preserve their rents on the city market. The Italian case shows mainly that these medieval institutions experienced, during the modern period, a "genetic mutation towards flexibility spurred on by mercantile capital" that allowed them to sustain the growth of specific sectors.[7] Furthermore, even within the city walls, regulation and freedom were deeply entangled as urban markets structurally integrated both guilded and non-guilded labour.[8]

The example of early modern Milan is illustrative of this dynamic, as the guild's stratification mainly reflected the functional adaptation to the redefinition of the productive and commercial environment of each sector on the international market.[9] More specifically, the definition of the gold and silk's guild landscape – between the sixteenth and seventeenth centuries – was characterized by a double process of polarization and hierarchization promoted by a small elite of merchants.[10] On the one hand, in little more than thirty years, four new guilds were created with no formal autonomy and were placed directly under the control of the silk and gold merchants' guild.[11] On the other hand, the members of the powerful silk weaver guild progressively lost their capacity to operate autonomously on the market and became either "proletarianized" workers or subcontractors on behalf of merchants.[12] Therefore in their fully matured period, between the seventeenth and eighteenth century, Milan's silk guilds became essentially tools to ensure control and discipline rather than protect the equality between their members.

The fading of the guild regime started in the early eighteenth century, when direct subsidies and tax exemptions were granted to some merchant-manufacturers as part of the mercantilist policy promoted during the reign of Charles VI.[13] The arrival of big, privileged manufactures in the textile sectors increased labour demand and the mobility of weavers between different firms. Before the abolition of the Milanese guilds, this motivated the creation of a parallel and competing regulation of the

---

[6]Angelo Moioli, "I risultati di un'indagine sulle corporazioni nelle città italiane in età moderna", in Paola Massa and Angelo Moioli (eds), *Dalla corporazione al mutuo soccorso. Organizzazione e tutela del lavoro tra XVI e XX secolo* (Milan, 2004), pp. 15–32.

[7]Luca Mocarelli, "Guilds Reappraised: Italy in the Early Modern Period", *International Review of Social History*, 53 (2008), pp. 159–178, 172.

[8]Andrea Caracausi, Matthew Davies, and Luca Mocarelli (eds), *Between Regulation and Freedom: Work and Manufactures in the European Cities, 14th–18th Centuries* (Cambridge, 2018).

[9]Angelo Moioli, "The Changing Role of the Guilds in the Reorganisation of the Milanese Economy throughout the Sixteenth and the Eighteenth Centuries", in Alberto Guenzi, Paola Massa, and Fausto Caselli Piola (eds), *Guilds, Markets and Work Regulations in Italy, 16th–19th Centuries* (Aldershot, 1998), pp. 32–55.

[10]Giuseppe De Luca, "Mercanti imprenditori, elite artigiane e organizzazioni produttive. La definizione del sistema corporativo milanese (1568–1627)", in Guenzi, Massa and Moioli, *Corporazioni e gruppi professionali*, pp. 79–116.

[11]*Ibid.*

[12]Simonetta Ortaggi Cammarosano, *Libertà e servitù. Il mondo del lavoro dall'ancien régime alla fabbrica capitalistica* (Naples, 1995), ch. 5; Luca Mocarelli, *Le attività manifatturiere a Milano tra continuità dell'apparato corporativo e il suo superamento (1713–1787)*, in Guenzi, Massa, and Moioli, *Corporazioni e gruppi professionali*, pp. 131–170.

[13]Luigi Trezzi, *Ristabilire e restaurare il mercimonio* (Milan, 1986).

workforce: the royal edict on the discipline of manufactures of 30 May 1764.[14] This edict reflected the particular condition of manufacturing work at the time, mixing elements typical of factory regulations with residues characteristic of guild statutes. As the state took over manufactures through direct financing, any infringement of their proper functioning could be construed as a direct attack on the sovereign will. Misbehaviour by workers was no longer seen as a matter for the guilds but rather as an attempt to "defraud Her Majesty's clear intentions", as written in the text's preamble.[15]

The first part of the edict is devoted to attendance at work. A worker could not be admitted to a new master without the previous master having released him from all duties. The circulation of practitioners had to be regulated, and their activity needed to be continuous. An inactive worker became a supposed culprit, the edict threatening to make the unemployed fall under the regime of idlers. The second part is devoted to "fidelity", which had to be "universally observed, but most unquestionably in this context". The edict threatens that anyone who stole "things from factories" or "returns a lesser weight of what has been delivered to him to be worked on" must be publicly whipped "with the sign 'thief of manufactures' around his neck". With the motivation of avoiding trafficking, the edict limited the legitimacy of informal trade. A presumption of guilt fell on those who bought from small traders who did not have a shop of their own. Finally, the third part of the edict attacks any possibility of a union or alliance between workers to increase wages: individual pay was not supposed to be influenced by any factor external to the contract.

The importance of this decree – in fact, the only legal basis mentioned in the disputes between employers and workers, at least until the 1830s – should not be underestimated. It completely discarded the statutory self-regulation of guilds in favour of sovereign legislation that made labour discipline a police matter. The edict was also the first attempt to define a new contractual form of managing the workforce, but a very particular contractual model emerges from the text. In Italy, before the civil law reform at the end of the nineteenth century, wage labour was fitted into the narrow limits of one of the rental contracts from Roman civil law, more specifically, the *locatio conductio operarum*.[16] The *locatio conductio operarum* presupposes, like any consensual contract in Roman law, *bona fides* (good faith).[17] *Bona fides* is a complex and stratified legal concept as it does not refer to respect for the terms of the agreement in the abstract space of the will but is configured as an attribute of the person. Hence, it is a notion deeply intertwined with social hierarchies: good faith can only be presumed of a person who is recognized as worthy of it.[18] The status of the merchant

---

[14]Royal Edict on the Discipline of Manufactures, 30 May 1764, SAMi, commercio, pm, c. 176.

[15]*Ibid.*

[16]Giovanni Cazzetta, "Società industriale e silenzio del codice. Lavoro e impresa", in *Scienza giuridica e trasformazioni sociali. Diritto e lavoro in Italia tra Otto e Novecento* (Milan, 2007), pp. 3–26.

[17]Reinhard Zimmermann, "contract," in *Oxford Classical Dictionary* (Oxford, 2012), p. 370.

[18]Roberto Fiori, "'Fides et bona fides'. Hiérarchie sociale et catégories juridiques", *Revue historique de droit français et étranger*, 86 (2008), pp. 465–481. Some thoughtful considerations about good faith as a "secular ethic" of social distinction in late modern society can be found in Daniele Baggiani, "Camere di Commercio in figura di corporazioni. Note sulla politica degli interessi all'inizio del XVIII secolo", in Danilo Zardin (ed.), *Corpi, "fraternità", mestieri nella storia della società europea* (Rome, 1998), pp. 253–256.

attested good faith and, unlike craftsmen, following the Lombard reform, merchants preserved their status even after the abolition of guilds through the maintenance of a special and separate jurisdiction in matters of trade.[19] In contrast, the new work regulations of the 1764 edict were directly transferred from the domestic service model, with its corollary of prison sentences and public whipping. Even though it was explicitly drafted for privileged factory workers, two decades later, the edict evolved into the only legal basis allowing for the functioning of the Lombard silk industry after the formal abolition of the guilds.[20]

Behind an "apparent universality", therefore, we observe the transition to a very peculiar form of contractual society.[21] Concerning trade, freedom of contract was based on the presumed good faith of merchants; concerning labour, however, such freedom was based on the putative disloyalty associated with domestic workers.[22]

From Labour Control to Product Control

In Lombardy, most guilds were gradually abolished from 1775 onwards. Even if the silk weavers' guild was not formally eliminated until 1787, the constraints previously set by the statutes were unofficially abandoned a few years earlier. In 1784, the State Chancellor Anton von Kaunitz (1711–1794) declared that the size and quality requirements for cloths were null and void because "the dealer must always comply with the buyer's wishes".[23] Workers who wanted to change their occupation could no longer be prevented from doing so because such a ban "does not seem to correspond to the principles of freedom that the industry demands".[24] The overcoming of the guild system was completed by the creation of eight Chambers of Commerce in 1786. They co-opted merchants, bankers, and large manufacturers (*fabbricatori nazionali*) into a single organization.[25]

These reforms were part of a vast fiscal, economic, and jurisdictional overhaul of the state spanning the eighteenth century.[26] From the early 1760s, the question of what institutional frame could ensure "public happiness" became pivotal for the young civil servants overcoming the old regulatory system.[27] For these representatives

---

[19]Giuseppe Paletta, "Repubblica dei mercanti e stato moderno: rappresentanza degli interessi commerciali a Milano nel periodo delle riforme", *Annali di storia d'impresa*, 5–6 (1989–1990), pp. 167–198.

[20]The scope of the edict was "to remedy the inconveniences prejudicial to the *new factories introduced in this capital city*", as stated in Carlo Maria Crivelli to Marquis Corrado, 17 May 1764, SAMi, Commercio, p.a., c. 3. Emphasis added.

[21]Bruno Veneziani, "The Evolution of the Contract of Employment", in Bob A. Hepple (ed.), *The Making of Labour Law in Europe: A Comparative Study of Nine Countries up to 1945* (London, 1986), pp. 31–72.

[22]The analogies with other cases are striking. See Simon Deakin and Frank Wilkinson, *The Law of the Labour Market: Industrialization, Employment, and Legal Evolution* (Oxford [etc.], 2005); Steven Kaplan, "Réflexions sur la police du monde du travail, 1700–1815", *Revue Historique*, 261 (1979), pp. 22–23.

[23]Copy of the letter from Kaunitz to Wilczek, 21 June 1784, SAMi, Commercio, p.a., c. 247.

[24]*Ibid.*

[25]Cesare Mozzarelli, "La riforma politica del 1786 e la nascita delle camere di commercio in Lombardia", in Cesare Mozzarelli (ed.), *Economia e corporazioni. Il governo degli interessi nella storia d'Italia dal Medioevo all'età contemporanea* (Milan, 1988), pp. 163–186.

[26]Carlo Capra, *La Lombardia austriaca nell'età delle riforme. 1706–1796* (Turin, 1987).

[27]Luigino Bruni and Pier Luigi Porta, "Economia civile and pubblica felicità in the Italian Enlightenment", *History of Political Economy*, 35:S1 (2003), pp. 361–385.

of an Enlightenment imbued with confidence in the new truths of political economy, the moral aim of reform was to reorganize economic life along competitive principles. As Verri put it, liberty was the "secret life of commerce", enforcing fairness and prosperity.[28] The general view of these intellectuals, working closely with Vienna to modernize the Duchy of Milan, was that the responsibility for dealing with the new economic freedoms should fall to each individual subject. The state was only supposed to take care of breaches of good faith through the severe punishment of acts of fraud.[29]

One of these civil servants was councillor Pietro Secchi (1734–1816), entrusted by Vienna to abolish the guilds. Alongside better-known figures such as Verri and Beccaria (1738–1794), Secchi was a member of the liberal intellectual circle Academy of Fisticuffs (Accademia dei Pugni).[30] He was involved, as most European pre-classical economists were, in political discussions about policies for the grain trade and was a strong supporter of freedom of labour.[31] However, some doubts about such an approach to industrial labour were voiced in Vienna. Chancellor Kaunitz, amid the abolition of the guilds, expressed his concern that excessive freedom to undertake a craft might jeopardize the reform. He asked, therefore, whether it would not be wiser to maintain some regulatory system to verify the dexterity of practitioners. The response to his concerns makes clear that the interlocking of regulations and guilds was typical of a time when the spirit of reform had not yet had to confront the everyday necessities of trade. Secchi explicitly opposed this idea and replied to Kaunitz that "all these verifications carried out by the current regulations have, with time, degenerated into a simple and expensive formality".[32] For Secchi, the maintenance of an entrance examination for the exercise of crafts would inevitably end up restoring those pernicious constraints that prevented industry from prospering. By opening the Pandora's box of "regulations" that had been closed so painfully, one could only spread the evil of the "monopoly".[33]

According to the plans of the Lombard reformers, what was previously supposed to be ensured by trade guild statutes should now be derived from the extrinsic characteristics of the objects traded on the market. A voluntary public mark should certify the quality of the goods. Yet, goods without such a mark could continue to circulate

---

[28]Pier Luigi Porta and Roberto Scazzieri, "Pietro Verri's Political Economy: Commercial Society, Civil Society, and the Science of the Legislator", *History of Political Economy*, 34 (2002), pp. 83–110.

[29]Elisabetta Merlo, *Le corporazioni, conflitti e soppressioni. Milano tra Sei e Settecento* (Milan, 1996), pp. 101–103.

[30]A brief biography of Pietro Secchi (also known as Pier Francesco Secco Comneno) can be found in Sergio Romagnoli and Gianni Francioni (eds), *Il Caffè*, 2 vols (Turin, 1998), I, pp. lxi–lxiii. On the Academy of Fisticuffs and the vibrant intellectual atmosphere in Milan, see Sophus A. Reinert, *The Academy of Fisticuffs: Political Economy and Commercial Society in Enlightenment Italy* (Cambridge [etc.], 2018).

[31]If his beliefs about liberalization of the industrial production were radical, Secchi's position on agricultural trade was more nuanced, probably because of his family interests, according to Franco Venturi, *Settecento riformatore. L'italia dei lumi*, 2 vols (Turin, 1987), I, pp. 771–774. The entanglement between the liberalization of grain trade and the abolition of guilds is highlighted in Steven L. Kaplan, "Social Classification and Representation in the Corporate World of Eighteenth-Century France: Turgot's Carnival", in *idem* and Cynthia J. Koepp (eds), *Work in France: Representations, Meaning, Organization, and Practice* (Ithaca, NY [etc.], 1986), pp. 195–197.

[32]Councillor Pietro Secchi to Chancellor Kauntiz, 4 October 1773, SAMi, Commercio, p.a., c. 4.

[33]*Ibid.*

since anyone who wanted to buy unmarked products "should attribute to himself the deceit to which he has exposed himself".[34]

Probably thanks to the intervention of Verri mentioned at the beginning of this paper, the 1786 edict that established the Chambers of Commerce provided for introducing two Expert Commissioners for Manufactures and Workers' Discipline (Commissari periti per le Manifatture, e disciplina degli operaj).[35] However, the conviction that compulsory and binding labour control had to give way to a more modest and voluntary product control was shown in Beccaria's approach, adopted in 1787, to rewrite a regulation for silk manufactures. The issues addressed to the Chambers of Commerce by the famous jurist in charge of the Milanese government's economic department focused mainly on how to guarantee the quality of cloth. And his reply to merchant-manufacturers who demanded the application of corporal punishment against recalcitrant workers sounds like an Enlightenment manifesto: "[L]et the manufacturers make such agreements with their workers as are in their own interest, and it will be easier for them to obtain from the obligation of a free man's contract what cannot be obtained, unless badly and rarely, from the force used against a slave."[36]

Silk Weaving in Lombardy

This period of profound institutional changes in the Duchy of Milan coincided with a time of intense growth for the Lombard silk industry as the Habsburgs' desire to encourage greater integration between the various regions of the empire opened the door to the Vienna market for Lombard silk fabrics. The export of silk textiles from the Duchy of Milan (Figure 2) almost quadrupled between 1769 and 1790.[37] The most significant increase took place in 1785 when, in just one year, export value jumped from 328,036 to 663,811 florins as Lombard manufacturers enjoyed an exemption to the import ban of foreign textiles in the Hereditary Lands (Erblande).[38] Even after the abolition of the guilds, Lombard silk weaving (Figure 3) remained mostly an urban affair.[39] The control exerted by the merchant class over the different silk guilds since the early modern period removed any incentive to relocate the last stage of production to the countryside, in contrast to several other textile cities of northern Italy.[40]

---

[34]Councillor Pietro Secchi to Chancellor Kauntiz, 22 November 1773, SAMi, Commercio, p.a., c. 4.

[35]Even though the edict of 30 May 1764 explicitly stipulated that the enforcement of the law should be entrusted to a public officer, it was the commissioner of the Chamber of Commerce who became responsible for applying the edict. See Regia intendenza provinciale to the Chamber of Commerce of Como, 22 November 1788, State Archive, Como [hereafter, SACo], Camera di commercio, c. 22, f. 13–25; Report of the session of the Chamber of Commerce of Milan, 25 November 1790, SAMi, Commercio, p.a., c. 135.

[36]1170 – Disciplina degli operai [14 May 1787], in Rosalba Canetta (ed.), *Opere di Cesare Beccaria*, Atti di governo, serie IV, 1787 (Milan, 1998), p. 374.

[37]Angelo Moioli, *Note sulla struttura del commercio estero dello Stato di Milano nella seconda metà del settecento*, in Giorgio Borelli (ed.), *Studi in onore di Gino Barbieri*, 3 vols (Pisa, 1983), II, pp. 1076–1079.

[38]Mocarelli, *Milano città atelier*, p. 152, n. 442.

[39]Alberto Cova, "L'alternativa manifatturiera", in Sergio Zaninelli (ed.), *Da un sistema agricolo a un sistema industriale. Il Comasco dal Settecento al Novecento*, 3 vols (Como, 1987), I, pp. 177–178.

[40]Carlo Marco Belfanti, "Rural Manufactures and Rural Proto-industries in the 'Italy of the Cities' from the Sixteenth through the Eighteenth Century", *Continuity and Change*, 8 (1993), pp. 253–280. In the

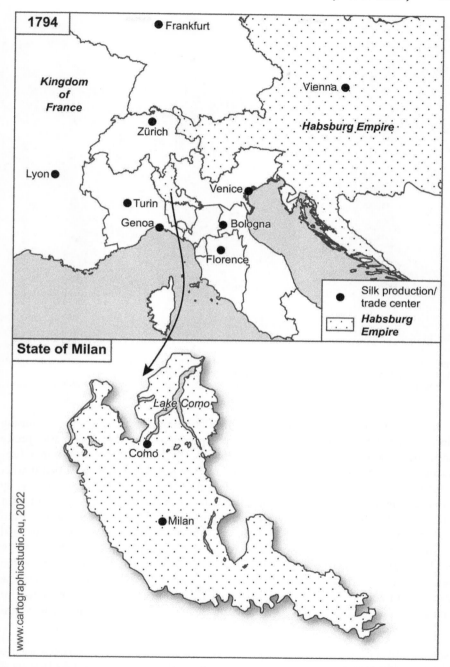

Figure 2. Map of the Duchy of Milan (Ducato di Milano) at the end of the eighteenth century, with silk production and trade centres and their trade connections throughout Europe.

Figure 3. A representation of a Lombard silk weaving workshop. In the back, a man working on a four-shaft weaving loom, in the front a woman winding some silk thread.
Arti e Mestieri m. 4-23, Civica Raccolta delle Stampe Achille Bertarelli, Castello Sforzesco, Milan. With permission.

In 1785, in Milan, there were 1384 active silk looms.[41] Even if it was not coming close to the high-quality products of Lyon, production in the capital was pretty diversified, featuring cloths of all kinds, ribbons, silk hosiery, and other minor productions. Exports played an important role, but the presence of a large urban market and the ability to modulate production according to a new domestic demand (i.e. by reducing the production of less popular fabrics such as damask in favour of light cloths and shawls) allowed a significant proportion of silk textiles to be sold within the city's walls. The new tariffs also allowed the development of another regional centre, Como, where 725 looms were in use this same year.[42] Here, the range of products was limited to plain fabrics. Production was highly dependent on foreign demand and proved volatile, with frequent booms and busts. Along with Vienna, the German fairs (especially Frankfurt) played a significant role. Another outlet for Como silk fabrics was Russia and the Baltic territories, where costumers were less

---

Duchy of Milan it was only the central stage of production (silk throwing) that was once urban and then delocalized in the countryside, but this was mainly for reasons linked to adverse taxation. See Luigi Trezzi, "Un caso di deindustrializzazione della città. I molini da seta a Milano e nel Ducato (secc. XVII e XVIII)", *Archivio storico lombardo*, 112 (1986), pp. 205–214.

[41]Bruno Caizzi, *Industria, commercio e banca in Lombardia nel XVIII secolo* (Milan, 1968), p. 108.
[42]*Ibid.*

exigent in terms of quality.[43] Despite the differences, when it comes to silk, Como and Milan formed one single labour market "since between these two cities there's always been a communication of artificers, if we can say, also of disorder and vices of the same kind", as the royal provincial delegate put it in 1787.[44]

The dominant form of work organization at the time was typical of what historians call the "putting-out system" (a means of subcontracting work). A small group of merchant-manufacturers (*fabbricatori*) were in charge of the commercialization of the product. They entrusted the silk yarn to the master weavers (*capi tessitori* or *capi fabbrica*), who turned it into cloth. The master weaver was a liminal figure somewhere between artisan and subcontractor. Sometimes, he worked at home on his own looms with the help of his relatives; other times, he was a middleman between weavers and merchant-manufacturers.[45] To fill the orders by the merchant-manufacturers, the master weaver hired salaried workers (*tessitori*) to work on his looms. Even if they did not have any form of stable organization, these workers could be likened to the French journeymen since, generally, they were very mobile, did not possess their own loom, and were paid by the piece. Production was most often carried out in the master house, but sometimes, following the wave of abolitions of several monastic orders, the main manufacturers started to concentrate looms in old urban monasteries in both Milan and Como.[46]

We must be cautious in fixing too static a picture of production and social classi- fication. Even before the abolition of the guilds, the structures of silk weavers' asso- ciations were very elastic according to the needs of merchant capital. Some weavers were allowed to be the master for a limited time, even without a formal inscription to the guild, and it was easy for foreigners to join the guild.[47] After the demise of the guilds, the ideal tripartition of the putting-out system (merchant-manufacturer, master weaver, weavers/workers) was continually reconfigured by variations in the demand for cloth and the supply of silk yarn. Since formal apprenticeships had dis- appeared, in times of high textile demand, all kinds of people came to work on the

---

[43] A report from 1792 mentions that among the 868 cloths that were weaved at that time, only 74 were for internal consumption: 426 were sent to Vienna, 17 to the Low Countries, 308 to the German fairs (232 in Frankfurt, 56 in Leipzig, and 20 in Augusta), and 43 to Russia. See Elenco delle stato attuale delle mani- fatture seriche risultante dalla perlustrazione fatta dall'infascritto commissario perito ..., 17 March 1794 SAMi, Commercio, p.a., c. 238. It seems likely that the eastern European market was even more important since another report from 1797 estimates that before the Napoleonic invasion, silk fabrics exported to Russia was a third of that shipped to Vienna. See Delegate Commission of the Commercial and Industrial Affairs to the Municipal Council of Como, SACo, civico, c. 294. Local chronicles mention that parts of the export to Austria were usually routed to Poland, Turkey, and other countries. See Giuseppe Rovelli, *Storia dei principali avvenimenti dopo l'ingresso dei francesi in Lombardia cioè dal Maggio 1796 a tutto il 1802 per servire di appendice alla storia di Como* (Como, 1808), p. 77.

[44] Report of the Political Intendant of Como Giuseppe Pellegrini, 20 February 1787, SAMi, Commercio, p.a., c. 4.

[45] In Milan, sixty-six per cent of master-weavers declared that they personally worked on a loom; see Elenco generale delle fabbriche esistenti nella città di Milano e corpi santi, Chamber of Commerce Historical Archive, Milan [hereafter, CCHAMi], registri, c. 405. In Como, it was ninety-two per cent; see Distina dello stato delle Manifatture di stoffa nella città, borghi e corpi santi di Como, 27 June 1789, SACo, Camera di commercio, c. 23.

[46] Cova, "L'alternativa manifatturiera", p. 179; Ortaggi, *Libertà e servitù*, pp. 11–112.

[47] Mocarelli, *Milano città atelier*, pp. 71, 150.

silk looms. Furthermore, merchant-manufacturers now issued their orders directly to the weavers without the intermediation of those who had qualified as master weaver under the former guild regime. On the contrary, in times of good cocoon harvest, master weavers started to act as manufacturers since falling silk prices meant they could afford to produce their own cloths and put them on the market.[48]

Desacralizing Saint Monday

Since one of the main features of the pre-industrial labour market was instability, it is only by considering market trends that we can make sense of working-class practices. In 1786, the merchant manufacturers of Como complained that the silk weavers were

> always insatiable about their pay (although they are increased for each quality [of cloth]), they disturb the manufacturers, inciting them to compete to increase wages. Once such an increase is obtained, workers try to improve it more and more, making their claims through intemperance and sloppy work [and] preventing commerce from flourishing.[49]

Merchant-manufacturers were echoed some months later in such views by the political authorities who noted that silk weavers not only plotted for more money and reduced their workloads, but also shortened their working week: "[I]nstead of being made up of six working days, as it is for everyone, it has become for them of three or four days."[50]

The voluntary inactivity at the start of the week (referred to as "Saint Monday") was a well-known practice in pre-industrial society and has been subject to multiple interpretations among scholars. In his seminal essay on time and work discipline, British historian E.P. Thompson argued that Saint Monday was embedded in the dense web of artisan customs and one mark of workers' resistance to the intensification of work.[51] Another interpretation, by the Italian historian Simona Cerutti, suggests that Saint Monday was instead a time of autonomous organization by workers. Monday was a very busy day. On this day, workers would meet outside their workplaces, redistribute workloads in taverns, or collect alms to help their fellow journeymen. Thus, Saint Monday was not just a chance to offer resistance, but also experience another form of work organization that was distinct and alternative from that of the masters.[52] The progressive disappearance of this practice has been primarily addressed in terms of a shift in the balance between toil and leisure in

---

[48]I have discussed these issues in Lorenzo Avellino, "Des ouvriers, des fabricants ou des oisifs? Roôles et hiérarchies dans la fabrique de soie lombarde après l'abolition des corporations (1780–1860)", Le Mouvement Social, 276 (2021), pp. 27–45.

[49]Silk Merchant-Manufacturers of Como, n.d. [1786], SAMi, Commercio, p.a., c. 237.

[50]Report of the Political Intendant of Como Giuseppe Pellegrini, 20 February 1787, SAMi, Commercio, p.a., c. 4.

[51]E.P. Thompson, "Time, Work-Discipline, and Industrial Capitalism", Past & Present, 38 (1967), pp. 56–97.

[52]Simona Cerutti, "Travail, mobilité et légitimité. Suppliques au roi dans une société d'Ancien Régime (Turin, XVIIIe siècle)", Annales. Histoire, Sciences Sociales, 65 (2010), p. 597.

working-class households.[53] Jan de Vries has cast this change in terms of economic growth, theorizing that the household choice to increase labour supply participated in an "industrious revolution" that paved the way to industrial take-off in Western Europe.[54] Since then, labour historians have returned to the issue of working time, putting forward less linear and univocal arguments. Several scholars have underlined that the intensification of work during the long eighteenth century is fuzzier than De Vries claims and that both masters and workers were fully aware of the centrality of the "struggle for time" earlier than what E.P. Thompson admitted.[55] This revisionism allows us to put forward a third explanation of Saint Monday since, in the case of the Lombard silk manufactures, this practice seems to have been followed for the more prosaic reasons of keeping wages in line with the high demand for cloths.[56]

The letter cited above by the Como intendant complaining about weavers' absences at the start of the week was written in early 1787 after several months of positive trends in the cloth market. Only a few months later, the situation changed radically and with it, the behaviour of the weavers. A poor cocoon harvest in the summer and the decrease in cloth demand because of the beginning of a new Russo–Turkish war (1787–1792) threw the silk factories into a rude economic crisis. At the beginning of the autumn, the Como intendant warned that the spinners had practically ceased work, that weavers would soon do so, and that crowds of unemployed workers had started to roam the towns and loot the fields.[57] What about the weavers still employed? Beccaria was told by the master weavers that the workers presently "have become more docile and active so that now that work is scarce, they not only work five full days of the week, but even on the famous Monday".[58] Remarkably, then, it was at the very moment of economic crisis and decreased labour demand that what was thought to be the ineradicable indolence of weavers on Mondays seemed momentarily to vanish.

In contrast, the years 1794 and 1795, just before Napoleon Bonaparte's First Italian Campaign, saw a further boom for the Lombard silk industry as French producers could no longer supply the European silk cloth market because of the war. As cloth demand rose again, complaints immediately resumed against Saint Monday.

---

[53]For example, Douglas A. Reid, "The Decline of Saint Monday 1766–1876", *Past & Present*, 71 (1976), pp. 76–101; idem, "Weddings, Weekdays, Work and Leisure in Urban England 1791–1911: The Decline of Saint Monday Revisited", *Past & Present*, 153 (1996), pp. 135–163; Hans-Joachim Voth, "Time and Work in Eighteenth-Century London", *Journal of Economic History*, 58 (1998), pp. 29–58.

[54]Jan de Vries, *The Industrious Revolution: Consumer Behaviour and the Household Economy, 1650 to the Present* (Cambridge, MA, 2008), pp. 91–92.

[55]Corine Maitte and Didier Terrier, *Les rythmes du labeur. Enquête sur le temps de travail en Europe occidentale, XIVe–XIXe siècles* (Paris, 2020). For the textile sector specifically, see Andrea Caracausi, "La lutte pour le temps. Réglémentation du travail et formes de la négociation dans les manufactures de l'Italie moderne", in Didier Terrier and Corine Maitte (eds), *Les temps du travail. Normes, pratiques, évolutions (XIVe–XIXe siècle)* (Rennes, 2014), pp. 395–414.

[56]Michal Sonenscher, in his monumental study of the Parisian trades, evokes a similar pattern when he points out that there was a likely relationship between Saint Monday and the urban demand of employment; Michael Sonenscher, *Work and Wages: Natural Law, Politics and the Eighteenth-Century French Trades* (Cambridge, 1989), p. 201, n. 64.

[57]Report of the Political Intendant of Como Giuseppe Pellegrini, 12 October 1787, SAMi, Commercio, p.a., c. 237.

[58]2140 – Disoccupazione a Como [3 December 1787], in Canetta (ed.), *Opere di Cesare Beccaria*, p. 861.

The Chamber of Commerce of Como criticized weavers "as never before [so] insolent, saying that they want to work whenever they like, and so they do, since the weavers' taverns are full on *the first days of the week*".[59] It seems that manufacturers even had to dismiss several orders as their employees were working "not even half of what they would have done in bad times".[60]

One could argue that the masters and manufacturers always complained about the lack of industriousness of their employees. But we can observe not just general grievances about the vicious nature of the workers – though these were not lacking, as we will see – but detailed allegations explicitly linking the state of trade to the voluntary modulation of working time. In my view, this complaint appears to be coherent with the interpretation of Saint Monday as a way to restrain labour supply in order to maintain high wages.[61]

The manufacturers, on their side, expressed their frustration that using wages as leverage seemed to have the opposite effect of what was expected: the more they were paid, the less the weavers worked. In the words of the Chamber of Commerce of Como:

> Experience has shown that in the years 1786 and 1787, during which time prices were raised by two *soldi* for every *auna*, the weavers abandoned themselves to all sorts of vice, they loaded themselves with debts, they worked very little, and badly. As further proof, in the scarcity of the year 1790, the merchants, with one-third fewer workers, had the same quantity of cloth and greater perfection.[62]

I argue that Saint Monday was then part of a dynamic form of wage negotiation that followed its own logic. That logic is certainly astonishing if looked at through the eyes of the nascent political economy, but it is entirely consistent with the cyclical variations of the silk fabric market.

Private Concerns and Public Unrest

If raising wages did not work as the merchants expected, what means of constraint could be considered to ensure that every worker remained committed to their assigned task?

A first punishment, strongly urged by the merchant authorities, was to treat absent workers as idlers in order to take advantage of the dissuasive effect of incarceration. However, this approach proved challenging to implement, given the social unrest it might provoke. At the end of 1790, faced with the insistence of the manufacturers to act, the government council intervened to demand "greater caution" in applying

---

[59]Report of the Commissioner of Chamber of Commerce of Como Giovanni Valentini, 16 July 1794, SAMi, Commercio, p.a., c. 238. Emphasis added.

[60]Silk Cloth Manufacturers Caroe and Scalini, Montefiori and Rubini, Pietro Rubini, Giovanni Maria Fischer to the Chamber of Commerce of Como, 20 February 1795, SAMi, Commercio, p.a., c. 238.

[61]Alongside other practices. See for instance the complaint about weavers who provoked fights against foreigners to scare them and make them "leave the city abandoning their work unfinished". Petition from Master-Weavers Cattena, Antonio Bianchi, etc., 13 May 1795, SACo, Camera di commercio, c. 20, f. 1795.

[62]Chamber of Commerce of Como to Municipal Congregation of Como, 15 July 1791, SACo, Camera di Commercio, c. 23. Twenty *soldi* equated to one Milanese *lira*, one *auna* to 0.53 meters.

the law.[63] This circumspection was undoubtedly dictated by an awareness that the social stability that permitted the functioning of the silk manufactures was somewhat precarious. The possibility that the private concerns of the merchants might turn into public unrest seemed to pose a persistent threat. A weaver's riot had shaken the town of Como only a few months earlier, with hundreds of workers demanding the head of the Chamber commissioner.[64]

The other option for constraining absentee workers was the sequestration of their loom shuttles.[65] Once again, it was the commissioner of the Chamber of Commerce who oversaw removing such tools to force the weavers to show up at the Chamber to recover them and, in the process, be served a formal injunction to respect their contractual commitments. In practice, such operations were often complicated due to the animosity of the weavers and their wives, who greeted the commissioner with insults and even stones.[66] In Como, during the summer of 1791, intimidation became so frequent that the commissioner was too scared to leave the Chamber, afraid of the threats he received "if he had dared to go to visit the looms and take possession of the shuttles of those whom he found absent from work".[67]

Moreover, it was precisely at times of intense work that absences were most serious and most challenging to constrain. In September 1795, orders abounded with the upcoming German fairs, and the Chamber of Como insisted that several absent weavers be imprisoned "to serve as an example to make the others maintain their commitments".[68] However, this show of force was cut short: one weaver spent a few days in jail before his master pleaded for his immediate release because he needed him to finish a cloth.[69]

The manufacturers were well aware of these contradictions and complained about the ineffectiveness of the measures available to them. When questioned about the alternatives that might be made available to them in a new regulation for silk workshops, they replied that

> if suspension from work were a punishment that did not encourage idleness and vice, it might be appropriate in this case. But experience has now shown the contrary. Therefore, to avoid such inconvenience, it is in the Chamber's opinion to

---

[63]Government Council to the Political Intendant of Como, 14 December 1790, SACo, Prefettura, c. 366.

[64]Protocolli in occasione del tumulto dei tessitori del mese di luglio 1790, July 1790 SACo, Prefettura, c. 355.

[65]See for instance the complaints against the weavers Pietro Fontana, Giuseppe Pedraglio, Abbroggio Lisasse, and Zaverio Peia in SACo, Camera di commercio, c. 22. One day they showed up for work "for only one hour" and then went to a tavern, so they had their shuttle sequestered. A few months later another weaver, Francesca Ceriani, got his loom shuttle seized by the Chamber for failing to attend the workshop of his master; he had promised to do so in the evening but never complied (Complaint against Francesca Ceriani, SACo, Camera di commercio, c. 22).

[66]As a result, the commissioner in Como started to carry a knife for protection on his visits to the fabrics manufactures; see Licenza d'armi n. 1556, 14 October 1790, SAMi, Commercio, p.a., c. 114.

[67]Chamber of Commerce of Como's Record, 22 July 1791, SACo, Camera di commercio, c. 22. Similar complaints by Milan's commissioners "insulted and even threatened lives", according to a report of the commissioners of the Chamber of Commerce of Milan, 21 May 1795, SAMi, Commercio, p.a., c. 238.

[68]Chamber of Commerce of Como to the Pretura, 7 September 1795, SACo, Camera di commercio, c. 21.

[69]Chamber of Commerce of Como to Pretura, 16 September 1795, SACo, Camera di commercio, c. 20.

punish those absent from work for a depraved cause (*causa viziosa*) by forcing them to work chained to the loom.[70]

Although one might have expected a liberal backlash to such a suggestion, much more pedestrian arguments seem to have prevented its implementation. As the intendant explained in his response to the Chamber of Commerce's proposal, chaining a worker to his loom "can be the cause of many disruptions: a grouping of his comrades with the aim of freeing him can take place any time". And his advice, at the time, was to "stay away from anything that can cause any excitement".[71]

Nevertheless, the Chamber's proposition was reiterated in 1794, but the Duchy government never accepted it.[72] On the contrary, the Milan authorities pushed for exclusively pecuniary sanctions against workers who did not respect their contractual commitments. As might be expected, the merchants of Milan and Como, when consulted, opposed what they deemed to be a relaxation of the rules, but it is the motivation for their opposition that is especially interesting. The Chamber political magistrate (*Magistrato politico camerale*) alleged that they considered that "the punishment in case of transgression seems to be the only one that can contain such people who have no property to lose" (*nulla ha da perdere dal lato della robba*).[73] Maria Luisa Pesante has identified the servile roots of the modern wage in a specific conception of the salaried worker's condition going back to natural jurisprudence. On the one hand, despite his engagements, the wage earner cannot entirely cede what he is renting, namely, his workforce. On the other hand, he lacks any other property entitlement that he could alienate.[74] It is this double deficiency that legitimates the legal coercion to work. The remark of the Lombard manufacturer about workers' insolvency, then, is crucial since it evokes the limits of any attempt to cast the transition to a contractual order as a peaceful and consensual one in which employer and worker exchanged on equal terms. For the merchants, the new "free labour" system could not function because one of the parties to the contractual relationship lacked the two prior and necessary attributes of the civil law regime: good faith and private property.

Debt, Pay, and Runaways

Even if incarceration and physical coercion were an ever-looming threat, such forms of punishment appeared unmanageable for commercial and political reasons. As such, and despite the manufacturers' petitions, debt remained the most common form of labour constraint. The use of wage advances was deeply rooted in the pre-industrial organization of work. Since any worker was officially prohibited from

---

[70]Protocol No. 61 of the Chamber of Commerce of Como, 12 May 1791, SAMi, Commercio, p.a., c. 117.

[71]Annex to the Letter from the Magistrato politico camerale to the Royal Delegate of Como, 16 May 1791, SACo, Prefettura, c. 366.

[72]Annex to the Letter from Chamber of Commerce of Como to the Magistrato politico camerale, 17 January 1794, SACo, Camera di commercio, 26.

[73]Magistrato politico camerale to the Conferenza di governo, 20 September 1795, SAMi, Commercio, p.a., 236.

[74]Maria Luisa Pesante, *Come servi. Figure del lavoro salariato dal diritto naturale all'economia politica* (Milan, 2013).

leaving his workplace while he was indebted to his master, advances were used to enforce loyalty, fix a highly mobile labour force to the workplace, and limit competition between employers.[75]

During the turbulent years in Lombardy immediately after the guild system's abolition, weavers' debts exploded because of the need to try to keep up with the growth of the textile market. In this regard, there was no discontinuity before or after the abolition of guilds; instead, the debt spiral of the end of the eighteenth century was mainly related to the instability of the international cloth market. As the market rose, "mainly instigated by manufacturers", master weavers started to propose to workers to pay their debts if they moved to their workshop.[76] At the same time, to try to convince them to stay, the master weavers were forced to increase the advances that, in times of buoyant economic activity, became a de facto pay raise. During one of these favourable trends, the master weavers in Como declared that they were "threatened by the workers to force their hand and give them what they wanted" and begged the authorities to intervene "by any means to be exempted from giving the workers any money".[77] This kind of petition opens up a more ambivalent interpretation of credit in the pre-industrial work organization. Andrea Caracausi has already pointed out that textile workers often pretended advances as insurance against insolvent masters or to face the cost of moving to a new town.[78] The Lombard case shows that they were not only a tool of labour constraint but were also a symptom of the capacity of the weavers to exploit the position of strength they had in certain moments since it was common that the debt was only partially refunded or not paid back at all as the workers ran away from the workshop. The continual complaints about the comings and goings of workers between Como and Milan are evidence of this credit-driven mobility.[79] Furthermore, the bond created by the debtor-creditor relationship was a reciprocal one. In times of low cloth demand, the masters were encouraged to continue to employ the indebted workers "with the hope of reducing or extinguishing the debt of each". At the same time, the weavers "resist[ed] any attempt to save anything on their wages in return for the debt".[80]

As has already been pointed out, the ubiquity of credit in the modern economy was not only motivated by the limited amount of money available. It constituted a

---

[75]Kaplan, "Réflexions sur la police", pp. 48–50; Cynthia M. Truant, "Independent and Insolent: Journeymen and Their 'Rites' in the Old Regime Workplace", in Kaplan and Koepp, *Work in France*, pp. 148–150; Sonenscher, *Work and Wages*, pp. 191–192; Andrea Caracausi, *Dentro la bottega. Culture del lavoro in una città d'età moderna* (Venice, 2008), pp. 64–67; idem, "I salari", in Renata Ago (ed.), *Storia del lavoro in Italia. L'età moderna* (Rome, 2018), pp. 112–115; Luca Mocarelli and Giulio Ongaro, *Work in Early Modern Italy, 1500–1800* (London, 2019), pp. 75–77.

[76]Report of the Political Intendant of Como Giuseppe Pellegrini, 20 February 1787, SAMi, Commercio, p.a, c. 4.

[77]Capi fabbrica o proprietari di telaro to the Chamber of Commerce of Como, 1 March 1787, SAMi, Commercio, p.a., c. 237.

[78]Caracausi, *Dentro la bottega*, p. 66.

[79]The clerks of the Chamber of Commerce in both Milan and Como were constantly corresponding with each other to track down the weavers and recover the debts; see Commissioner Giovanni Valentini to the Chamber of Commerce of Como, 21 March 1796, SACo, Camera di commercio, c. 21.

[80]Report of the Political Intendant of Como Giuseppe Pellegrini, 20 February 1787, SAMi, Commercio, p.a., c. 4.

means to cement economic relationships and mediate the uncertainty that was necessarily inherent to such exchanges at any level.[81] According to Craig Muldrew, the social trust at the base of this "economy of obligation" was inextricably linked to communitarian bounds placed under strain by increasing market activity.[82] While it is true that this movement pushed towards an increasingly contractual society, as far as labour was concerned, the form of the contract was influenced by the peculiar relationship of the parties to "good faith", as I have emphasized in this article. Freedom of contract could not go along with freedom of movement for workers, as demonstrated by the fact that limitations imposed on the displacement of working men and women were not only maintained after the abolition of the guilds but started to be directly enforced by the state through specific devices combining mobility restraint, identification, and debt control.[83]

In Lombardy, it was only at the beginning of the nineteenth century, amid the Napoleonic conquest, that the prefecture began to track down missing workers. Some weavers were jailed; many more were returned to work by the police authorities.[84] The chief of police even started to settle arrangements to stagger the debts owed to the masters with money deposited monthly by the debtors to the prefecture office.[85] The involvement of police authorities in punishing breaches of contract represents a persistent and significant infringement of the legal logic that distinguishes civil from penal law.[86] Furthermore, the manufacturers go as far as to suggest that the scope of labour discipline should no longer be limited to the workshop but may embrace the whole town. Any weaver caught in places like taverns should be brought back to his master:

> [I]t would also be good for the universal benefit of the workers themselves if the police could keep an eye on them and, if they find them idle and wandering on weekdays outside of mealtimes, they [should] send them back to their respective jobs. They [should also] frequently visit the taverns and inns, and if they see workers drinking and gambling outside the aforementioned hours, they [should]

---

[81]Renata Ago, "Enforcing Agreements: Notaries and Courts in Early Modern Rome", *Continuity and Change*, 14 (1999), pp. 191–206; Laurence Fontaine, *L'économie morale. Pauvreté, crédit et confiance dans l'Europe préindustrielle* (Paris, 2008); Anne Montenach, *Espaces et pratiques du commerce alimentaire à Lyon au XVIIe siècle. L'économie du quotidien* (Grenoble, 2009); Pierre Gervais, "Crédit et filières marchandes au XVIIIe siècle", *Annales. Histoire, Sciences Sociales*, 67 (2012), pp. 1011–1048; Anaïs Albert, *La vie à crédit. La consommation des classes populaires à Paris (années 1880–1920)* (Paris, 2021).

[82]Craig Muldrew, *The Economy of Obligation: The Culture of Credit and Social Relations in Early Modern England* (London, 1998).

[83]Martino Sacchi Landriani, "Rethinking the Livret d'ouvriers: Time, Space and 'Free' Labor in Nineteenth-Century France", *Labor History*, 60 (2019), pp. 854–864. For the Lombard case specifically, see Simona Mori, "Dal benservito al libretto di scorta. Mobilità del lavoro e pubbliche discipline nella Lombardia preunitaria", in Livio Antonielli (ed.), *La polizia del lavoro. Il definirsi di un ambito di controllo* (Catanzaro, 2011), pp. 81–116.

[84]See the series for the years 1803 and 1805 conserved in SACo, Camera di commercio, c. 21.

[85]Report No. 5196 from the Prefect of Police of the Olona Department to the Police Delegate of Larius Department, 8 April 1805, SACo, Camera di commercio, c. 21.

[86]Thorsten Keiser, "Between Status and Contract? Coercion in Contractual Labour Relationships in Germany from the 16th to the 20th century", *Rechtsgeschichte-Legal History*, 21 (2013), pp. 33–36.

chase them away from there and send each one to his job, threatening the most reluctant with prison.[87]

Such punishment was characterized as being inflicted for the worker's own benefit. "Working the whole week, they would spend less and earn a lot more", thanks to which "gradually we would remove that ~~innate~~ [*sic!*] rooted indolence which unfortunately rules them".[88]

Weavers or Idlers?

The French domination was not only a period of police reform but ushered in a time of deep crisis for the Lombard silk fabrics industry. In addition to the loss of the crucial Viennese market, Northern Italy suffered from a shift in French economic policy to turn the region into a simple supplier of cheap raw silk for Lyon. By 1800, in Como, there was only a third of the number of active looms that had existed on the eve of the French invasion in 1795.[89] Faced with unemployment, some weavers set off for Veneto while others went to Northern Europe. However, the Chamber of Commerce of Como declared that among the workers who remained in town, there were "some who would be well suited to work [but] they prefer to go to begging in [the] town and in the countryside [...] and, rather than conform with their profession, decide to become peddlers or boatmen".[90] The master weavers hunted workers for their workshops, especially for auxiliary tasks, "but with no success because those people replied that *they would work when they are paid as in the past*".[91]

During the summer of 1810, the parishes of Como were asked to classify the poor; all beggars who wanted to keep asking for alms had to present themselves to the municipal authorities.[92] In November, the Chamber of Commerce pointed out again that "today there would be work to occupy some of those who remain idle, and who, because of the decrease in the price of work, prefer either to take up another craft or to become vagabonds by begging".[93] A month later, in December 1810, the interior minister decided to "repress the idleness and vagrancy of silk workers" and asked the police commissioner to imprison the workers circulating in the town.[94]

---

[87]Draft of the Observations by Guaita and Comini about the New Disciplinary Regulation for the Workers, n.d. [1808], SACo, Prefettura, c. 912. The suggestion came from the owner of the main woollen firm of Como and was adopted by Chamber of Commerce in 1812; see Draft of the Letter from the Chamber of Commerce to Larius Prefect, 8 May 1812, SACo, Camera di commercio, c. 82.

[88]Minister of Interior to the Prefect of the Larius Department, 4 November 1812, SACo, Camera di commercio, 82. Strikethrough in the original.

[89]Chamber of Commerce of Como to the Regia direzione provinciale di finanza, 21 February 1800, SACo, Camera di commercio, c. 23.

[90]Report of Commissioner Giovanni Valentini, [n.d., but 1800], SACo, Camera di commercio, 26.

[91]*Ibid.* Emphasis added.

[92]The statistics sent out after this vast survey confirm the miserable state of the silk workers. In Larius Department, the poor "capable of working" numbered 269 (158 of them, textile workers); see Giancarlo Galli, "Forestieri, inabili, miserabili del mestier della seta. La mendicità nel comasco durante il periodo rivoluzionario e napoleonico (1796–1814)", *Periodico della società storica comense*, 47 (1980), pp. 39–71.

[93]Chamber of Commerce of Como to Larius Prefect, 16 November 1810, SACo, Prefettura, 912.

[94]Interior Minister to the *Gendermeria* Commander, Police Commissioner and Como's *Podestà*, 5 December 1810, SACo, Prefettura, 912.

However, this drastic measure failed to dissuade the weavers. Less than a year later, in November 1811, the Chamber of Commerce once again complained about silk workers who, invited to return to their looms, refused because "the ordinary and common wage does not give them enough to live on".[95]

Because the Lombard cloth manufacturers managed to reduce wages to cope with the economic crisis, becoming a silk weaver was no longer an advantageous option for the urban worker. As many workers weaved only in times of high demand for cloth, during crises, they could return to their former profession, find a new one, or start to beg.[96] Because this form of voluntary inactivity played off when wages fell below subsistence levels, the political authorities had to deal with another form of disguised wage negotiation through the modulation of working time.

Conclusion

Through the preceding analysis of the constraints imposed on work in a significant and growing industry, I have highlighted the gap between the principles of liberty enunciated by the Lombard state reformers like Verri and Beccaria and the pragmatic appeal of constraints imposed on workers' right to ensure the regularity of their production. Different conceptions of legal responsibility are relevant to investigate how the formal unity of civil law hides the "tutelage of a society to be fortified in its new hierarchies and its new proprietary certitudes".[97] In Lombardy, the discussion between the political authorities and the merchant-manufacturers continued for several decades, forcing the constant affirmation of the distance between the officially applied "free labour" regime and the demands to force workers to perform their tasks. In particular, the lack of property and presumed good faith on the part of workers were central elements to explain why manufacturers never claimed that a contractual relationship in a proper civil law regime was possible.

Despite the pressure to reinforce punishment, the debt relation, taking the form of salary advances, stood as the most effective means to try to discipline the workers. In this regard, there was no significant disruption compared with the guild regime, but a dynamic assessment of weaver behaviour suggests a more active role played by workers. For instance, if we consider the state of the international cloth market, we observe that the debts were not only undergone by workers but sometimes obtained as a form of disguised pay raise. A similar approach can help make sense of practices like Saint Monday as a form of struggle to keep wages high or to frame begging by weavers as a decision not to accept low pay under a given amount.

---

[95]As cited in Galli, "Forestieri, inabili, miserabili", p. 63.

[96]Pluri-activity was so widespread in silk manufactures that the authorities started to distinguish by a special certificate the "real weavers by profession" from the rest of the workers; see Avellino, "Des fabricants, des ouvriers ou des oisifs?". A 1792 list of silk workshops and weavers compiled by the Chamber of Commerce of Como is full of annotations beside the names of the workers like "now he does tailoring", "now he is a sexton", "he does hairdressing too", "butcher", "now he is a fisherman", and so on; see Dello stato attuale delle manifatture di stoffe di seta, telai battenti e lavoranti …, SAMi, Commercio, p.a., 238.

[97]Giovanni Cazzetta, "Danno ingiusto e 'governo' della società fra distinzioni e unità valoriale del sistema", in Alessandro Somma et al. (eds), Dialoghi con Guido Alpa (Rome, 2018), p. 66.

Concerning institutions, by looking beneath the fiction of a contract between equals, it becomes clear that, after the guilds' abolition, the wage relationship's inherently asymmetric nature was not compensated by political authorities but reinforced by police measures, particularly concerning the mobility of workers.

Cite this article: Lorenzo Avellino. "They Have No Property to Lose": The Impasse of Free Labour in Lombard Silk Manufactures (1760–1810). *International Review of Social History*, 68:S31 (2023), pp. 135–155. https://doi.org/10.1017/S002085902200092X

International Review of Social History, 68:S31 (2023), pp. 157–175
doi:10.1017/S0020859022000906

RESEARCH ARTICLE

Mercenary Punishment: Penal Logics in the Military Labour Market

Johan Heinsen

University of Aalborg, Denmark, e-mail: heinsen@dps.aau.dk

Abstract
This article examines the entangled logics of corporal and carceral punishments of mercenary soldiers in eighteenth-century Denmark. Beginning with the story of a single man and his unfortunate trajectory through a sequence of punitive measures before his death as a prison workhouse inmate, the article looks at how punishments of soldiers communicated in multiple ways and were used to a variety of ends that were both typical and atypical within eighteenth-century society. It argues that soldiers experienced a breadth of both corporal and carceral punishments that were, in many cases, designed to limit otherness while communicating exemplarity along a fine-tuned spectrum of pain. The clearest example of this was running the gauntlet; a harrowing physical ordeal meted out by the offender's fellow soldiers. Turning to the carceral experiences often initiated by this ritual, it then examines how former mercenaries experienced convict labour differently from other occupational groups based on several factors. Their gender and occupational belonging meant they were funnelled towards specific penal institutions. Yet, their status as migrants and potential military labour meant they would often exit these institutions in specific ways. Whereas civilians often endured dishonouring punishments, ex-military convicts experienced punishments designed to inflict great pain without rendering them unfit for later military labour.

Introduction

By the mid-seventeenth century, the Danish state had created a standing army of mercenary soldiers. At the time, the Danish king's conglomerate included the separate kingdom of Norway, the German duchies of Schleswig and Holstein, and soon-to-be lost possessions in Sweden. These sprawling territories needed protection from the Swedish arch-enemy, with whom Denmark fought many wars. However, in creating a modern standing army, there were several precautions. Denmark's rural population (about eighty-five per cent of the total) was already bound, in various ways, to the land.[1] In 1733, this culminated in the system of *Stavnsbåndet* (sometimes translated as "Adscription"), in which all unmarried men outside of the major towns were bound to the estates on which they were born. In turn, for an immobilized male

---

[1] The legal frameworks binding peasants to both land and state until the coming of *Stavnsbåndet* is described at length in Thomas Munck, *The Peasantry and the Early Absolute Monarchy in Denmark 1660–1708* (Copenhagen, 1979).

workforce, estate holders were to organize a conscripted military reserve made up of such farmhands. If male peasants married, their constraints changed character as they typically became regulated by the tenant contracts with the landowners.[2] For this reason, recruiting Denmark's rural population to the standing army's regular regiments was impossible.[3] And while the towns grew over the period, most notably the capital of Copenhagen, this was far from a sufficient population basis for recruitment. Instead, migrant labour came to form the backbone of the state's military. The most important military labour market was Germany's patchwork of polities. There, Danish recruiters competed with those of other European powers for the labour of young men. The competition was cut-throat.[4]

Signing on, an act known as *kapitulation*, bound soldiers, typically for eight years at a time.[5] During this period, they had no right of resignation. They were stationed in garrisons highly concentrated on the Swedish borders, in Copenhagen, and in the duchies. The lives of mercenary soldiers were defined by the settings of the garrisons and by the poverty they experienced at the bottom of the urban labour market. One eighteenth-century observer, an Icelandic traveller and naval sailor, likened the whole thing to a trap.[6] The regiments regulated the ability of soldiers to establish their own households, as their employers had to grant them the right to marry.[7] While Lutheranism was a state religion, many mercenaries belonged to other creeds. Actual military work, in the sense of exercising and fighting, was, in most cases, limited, especially during the long period of peace that followed the conclusion of Denmark's conflict with Sweden as part of the Great Northern War in 1720. Instead, mercenaries formed an integral part of the urban markets for manual labour as day labourers or servants, although they always remained distinguishable by their uniforms. In his memoir, mercenary soldier Theodor Nübling recounted his experiences in Copenhagen in the 1780s; taking extra jobs was the only alternative to starvation. In a harrowing passage, he describes the effect of his first day as a hand at a shipyard, which literally stripped the skin off his shoulders. The following day, he had to participate in a drill, wearing his full uniform and musket. Similarly, the typical job as a removal man left him with open sores and tattered fingers. However, in such cases, at least he was able to eat. Looking back, he paints the hard labour and poverty

---

[2]Birgit Løgstrup, *Bundet til Jorden. Stavnsbåndet i praksis* (Copenhagen, 1787); Peter Henningsen, *Stavnsbåndet* (Aarhus, 2020).

[3]Karsten Skjold Petersen, "Den danske hærs hvervning af soldater i slutningen af 1700-tallet", *Fortid og Nutid* (2001), pp. 171–192, 172.

[4]On recruitment practices in this labour market, see Jeannette Kamp, "Between Agency and Force: The Dynamics of Desertion in a Military Labour Market, Frankfurt am Main 1650–1800", in Matthias van Rossum and Jeannette Kamp (eds), *Desertion in the Early Modern World: A Comparative History* (London, 2016), pp. 49–72. See also Michael Sikora, "Change and Continuity in Mercenary Armies: Central Europe, 1650–1750", in Erik-Jan Zürcher (ed.), *Fighting for a Living: A Comparative History of Military Labour 1500–2000* (Amsterdam, 2013), pp. 201–242.

[5]On *kapitulation*, see Petersen, "Danske hærs", p. 182; Karsten Skjold Petersen, *Geworbne Krigskarle. Hvervede soldater i Danmark 1774–1803* (Copenhagen, 2002), pp. 92–95.

[6]Arni Magnusson, *En Islandsk Eventyrer. Arni Magnussons Optegnelser* (Copenhagen, 1918), p. 103.

[7]On marriage status of soldiers, see Petersen, *Geworbne Krigskarle*, pp. 220–222.

as a punishment for the youthful recklessness that had led him to sign on.[8] There were alternative strategies, though: soldiers were notorious for stealing and other crimes such as fornication, fighting, and desertion, which scholars have recently interpreted as expressions of their social conditions.[9]

This article examines the logics that influenced their punishments. These employed a wide range of evolving and entangled punitive measures to various ends.[10] It is argued that three factors shaped these patterns: (a) that soldiers were men and that punishment in early modern Europe was fundamentally gendered; (b) that they were migrants and that, as unmarried, they were not themselves obligated by duties to care and coerce others; and (c) that they were military labourers in a context of immediate labour scarcity. Combined, these three elements help explain the variety of, sometimes contradictory, punishments experienced by mercenaries.

The article is structured in three parts. First, it looks briefly at the life story of a single man who experienced many of these punishments. He was not typical, but his punitive trajectory can help us tease out how different punitive practices intersected and entangled. The second part explores the evolving repertoire of corporal punishment exacted on mercenaries. Here, the article uses the framework developed by Guy Geltner in his book *Flogging Others* (2014) to highlight how these punishments were far from devoid of logics, despite their seemingly draconian character. Most importantly, it shows that while military labourers were subjected to a high degree of formalized physical punishment, their specific implementation often aimed at preserving their labour by limiting the production of social and legal otherness. The third and final part compares the experiences of those soldiers who became subject to penal labour with civilians suffering similar punishments. It is argued that the way that penal labour and incarceration were combined with specific forms of corporal violence, dishonouring, and deportation was often specific to this group and can only be understood by examining the interplay of gender, labour, and migrant status.

A Trajectory of Punishment

In the late afternoon of 20 July 1787, a group of convicts were working at the fortress of Kronborg by Elsinore. They were carting gravel. Convicts like these were known to their contemporaries as "slaves" and were immediately recognizable by the light chains they wore over their prison uniforms (see Figure 1).[11] Only men were

---

[8]Karsten Skjold Petersen, *Otte år i Danmark. En hvervet tysk soldats erindringer 1783–1791* (Copenhagen, 2005), pp. 43–49.

[9]Most notably, Tyge Krogh, "Larcenous Soldiers: Crime and Criminal Cultures in Copenhagen in the First Half of the Eighteenth Century", in Tyge Krogh, Louise Nyholm Kallestrup, and Claus Bundgaard Christensen (eds), *Cultural Histories of Crime in Denmark, 1500–2000* (London, 2018), pp. 129–144.

[10]On punitive pluralism, see Christian G. De Vito, "Punishment and Labour Relations: Cuba Between Abolition and Empire (1835–1886)", *Crime, History & Society*, 22:1 (2018), pp. 53–79. On the connection between punishment and labour, see also *idem* and Alex Lichtenstein, "Writing a Global History of Convict Labour", *International Review of Social History*, 58 (2013), pp. 285–325.

[11]On the semantics of penal "slavery", see Johan Heinsen, "Penal Slavery in Early Modern Scandinavia", *Journal of Global Slavery*, 6:3 (2021), pp. 343–368.

Figure 1. Nicolai Abildgaard (1743–1809), *En slave skubbende en trillebør* (A Slave Pushing a Wheelcart), undated.
Statens Museum for Kunst, Copenhagen.

subjected to this punishment, typically administered by the army, even if not all such convicts had military backgrounds. At night, the convicts slept in prison barracks. During the day, they laboured, typically on fortifications or other military infrastructure sites. Their work was overseen by soldiers and the so-called *slavegevaldigere* – a job often given to elderly petty officers. The convicts in question were working under a *slavegevaldiger* named Johannes Rungrafft. He was sixty-one years old and had served more than thirty years in Denmark's mercenary army. The convicts liked him because, in his own words, he "did not maltreat any slave that worked under him".[12]

In Rungrafft's work gang were many ex-soldiers. One of them was Johan Lichtmannicke. He had been born in Vienna forty-three years prior. He had never married. Like most foreign mercenaries, he had been recruited in Germany. He had served six of his eight years when he "sold a pair of shoes and therefore had to run the gauntlet, but then pretended to have killed a person", as he later recounted.[13] He appears to have served in the garrison of the capital. Thus, Lichtmannicke had resorted to crime but had attempted to manipulate the logics of punishment. Running the gauntlet was feared by many. It consisted of having to pass multiple times between two columns of fellow soldiers who were to strike you

---

[12]Rigsarkivet, Generalauditøren, Auditøren for Kronborg Fæstning, 1716–1912, F. Justitsprotokoller, 1752–1770 mm., nos 3–4, p. 108ff. Unless otherwise stated all translations are my own.

[13]*Ibid.*, pp. 110–112.

with a rod. Lichtmannicke was to do twelve passes. To avoid this, he had feigned murder, seemingly expecting to end his life at the hand of an executioner instead. To us, this choice, along with its method, seems puzzling. Still, in the eighteenth century, the spectacle of the gallows promised the individual a well-prepared end, assisted by a priest who would prepare you for the grace that Lutheran theology promised. This was such an alluring death that people would sometimes attempt to kill in order for themselves to be killed properly, instead of regular suicide, which carried a heavy stigma. This misuse of the law prompted a change in 1767 when it was decided that killing in order to kill yourself was no longer to prompt a swift end at the gallows but a lifetime in the slaveries or the prison workhouse, along with yearly floggings at the site of the murder.[14] Lichtmannicke was Catholic but evidently preferred Lutheran grace to the prolonged pain of the birches in the hands of his fellow soldiers. However, his story "was investigated and could not be proven, and therefore, he was sentenced to a lifetime of slavery".[15] Because he had not actually committed the fictitious murder, he was spared the yearly flogging. From his entry into the muster of the Copenhagen Slavery, it does, at least, appear as if he was not made to run the gauntlet. He entered the prison in northern Copenhagen on 11 January 1785. He worked the Copenhagen ramparts and military construction sites for about two years until, on 10 April 1787, he was transferred to Kronborg.[16]

As their crew was about to pick up and haul the last sleigh of gravel for the day, Lichtmannicke approached a fellow convict, Lars Brynildsen. Brynildsen had also been a mercenary soldier. He was Norwegian. Because *Stavnsbåndet* did not include the Norwegian parts of the composite state, regiments in Norway had a different composition than those in Denmark. Sometimes, Norwegians even found their way into the regiments garrisoned on Danish territories. Brynildsen had been part of a regiment based in rural Zealand when he had stolen and then deserted. Caught, he was sentenced to slavery in Copenhagen. There he had been part of a spectacular escape attempt in which he, along with four fellow ex-soldiers, had run from a worksite at the ramparts before trying to cross the channel separating Zealand and the smaller island of Amager. Each of Brynildsen's running mates drowned, but the Norwegian lagged behind and realized the danger just in time to turn back, making his way to shore where his pursuers apprehended him, beat him, and returned him to the prison.[17] Like Lichtmannicke, he was transferred to Kronborg, but for longer. He would later argue that he had not yet really come to know the Austrian newcomer. However, when Lichtmannicke asked Brynildsen if he could borrow his knife, he complied. Normally, Brynildsen used the small blade, about three inches long, to make wooden spoons in his spare hours in the slavery, thereby earning a little cash

---

[14]Tyge Krogh, *A Lutheran Plague: Murdering to Die in the Eighteenth Century* (Leiden, 2012). On the implementation of the punishment, see Emilie Luther Valentin, "Feelings of Imprisonment: Experiences from the Prison Workhouse at Christianshavn, 1769–1800" (Ph.D., Aalborg University, 2022), p. 91.

[15]Rigsarkivet, Generalauditøren, Auditøren for Kronborg Fæstning, 1716–1912, F. Justitsprotokoller, 1752–1770 mm., nos 3–4, pp. 110–112.

[16]Landsarkivet for Sjælland, Københavns Stokhus, Slaverulle, nos 34–35, 1777–1826, p. 686.

[17]Brynildsen's story is told at length in Johan Heinsen, "Runaway Heuristics", *Annals of the Fondazione Luigi Einaudi* (forthcoming).

to supplement the allowances on which convicts lived. Lichtmannicke claimed that he needed the knife to remove a corn.[18]

As the work concluded for the day, the convicts were mustered to return to the prison barracks. The *slavegevaldiger* Rungrafft walked next to the convicts. However, suddenly the officer felt acute pain "as if someone had hit him with a club". He waved his arms around, and the convicts were alerted. The convict Per Persen Broballe then noticed "that there was a knife in Rungrafft's neck" and immediately pulled it out. No one had seen Lichtmannicke stab the officer, but he immediately confessed to his fellow convicts amid the confusion. The next day, a summary court was held in the sick ward where Rungrafft had been placed. The wound was bad but not fatal, and the officer was conscious as he heard Lichtmannicke recount his story. The convict was suicidal and had hoped to end his life. He held no grudges against Rungrafft, who had "never done him anything wrong". Instead, he felt wronged on a different level: he had wanted to die since he was sent to the slavery, which he felt was "for a very small crime".[19] Two weeks later, when a follow-up interrogation was held, he still regretted nothing but added that his troubles had continuously worsened. His initial crime of selling his shoes, which, being part of his uniform, were not his to sell, had been committed from "need and starvation". He found his transfer to Kronborg had been an added punishment because "the slaves in Copenhagen have a better time and get a better allowance even if their work is much easier".[20] Indeed, the taxing work of securing the fortress against coastal erosion made Kronborg the worst place in Denmark to serve a sentence. While, seemingly, Lichtmannicke had done nothing to warrant his transfer, other convicts, like Brynildsen, were sent to the Elsinore fortress as an added punishment if they ran away, caused unrest, or acted violently.[21]

Of course, the 1767 decree meant that Lichtmannicke's hopes of using the law to his perceived advantage were futile. While he had committed a textbook suicide murder attempt, striking a well-liked officer without any premeditated ill feelings between them and, therefore, no ulterior motive, it was no longer possible to attain execution by such means. Instead, Lichtmannicke was transferred again. This time he was sent back to Copenhagen, but instead of going to another slavery, he was transferred to the other strand within Denmark's two-pronged prison system: the prison workhouse. While the military administered the slaveries, this composite institution had ties to the system of poor relief. Through the eighteenth century, the institution, especially the largest prison workhouse in the Copenhagen district of Christianshavn, had been found suitable to hold an ever-growing number of felons, made to perform intramural convict labour. In the courtyard of the towering complex, a *Rasphus* (rasp house; a small site for the punishment of male prisoners employed in hard labour) was used to hold some of those men considered too dangerous to incarcerate anywhere else. The rasp house inmates slept in cells at night and were made to rasp colonial dye-

---

[18]Rigsarkivet, Generalauditøren, Auditøren for Kronborg Fæstning, 1716–1912, F. Justitsprotokoller, 1752–1770 mm., nos 3–4, p. 113.

[19]*Ibid.*

[20]*Ibid.*, p. 112.

[21]Heinsen, "Runaway Heuristics".

woods to a fine powder. Lichtmannicke was spared the ritual of a yearly return to and flogging at the crime scene. After all, Rungrafft had lived, and, besides, an annual trip to Kronborg would have been a costly endeavour. Furthermore, this practice was falling out of favour.[22] He was, however, flogged and branded by the executioner before entry. This meant that he was legally stripped of honour. In eighteenth-century Denmark, honour was an almost material currency. You could have a lot or a little of it, or none, as was the case with people corporally punished by an executioner – typically in the form of public flogging, known as *kagstrygning*, sometimes combined with branding on the face or the back.[23] In the eighteenth century, dishonouring punishments were typically tied to lifelong convict labour without the chance of pardon. There was no way back after losing one's stake in the game of honour.

Now in the prison workhouse, Lichtmannicke was done trying to hack the law. Maybe he finally realized that suicide was not attainable by execution, as he had previously believed. However, he did not find that his fate had eased. On 23 April 1792, he "cut his own hand to avoid work".[24] We do not know for how long he was unable to dodge the labour, but since he was never transferred again, it cannot have been for long. He died a rasp house inmate on 29 October 1799. Most likely, he was buried by other convicts in the so-called Slave Churchyard on the outskirts of Copenhagen.[25] His story is exceptional but not unique. While his life trajectory suggests that he had a somewhat frail psyche, he is presented in the sources as coherent and makes a clear argument about his rationale. He was not alone either, as we know of a few handfuls of ex-soldiers who, as convicts, tried to kill in order to be killed, thereby trying to leverage the law in their attempts to avoid a lifetime of penal labour.[26] Furthermore, suppose we break Lichtmannicke's unusual trajectory into smaller parts. In that case, his experiences resonate with thousands of soldiers in eighteenth-century Denmark, accentuating common themes of poverty, otherness, and desperation.

Recent scholarship has highlighted these themes. For a long time, the history of the Danish military state and its workforces was written without paying much attention to the mercenary soldier. This has changed in the last twenty years. While this work predates or is otherwise unconnected to the recent concerns of military labour historians, the insights produced resonate clearly with the recent agenda of seeing soldiers first and foremost as workers.[27] The work of Karsten Skjold Petersen, culminating in

---

[22]Rigsarkivet, Generalauditøren, Auditøren for Kronborg Fæstning, F. Slavesager, 7, sentence of Lichtmannicke, 21 September 1787. On the easing of such punishments, see Valentin, *Feelings of Imprisonment*, p. 203.

[23]Tyge Krogh, *Oplysningstiden og det magiske. Henrettelser og korporlige straffe i 1700-tallets første halvdel* (Copenhagen, 2000), pp. 328–352.

[24]Rigsarkivet, Tugt-, Rasp- og Forbedringhuset på Christianshavn, Mandtalsbog for Børne- og Rasphuset, 1778–1811, p. 16.

[25]Valentin, *Feelings of Imprisonment*, pp. 160–161.

[26]For example: Rigsarkivet, Generalauditøren, Auditøren for Kronborg Fæstning, 1716–1912, F. Justitsprotokoller, 1752–1770 mm., nos 3–4, p. 78ff.; Rigsarkivet, Forsvarets Auditørkorps, Auditøren for Københavns fæstning, Justitsprotokol, no. 21, p. 52ff.; Rigsarkivet, Forsvarets Auditørkorps, Auditøren for Københavns fæstning, Justitsprotokol, no. 21, p. 826ff.; Rigsarkivet, Admiralitetet (Søetaten), Overadmiralitetsretten, Standretsprotokoller, 1724–1727, no. 49, fo. 137; Rigsarkivet, Forsvarets Auditørkorps, Auditøren for Københavns fæstning, Justitsprotokol, no. 19, p. 662ff.

[27]Zürcher, *Fighting for a Living*, pp. 11–14.

his doctoral thesis, subsequently published as *Geworbne Krigskarle* (2004), has high-lighted the integral part played by mercenaries in the Danish army while making a thorough examination of their social conditions. From his work emerges the image of the mercenary as a labourer used strategically by the state. Besides the work we would expect soldiers to perform, they were used in various settings. Regiments used soldiers as part of their recruitment efforts abroad, handing them over to the navy for use on their ships and using them as "crown workers" – cheap manual labourers in infrastructure construction and maintenance.[28] In the latter respect, they were part of logics of deployment that also included the convicts in the slaveries. For instance, crown workers were part of the large-scale project of creating a new naval base at Holmen in Copenhagen – a work that consisted, in part, of land recla-mation in the shallow waters north of Christianshavn. Convicts and naval sailors worked alongside them. Lichtmannicke is likely to have worked this site as a convict and, before that, possibly as a soldier too. At the same time, soldiers could also be commanded to interact with convicts as guards. To alleviate upkeep, a large part of the mercenary labour force was given the status of *frifolk*, literally "free people". The percentage varied but could be as high as fifty per cent.[29] When "free", the mer-cenary was unpaid but was allowed to work for wages, except when called on to exer-cise. This was attractive because the pay was much better, even at the lowest tiers of the urban labour market. Petersen describes their work: they worked in crafts (if they knew one), as manual workers in factories and workshops, as hands in construction or at the docks, and, in some settings, as rural servants. They could not become mas-ters or merchants but were employed as servants or day labourers. Much of this work was seasonal.[30] The possibility of roaming was limited since the soldier needed a passport to go beyond the garrison. If given passports, these would stipulate the con-ditions of the soldier's travels and violating them effectively made the person a deserter. Thus, while soldiers worked as integral parts of urban and rural labour mar-kets, their integration within local communities was limited by their military status. The same was the case in terms of their options to marry. A mercenary could not marry without the consent of the head of his regiment, who was only allowed to grant such permissions to thirty per cent of their workforce. This can be attributed partly to the state's realization that the soldier's pay could not provide for a family.[31]

Other scholars have highlighted how the presence of soldiers was a disruptive force in the urban community. Most soldiers lived as tenants in the households of others. This meant that they were subject to the authority of the head of their household while simultaneously subjected to the authority of their officers. As Camilla Schjerning has shown, this was a cause of disputes as the social geographies of the city blurred in ways exacerbated by the culture of violence and masculinity that defined the military community.[32] Furthermore, the legal pluralism of the cities'

---

[28]Petersen, *Geworbne Krigskarle*, pp. 160–162.

[29]*Ibid.*, pp. 167–69.

[30]*Ibid.*, pp. 206–207.

[31]*Ibid.*, p. 217.

[32]Camilla Schjerning, "Følelsesgeografier og Fællesskaber i København 1771–1800", *Temp – Tidsskrift for Historie*, 6 (2016), pp. 26–49; *idem*, "Moralske følelser og sociale relationer I København 1771–1800" (Ph.D., Copenhagen University, 2013).

complicated tangles of jurisdictions would sometimes spill into the streets. As high-lighted by Ulrik Langen, officers and their soldiers would sometimes compete for ter-ritory with their civilian counterparts.[33] In other instances, they would fight sailors in what can be considered turf wars tied to occupational identities.[34] Perhaps, the ambiguous presence of soldiers in the urban environment is most evident from stud-ies of their crimes. Historian Tyge Krogh has conducted an in-depth analysis of sol-diers' thefts in Copenhagen. Owing to the conditions under which they lived, Krogh traces a culture of larceny and fencing that was, ultimately, a product of the state but also a competitive European labour market for recruits that meant that recruiters did not always enquire deeply into the past of the potential recruit.[35] Therefore, it is not surprising that mercenaries formed the backbone of several gangs operating in the capital. Krogh argues that this was not "organized crime" in the modern sense but that social conditions perpetuated a widespread crime culture that enabled a market for stolen goods in which it was rarely hard to find a buyer.[36]

Thus, the seemingly draconian punishment meted out against Lichtmannicke when he sold his shoes in order to eat expressed a marked unease among urban elites facing an amorphous crowd of soldiers roaming the streets of the garrisons and deal-ing in things that often could not be accounted for. They upset a social order that still ultimately hinged on the household.

Violent Communication

Crucially, punishments cannot be understood only in the context of the ills they were to combat. Punitive forms were defined by law, but in reality, they were complex and evolving assemblages of practices, and care is needed to avoid the projection of sim-plified schemata.[37] Notably, we might be tempted to conjure up a clear divide between corporal punishments and forms of incarceration. Popular modernization narratives state that penal modernity was marked by a transition from one to the other: from the outward spectacle of the body at the gallows to the inward world of the penitentiary cell.[38] However, in Denmark, the prison (starting as a kind of

---

[33]Ulrik Langen, "Den æreløse ordensmagt. Kampen om byrummet mellem vægtere, gardere og pøbel i 1700-tallets København", *Fortid og Nutid*, 1 (2009), pp. 83–196. See also Petersen, *Geworbne Krigskarle*, p. 261ff.

[34]Joen Jakob Seerup, "Søetaten i 1700-tallet. Organisation, personel og dagligdag i 1700-tallets danske flåde" (Ph.D., Copenhagen University, 2010), pp. 207–209.

[35]Krogh, "Larcenous Soldiers", p. 141.

[36]*Ibid.*, p. 136.

[37]On punishment as assemblage, see Johan Heinsen, "Historicizing Extramural Convict Labour: Trajectories and Transitions in Early Modern Europe", *International Review of Social History*, 66:1 (2021), pp. 111–133.

[38]Michel Foucault, *Discipline and Punish: The Birth of the Prison* (London, [1975] 1977); Michael Ignatieff, *A Just Measure of Pain: The Penitentiary in the Industrial Revolution 1750–1850* (New York, 1978). While in the works of Foucault and Ignatieff this opposition undergirds an understanding of a rela-tively sudden change around 1800, linked to new institutional forms, it also structures narratives with longer arcs. For instance, a similar understanding underpins the interpretations inspired by the works of Norbert Elias. See, for example, Pieter Spierenburg, *The Prison Experience: Disciplinary Institutions and Their Inmates in Early Modern Europe* (Amsterdam, 1991).

auxiliary technology of convict labour) had existed since the mid-sixteenth century. It had grown incrementally since this point, while the uses of corporal punishments evolved alongside it in a pattern that appears far from linear.[39] As I have argued elsewhere, historians trying to understand the emergence of carceral institutions need to take stock of the empirical fact that their evolutions were often glacial and challenging to link to any one moment of modernity, in part because there was never just a single "prison" corresponding to a single "modernity".[40] In the early modern Danish case, there was no clear separation of the corporal and the carceral. Felons who arrived at the gates of prisons had often received corporal, sometimes dishonouring punishments as part of their journeys there, and discipline within the prisons was always upheld by the threat of violence mimicking the way punishments communicated outside the walls.

We should not be surprised by this. As the Danish prison system found its many forms only gradually, beginning in the sixteenth century, such institutions evolved in a culture that thought of violence as integral to social order.[41] In Lutheran Denmark, it was understood that authorities on all levels had a religious duty of both care and coercion, to the point that the two cannot be disentangled. As argued by cultural historian Nina Koefoed, this entanglement and obligation is embedded within the concept of *tugt* – a notion of religious discipline that accompanied the prison workhouses everywhere in continental Northern Europe, beginning in the late sixteenth century.[42] In Denmark, the prison system was bifurcated, with the notion of *tugt* clearly embedded in the prison workhouses, while understandings of military discipline underpinned the slaveries.

The Danish Code of 1683 marked an explicit formalization of the use of convict labour and thus incarceration. However, it also highlights the overlap between punishments targeting the body and those concerning labour: in no way did it do away with corporal punishments. The breadth of corporal punishments sanctioned by the code and its continuous modifications are staggering. They include various forms of whippings, some clearly tied to the logics of household *tugt*. The body, as a subject of pain and exemplarity, also played a clear role in punishments such as being locked in the pillory (*gabestok*) and in a set of punishments that, while not mentioned in the code, were still used widely in rural Denmark, such as being put on the "wooden horse" or in the "Spanish mantle", which similarly married degrees of physical discomfort with public shaming.[43] The body also played a role in the practice of punishing with hunger through short stints of incarceration on a diet of water and bread,

---

[39]Johan Heinsen, *Det første fængsel* (Aarhus, 2018); Fr. Stuckenberg, *Fængselsvæsenet i Danmark 1550–1741* (Copenhagen, 1893).

[40]Heinsen, "Historicizing Extramural Convict Labour", pp. 114–117.

[41]*Ibid.*

[42]Nina Koefoed, "I Trust You with My Child: Parental Attitudes to Local Authorities in Cases of Disobedient Children in 18th Century Denmark", *Journal of Historical Sociology*, 33:4 (2020), pp. 489–504; Maria Nørby Pedersen, "En Kristen Forsørgelse af Alle Fattige", in Nina Koefoed and Bo Kristian Holm (eds), *Pligt og Omsorg - Velfærdsstatens Lutherske Rødder* (Copenhagen, 2021), pp. 209–239. On the broader European context, see Spierenburg, *Prison Experience*; Falk Bretschneider, *Gefangene Gesellschaft. Eine Geschichte der Einsperrung in Sachsen im 18. und 19. Jahrhundert* (Konstanz, 2008).

[43]Valentin, *Feelings of Imprisonment*, p. 65.

and even in the practice of public confession, in which a sinner was forced to proclaim their sins in front of their congregation. The latter form was sometimes connected to punishments in the prison workhouse, where the ritual took place in the prison church.[44] Thus, most of these punishments could be experienced on one's path to prison, but they did not automatically lead one there. By contrast, that was, in effect, the case for all corporal punishments involving whippings by the executioner at the public shaming post known as the *kag* and for those who were branded, typically on the face or the back. These two forms often went together. In a few instances, the similarly dishonouring dismemberment of noses, ears, fingers, or hands could also be used in conjunction with convict labour. These mutilations predated prisons and had initially often been used in conjunction with banishment from one's local community but were reconfigured as the state took the reins of the penal system.[45] In this way, the carceral domain was intricately related to a range of corporal and shaming measures varying in severity and impact on the life trajectory of the punished. Prisons did not obsolete the use of executions either. The Danish code sanctioned various executions similarly connected to particular forms of maiming, such as severing specific limbs and multiple forms of public torture. Drowning and burning were also sanctioned for specific crimes, typically of a religious nature. Peculiarly, all these bloody theatres were scenes of grace. Sovereignty manifested doubly: in the excess of violence and the moderation of said violence. And grace often related the use of corporal and capital punishment to convict labour, as the latter was used as an alternative to the former, especially in the case of capital punishment. This had the added effect of preserving labour, though this only seems to have been the explicit logic of the practice in the late sixteenth and early seventeenth centuries.[46] The widespread use of commutations was, however, checked by religious orthodoxy, which dictated specific retribution in the cases of certain crimes.[47]

The military also employed many of these punishments, but their codes adjusted and added to the repertoire, sometimes pointing to different logics. Some corporal punishments could be meted out without a formal sentence. These were known as "corrections" and "arbitrary punishments". Their uses were regulated by a series of decrees to limit excessive use. Corrections were punishments meted out daily by officers, who used their canes to beat soldiers for disobedience or negligence. This parallels the right of heads of households to chastise their subjects. On the other hand, arbitrary punishments were decided only by the head of the regiment. The punishments employed in such instances were also less personal. They included being put on the wooden horse, being forced to carry weapons, a form known as *pælslutning*, in which the punished was chained to a pillar with their feet barely touching the ground, and *krumslutning*, in which the punished had their hands

---

[44]*Ibid.*, pp. 71–72.

[45]Tyge Krogh, *Staten og de besiddelsesløse på landet* (Odense, 1987).

[46]Heinsen, "Historicizing Extramural Convict Labour", p. 118.

[47]Bo Kristian Holm and Nina J. Koefoed, "En Luthersk Autoritet i Dansk Enevælde", in *idem* (eds), *Pligt og Omsorg. Velfærdsstatens Lutherske Rødder* (Copenhagen, 2021), pp. 79–101; Krogh, *Oplysningstiden*, pp. 99–118.

and feet fixed together and were left in this painful position for a set duration.[48] Crucially, these forms hinged on combining pain and shaming. If the soldier facing arbitrary punishments demanded to be brought before a formal court and sentenced according to the military articles, he had a right to be so. However, because a court procedure would leave a paper trail, this was usually not in his interest, given that many punishments were graded based on the offender's past run-ins with the law. Of course, some offences, like theft and desertion, were too grave not to warrant proper procedure.

The punishments enabled by the military codes included the disciplinary punishments mentioned above. However, they also contained graver measures directed principally at deserters and thieves. These included the practice of punishing deserters in absentia. In such cases, the runaway's name would be put to paper and the note posted on the gallows. The punishment communicated in several ways. First, it evoked the clauses in the law codes that enabled the hanging of deserters. Second, the association between the gallows and dishonour added a stigma to the punishment. Ironically, both these messages were somewhat blunted by two related facts: (1) deserters were very rarely hanged in peacetime, with commutations being standard practice and hanging being replaced with a lifetime in the slavery in 1763, and (2) while there was a perception of dishonour associated with the gallows, this practice did not legally dishonour the deserter perpetually, if he returned.[49] Thus, the lines of demarcation invoked by the punishment had, in practice, a degree of elasticity. Fundamentally, this meant that a deserter could still be taken back if he were apprehended or returned willingly. His labour would have been lost if he had been dishonoured (or hanged).

Similarly, the punishment of running the gauntlet communicated in specific ways. It was a harrowing ordeal.[50] Fears like the ones experienced by Lichtmannicke as he faced his initial punishment gain even more importance in light of a society where beatings were not unusual. Indeed, the repeated runs between one's fellow soldiers were painful, probably also more so than the counterparts in the civilian law codes in which an offender could be sentenced to public whippings by an executioner. With repeated runs, the number of strikes could range in the thousands, even on a single day. The fact that the codes included the standard practice of spreading the runs over several days if they exceeded a certain number indicates that lawmakers understood how much the practice placed a strain on the body. However, while deterrence hinged on this violence, the practice, in fact, preserved the potential labour power of the punished by not legally dishonouring them, given that the executioner was not involved.[51] Being dishonoured took away legal rights, such as the ability to bear witness against those with honour.[52] In the eighteenth century, dishonour effectively always entailed a lifetime prison sentence. Only in the last decade of the century did authorities slowly begin to commute such sentences and return the honour lost.

---

[48]Petersen, *Geworbne Krigskarle*, p. 133.

[49]Krogh, *Oplysningstiden*, p. 81.

[50]*Ibid.*, p. 80.

[51]On dishonourable professions, see Tyge Krogh, *The Great Nightmen Conspiracy: A Tale of the 18th Century's Dishonourable Underworld* (London, 2019); Tyge Krogh, "Bødlens og Natmandens Uærlighed", *Historisk Tidsskrift*, 3 (1994), pp. 30–51.

[52]Heinsen, "Penal Slavery in Early Modern Scandinavia".

Effectively, the dishonoured person left their community, never to return. A dishonoured soldier would never again be available to his regiment. While his labour could still be exploited as convict labour, he was a perpetual outsider. By contrast, a person who had run the gauntlet could be back on duty as soon as he had healed. And even those for whom running the gauntlet was the first step to a prison sentence could still be released back into the army. Further, the stigma of running the gauntlet was checked by the communal nature of the ritual. By making soldiers carry out the punishment, there was a limit to the ability to "other" the punished. Anecdotal evidence even suggests that soldiers felt sorry for those they were to punish.[53]

In this way, the seemingly draconian punishments enabled by the military codes communicated in ways that mediated the othering inherent to exemplary punishments. Historian Guy Geltner argues that a critical feature of corporal punishments is their use of the body to communicate. They do so in three "discrete yet often overlapping ways".[54] Corporal punishments *index* social otherness to an audience. In this way, they make the borders of a community tangible. This would be true of all punishments that involved an audience. The infliction of dishonour heightened the effects of indexing, while the brand could make such a limit perpetually readable on the punished body or face. Of course, the most extreme versions of indexing were in capital punishments, but these would sometimes also involve further reasoning. For instance, when crimes were collective, it was common practice to attempt to single out ringleaders and pardon those understood to have been seduced. When no ringleader could be identified, punishments would sometimes still play on this dynamic. For instance, groups of soldiers facing execution were, on rare occasions, made to publicly play dice with who was to die, while the rest would be sentenced to life in prison.[55] To draw the lines of a social world, authorities only needed to communicate in examples, and potential inclusion was often part of the message. Thus, while striking us as unjust, such measures would still "eliminate ambiguities regarding that society's normative boundaries".[56] Military corporal punishments communicated exemplarity to fellow soldiers but, at the same time, often took care not to create a perpetual other from the punished body unless this was perceived as absolutely necessary. At stake was the potential of inclusion and therefore labour. The scars on one's back left after running the gauntlet might achieve indexing, but not in ways that severed the scarred from normal work relations. Fundamentally, this hinged on the fact that the person to whom those scars communicated was themselves an insider to inflicting such marks.

The second mode of communication outlined by Geltner is that of *mimesis*. In this mode, corporal punishments communicated by mirroring the crime in the punishment. This could be literal or symbolic, as when, for instance, the hand of a person guilty of forgery was severed. Both military and civilian codes used mimesis in crimes relating to violence, most explicitly in cases of murder where the Old Testament

---

[53]Petersen, *Otte år i Danmark*, p. 43.

[54]Guy Geltner, *Flogging Others: Corporal Punishment and Cultural Identity from Antiquity to the Present* (Amsterdam, 2014), p. 26.

[55]Krogh, "Larcenous Soldiers", p. 139.

[56]Geltner, *Flogging Others*, p. 26.

underpinning of the codes meant that blood spilled had to be repaid in kind. Part of the importance of the 1767 decree under which suicide murderers were *not* to be executed lies in breaking with this orthodox principle of mimesis.

If mimesis played only a minor part in the communications of corporal punishments of soldiers in eighteenth-century Denmark, the obverse is the case with the third mode of communication: *numerical proportionality*. As Geltner points out, scholars have often overlooked this dimension of corporal punishment, understanding proportionality as an inherently modern principle of justice incompatible with the spectacle of violence.[57] However, almost all the punishments mentioned here could be graded according to the severity of the crime or circumstances meriting grace or escalation. This appears to have been especially true of military punishments in which the time on the wooden horse or locked in fetters could be modulated along with the number of passes through the gauntlet, the number of men in each column, and the duration over which the ritual of violence was to take place. In this way, military authorities operated a carefully tuned spectrum of pain. By contrast, the indexing dishonour inflicted by an executioner was not tied to a number.

Put together, we can say that the semiotics of military punishments in the period suggested an emphasis on creating a clear example, grading severity numerically, yet, ultimately, in the name of labour, limiting the otherness that exemplary punishments imparted, at least legally. As a result, corporal punishments could work as an integral part of the disciplinary machinery of the mercenary army without producing a further need for new recruits.

Mercenaries' Experiences of Penal Slavery

As highlighted by Lichtmannicke's trajectory, Denmark's carceral system consisted in two parallel tracks, of which he saw the worst parts. Both revolved around the performance of labour as punishment, but on other matters, they were fundamentally different. One was the prison workhouses, where convicts performed intramural labour in textile manufacturing. The other was the so-called slaveries, where convicts laboured for the military state. The prison workhouse was directed at the civilian population. At the start of the century, it housed a distinctly gendered population of women and children, but as the century marched on, it came to house more and more men sentenced for graver and graver offences.[58] The largest of the kind was the multitiered institution at Christianshavn, where upwards of 600 inmates worked in various wards, including the rasp house that housed Lichtmannicke for the last twelve years of his life. However, as a former soldier, the Austrian was a rare sight within the walls. Mostly, ex-soldiers were put in chains and sent to the slaveries. There they joined a homosocial world directed by the military, though it was not only soldiers that became "slaves". Looking at the inmates' registers of the Copenhagen Slavery (Stokhusslaveriet), ex-soldiers experienced 1181 of the 3190 stays recorded in the institution from 1741 (when the institution opened and took over the duties and population of the naval dockyard slavery known as Trunken)

---

[57]*Ibid.*, p. 27.
[58]Valentin, *Feelings of Imprisonment*, pp. 75–114.

to 1800.[59] In the same period, civilians experienced 1185 stays, while former naval workers accounted for 437 stays. People listed as recidivists and those transferred to the institution from other prisons accounted for the remainder, with a small number (forty-one) having no disclosed background.[60]

Through this period, the musters were systematic in listing the sentence as well as the corporal punishments the newly arrived inmate had endured just prior to entry. They were also systematic in noting how the stay ended. This data can therefore be used to sketch out how the carceral experiences of ex-soldiers related to their prior experiences of punishment and compared to the other main social groups within the institution. The notes about corporal punishments can be sorted into three distinct categories: no corporal punishment (as part of the sentence at least), non-dishonouring corporal punishments (such as running the gauntlet or naval flogging with the cat), and dishonouring punishments (typically whipping and/or branding by the executioner, but in some cases of people already dishonoured, flogging by a dishonoured convict within the prison itself).

The numbers support the above reading that prison was far from an alternative to corporal punishment. More than half of the inmates arrived as part of punitive sequences involving corporal punishment as part of their sentence. However, as shown in Table 1, the occupational divides presented a divide in degree and kind.

Naturally, we would expect a kind of hierarchy of pain in which having undergone no corporal punishment before entry would entail a milder prison sentence. This was the case for civilians and sailors but not for soldiers. Here, we see that those who arrived without having undergone corporal punishment as part of the sentence were, in fact, more likely to carry lifetime sentences than those who had received military corporal punishments. By far the most common of these punishments was to have run the gauntlet. However, those who had done so were often still considered to belong to the military. In this sense, the 51.6 per cent of the ex-military convicts who had received non-dishonouring corporal punishments were, in many cases, still considered by their regiments as potential workers. Had they received dishonouring corporal punishment, no ordinary release would have been possible. Thus, we can say that while soldiers (and sailors) were more likely to enter convict labour with scarred backs, those scars did not communicate perpetual otherness as the scars or brands carried by their civilian counterparts. Rather, they effectively communicated a kind of "suspended belonging" to the military sector.

This becomes clear as we look at the mode of final exit of soldiers. Exit has been categorized into death, escape (in which case the escape was the final mode of exit, discounting failed attempts), release, deportation, recapitulation (meaning entering back into mercenary service), and transfer to another prison. Of course, that last category was not really a final exit, but the sources do not allow us to systematically trace all men who, like Lichtmannicke and Brynildsen, were sent elsewhere. Deportation and recapitulation must be considered as variants of release. They have been noted

---

[59] The reason for dealing with "stays" instead of people, is that there were quite a lot of people with the same common patronyms. In the case of native Danes especially, it can be difficult to surmise whether the same person accounted for multiple stays.

[60] The musters are found in Landsarkivet, Københavns Stokhus, Slaverulle, boxes nos 32, 33, and 34–35.

Table 1. Corporal punishment at entry into the Copenhagen Slavery by occupational group, 1741–1799.

	Army	Navy	Civilian
No corporal punishment	430 (36.7%)	145 (33.2%)	810 (69.0%)
Non-dishonouring corporal punishment	605 (51.6%)	241 (55.1%)	65 (5.5%)
Dishonouring corporal punishment	138 (11.8%)	51 (11.7%)	299 (25.5%)
Total	1173 (100%)	437 (100%)	1174 (100%)

only when the musters explicitly mention such exits, but a greater number of such exits are likely to be hidden in the data on instances when a convict is simply noted as "released". In Table 2, the mode of exit of ex-soldiers is listed according to their experiences of corporal punishment prior to entry.

Fundamentally, dishonour was a determinant of exit. The dishonoured ex-soldiers, almost all of whom carried life sentences, were more likely to die or be transferred than their non-dishonoured counterparts. Because there were no hopes of getting a pardon until 1791, this makes sense. So does their propensity to escape. However, it should be noted that dishonoured ex-soldiers were more likely to escape than their civilian and naval counterparts (twenty-one and eighteen per cent of those escaped as final exit). The reason might be that, as foreigners, few had families in Denmark. Therefore, they would be harder to track and have fewer qualms about leaving the country.

Their status as migrants also explains the common use of deportation for ex-soldiers. Deportation was used in the cases of migrant ex-soldiers who were deemed of no potential use to the military. As shown here, even dishonoured convicts could be released this way, but usually, only soldiers were, owing to their status as foreigners. Only four dishonoured non-soldiers are mentioned to have been deported in the muster. Ex-soldiers who had received non-dishonouring corporal punishments were also deported, while it appears less common that those who had received no corporal punishments were deported. Deportation happened by boat. In a few instances, deportation is listed as part of a sentence that was to conclude after a set duration. This was the case for several ex-soldiers who had been found to have already been dishonoured prior to their recruitment but had tried to hide their past. They were also the only exceptions to the rule that dishonour entailed a lifetime sentence. For instance, the soldier Gottfried Schreiber, originally from the town of Legnica in what is today Poland, arrived in March 1769 on account of a case of theft and desertion, but during the trial, it had been revealed that he had previously been whipped by an executioner in Danzig. His sentence was explicit about his eventual deportation, which was natural given his dishonour. However, first, he was to endure three days' worth of whippings by a dishonoured convict before spending a year in prison. In April of the following year, he was sent on a packet boat to Lübeck.[61] Typically, however, deportation concluded a lifetime sentence and was therefore contingent on a pardon given by the king. Petitions could influence such a pardon. For instance,

---

[61]Landsarkivet for Sjælland, Københavns Stokhus, Slaverulle, no. 32, 1741–1770, entry #1319.

Table 2. Exit of ex-soldiers from the Copenhagen Slavery, having entered 1741–1799.

	Death	Escape	Release	Deportation	Recapitulation	Transfer	Total
No corporal punishment	58 (14%)	64 (15%)	160 (38%)	31 (7%)	33 (8%)	78 (18%)	424 (100%)
Non-dishonouring corporal punishment	79 (13%)	39 (6%)	120 (20%)	101 (17%)	181 (30%)	81 (13%)	601 (100%)
Dishonouring corporal punishment	41 (30%)	37 (27%)	6 (4%)	19 (14%)	0 (0%)	33 (24%)	136 (100%)

the ex-soldier Johan Paul Ritter was pardoned from the slavery at Kronborg in 1758 after a petition from his brother, who pledged to follow him to Königsberg.[62] In this way, the acts of grace that were a key component of the communicative workings of corporal punishments also defined many carceral trajectories. It appears as part of the condition that the deported person would face a lifetime in a slavery if they returned.[63]

Deportation was an end specific to (some) soldiers on account of their migrant status. Recapitulation, on the other hand, was an exit defined by their status as potential labourers. While naval men could also be released on condition of returning to naval service, this appears significantly more common for soldiers.[64] Recapitulation typically appears to have been conditioned on the period of capitulation being reset to begin from the start. For instance, when Mathias Hauschildt was pardoned after enduring seven years of a lifetime sentence and released from Kronborg into a regiment in 1758, the note to the fortress commander explicitly stipulated that his bondage to the regiment was to start over.[65] This practice reflected the standard practice that all punishments for desertion would reset the period of service.[66] Sometimes pardoned convicts would enter into new regiments, but in cases of convicts carrying sentences for a set duration, the regiments explicitly stated at the initiation of the stay whether they wanted the convict to return at the conclusion of the stay.[67] In such cases, sentences were sometimes cut short at the request of heads of regiments.[68]

Both recapitulation and deportation were more common for those who had received a non-dishonouring corporal punishment than those who had not received any corporal punishment at all. We can interpret this as a consequence of what was communicated by the scars of those convicts whose punishment started with running the gauntlet. They were still considered military workers, but their potential use was to be evaluated. If deemed useful, they would re-enter the regiments. If not, they would be expelled from the realms.

Conclusion

The (entangled) corporal and carceral punishments of mercenary soldiers were related to three (entangled) attributes. First, they were defined by their gender, as both corporal punishments and carceral institutions were divided based on sex. This was accentuated by their military affiliation, as few ex-soldiers entered the prison workhouse but remained in the military domain as convict labourers in the homosocial world of the slaveries. Second, the migrant status of many mercenaries

---

[62]Rigsarkivet, Generalauditøren, Auditøren for Kronborg Fæstning, F. Slavesager, 7, pardon for Johan Paul Ritter, 13 September 1758.

[63]This is for instance explicit in Rigsarkivet, Generalauditøren, Auditøren for Kronborg Fæstning, F. Slavesager, 7, pardon for Frantz Ladeberg, 18 April 1759.

[64]An example of a sailor doing so is the famous case of Arni Magnusson who describes it in his memoir. See Magnusson, *Eventyrer*, p. 116.

[65]Rigsarkivet, Generalauditøren, Auditøren for Kronborg Fæstning, F. Slavesager, 7, release note for Mathias Hauschildt, 26 November 1759.

[66]Petersen, *Geworbne Krigskarle*, p. 139.

[67]Rigsarkivet, Generalauditøren, Auditøren for Kronborg Fæstning, F. Slavesager, 7, instructions for the commander at Kronborg, 21 January 1741.

[68]Rigsarkivet, Generalauditøren, Auditøren for Kronborg Fæstning, F. Slavesager, 7, pardon for Johan Jacob Bernhardt, 25 January 1755.

meant that they were seen as potential subjects for deportation. This option was not explicitly listed in the codes. Still, it came into existence through the widespread use of pardons and commutations by which the sovereign performed his grace while simultaneously getting rid of unwanted people. Ironically, this meant that while dishonoured civilians had no way to exit alive except through escape, dishonour meant something else to migrant mercenaries. Third, the labour resource of mercenary soldiers inflected on punishments in several respects. This makes sense, given the competitive nature of the international military labour market and the upfront costs of bringing in a new recruit from abroad. The heavy use of running the gauntlet, a measure that was spectacularly violent but not dishonouring, is explained by this. This punishment also combined with stints in the slaveries in specific ways. In many cases, the convict whose prison stay had ritually been instated by the rods held by his fellow soldiers was still seen as one of them.

It should be noted that military punishments also inflected on the penal system. The practice of having convicts punished by the hands of other convicts, as was the case of Schreiber, might be an example of this, though the connection is unclear. The use of various forms of flogging when convicts in the slaveries transgressed the rules of the prison were clearly shaped by military practices, just as the everyday "correction" exerted fell under the auspices of the mandates for officers to correct their soldiers.[69] A less one-to-one transfer occurred as the prison workhouses in the early nineteenth century implemented new disciplinary codes that carried an evident influence from the military, including the use of specifically military forms of corporal punishment such as *krumslutning*. This might be connected to the fact that the man appointed as director of the central prison workhouse at Christianshavn in 1810 was a former commandant from the fortress of Kronborg, while his predecessors had been civilian officials.[70] How the naval instrument of the cat o' nine tails migrated into the carceral domain is less clear, though it appears to have happened around the same time.[71] It was commonly used to discipline penitentiary inmates throughout the nineteenth century.[72] More puzzling is how informal military codes shaped the hierarchies among inmates themselves. In the slaveries, ex-soldiers were over-represented among ringleaders in mutinies and collective escapes.[73] From a few cases dating to the 1720s, we know that such leaders among the inmates enacted their internal discipline against their fellow convicts in cases of suspected theft or snitching by using military forms of punishments. Thus, when ex-soldiers were to discipline their fellow convicts, they made them run the gauntlet too.[74]

---

[69]Heinsen, "Penal Slavery in Early Modern Scandinavia".

[70]Valentin, *Feelings of Imprisonment*, p. 279.

[71]Its use in the prison workhouse in the 1830s is described in detail from the perspective of an onlooker in Christian Kjær, *Forbryderen Christian Kjer hans Liv og Levnet* (Rudkjøbing, 1860), p. 108.

[72]The penitentiary museum Fængslet in the defunct penitentiary in the town of Horsens displays the cat o' nine tails used in the institution as part of its permanent collection.

[73]Johan Heinsen, *Mutiny in the Danish Atlantic World* (London, 2017), pp. 125–144.

[74]The case is described in detail in Heinsen, *Første Fængsel*, p. 50.

Cite this article: Johan Heinsen. Mercenary Punishment: Penal Logics in the Military Labour Market. *International Review of Social History*, 68:S31 (2023), pp. 157–175. https://doi.org/10.1017/S0020859022000906

International Review of Social History, 68:S31 (2023), pp. 177–195
doi:10.1017/S0020859022000918

Absolute Obedience: Servants and Masters on Danish Estates in the Nineteenth Century

Dorte Kook Lyngholm (ID)

Viborg Museum, Viborg, Denmark, e-mail: dkl@viborg.dk

Abstract

This article examines legal relations between estate owners and their servants and workers on Danish estates in the nineteenth century. From the end of the eighteenth century onwards, the traditional privileged role of Danish estate owners was changing, and their special legal status as "heads of household" over the entire population on their estates was slowly being undermined. The article investigates the relationship between estate owners and their servants and workers in legislation and court cases during these times of change. It examines the Danish servant acts from 1791 and 1854 and identifies the asymmetric order of subordination and superiority in this legislation. The core of the relationship was still a "contractual submission" that, to some extent, was private and unregulated by law, and estate owners were entitled to impose sanctions and physical punishment on their servants and workers according to their own judgement. When the Servant Law of 1854 abolished estate owners' right to punish adult servants physically, it was a significant break from the old legal order. However, a central element in the legislation, before and after 1854, was that servants' and workers' disobedience towards estate owners was illegal. By analysing court cases, the article examines the borderlands of the legal definition of disobedience. The elasticity in the legal system was substantial – and frequently favoured the owners. In the legal system, the notion of disobedience served to protect the last remnants of the traditional legal order of submission and superiority.

In early modern Denmark, the masters' right to punish workers and servants was protected by state law. In rural districts, the private noble estates and the estate owners' personal privileges constituted the framework of this punitive system. Private estates were the mainstay of the lives of the rural population, and the copyhold system was the foundation of the economic, social, and working conditions of large parts of the population. During the time of absolute monarchy in the 1700s, the expanding state's local administrative structure and judicial system were largely based on the existing system of estates and estate owners' personal authority.[1] State and private justice on the estates were intertwined, and the estate owners administered important

---

[1] Birgit Løgstrup, *Jorddrot og offentlig administrator. Godsejerstyret indenfor skatte- og udskrivningsvæsenet i det 18. århundrede* (Copenhagen, 1983); Lotte Dombernowsky, *Lensbesidderen som amtmand. Studier i administrationen af fynske grevskaber og baronier 1671–1849* (Copenhagen, 1983); Jonathan Finch and Kristine Dyrmann, "Estate Landscapes in Northern Europe: An Introduction", in Jonathan Finch et al. (eds), *Estate Landscapes in Northern Europe* (Aarhus, 2019), pp. 13–36.

parts of criminal justice.[2] In Danish research, this system has been referred to – inspired by Max Weber's ideal type – as "the patrimonial household".[3] In this system, the estate was perceived as a parallel to the small individual household, with the estate owner being the head of a "family" that included the entire estate population. In the 1700s, the estate population was thus part of two punitive systems: the emerging "public" criminal justice system of the state and the traditional "private" punitive system of the estate owners. The private punitive system was protected by state laws that, in certain matters, left the estates as enclaves with considerable legal autonomy.

The agrarian revolution beginning in the latter part of the 1700s eroded the foundation of this social and legal order. The public administration of criminal justice was transferred to the state exclusively, and the estate owners' private right to inflict corporal punishment on the copyholders was abolished. These changes and their effect on punishment as a tool for managing the workforce on Danish estates is the point of departure for this article. The article examines the development of the punitive structure between estate owners and their workforce from the late 1700s to the late 1800s. The analysis includes punitive measures towards the two main groups of workers on Danish estates in the period: live-in servants and corvée workers. It examines the development of the traditional punitive system in the legislation from 1791 to 1854 and in court cases between estate owners and workers from the 1830s and 1870s. During these times of change, the article identifies *obedience* as an important entry point into the study of punishment and labour management. It examines how the legal demand for workers' obedience was a crucial tool in the estate owners' efforts to remain in control of their workforce during the process that led to the final elimination of the traditional private punitive system.

The Legal Privacy of the Household

The legal relationship between Danish estate owners and their workers after the agrarian revolution features in Anette Faye Jacobsen's research on the evolution from a collective to an individual legal culture from the late 1600s to the early 1900s. Her work is mainly based on normative sources but also includes some interesting examples of local legal practice in 1797 and 1853.[4] Jørgen Mührmann-Lund has dealt extensively with the procedures of the urban police courts, investigating the legal practice in trials concerning rural servants and corvée workers around 1800.[5] Hanne Østhus has examined master–servant relationships in Danish–Norwegian cities in law and practice between 1750 and 1850.[6] And Vilhelm Vilhelmsson has investigated labour relations in Iceland in the 1800s and master–

---

[2]Dorte Kook Lyngholm, *Godsejerens ret. Adelens retshåndhævelse i 1700-tallet. Lov og praksis ved Clausholm birkeret* (Viborg, 2013).

[3]Anette Faye Jacobsen, *Husbondret. Rettighedskulturer i Danmark 1750–1920* (Copenhagen, 2008), pp. 31–36. Unless otherwise stated, all translations are mine.

[4]Jacobsen, *Husbondret*, pp. 153–186, 293–310.

[5]Jørgen Mührmann-Lund, *Borgerligt regimente. Politiforvaltningen i købstæderne og på landet under den danske enevælde* (Copenhagen, 2019), pp. 377–381.

[6]Hanne Østhus, *Contested Authority: Master and Servant in Copenhagen and Christiania, 1750–1850* (Florence, 2013).

servant relations in rural Sweden during the agrarian revolution by Carolina Uppenberg.[7]

Some Scandinavian research has interpreted the relationship between masters and servants in the light of the Lutheran doctrine of the three estates consisting of commanding and obeying positions, often emphasizing the mutual duties and obligations within the household.[8] The asymmetrical power relationship between servants and masters has been addressed with analyses of the special character of the private sphere surrounding this relationship. Anette Faye Jacobsen has argued that (small and large) households were basic social and legal entities that constituted parallel orders with considerable legal autonomy from the state.[9] Sølvi Sogner has made similar observations in her research on the legal status of servants in Norway, where she describes the world of the household in the following terms: "a very private arena [...] where angels, let alone lawmakers, might well fear to tread".[10]

Other studies have considered the special status of the household and the apparent opposition between the contractual and patriarchal elements of the relationship between master and servant within the household. In his studies of the Augustenborg castle, Mikkel Venborg Pedersen has noted that the great households of the early modern period rested on an unclear duality of contractual relationships and family ties that held advantages for the servant but also contained control and risk of abuse from the master.[11] In his research on the conditions of Swedish servants, Börje Harnesk has also emphasized that, as compensation for wages, a servant had to submit to an unequal patriarchal structure.[12] Christer Lundh has described the legal implications of the specific contractual conditions of servants in his studies of Swedish servant legislation: "The decision to take up service or to hire a servant was made freely, but as soon as the employment agreement was made, a relation of subordination and superiority was also established."[13] To take up service involved entering into a contract, one consequence of which was that the contractee entered into an area where state legislation provided a framework but left important measures – such as the punishment of the servant – to the masters' judgement.

---

[7]Vilhelm Vilhelmsson, "The Moral Economy of Compulsory Service: Labour Regulations in Law and Practice in Nineteenth-Century Iceland", unpublished paper presented at the European Social Sciences History Conference, Leiden, 2021; Carolina Uppenberg, *I husbondens bröd och arbete. Kön, makt och kontrakt i det svenska tjänstefolksystemet 1730–1860* (Gothenburg, 2018); idem, "The Servant Institution During the Swedish Agrarian Revolution: The Political Economy of Subservience", in Jane Whittle (ed.), *Servants in Rural Europe 1400–1900* (Woodbridge, 2017), pp. 167–182, 171.

[8]Nina Javette Koefoed, "Authorities Who Care: The Lutheran Doctrine of the Three Estates in Danish Legal Development from the Reformation to Absolutism", *Scandinavian Journal of History*, 44:4 (2019), pp. 430–453.

[9]Jacobsen, *Husbondret.*

[10]Sølvi Sogner, "The Legal Status of Servants in Norway from the Seventeenth to the Twentieth Century", in Antoinette Fauve-Chamoux (ed.), *Domestic Service and the Formation of European Identity* (Bern, 2004), pp. 175–187, 187.

[11]Mikkel Venborg Pedersen, "Det augustenborgske hof. Organisation og praksis", *Herregårdshistorie*, 17 (2021), pp. 77–91; idem, *Hertuger. At synes og at være i Augustenborg 1700–1850* (Copenhagen, 2005), pp. 177–185.

[12]Börje Harnesk, "Patriarkalism och lönarbete. Teori och praktik under 1700- och 1800-talen", *Historisk Tidskrift*, 3 (1986), pp. 326–355.

[13]Christer Lundh, *Life Cycle Servants in Nineteenth Century Sweden: Norms and Practice* (Lund, 2003), p. 2.

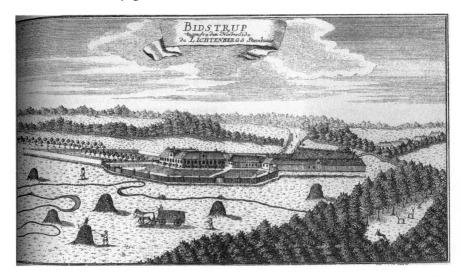

Figure 1. Bidstrup Manor in 1767, harvest time on the estate's main farmland. In the 1700s, the workforce on Danish estates could be punished physically by their masters, the estate owners. In the legislation, chastisement was linked specifically to the workers' duty to show obedience towards their masters. *Copper engraving by Jonas Haas from Erik Pontoppidan's Danish Atlas 1763–1781.*

This article examines this private arena of masters and servants. Analysing legislation and court cases, it investigates the boundaries of this private space and the changing connections to the state surrounding the large households of the estates.[14] Within this private area, the article specifically studies punishment as a tool for managing and controlling the workforce. It examines how the intimate connection between punishment and the demand for obedience could provide an effective strategy for the masters in a legal context during these times of change (Figure 1).

The Prohibition of Disobedience in the Laws of 1791 and 1854

During the 1800s, the legislation of the Danish state was the framework for controlling the workforce. The legislation contained specific rules for certain elements of the relationship between heads of household and the workforce. At the same time, it left a private area of control and punishment. This article deals with the two large groups of workers on the estates of the 1800s: (1) live-in servants (*tjenestefolk*) and (2) corvée workers (*hoveriarbejdere*). These two groups performed very different types of work and were subject to different legislation. Some were parts of other hierarchies and families, but their roles were similar regarding their position in the patrimonial household. When performing work at the estates, they were all subordinates of the estate owner.

---

[14]Lorenzo Avellino's contribution to this Special Issue is an interesting example that this transition from "private" to "state" punitive systems has striking parallels in different legal, social, and economic settings.

(1) The first group included unmarried, contractually employed women and men who lived and worked at the estates and had long-term contracts. Most of these servants were young, working at the estates before they married and established their own households. This type of servant has been identified as an integral element in the so-called European Marriage Pattern, where relatively late marriage was preceded by the circulation of young unmarried men and women as servants between households.[15] They have been referred to as "life-cycle servants" as their employment was not permanent but reflected a specific period in the lives of society's young women and men.[16] This group included the domestic servants in the estate owner's household and those who provided labour in the farm production.

During the first half of the 1800s, all servants in rural Denmark were covered by a special law defining the legal framework of their lives: the regulation relating to several aspects of the police work in rural Denmark of 23 March 1791 (the Police Regulation of 1791).[17] The introduction of this regulation mentions the "mutual rights and obligations" of the head of the household and the servants. However, this is mainly a law that defined servants as subordinate to their heads of household, and the basic premise of this regulation was that it was illegal to be unemployed. It was the duty of the landless rural population to enter into permanent employment, and if they did not, they could be punished for vagrancy. It was only possible for servants to change their jobs twice a year, either on 1 May or 1 November, and notice had to be given at least twelve weeks in advance and with witnesses. Specific sections of the regulation define the rules for observance and breach of the service contracts.

(2) As mentioned above, the second group of workers were people connected to the estates through the corvée system. Corvée was the work that copyholders (*fæstebønder*) and smallholders (*husmænd*) were obliged to carry out for the estate owner as a part of their copyhold arrangement. This form of work was still widely practised on estates during the first half of the 1800s.[18] The corvée of the copyholders was subject to a regulation that, like the Police Regulation mentioned above, was passed on 23 March 1791: the regulation regarding the enforcement of good conduct in connection with corvée at the Danish estates (the Corvée Regulation of 1791).[19] On

---

[15]John Hajnal, "Two Kinds of Preindustrial Household Formation System", in Richard Wall *et al.* (ed.), *Family Forms in Historic Europe* (Cambridge, 1983), pp. 65–104; Whittle, *Servants in Rural Europe*, p. 2.

[16]Peter Laslett, *Family Life and Illicit Love in Earlier Generations* (Cambridge, 1977), p. 34; Sheila McIsaac Cooper, "From Family Member to Employee: Aspects of Continuity and Discontinuity in English Domestic Service, 1600–1800", in Antoinette Fauve-Chamoux (ed.), *Domestic Service and the Formation of European Identity* (Bern, 2004), particularly p. 278ff.; Sogner, "The Legal Status of Servants", p. 184; Lundh, *Life Cycle Servants*, pp. 1–14; Kussmaul, *Servants in Husbandry*, p. 4; Hanne Østhus, "Servants in Rural Norway c.1650–1800", in Whittle, *Servants in Rural Europe*, pp. 113–130, 113.

[17]Published in Jacob Henrik Schou, *Chronologisk Register over de Kongelige Forordninger og Aabne Breve, samt andre trykte Anordninger, som fra Aar 1670 af ere udkomne*, vols 1–28 (Copenhagen, 1777–1850). Available at: https://www.hf.uio.no/iakh/tjenester/kunnskap/samlinger/tingbok/lover-reskripter/schous-forordninger/ (Forordning om adskilligt, der vedkommer Politievæsenet paa Landet i Danmark); last accessed 17 November 2022.

[18]Carsten Porskrog Rasmussen, "Gård og gods", in John Erichsen and Mikkel Venborg Pedersen (eds), *Herregården*, 4 vols, I: *Gods og samfund* (Copenhagen, 2009), pp. 163–240.

[19]Published in Schou, *Chronologisk Register* (Forordning ang. hvorledes god Orden skal haandthæves ved Hoveriet paa Jorde-Godserne i Danmark).

31 January 1807, a separate regulation was passed regarding the corvée of the small-holders: the regulation regarding the enforcement of good conduct in connection with the weekly or other compulsory work carried out by smallholders in Denmark (the Smallholder Regulation of 1807).[20]

These two regulations primarily aimed at safeguarding the interests of the estate owners by ensuring that work in the fields of the estates was carried out without irregularities. The main rule for the copyholders was that they had to be notified the evening before the work had to be carried out, but that the estate owner had the right to summon them immediately with unexpected work. The working hours in the field were set at ten hours a day, excluding breaks. However, the Corvée Regulation of 1791 also stipulated that the servants of the copyholders could not refuse to work longer hours if the copyholders thought that they were able to work more than ten hours a day. In addition, the regulation included detailed provisions regarding punishments for carelessness, being late for work, or not turning up.

By the mid-nineteenth century, the legislation on servants' disobedience was revised. The 1800s was a turbulent period for the Danish estates, and the transition of copyholds to freeholds gradually removed the structural foundation of the rural population's corvée until it was finally abolished by law in 1850. However, during the second half of the century, the estates continued to farm on a large scale, and the workforce primarily consisted of contractually employed live-in servants.[21] To cover this group, a new law was passed on 10 May 1854: the Servant Law for the Kingdom of Denmark (the Servant Law of 1854).[22] The new law abolished compulsory service and the system that only allowed servants to change their jobs twice a year. The existing regulations regarding service contracts were expanded, but the fundamental inequality enshrined in the Police Regulation of 1791 was maintained.

One of the most notable expressions of the subordinate role of the rural servants and corvée workers in the legislation of the 1800s was their legally defined duty to show obedience towards the estate owners. For the copyholders, the demand of obedience had been fixed by law as early as 1683 in the Danish Code's section 3-13-1, which stipulates that a copyholder owed submissiveness and obedience to his estate owner. This section was repeated in the first paragraph of the Corvée Regulation of 1791. The Smallholder Regulation of 1807 §1 included a similar statement ordering submissiveness and obedience. The same demands were put on the servants, who, in §14 of the Police Regulation of 1791, were ordered to show obedience towards their head of household.

The legislation allowed the servants and corvée workers in rural Denmark to be subjected to corporal punishment, and the estate owners and their representatives could execute this punishment themselves. This piece of legislation rests on an

---

[20]Published in Schou, *Chronologisk Register* (Forordning ang. hvorledes god Orden skal haandthæves ved det Ugedags- eller andet Pligtsarbeide, som Huusmænd eller Huusbeboere i Danmark, efter deres Fæstebreve eller Leiecontracter, ere skyldige at forrette for Jorddrotterne).

[21]Carsten Porskrog Rasmussen, "Storlandbrugets storhedstid. Danske godser og godsejere 1849–1919", in Britta Andersen *et al.* (eds), *Herregårdenes Indian Summer. Fra Grundloven 1849 til Lensafløsningsloven 1919* (Gylling, 2006), pp. 101–117.

[22]Published in Tage Algreen-Ussing, *Love og Anordninger, samt andre offentlige Kundgjørelser Danmarks Lovgivning vedkommende* (Copenhagen, 1850–1871) (*Tyendelov for Kongeriget Danmark*).

older legal order, as the sections on physical punishment in both regulations from 1791 are based on the article regarding domestic discipline in the Danish Code of 1683. Section 6-5-5 reads: "The head of household can chastise his children and servants with a cane or rod, but not with an actual weapon. However, if he inflicts upon them a wound with a pointed weapon or a stick, breaks their bones, or otherwise damages their health, he will be punished as if he had hurt a stranger."[23] The article gives the head of household the right to chastise his servants but defines limits on which instruments may be used for this purpose and the severity of the punishment.

In §14 of the Police Regulation of 1791, the right to chastise servants was linked directly to the requirement of servant obedience: "It is the distinct wish of the King that all servants must be obedient to their head of household, who has the legal right to punish his servants as put in the Law's section 6-5-5." Furthermore, §15 of the regulation links the right to chastise servants to disobedience: "Servants must show their head of household due respect and obedience, and the head of household may enforce his authority as the Law entitles him to." Moreover, the Police Regulation of 1791 dictated that servants could not oppose such punishment. If a servant openly disobeyed or resisted chastisement, they could be sentenced to prison on "bread and water" or even hard labour.

At the time of the Danish Code of 1683, the population on the estates was considered part of the household of the estate owner – the patrimonial household – and with the articles in the Corvée Regulation of 1791 regarding chastisement, this understanding was put into law. However, in §13, the copyholders and their wives were exempted from the estate owners' chastisement rights, as the respect they were entitled to as heads of their own households on their copyhold farms would otherwise have been eroded. This was an important step for the state to cross the boundary into the traditional private area of the estates. Regarding labour conditions on the estates, this change probably had little practical effect, as the copyholders rarely did corvée work themselves but sent their servants. For these servants, the regulation simply confirmed the chastisement article from the Danish Code of 1683. The servants of the copyholders were still subjected to the right of chastisement when working for the estate owner. The same applied to the smallholders. Even though they were also heads of their own households, they were not exempted from the estate owner's right of chastisement when they were performing corvée work on the estates.[24]

As mentioned above, the Danish Code of 1683 set certain limits for how the right of chastisement could be practised and specified where infringement could lead to the punishment of a head of household. The law's section 6-5-10 read: "If a head of household behaves in an illegal or unseemly manner towards his servants or peasants, then it is as if such an act had been committed towards a stranger, and it is in their power to seek justice against their head of household as if he had been a stranger." This meant that if the limits of the right to chastise servants were breached, workers on the estate had the right to take legal action against their head of household, who could then be punished as if he had committed an offence against a "stranger", that is,

---

[23]This article is based on even earlier sources in Danish law, as it is also known from the Law of Jutland from 1241 (sections 2–86).

[24]See Jacobsen, *Husbondret*, pp. 126–128.

a person outside the household. The Corvée Regulation's §14 also dealt with breach of the limits of the right of chastisement, such as if the estate owner or his representative "punished an innocent". For cases like this, the regulation referred to the provisions of the Danish Code of 1683 and the right of people on the estate to sue the estate owner.

When the Servant Law of 1854 replaced the Police Regulation of 1791, disobedience was still a core issue. The question of the scope of the servants' work obligations was not covered by the Police Regulation of 1791. Still, the Servant Law's §22 specified that they were practically unlimited: "Even if a servant was employed to carry out certain tasks, he/she is bound also to carry out other tasks relevant to his/her position and abilities, should circumstances require this." And finally: "Every servant is bound by the domestic order of the household." In the Servant Law of 1854, disobedience was still covered by the right of the head of household to chastise his servants. §27 stipulates that, in connection with disobedience, chastisement could be practised towards servant girls aged less than sixteen and servant boys aged less than eighteen. However, the older adult servants were now covered by a new rule. Disobedience was still illegal, but the law introduced a new fundamental principle: estate owners and other heads of household were not allowed to carry out the punishment themselves. The centuries-old right of heads of household to deal with the conflict situations of everyday life and to punish their servants themselves had been abolished, and this was now in the hands of the state and the courts. From this point onwards, a head of household who submitted an adult servant to corporal punishment could be convicted of violence.

Until 1854, corporal punishment was the predominant form of punishment towards servants and corvée workers, but the laws also included other forms. In terms of offences committed during corvée work, the Corvée Regulation of 1791 allowed fining as one form of punishment. As mentioned above, the estate owners' right to chastise their copyholders was abolished with the introduction of this regulation. Still, the duty of the copyholders to observe obedience towards their estate owners remained. The regulation's §9 stipulated that if a copyholder behaved in a disobedient or insubordinate manner during work, he could be fined between two *mark* and two *rigsdaler*. Furthermore, if servants and smallholders committed the same offence, they could be fined slightly less severely, between eight *skilling* and half a *rigsdaler*.[25] If the disobedient act was witnessed by others and thereby set a "wicked example", this was considered an aggravating circumstance, which could lead to a doubling of the fine and, in the worst cases, copyholders and smallholders could have their copyhold forfeit. The worst possible case of disobedience was to attempt to induce others to disobedience, which was punishable by fines of up to ten *rigsdaler*, a prison sentence, years of hard labour, or the forfeit of the offender's copyhold.

With §26 of the Servant Law of 1854, disobedience towards the head of the household was punishable by fines of between one and ten *rigsdaler*. Defiance and insults resulted in the same punishment or a prison sentence on an ordinary prison diet or on "water and bread" for up to five days. Finally, physical resistance or violence might

---

[25]One *rigsdaler* was ninety-six *skilling*, and one *mark* was sixteen *skilling*. The annual wage for a male servant in Denmark in the late 1700s varied from nine to twenty-eight *rigsdaler* (paid both in money and kind).

Figure 2. Workers and servants in front of Gammel Estrup Manor in 1918. The Servant Law of 1854 abolished Danish estate owners' right to punish servants with a physical chastisement. However, servants' disobedience towards estate owners continued to be illegal and could now be sentenced in court.
Photo: Gammel Estrup. The Danish Manor & Estate Museum.

result in a prison sentence on a diet of "water and bread" for five to ten days unless other paragraphs in the law dictate more severe punishment for a similar offence. However, regarding the punishment of underage servants, §27 stipulated that if they had been subjected to corporal punishment for one of the offences mentioned in §26, they could not also be fined. This meant that the heads of household could choose whether to chastise or fine underage servants – but they could not subject these servants to both forms of punishment for the same offence.

The right of a head of household to punish his servants also included the right to dismiss them without notice. This was not specified in the Police Regulation of 1791, but it was covered indirectly by the regulation's §10 on the illegal dismissal from service. This section stipulates: "If a head of household, without legal cause, dismisses a servant before the end of term, he must, in addition to outstanding wages, pay the servant a further half a year's wages and twelve weeks of subsistence allowance." This meant that if a head of household dismissed a servant, the law committed him to pay half a year's wages and twelve weeks of subsistence allowance in addition to the wages owed to the servant on the day of dismissal. However, the mention in §10 of illegal dismissal suggests that there were also legal reasons for dismissal.

The Servant Law of 1854 clarified these matters. The law retained the right of heads of household to dismiss their servants without notice and listed no less than seventeen different legal reasons for doing so. Among other things, a dismissal would be considered legal if it turned out that the servants did not possess the skills they had claimed to have, if they seduced the children of the household to misbehave, or if a servant girl became pregnant.[26] §46 made clear that if a head of household dismissed a servant for other than the seventeen legal reasons, he had to pay the wages and the subsistence allowance the servant would have been due on the day when they could have been dismissed legally. In the Servant Law of 1854, disobedience is mentioned as one of the main reasons for dismissal. The law's §5 stipulates that servants who refused to obey the head of household or his representative could be dismissed. Persistent carelessness during work is mentioned in the same article as a legal reason for dismissal. In addition, §4 allows servants to be dismissed if "they behaved in a physically threatening or offensive manner" or if "during work they insulted" the head of household, his family, or representative.

In several areas where the state legislation protected a private domain where the heads of household were allowed to punish servants and corvée workers, disobedience was a key concept. The legislation's various provisions overlap to a certain degree and generally allow the head of household to either chastise or dismiss the worker. If a case was brought before a court, disobedience could be fined, or the worker could be imprisoned (Figure 2).

Punishment and Disobedience in Trials in the 1830s and 1870s

The estate owners were the masters of both servants and corvée workers. However, the practical administration of the different kinds of work on the estates was often performed by his representatives: a bailiff (*forvalter/ridefoged*) or a leaseholder (*forpagter*).[27] When bailiffs and leaseholders organized work on the estates, the rights of the estate owners were transferred to them. In the 1791 legislation, it is specified that the right of chastisement could be performed by the estate owner and by these particular representatives.[28] In the following analyses of court practice, both kinds of representatives – bailiffs and leaseholders – are thus considered masters of the estates. In work-related matters on the estates, these representatives operated with the authority of a head of household towards all workers.

As the survey of the legislation has shown, servants' and corvée workers' disobedience towards their masters was clearly illegal and punishable in the 1800s. But what was the legal definition of obedience? Which acts were defined by the legal system as representing disobedience? What were the consequences of these definitions regarding how legal disputes between estate owners and their servants and corvée workers were solved? Below, this chapter deals with these questions based on an investigation of court cases between estate owners and workers from the area covered by the lower court of Rougsø, Sønderhald, and Øster Lisbjerg districts ("Rougsø and other

---

[26]See also Dorte Kook Lyngholm, "Når herregårdenes tjenestepiger kom i ulykkelige omstændigheder", *Herregårdshistorie*, 8 (2013), pp. 23–31.

[27]The bailiff was the top administrator responsible for all estate matters. On some estates the farming was organized directly from the state administration and in these cases the bailiff was in charge. On other estates the entire farm production or parts of it was put in the hands of a leaseholder. The leaseholder organized and had financial responsibility for the production.

[28]Corvée Regulation, §13.

districts") in eastern Jutland.[29] Cases concerning service relationships appeared before the local police court, and the archives from this court form the empirical basis for the investigation.[30] Two periods were selected for scrutiny, 1830–1835 and 1870–1875, and within these periods, all court cases concerning conflicts in service relationships or corvée work on the area's estates were examined.[31]

The total number of examined court cases was eighty-four, distributed equally between the two periods, with forty-three cases in the 1830s and forty-one cases in the 1870s. With twenty-five cases concerning absence from or insufficient corvée work, this is the largest group of cases in 1830–1835. In these cases, the estate owner was the plaintiff, and proceedings were finished quickly before the court. The court cases reveal no legal excuses for the neglect of corvée work, and the workers were found guilty in all the trials. A similar group of cases concerns servants sued for illegally leaving their jobs. These cases were also all won by the estate owners.[32]

Many other trials concerning conflicts within the large household of the estates concern the right of estate owners and their representatives to sanction or punish servants or corvée workers. The examined court records include several trials that deal with the right of chastisement held by the estate owners, which were brought before the court by workers who found that the limits of this right had been breached. The cases show that one of the most important points of the investigations of the courts was to clarify whether the limits of the Danish Code's section 6-5-5 had been breached – that is, partly the question as to whether the chastisement had been carried out with an appropriate instrument, and partly whether the chastisement had caused serious physical injury to the claimant. The sentencing in these cases shows that – in the 1830s as well as in the 1870s – this was an area where the courts were very hesitant to intervene, and even very severe chastisement did not necessarily lead to the head of household being found guilty.

One such case dates to 1874, when the Sorvad estate's leaseholder chastised the sixteen-year-old servant Frederik Simon Stemme and was subsequently charged

---

[29] Danish Rougsø, Sønderhald og Øster Lisbjerg herreder. This area was considered suitable for the investigation of legal relations between estate owners and their workforce since it had a high density of traditional estates throughout the century. In a Danish context, this area (Djursland), along with parts of the islands Funen (Fyn) and Zealand (Sjælland), had the highest concentration of estates. See Carsten Porskrog Rasmussen *et al.* (eds), *Det Danske Godssysten* (Aarhus, 1987), pp. 13–38.

[30] In other Nordic studies investigations of the archives from the arbitration courts have given valuable insights into labour conflicts. See Vilhelmsson, *The Moral Economy*. Studies in Danish arbitration courts also include examples of conflicts between estate owners and copyholders. See Lotte Dombernowsky, *Slagsmaale ere nu om Stunder langt sjældnere...* (Odense, 1995). However, all police matters including conflicts concerning servants and corvée workers were exempt from the arbitration courts established in Denmark in 1795. Hence the archives from the arbitration courts have not been included in this study. See Forordning om Forligelses-Commissioners Stiftelse overalt i Danmark, samt i Kiøbstæderne i Norge of 10 July 1795, §§26–28. (Published in Schou, *Chronologisk Register*.)

[31] The term "estates" includes both Danish nineteenth-century terms: *godser* and *proprietærgårde*. The choice of the two periods was made to investigate the development both over time and before and after the Servant Law of 1854. The specific period 1830–1835 was chosen to study estates after the agrarian revolution and the second period 1870–1875 to ensure that the Servant Law of 1854 had been an integrated part of the legal practice.

[32] See also Dorte Kook Lyngholm, "Pligten til lydighed. Tjenestefolk og landarbejderes retsstilling på danske herregårde i 1800-tallet", *Temp – tidsskrift for historie*, 13 (2016), pp. 27–59.

with grievous bodily harm.[33] The leaseholder was unhappy with how the boy performed when he was asked to bring food to some of the estate's cattlemen, and he, therefore, chose to chastise him. He grabbed the boy's whip, and when the latter resisted, the leaseholder pushed him over and struck him several times on his body with it. According to the boy, he also stepped on his chest with his boot. The boy subsequently fell ill, and a doctor examined him and found clear signs of violence. However, during the case, the judge emphasized that the instrument used to chastise the boy had been suitable, and that the boy's injuries were no more serious than would usually be accepted in such cases. The leaseholder was therefore acquitted.

The cases concerning chastisement shed light on how the courts in the 1800s assessed the question of disobedience and which forms of disobedience the courts accepted as justification for chastisement. One of the judgements states that "it is accepted that it is not the head of household's duty to prove whether he had reason to chastise his servant, as long as he did not go beyond the limits of his chastisement right".[34] This means that, in principle, a head of household did not have to prove whether chastisement had been justified in a specific case but simply whether he had gone too far. However, this specific question was the focus of several court cases where servants claimed chastisement was unjustified.[35]

One of these cases was brought before the court in 1832, where the servant Søren Nielsen Dahl from the Stenalt estate sued leaseholder Bræmer, who had beaten him with a cane.[36] During the court case, the servant explained that he found the punishment unjustified as he had not given the leaseholder any reason to chastise him. The leaseholder's explanation took as its point of departure that the servant had been drunk and beaten one of the farm's pigs so hard that it might have been killed. He later elaborated on the explanation by claiming that the servant, due to his drunkenness, was incapable of carrying out his duties. Furthermore, the servant had answered back several times, for example, when he, after the chastisement, had been ordered back to work, to which he had replied that he "would not be ordered around by him".[37]

---

[33]Danish National Archives, Viborg [hereafter, DNAV], Rougsø, Sønderhald, and Øster Lisbjerg lower court, Register of Judgements (*domprotokol*) [hereafter, RSØ RJ] 1872–1875, pp. 146b–148.

[34]DNAV, Rougsø, Sønderhald, and Øster Lisbjerg lower court, Register of Police Trials (*politiprotokol*) [hereafter, RSØ RPT] 1831–1833, p. 102.

[35]A comparison of the estate owners' and the copyholders' rights of chastisement could reveal similarities and differences between the perception and practice of the punishment in "small" and the "big" households. However, no separate study has yet been conducted on court practice concerning masters and servants in Danish copyhold farms and the existing research on rural court practice does not systematically draw a distinction between estates and copyhold farms in the analysis. Hanne Østhus's studies of urban households in Denmark–Norway has, however, shown many similarities in court practice in trials concerning chastisement. She has shown that the courts in the cities operated with three criteria when identifying the boundary between illegal violence and chastisement: the instrument used, the severity of the injuries, and the question of the justification of the punishment. She has also emphasized that drawing the line between violence and chastisement was a question of interpretation. And she has shown that court cases concerning chastisement stand out as a category were the servants almost never won. Hanne Østhus, *Vanartige tjenestefolk eller uordentlige husbønder? Tjenestefolk i arbeidskonflikter i Christiania på sluten af 1700-tallet* (Oslo, 2007), pp. 44–46, 104–106.

[36]DNAV, RSØ RPT 1831–1833, pp. 39b–102b; DNAV, Rougsø, Sønderhald, and Øster Lisbjerg lower court, Police Cases (*sager til politiprotokoller*) [hereafter, RSØ PC] 1832–1833.

[37]DNAV, RSØ RPT 1831–1833, p. 47b.

In court, the servant confirmed that he had beaten the pig to prevent it from eating the grain in the barn. He also admitted that, on the day, he had had "a dram"[38] but claimed that he had not been too drunk to be able to carry out his work. The following day he had been so done in by the beating that he had been unfit for work. None of the witnesses could shed any light on the cause of the chastisement. To the judge, the conclusive point was that the servant had neglected his work commitments. The leaseholder was entitled to beat the servant as "it is the court's decision that there is no doubt that the head of household had the right to chastise the servant, as he had not carried out his work".[39] As this example shows, neglecting one's work was a form of disobedience that was clearly perceived as an acceptable reason for corporal punishment.

Other forms of disobedience might also justify chastisement in the legal system of the 1830s. In a court case from 1833, the servant Thomas Pedersen sued the estate owner J.M. Secher and his son after he had been chastised on the Julianeholm estate.[40] The servant claimed that he had been violently attacked with a cane by the estate owner and his son without having offended them in any way. He found the chastisement unjustified and focused his complaint on the following point: "As head of household, Conscription Commissioner Secher may have the right to chastise, but the chastisement has to have a legal cause."[41] According to the servant, there was no such cause in the present case where he had been beaten after a row with the head farmhand. He considered this row a private matter between him and the head farmhand, of no concern to the estate owner.

However, the estate owner accused the servant of several other offences, which he found justified the chastisement. During the trial, it was revealed that, on the previous day, the servant had left the horses and cart in his care to take a nap in a haystack. According to several witnesses, he had called the head farmhand names and called him a scoundrel when he was ordered to return to work. Following this, the head farmhand sent for the estate owner, and an incident occurred in which the owner removed a hayfork from the servant. The servant fled, followed by the estate owner with the fork, who repeatedly ordered him to stop, before pursuing him on horseback. In addition, the court also heard that on several occasions, the servant had, without permission, taken off by night on one of the horses grazing near Julianeholm. In the past, the tense relationship between the servant and the head farmhand had resulted in the servant deliberately dulling the edge of the farmhand's scythe.

All these counts formed part of the estate owner's accusations against the servant, and they were all confirmed by witnesses and by the servant's own admissions in court. They all formed part of the judge's evaluation, and in the verdict, they were listed as the basis for the outcome of the case. The verdict stated that the sum of the servant's behaviour towards the estate owner was irreconcilable with "the submissiveness and obedience he as a servant, according to the regulation of 25 March 1791 §14, was duty-bound to observe towards his head of household

---

[38]*Ibid.*, p. 40.
[39]*Ibid.*, p. 102b.
[40]*Ibid.*, pp. 290–301b; DNAV, RSØ RPT 1833–1836, pp. 30–31b; DNAV, RSØ PC 1833–1834.
[41]DNAV, RSØ PC 1833–1834.

and his bidding".[42] Furthermore, as the chastisement had not breached the limits of the law, in terms of which instrument was used and the damage caused, the case went against the servant. In addition, the servant's "entire attitude, as described to the court, must be considered of a kind which a head of household would be fully justified to perceive as unseemly, and that a servant behaving in such a manner would be liable to punishment for this behaviour".[43] In effect, the court ruled that the estate owner was justified in chastising the servant. The servant's disobedience included several examples of improper behaviour, culminating in the incident in the field.

A case from 1833 represents an example of servant disobedience that could trigger a different kind of justified sanction from an estate owner. In this case, the servant Anders Pedersen Rytter brought an action against his former master, the owner of the Vosnæsgård estate, Ditmar Friedrich von Ladiges, for illegal dismissal.[44] The servant described the estate owner's conduct in the following way: "Yesterday he took the liberty, without any cause from me, to dismiss me from his service and to only pay me the wages I was due yesterday."[45] During the court case, the estate owner argued that he had been justified in dismissing the servant. The so-called unseemly behaviour of the servant was illustrated thus: He thought he had the right on his own to "decide when to appear for work, disregarding the fact that everybody else did the work they were ordered to do, and he also thought he had the right on his own to decide when it was time to take a break".[46] In addition, he opposed the orders of the bailiff to collect some manure, which had been dropped on the road in connection with muck spreading. On this occasion, he even referred to the order as "nonsense", and asked the bailiff to speak Danish as, according to one of the interviewed witnesses, he did not understand "his German gibberish".[47] The servant denied that he had opposed the order, and none of the interviewed witnesses could confirm his refusal to carry out the task.

No witnesses supported the bailiff's claim that the servant had refused to carry out the work he had been ordered to do, and, subsequently, he was not convicted for neglect of work. He was, however, convicted for having referred to work he had been ordered to do as nonsense. In the verdict, it was put that "his behaviour suggested an inclination to reason in a way which was not in line with the submissiveness, obedience, and respect the law impresses on servants that they must show towards their head of household".[48] The premises of the verdict also considered that the servant had frequently been seen arguing with the bailiff. In summary, the court found that the improper attitude and behaviour of the servant had given the estate owner good reason for the dismissal. The servant's claim of payment of outstanding wages was not accepted, and the estate owner was cleared of the charge of illegal dismissal. In this case, the punishable disobedience was thus not the servant's refusal to work but his improper and disrespectful attitude.

---

[42]DNAV, RSØ RPT 1833–1836, p. 31.

[43]*Ibid.*, p. 31b.

[44]DNAV, RSØ RPT 1831–1833, pp. 255b–279; DNAV, RSØ PC 1832–1833.

[45]DNAV, RSØ PC 1832–1833.

[46]DNAV, RSØ RPT 1831–1833, p. 256b.

[47]*Ibid.*, p. 268.

[48]DNAV, RSØ PC 1832–1833.

The right of chastisement and the right to dismiss servants therefore gave the masters two different ways of sanctioning their workers. The above case shows that the head of household had the right to choose between the two different forms of punishment. The verdict stated that "it is in [the] hands of the accused [the estate owner] whether he will punish him [the servant] for the neglect of his duties, or whether he will declare the contract null and void".[49] During the case, the estate owner demanded that the servant be fined for his behaviour. However, the court rejected this for the following reason: "Although the behaviour of the plaintiff [the servant] may be punishable by law, the defendant [the estate owner] has, by dismissing him, renounced further charges against him."[50] Servants who had breached the limits of acceptable behaviour could not be punished twice for the same offence, but it was up to the estate owner to decide the nature of the punishment; that is, whether the servant should be chastised, dismissed, or fined by the court.

As shown above, the estate owners had the right to punish their servants without involving the courts. Court cases based entirely on charges of disobedience were thus rare in the investigated districts in the 1830s. However, the records do include examples of disobedience brought before the court, where the judge – and not the estate owner – was expected to sentence the servant. In 1834, the owner of the Stenalt estate, Malte Bruun Nyegaard, sued the corvée workers Frantz Sørensen and Peder Nielsen.[51] The workers were not employed by the estate owner but were the servants of two copyholders in the village of Ørsted who had sent them to do corvée work during the harvest on the main farm on the estate. They were charged with disobedience and insubordination in connection with the corvée work since they had refused to carry out the estate owner's order to separate grain from hay. In addition, they "induced other corvée workers to also behave in a disobedient manner, and when I [the estate owner] ordered them to do this work, they replied in a rude tone of voice that 'they chose to do otherwise'".[52] During the court case, the workers denied that they had been disobedient or said that "they chose to do otherwise". They explained that on the day in question, work had been distributed in such a way that they would have had to process twice as much hay as the other corvée workers, which they had found unfair.

The judge agreed in principle that one corvée worker could not be ordered to carry out harder work than the others. Still, he found that, in practice, it would be impossible to distribute the work entirely evenly. In the present case, he noted that one witness had mentioned that there was a good reason why the work had been distributed unevenly, as one of the haystacks would otherwise have tumbled over. Against this background, the judge assessed that the two charged workers had no legal reason to refuse to work. He also pointed out that there were aggravating circumstances in connection with the workers' refusal to work, namely, that their refusal had taken place in front of other people. As mentioned above, disobedience and insubordination in the presence of others carried higher penalties, and, in accordance with

---

[49]*Ibid.*
[50]*Ibid.*
[51]DNAV, RSØ RPT 1833–1836, pp. 136b–160b; DNAV, RSØ PC 1833–1834.
[52]DNAV, RSØ PC 1833–1834.

§9 of the Corvée Regulation of 1791, the two workers were each sentenced to pay a fine of two *mark*. The case is remarkable since nothing suggests that this was a total work stoppage or that the accused's behaviour had negatively influenced the other corvée workers' performance. However, the fear of collective action by the workforce was deeply ingrained in the society of absolute monarchy. In the case against the two workers from Stenalt, an example had to be made of them.[53] In this case, the estate owner used the court system to ensure that those who witnessed the episode knew precisely who was in command and to confirm the established relationship between superiors and subordinates.[54]

Following the Servant Law of 1854, the heads of household were no longer allowed to punish their servants with chastisement. An accusation of disobedience could therefore be brought before the courts. The records from the courts in Rougsø and other districts in the 1870s include several trials where estate owners sued their servants for disobedience with reference to the Servant Law's §26. Most of these cases concern refusal to work, where servants refused to carry out certain tasks and stated that they had been employed to carry out other types of work. However, as shown above, it was specified in §22 that the scope of the servants' work obligations was unlimited. The examined court practice confirms this principle since the estate owners won all cases of this kind. One interesting exception to this rule was from 1873 when estate owner Schytte from Ejstrupgård sued his servant Nicoline Petersen who had refused his order to spread manure on the field.[55] The servant won this case when she claimed she was hired as a parlourmaid and thus had no obligation to work in the field. Another female servant, Ane Kirstine Andersen, was sued in this case as she denied spreading manure on the same occasion. She, however, lost the case. She was hired as a kitchen maid, which probably made a difference. The case suggests the special status of some of the domestic servants and illustrates that the courts drew a thin line between the functions in the house and stated that a parlourmaid could not be obliged to work outside.

Some of the other trials on disobedience concerned offensive or rude behaviour, and the charged servants were fined between three and ten *rigsdaler*. The most severe sentence was passed in a case from the Holbækgård estate in 1873.[56] In this case, disagreements over food developed into a more substantial conflict, with one servant throwing the meat on the floor during a meal, claiming it smelled off. When the estate bailiff reprimanded him, the servant threatened him and called him "a red-bearded donkey" and "a lecher".[57] Later that evening, after the servant had drunk some schnapps, he broke a window in the bailiff's room and struggled so that it took two other servants to restrain him and lead him to bed. For this behaviour, the

---

[53]Mührmann-Lund, *Borgerligt regimente*, pp. 370–376; Claus Bjørn, *Bonde Herremand Konge. Bonden i 1700-tallets Danmark* (Copenhagen, 1981), pp. 26–35; Lyngholm, *Godsejerens ret*, pp. 200–244.

[54]Mührmann-Lund concludes that the police courts very often judged in favour of the masters in corvée cases compared to servant cases. *Borgerligt regimente*, p. 370. A similar pattern can be found in the investigations presented in this article since all cases between estate owners and corvée workers were won by the estate owners.

[55]DNAV, RSØ RJ 1872–1875, p. 133b.

[56]*Ibid.*, pp. 125b–126.

[57]*Ibid.*, p. 125b.

servant was sentenced to pay for the damaged window and to spend five days in prison. The sentence was served in Randers prison the same month as the sentence was passed.[58]

The trials from the 1870s also show that servants could be sentenced for disobedience for matters less serious. Such a case was brought before the court in 1873, where estate owner Poulsen of Dalsgård sued four of his servants for defiance and insubordination in service.[59] The reason was that the servants had written to the estate owner and complained about the food. During the court case, the servants admitted that the food had been adequate and that they had, therefore, no reason to complain. However, the court found that the most aggravating point of the case was that the letter had been put in improper and indecent language and contained threats to stop work. The four servants were therefore sentenced for disobedience according to §26 and made to pay a fine of three *rigsdaler*. In this case, the servants were punished for disobedience because they displayed an improper attitude towards the estate owner. The courts' definitions of obedience were still very broad, and in trials during the 1870s where servants were charged for this offence, the estate owners were the winners in all cases.

In the trials from the 1870s where servants sued their masters for illegal dismissal, the counterargument from the masters in most cases was that the servant had been disobedient. As in the trials from the 1830s, the refusal to work was considered a form of disobedience which clearly justified dismissal. However, a trial from the 1870s suggests that the court now observed a kind of triviality limit regarding which forms of disobedience could justify a dismissal. This trial was from the Gammel Estrup estate, where the servant Niels Jørgensen sued dairy leaseholder Hein for illegal dismissal.[60] During the case, the leaseholder stated that he had dismissed the servant due to disobedience. However, it turned out that all the servant had done was inform the leaseholder that he intended to leave his job half a year earlier than he had said. The judge ruled that this statement could not be defined as disobedience and justify dismissal. The leaseholder lost the case and was sentenced to pay the servant's wages until the contract expired.

Although the right of heads of household to chastise adult servants was abolished with the introduction of the Servant Law of 1854, cases brought before the court of Rougsø and other districts in the 1870s show that the centuries-old practice of corporal punishment was not discontinued automatically with the introduction of the new rules. The records show that the servants used their newly obtained right to sue the estate owners for violence if they subjected them to corporal punishment.[61] All these cases had the same outcome: the servants won the cases, and the accused were sentenced according to §200 of the Penal Code of 1866. In all these cases, it

---

[58]DNAV, Records from Randers Prison (*arrestjournal*) 1869–1877, serial number 826.
[59]DNAV, RSØ RJ 1872–1875, pp. 137b–138.
[60]DNAV, RSØ RJ 1867–1872, pp. 13–13b.
[61]The development of the workers' role as plaintiffs is remarkable, not only in cases concerning chastisement. Between 1830 and 1835, seven workers sued their masters; between 1870 and 1875 this number had increased to twelve. This means that in cases from the 1870s, the workers were plaintiffs in almost a third of cases.

was the representative of the estate owner – a bailiff or a leaseholder – who was sentenced, and they were either fined or sentenced to two days in prison.

One such case shows how the built-in inequalities of the service legislation could still have serious consequences for the servants. In this case, the servant S.N. Ytte sued bailiff Olsen from the Estruplund estate for beating him with a cane during work in the field.[62] According to the servant, the bailiff dismissed him on the spot when he asked to see a doctor after the incident. The bailiff admitted that he had beaten the servant but denied dismissing him. Instead, he accused the servant, referring to §47 of the Servant Law, of leaving his job illegally. The outcome was that the bailiff was fined according to the Penal Code's §200 to pay a fine of four *rigsdaler*, but the servant received a much harsher sentence, as it could not be proven that he had been illegally dismissed. He was sentenced for illegal absence from work and had to pay fifteen *rigsdaler* – half a year's wages – to the estate owner, as well as a fine of nine *rigsdaler*. Although the Servant Law of 1854 had made it illegal for an estate owner to chastise his servants, the courts did not consider a breach of this rule severe enough to allow the wronged servant to leave the service.

Conclusion: The Obligation to Be Obedient

Throughout the nineteenth century, the relationship between estate owners and the workforce was regulated by special laws that defined servants and corvée workers as subordinate to the estate owners. The inequality between the two parties was the foundation of this legislation, which provided the owners with an effective tool for binding the workforce to the estates. An important part of this legislation was the continuation of the estate owners' centuries-old right to – independently from the courts – punish their workforce with corporal chastisement or dismissal.

The right of the estate owners to chastise their workers was protected by law, even if the law did not specify in which contexts chastisement was permitted. However, in the legislation, chastisement was explicitly linked to workers' duty to show obedience towards the estate owners. The servants and corvée workers who were subjected to the right of chastisement were protected by law in the sense that the workers had the right to sue the estate owner if he breached the limits of this rule. Most trials from the court in Rougsø and other districts show that the courts trod very cautiously in cases like these. Even a very brutal chastisement did not necessarily lead to an estate owner being found guilty.

The demand for obedience from servants and corvée workers was fixed by law throughout the entire century, and the court cases show which offences the courts defined as disobedience. The kind of obedience defined as indisputable throughout the century was the demand that workers carry out the work they were ordered to do. In almost all cases where servants or corvée workers had neglected or refused to carry out work, they were found guilty of disobedience. During the first half of the century, it was perceived as an aggravating circumstance if others witnessed the disobedience. In these cases, the courts were used to make an example and to emphasize the estate owners' indisputable superiority. In addition to refusals to work, the

---

[62]DNAV, RSØ RJ 1867–1872, pp. 53b–54b.

courts recognized more diffuse forms of disobedience. In cases from the 1830s and the 1870s, servants were found guilty of disobedience or insubordination if they displayed a disrespectful attitude by, for example, insulting or behaving provocatively towards the estate owner and/or his representatives.

When the Servant Law in 1854 abolished the right of estate owners to chastise adult servants, the courts took over the authority of punishment in cases of disobedience. The courts' definition of disobedience did not change significantly, and in all examined cases where servants were accused of disobedience, they were found guilty. The pattern was broken in one trial from the 1870s concerning dismissal, where the court rejected the head of household's claim of disobedience. However, the general picture of legal practice through the entire period is that the courts accepted the accusations made by estate owners regarding disobedience. Particularly during the 1830s, the articles regarding disobedience could function like "rubber paragraphs", where accumulated small-scale provocations over an extended period could legitimize an estate owner's claim of disobedience in court and justify punishment.

The court practice in Rougsø and other districts shows how the court's interpretation of the service and corvée legislation's provisions regarding disobedience predominantly favoured the estate owners. If the servants and corvée workers challenged the independent legal powers of their heads of household, and the case was brought before a court, the likelihood of winning the case was small. Concerning the legally fixed duty of obedience, the courts of the 1800s protected the final remnants of the estate owners' legally defined special status and their right to determine whether their workforce should receive a punishment.

Cite this article: Dorte Kook Lyngholm. Absolute Obedience: Servants and Masters on Danish Estates in the Nineteenth Century. *International Review of Social History*, 68:S31 (2023), pp. 177–195. https://doi.org/10.1017/S0020859022000918

International Review of Social History, 68:S31 (2023), pp. 197–212
doi:10.1017/S0020859022000876

RESEARCH ARTICLE

The Political Economy of Punishment: Slavery and Violence in Nineteenth-Century Brazil and the United States

Marcelo Rosanova Ferraro

Center for the Study of Slavery and Justice, Watson Institute for International and Public Affairs, Brown University, e-mail: marcelo_rosanova_ferraro@brown.edu

Abstract

This article analyzes slave resistance, capital crimes, and state violence in the Mississippi Valley and the Paraíba Valley – two of the most dynamic plantation economies of the nineteenth century. The research focused on the intersection between slavery and criminal law in Brazil and the United States. The analysis of capital crimes committed by enslaved people in Natchez and Vassouras revealed changing patterns of resistance and judicial punishment through the decades. This investigation demonstrated that local experiences of violence on plantations and in courtrooms were connected to the dynamics of national politics and the world economy. Moreover, this comparative study illuminated differences between these racialized slave societies and their political systems and revealed the essence of distinct regimes of racial violence in the Americas.

Introduction

In early January 1852, Bill was under the whip of his owner, Matthew Lassley, when he struck back with lethal effect. In the courthouse of Natchez, Mississippi, he and his counsel justified the killing for maltreatment on the plantation, presenting a medical certificate for fractured bones and wounds. The testimonies of his fellow enslaved supported his claims. The prosecutor even considered the hypothesis of a conspiracy among Lassley's enslaved men against his life. Yet, he failed to prove it. The evidence against Bill convinced the jurors to acquit him of murder. He was instead convicted of manslaughter – a non-premeditated crime. Based on technical errors, his counsel succeeded in petitioning for a new trial. In December, the defendant re-entered the courthouse. Once again, he pleaded self-defense, the jurors acquitted him of murder, and he was convicted of manslaughter. These two crimes had different penalties for free defendants, but not if they were committed by enslaved men. Both offenses were punishable by death. Still, a second jury voted for a symbolic minor conviction. A motion for a third trial postponed Bill's fate, but before he headed to court again, he died in jail, the victim of a yellow fever epidemic. It was the early 1850s when an enslaved man had killed his master in the Mississippi Valley, two white juries had refused to convict him of murder, and he did not find his end at the gallows.[1]

More than two decades later, in October 1879, José Bastos Oliveira was chastising Manoel on a coffee plantation in the Paraíba Valley when Gil attacked him, followed by his fellow enslaved, Justiniano, Marciano, and Joaquim. Leaving the overseer's corpse behind, they marched toward the city of Vassouras – according to them, to be free. Carrying hoes and sticks, they met their owner on a horse along the way. They refused to take off their hats and challenged their master. He had hired the overseer to beat them; instead, the overseer was beaten. They continued on their way until they arrived at the police station, where they put down their weapons and surrendered. The prosecutor accused only Manoel and Gil of murder, assured that the others had hit the overseer's body after he died. During the trial, both confessed to the crime. They planned to kill the overseer previously if his unfair punishments continued. Witnesses registered that the crime was part of their strategy to be convicted and leave slavery behind. Their counsel convinced the jurors that the victim was no longer the overseer of the plantation, thus it was not a capital crime. The judge sentenced them to suffer 400 lashes each and to carry irons on their necks for two years. It was the late 1870s when those enslaved men had killed an overseer, a jury of freeholders had convicted them for a minor crime, and, after their whipping, they had returned to their plantation.[2]

Violence was constitutive of every slave society. However, patterns of punishment and resistance differed across time and space. Separated by decades and thousands of miles, both crimes reveal similarities and differences between slavery and criminal justice in nineteenth-century Brazil and the United States. In the Mississippi Valley's cotton fields and the Paraíba Valley coffee plantations, enslaved people worked under the lashes of masters and overseers, fighting for degrees of autonomy. The plantation's unwritten rules were constantly under negotiation, and their violation could result in violent reactions. Bill, Manoel, and Gil had had enough. The murder of masters and overseers was the ultimate crime in slave societies, along with insurrections. The freemen community eventually responded with extralegal violence; more frequently, the enslaved criminal faced trials and suffered harsh legal penalties.

Bill, Manoel, and Gil made their own history, albeit under extreme circumstances. It is the historian's privilege to reframe stories as part of a broader narrative, revealing their historical significance. An early generation of historians has emphasized the structural constraints of slavery, while, in recent decades, scholars have focused on the agency of enslaved people. These episodes seem to reinforce the latter perspective. Still, without disregarding the individual experiences of these men under captivity, their resistance can only be fully comprehended within the material constraints that conditioned their actions. Second, a social history of legal systems must avoid abstractions of formal procedures and the law by analyzing their dynamic in social life. In this sense, plantations and courthouses were political arenas wherein enslaved people, overseers, masters, and judicial authorities disputed notions of justice. Finally,

---

[1] *State v. Bill* [1852], Adam County Courts Record, Historic Natchez Foundation.

[2] Criminal Record for Murder, Manoel and Gil, 1879, Arquivo do Tribunal de Justiça do Rio de Janeiro / Instituto do Patrimônio Histórico e Artístico Nacional [hereafter, IPHAN], Vassouras, Rio de Janeiro.

the relationship between crime and punishment must be denaturalized since violence results from both individual actions and a complex network of economic, political, and cultural variables.[3]

This research therefore analyzed capital crimes committed by enslaved people and judicial punishment in the Mississippi Valley and the Paraíba Valley – two of the most dynamic slave economies in the Americas during the nineteenth century. This article is organized into three parts. The first part narrates the expansion of slavery and the remaking of slave and criminal law under the constitutions of Brazil and the United States. The second and third parts analyze capital crimes in two paradigmatic cities of those plantation societies: Natchez and Vassouras (Figures 1 and 2). Finally, the concluding section presents the results of this comparative study by revealing patterns of slave resistance and state violence in these slave societies during three periods: the expansion of agricultural frontiers in the early nineteenth century; the formation of mature slave societies in the mid-nineteenth century; and the crisis of slavery in the late nineteenth century.

Slavery and Criminal Law in the Age of Revolutions

When enslaved men and women of Saint Domingue rose up in arms in the late eighteenth century, the United States was the only independent country in the Americas, and Brazil was still a Portuguese colony. From the Caribbean, contradictory forces announced the end of colonial slavery, creating the conditions for the expansion of new slave regimes connected to the world market after the Industrial Revolution. Napoleon's defeat in the Atlantic reoriented the French empire toward Europe, which led to the Louisiana Purchase, the Continental Blockade against Britain, and the invasion of the Iberian Peninsula, forcing the Portuguese royal family to flee to Brazil. Seeking supplies, the colonial government built roads connecting Rio de Janeiro, the new capital, to Minas Gerais, opening lands through the Paraíba do Sul River, where sugar and coffee plantations were established. In the southern Mississippi Valley, now fully controlled by the United States, sugar production spread in areas near New Orleans while cotton fields took over the landscape of Natchez.[4]

The spectrum of insurrection still haunted the continent in the first decades of the nineteenth century, as rebels demonstrated in the mature slave societies of Bahia,

---

[3]On the political economy of slavery in nineteenth-century Brazil and United States, see Rafael Marquese and Dale Tomich, "O Vale do Paraíba Escravista e a Formação do Mercado Mundial do Café no Século XIX", in Keila Grinberg and Ricardo Salles (orgs), *O Brasil Imperial, Volume II – 1831–1870* (Rio de Janeiro, 2009), pp. 339–383; Ricardo Salles, *E o Vale era Escravo, Vassouras, Século XIX, Senhores e Escravos no Coração do Império* (Rio de Janeiro, 2008); Tâmis Parron, "A política da escravidão na era da liberdade. Estados Unidos, Brasil e Cuba, 1787–1846" (Ph.D., Universidade de São Paulo, 2015); Walter Johnson, *River of Dark Dreams: Slavery and Empire in the Cotton Kingdom* (Cambridge, 2013); Edward Baptist, *The Half Has Never Been Told: Slavery and the Making of American Capitalism* (Boulder, CO, 2014); Adam Rothman, *Slave Country: American Expansion and the Origins of the Sul Profundo* (Cambridge, MA, 2005); Sven Beckert and Seth Rockman (eds), *Slavery's Capitalism: A New History of American Economic Development* (Philadelphia, PA, 2016).

[4]See Dale Tomich, *Through the Prism of Slavery: Labor, Capital, and World Economy* (Lanham, MD, 2004), pp. 56–71; Johnson, *River of Dark Dreams*, pp. 18–45; Marquese and Tomich, "O Vale do Paraíba Escravista".

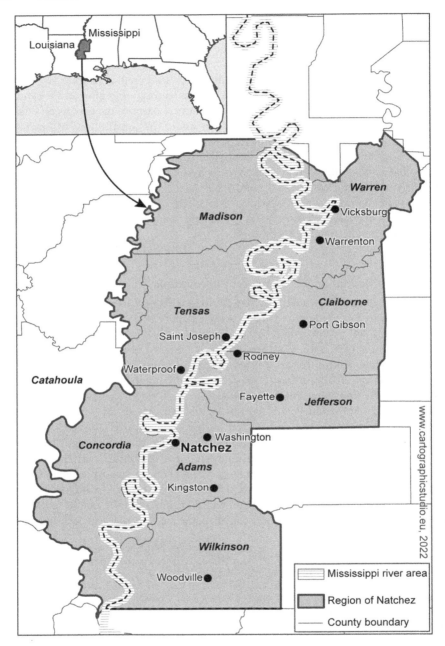

Figure 1. The region of Natchez, between the states of Louisiana and Mississippi, in the Mississippi Valley, nineteenth century.

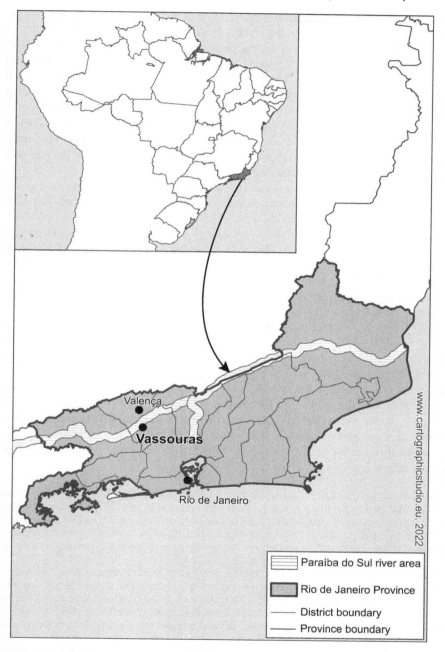

Figure 2. The region of Vassouras and the Paraíba Valley in the Province of Rio de Janeiro, nineteenth century.

Minas Gerais, South Carolina, and Virginia, and in the new slave zones of the Mississippi Valley and the Paraíba Valley. However, slave resistance in Brazil and the United States did not have the same disruptive effect as it did in Haiti. Instead, the struggles of the enslaved reinforced planters' alliances and informed the building of repressive state apparatuses. Strategic constitutional silences not only legitimized enslaved people as private property, but also the expansion of slavery itself, assuring legal certainty for the continuity of the slave trade. The prohibition of the Atlantic commerce of Africans – in 1808 in the United States and 1850 in Brazil – did not include the national trade. Moreover, the infraconstitutional legislation reinforced state institutions in favor of slaveholders and as a system of control over the enslaved population, especially in criminal law.[5]

In the United States, each state assembly created local legislation. The slave codes prevailed, establishing specific norms, crimes, and punishments for the enslaved. This dual system was a colonial tradition in Virginia, South Carolina, and Louisiana. Capital crimes were similar in all slave states, including insurrection, murder, or assault of masters and their families, murder of white people, arson, and rape of white women. Most violations were solved by "plantation law", under the domestic sovereignty of masters, while the justices of the peace were responsible for judging crimes, ruling a jury of freeholders. Mississippi was exceptional for including references to the enslaved in the general state code, and for making capital crimes committed by enslaved defendants a jury's responsibility.[6]

The Brazilian Congress, on the other hand, approved one criminal code and one criminal procedure code for the entire territory in the early 1830s, including few references and specificities for enslaved people. Only insurrection and murder were capital crimes, and both enslaved and free defendants were tried by jury. After a series of slave rebellions, the parliament approved a special law in 1835 that imposed special courts for crimes committed against masters, overseers, and their families. Legal procedures were accelerated and simplified: there would be no right to appeal, and the execution of the death penalty would be immediate – except by the emperor's prerogative of grace.[7]

---

[5] For studies on slave resistance, see João José Reis, *Rebelião Escrava no Brasil. A História do Levante dos Malês em 1835* (São Paulo, 1986); Eugene Genovese, *From Rebellion to Revolution: Afro-American Slave Revolts in the Making of the Modern World* (Baton Rouge, LA, 1979). On slavery and the constitutions, see Parron, "A Política da Escravidão"; David Waldstreicher, *Slavery's Constitution: From Revolution to Ratification* (New York, 2009); James Oakes, "'The Compromising Expedient': Justifying a Proslavery Constitution", *Cardozo Law Review*, 17:6 (1996), pp. 2023–2056.

[6] On the slave law in British colonies and the United States, see Edward Rugemer, *Slave Law and the Politics of Resistance in the Early Atlantic World* (Cambridge, MA, 2018); Thomas Morris, *Southern Slavery and the Law, 1619–1860* (Chapel Hill, NC, 1996); Mark Tushnet, *The American Law of Slavery, 1810–1860* (Princeton, NJ, 1981); Philip Schwarz, *Twice Condemned: Slaves and the Criminal Laws of Virginia, 1705–1865* (Baton Rouge, LA, 1988); Daniel Flanigan, "The Criminal Law of Slavery and Freedom, 1800–1868" (Ph.D., Rice University, 1987). For a comparative perspective of slave law in the Americas, see Ariela Gross and Alejandro de la Fuente, *Becoming Free, Becoming Black: Race, Freedom, and Law in Cuba, Virginia, and Louisiana* (Cambridge, 2020).

[7] On the Portuguese slave law tradition, see Silvia Hunold Lara, "Legislação sobre Escravos Africanos na América Portuguesa", in José Andrés-Gallego (org.), *Tres Grandes Cuestiones de la Historia de Iberoamérica* (Madrid, 2005). On the slave criminal law in the Brazilian empire, see Jurandir Malerba, *Os Brancos da Lei. Liberalismo, Escravidão e Mentalidade Patriarcal no Império do Brasil* (Maringá, 1994); Vivian Costa,

Despite the different legal traditions and institutional framings, both countries built criminal justice systems that legitimized slavery and subjected enslaved people to corporal punishment and regimes of exception under the rule of law. The monopoly of violence principle was adapted in these slave societies since slaveholders and legal authorities shared the right to punish and control enslaved people. Thus, public security in both Brazil and the United States depended on an *oligopoly of violence*. The overlapping sovereignties of slaveholders and the state reinforced an alliance that sustained slavery in the first half of the nineteenth century. However, this alliance became fractured during the later political crisis, as the Mississippi Valley and Paraíba Valley courthouses and the trials of Bill, Manoel, and Gil reveal.[8]

Capital Crimes and Punishment in Natchez, Mississippi

Natchez was founded by the French in 1716 and governed by Spain and then the British in the second half of the eighteenth century. Following the independence of the United States, the city became the capital of the Mississippi Territory when the cotton frontier expansion reframed its landscape. The Louisiana Purchase nationalized the port of New Orleans and navigation through the Mississippi River, intensifying the cotton economy and the internal slave trade. Stimulated by high cotton prices in the 1830s, planters expanded fields and intensified their workers' productivity. Recently arrived from the Upper South trade, many enslaved workers registered the higher labor intensity in the Deep South. Slavery became a major political topic in that same decade after the rising of Garrisonian abolitionism and Nat Turner's rebellion. The convergence of contradictory forces made the cotton frontier a terrain of struggle.[9]

In February 1833, Thomas Coats was working as an overseer on William Lintol's plantation when he decided to chastise Nat for not answering his calls. The enslaved man tried to bargain for fair punishment, keeping his clothes on. Coats insisted he stripped and laid down. Nat refused and attacked the overseer with a knife, injuring his hand, before fleeing to the woods. Almost one year later, he shot his fellow

"Codificação e Formação do Estado-Nacional Brasileiro. O Código Criminal de 1830 e a Positivação das Leis no Pós-Independência" (Master's thesis, Universidade de São Paulo, 2013); Maria Helena Machado, *Crime e Escravidão. Trabalho, Luta e Resistência nas Lavouras Paulistas, 1830–1888* (São Paulo, 2014); João Luiz Ribeiro, *No Meio das Galinhas as Baratas não têm Razão. A Lei de 10 de Junho de 1835, os Escravos e a Pena de Morte no Império do Brasil (1822–1889)* (Rio de Janeiro, 2005); Ricardo Pirola, *Escravos e Rebeldes nos Tribunais do Império. Uma História Social da Lei de 10 de Junho de 1835* (Rio de Janeiro, 2015).

[8]On the intersection between private and public prerogatives of violence, see Orlando Patterson, *Slavery and Social Death: A Comparative Study* (Cambridge, MA, 1982). On the concept of "regime of exception" in slave societies, see Achille Mbembe, *Necropolitics* (Durham, NC, 2019), pp. 66–92. An analysis of slavery and criminal law in the nineteenth century must include Cuba and the specificities of this colonial regime. Enslaved defendants who committed capital crimes on the island were subjected to colonial laws and eventually tried by military courts. This was a more explicit regime of exception since these legal institutions were not under the Spanish constitutional regime. Despite these differences, criminal justice systems in Cuba, Brazil, and the American South were founded on regimes of exception.

[9]See Anthony Kaye, *Joining Places: Slave Neighborhoods in the Old South* (Chapel Hill, NC, 2007); Charles Sydnor, *Slavery in Mississippi* (Columbia, SC, 2013); Johnson, *River of Dark Dreams*.

enslaved Issac and was captured before fulfilling his goal of killing the slave driver and the overseer. In court, the jury condemned the defendant for assault with the intention to kill a white person, a capital crime punishable by death in Mississippi. Nat's story is one among others that reveal the social tensions in Natchez during the 1830s cotton boom.

The struggle between the enslaved population, overseers, and masters reshaped the Mississippi Valley. If the plantation represented domestic sovereignty, enslaved men turned cabins and woods into spaces of relative autonomy. On the other hand, the city of Natchez was the state's domain. Capital crime exceeded the jurisdiction of the plantation, and restoration of the slave order took place at courthouses, prisons, and gallows. In August 1838, Eliza left the public jail after one year of responding in court for the attempt to murder her mistress. Followed by a crowd and a military force, she walked toward the Bluff near Fort Rosalie. After pronouncing some inaudible words, the executioner hanged her. Among the viewers were enslaved people brought by their masters to witness the spectacle, who, according to a local newspaper, "appeared suitably affected". She was fourteen years old.[10]

The justice system followed constitutional and legal procedures, not always fulfilling the expectations or reducing the anxieties of the white population. In the summer of 1835, rumors of a large slave conspiracy in Madison County spread panic in the Mississippi Valley, including Natchez. A vigilance committee performed an extralegal investigation and condemned a few poor whites and dozens of enslaved men to death. Two years later, Eliza Horn accused Peter of assault, but he left jail after his master presented a habeas corpus in his favor, promising to bring him to trial. He never presented himself again. One year later, the case was dismissed under the formal register that "to the satisfaction of the court", the defendant "hath departed this life". Apparently, the attack on a white woman, possibly rape, demanded a parallel system of justice with the discreet consent of the court.[11]

Information on criminality before 1835 is scarce in Natchez. Still, there were at least six capital crimes committed by enslaved defendants between 1832 and 1838, three against overseers and two against masters. However, between 1838 and 1849, there was only one case. Mr. Ward was overseeing the wood chopping on George Tarleton's plantation in 1846 when David killed him with an ax. Despite his lawyer's attempt to challenge his coerced confession, he was condemned for murder. Unlike the 1830s hangings, his execution occurred discreetly in the jail yard. The decrease in slave criminality and trials for capital crimes demands explanations, as does the shift in the death penalty procedures.[12]

---

[10] *State v. Nat* [1834], *State v. Eliza* [1837], Adam County Courts Record, Historic Natchez Foundation. On the intersection between gender and slavery, see Deborah White, *Ar'n't I a Woman?: Female Slaves in the Plantation South* (New York, 1985); Stephanie Camp, *Closer to Freedom: Enslaved Women and Everyday Resistance in the Plantation South* (Chapel Hill, NC, 2004).

[11] *State v. Peter* [1837], Adam County Courts Record, Historic Natchez Foundation. On the 1835 panic, see Joshua Rothman, *Flush Times and Fever Dreams: A Story of Capitalism and Slavery in the Age of Jackson* (Athens, GA, 2012); Johnson, *River of Dark Dreams*, pp. 46–62. Also see Kaye, *Joining Places*, pp. 169–170.

[12] *State v. David* [1846], Adam County Courts Record, Historic Natchez Foundation. Criminal Court Minutes, Books from 1835 to 1860, Adam County Courts Record, Historic Natchez Foundation. On the intersection between slavery, race, and sexual violence, see Diana Sommerville, "The Rape Myth in the

After the financial crisis of 1837, an economic depression extended through the 1840s. Planters slowed the expansion of cotton fields, and labor tasks stabilized. The decrease in the slave trade and the passing of time allowed enslaved men and women to establish families, creating community bonds. Natchez became a mature slave society based on an unwritten code negotiated through conflicts and bargains in previous decades. Criminality decreased partially because tensions were solved within the boundaries of plantations, subject to the negotiated unwritten rules that constituted a *moral economy of slavery*.[13]

Simultaneously, the formation of the Second Party System took the form of a *politics of slavery*, by silencing abolitionists and avoiding conflicts between northerners and southerners. The expansion of antislavery and abolitionist institutions encouraged politicians and jurists in the South to elaborate proslavery ideologies and promote legal reforms to legitimize slavery under liberal principles and prove the modernity of southern civilization. Supreme Courts extended guarantees to enslaved defendants, quashing coerced confessions and convicting overseers and masters for unusual punishments and killings. These cases were exceptional but politically symbolic. Social sensibilities toward state violence also led authorities to avoid public spectacles of punishment, preferring prison sentences and death penalty executions within jail walls.[14]

However, when Bill entered the courthouse in 1852 having murdered his owner, Natchez and the United States were not the same. The increasing price of cotton, the expansion of the internal slave trade, and national political tensions in the 1850s affected the precarious balance of this mature slave society. After decades of agriculture, lands were not as fertile anymore, and the higher pressure in productivity destabilized the relationship between the enslaved, overseers, and masters. The killing of Matthew Lassley was the third capital crime in two years, but Bill benefited from the legal guarantees extended by courts in the previous decade. His lawyer convinced the jurors not to convict him of murder and succeeded in petitioning for new trials. The *moral economy of slavery* informed Bill's justification, reframed in a self-defense legal rhetoric. His death in jail was not an acquittal, but neither did it represent an immediate and violent restoration of the slave order. The absence of a public hanging had different meanings to the enslaved community and the white population, reinforcing anxieties.[15]

Old South Reconsidered", *Journal of Southern History*, 61:3 (1995), pp. 481–518; *idem, Rape and Race in the Nineteenth-Century South* (Chapel Hill, NC, 2004).

[13]On the 1837 crisis, see Johnson, *River of Dark Dreams*, pp. 280–302; Baptist, *The Half Has Never Been Told*, pp. 75–144. On the making of enslaved families and communities and the political stability in mature plantation societies, see John Blassingame, *The Slave Community: Plantation Life in the Antebellum South* (New York, 1972); Eugene Genovese, *Roll, Jordan, Roll: The World the Slaves Made* (New York, 1974); Herbert Gutman, *The Black Family in Slavery and Freedom, 1750–1925* (New York, 1976), pp. 3–44; Kaye, *Joining Places*, pp. 21–50. On abolitionism in the United States, see Manisha Sinha, *The Slave's Cause: A History of Abolition* (New Haven, CT, 2016). On slave resistance in court, see Ariela Gross, *Double Character: Slavery and Mastery in the Antebellum Southern Courtroom* (Princeton, NJ, 2000); Kimberly Welch, *Black Litigants in the Antebellum American South* (Chapel Hill, NC, 2018).

[14]On the politics of slavery, see Parron, "A Política da Escravidão"; William Cooper, *The South and the Politics of Slavery, 1828–1856* (Baton Rouge, LA, 1992).

[15]*State v. Bill* [1852], Adam County Courts Record, Historic Natchez Foundation. On the concept of moral economy, see Edward Thompson, "The Moral Economy of the English Crowd in the Eighteenth Century", *Past & Present*, 50:1 (1971), pp. 76–136. On the intersection between the internal slave trade

In November 1854, Frank and General met at the Natchez jailhouse. One had killed his master, the other, his overseer. The jury condemned both for murder, and the judge sentenced them to public hanging. On 22 December, they marched a mile south of Natchez, followed by a crowd of roughly 3,000, who witnessed their bodies being simultaneously dropped on the gallows. This was the first public execution of the death penalty in more than a decade. In the years that followed, political tensions reached a new level after the rise of Free Soil ideology and the Republican Party, especially during the elections of 1856 and the subsequent insurrection scares. A year later, Natchez's white population was scandalized by the murder of two overseers in the same neighborhood where Bill had killed his master. Henderson, Anderson, and Reuben murdered Duncan Skinner and simulated an accident, deceiving the investigator. When the body of a second overseer was found in a neighboring plantation, a private investigation led by planters and overseers discovered that Tom, John, and Reuben were responsible and that the previous crime had inspired them. In December 1857, six enslaved defendants entered the courthouse, and the jurors accepted as evidence the confessions obtained under torture by the extralegal committee, condemning five of them to be hanged. Weeks later, they marched toward their respective plantations, where white crowds and their fellow enslaved witnessed their hangings close to where the overseers were murdered. The spectacle of the death penalty was back, taking place in the slaveholders' domestic domain.[16]

During the 1860 election, insurrection scares became epidemic in the Mississippi Valley. It was after the beginning of the Civil War that anxieties climaxed, when talk of enslaved people gaining freedom led to white hysteria in Natchez. A vigilance committee imprisoned and tortured hundreds of enslaved and free black men and women for an alleged conspiracy in 1861, extending their investigations over every rumor or misbehavior until the arrival of Union troops. Between fifty and 209 black people lost their lives under the white terror.[17]

Analyzed through multiple lenses and scales, Bill's trajectory becomes part of a broader narrative. He was tried for one of the first capital crimes of the 1850s, as economic pressure and political tensions increased. The legal procedures and his rights were respected in court. However, the political and symbolic significance of slave resistance increased after the rise of abolitionism. Enslaved men from Bill's neighborhood murdered their overseers, trying to hide their crimes and pleading maltreatment – perhaps remembering Bill's fate. The eight capital crimes committed in that decade are far from representing a slave insurrection but they were symptoms of underlying tensions. Criminal justice became harsher, and the spectacle of the public gallows

---

and slave resistance, see Michael Tadman, *Speculators and Slaves: Masters, Traders, and Slaves in the Old South* (Madison, WI, 1996).

[16]*State v. Frank* [1854], *State v. General* [1854], *State v. Henderson, Anderson, Reuben* [1857], *State v. Tom, John, Reuben* [1857], Adam County Courts Record, Historic Natchez Foundation. Also see the interpretation of Michael Wayne, *Death of an Overseer* (Oxford, 2001).

[17]On the alleged conspiracy and the extralegal investigation in Natchez, see Winthrop Jordan, *Tumult and Silence at Second Creek: An Inquiry into a Civil War Slave Conspiracy* (Baton Rouge, LA, 1993); Justin Behrend, "Rebellious Talk and Conspiratorial Plots: The Making of a Slave Insurrection in Civil War Natchez", *Journal of Southern History*, 77:1 (2011), pp. 17–52.

Figure 3. Enslaved workers on a coffee plantation in the Paraíba Valley, photograph by Marc Ferrez, c.1880s. Public domain.

returned. During the Civil War, the anxieties of the white population emerged, and formal justice was left behind.

Capital Crimes and Punishment in Vassouras, Rio de Janeiro

The city of Vassouras was founded in 1833, becoming one of the most important coffee districts in the Paraíba Valley. The natural Atlantic Forest was preserved in the region until the arrival of the Portuguese royal family in 1808, when the first sugar and coffee plantations were established (Figure 3). The expansion of the agricultural frontier was connected with the Atlantic slave trade that sealed the fate of thousands of African men and women. Ethnic diversity created tensions within the enslaved population, but the majority of Central West Africans also facilitated alliances and collective actions. The high prices of coffee in the 1830s stimulated planters to expand their fields and force their workers to produce more. The economic dynamism eventually backfired against masters and overseers in episodes of slave resistance. Moreover, the political crisis during that decade, the British anti-slave trade policy, and slave insurrections pushed slaveholders against the wall. Under pressure, they formed alliances, lobbying for legal reforms that centralized the judiciary and reinforced the severity of criminal justice against enslaved people.[18]

[18]On the formation of the Paraíba Valley, see Stanley Stein, *Vassouras: A Brazilian Coffee County, 1850–1900* (New York, 1976); Salles, *E o Vale era Escravo*. On the Atlantic slave trade in Brazil, see Jaime Rodrigues, *O Infame Comércio. Propostas e Experiências no Final do Tráfico de Africanos para o Brasil (1800–1850)* (Campinas, 2000); Manolo Florentino, *Em Costas Negras. Uma História do Tráfico Atlântico de Escravos entre a África e o Rio de Janeiro, séculos XVIII e XIX* (São Paulo, 1997); Beatriz Mamigonian, *Africanos Livres. A Abolição do Tráfico de Escravos no Brasil* (São Paulo, 2017). On the African ethnicities in Southeast Brazil, see Robert Slenes, "Malungu, Ngoma Vem! África Coberta e

In 1836, Matheus Rebollo and João Congo left the local jail surrounded by a military guard. Led by the judge, his clerk, and a priest, they marched through the streets of Vassouras, listening to their sentence at every corner. Finally, the executioner hanged both men in front of a crowd of free and enslaved people. They were the second and third Africans to lose their lives on the gallows in two years. Two of them had attacked their masters, and João Congo was condemned for killing his enslaved wife. This was an unusual punishment for a crime committed by one enslaved person against another, revealing the harshness of the judiciary at the time. Two years later, Manoel Congo led the biggest slave insurrection in the Paraíba Valley's history, escaping along with hundreds of enslaved men and women to the woods, seeking to build a maroon community. Defeated by a militia of slaveholders and a regiment of the National Guard, they were taken to the city, where the jury condemned seven men to public whipping. Only Manoel Congo was sent to the gallows.[19] Individual and collective resistance continued in the following decade. Bento Luiz Martins was hired as the overseer on the plantation of Barão de Massambará, one of the most important slaveholders of Vassouras. In two months, he intensified both labor productivity and punishments. After shortening the lunchtime, he humiliated those who disobeyed him, feeding his horse with their food. When he began whipping one of them, Januario and Antonio attacked him, stripped his clothes, and tied him down. Reversing the ritual, more than fifty enslaved people took turns whipping the overseer and left his body behind, believing he was dead. Under the orders of Massambará, all of them were punished, and only Antonio and Ciro were taken to court. Januario died before the trial, probably whipped to death on the plantation. The jury condemned Antonio to hang. However, the non-unanimous voting forced the commutation of the penalty to galleys for life. Ciro suffered 800 lashes and carried irons on his neck for three years.[20]

Between 1835 and 1850, capital crimes demonstrated local tensions, while the death penalty frequency revealed slaveholders' and authorities' anxieties in dealing with a great majority of enslaved African young men in Vassouras. More than a dozen enslaved people were accused of committing seven capital crimes and tried by jury; most of them were hanged. However, slave criminality decreased in the following decades for different reasons. The prohibition of the slave trade in 1850 changed the demography of the Paraíba Valley with the creolization of the enslaved population and the making of families and communities. The high prices of enslaved workers discouraged planters from expanding their fields, reducing pressure on labor productivity. The formation of a mature slave society after decades of conflicts and

Descoberta do Brasil", *Revista USP*, 12 (1992), pp. 48–67; *idem, Na Senzala, uma Flor. Esperanças e Recordações na Formação da Família Escrava, Brasil Sudeste, Século XIX* (Rio de Janeiro, 1999).

[19] Criminal Record for Murder, João Congo, 1836; Criminal Record for Attempted Murder, Matheus Rebollo, 1836, both in Arquivo do Tribunal de Justiça do Rio de Janeiro / IPHAN, Vassouras, Rio de Janeiro. Also see Keila Grinberg, Magno Fonseca Borges, and Ricardo Salles, "Rebeliões Escravas Antes da Extinção do Tráfico", in Keila Grinberg and Ricardo Salles (orgs), *O Brasil Imperial* (Rio de Janeiro, 2009), I, pp. 235–267. On the Manoel Congo Rebellion, see Flávio dos Santos Gomes, *Histórias de Quilombolas. Mocambos e Comunidades Escravas no Rio de Janeiro, Século XIX* (Rio de Janeiro, 1995), pp. 144–247.

[20] Criminal Record for Murder, Antonio and Ciro, 1844, Arquivo do Tribunal de Justiça do Rio de Janeiro / IPHAN, Vassouras, Rio de Janeiro. Also see Dos Santos Gomes, *Histórias de Quilombolas*, pp. 235–237.

negotiations created an unwritten code between the enslaved, overseers, and masters – a *moral economy of slavery*. At the same time, the political consensus that allowed the expansion of slave smuggling in the previous decade was reframed as a *politics of slavery* that silenced opposition voices for two decades. In the 1860s, jurists and politicians worked to legitimize state institutions based on liberal principles, defending gradual emancipation and penal reform. The emperor used his prerogatives to reduce the death penalty frequency as a strategy to legitimize Brazil among modern nations, despite the continuity of slavery. Under such conditions, trials for capital crimes and the execution of the death penalty decreased in Vassouras in the 1850s and 1860s.[21]

The only capital crime committed between 1857 and 1869 was the murder of Manuel Duarte Simões, a newly hired overseer who increased labor productivity and built a punishment pole in the coffee fields. He was ambushed and killed by gunshot, and seven enslaved men were taken to court. Accusing the overseer of violence, they managed to postpone a verdict until a prisoner revealed a conversation between the defendants who had agreed to keep silent, believing they would be released and chastised at the plantation. The jury acquitted most of them, condemning only Lucio and Sebastião, who were sentenced to perpetual galleys. The case reveals that the defendants not only succeeded initially in misleading the authorities, but also had a certain knowledge of the legal system. In a few years, other enslaved men would be even more audacious.[22]

The Civil War in the United States isolated Brazil as one of the last slave countries in the Americas, and the Paraguay War exposed its social contradictions internationally. The political consensus over slavery was broken, resulting in the Womb Law of 1871 – which established legal principles for gradual emancipation and expanded the rights of enslaved people. The increasing price of coffee stimulated planters to impose higher productivity on their workers. These enslaved people were born in Brazil, belonged to local enslaved communities, or were brought in by the interprovincial trade. This forced migration contributed to politicizing enslaved communities in the Paraíba Valley and expanding their resistance strategies, especially by encouraging them to claim their rights in court. Attacks on overseers recently hired became the major symptom of tensions on plantations in the 1870s. The last execution in the region happened in 1856, and according to the common sense among enslaved

---

[21]On the intersection between enslaved families and political stability in mature plantation societies in Brazil, see Manolo Florentino and José Roberto Góes, *A Paz das Senzalas. Famílias Escravas e Tráfico Atlântico, Rio de Janeiro, 1790–1850* (Rio de Janeiro, 1997); João José Reis and Eduardo Silva, *Negociação e Conflito. A Resistência Negra no Brasil Escravista* (São Paulo, 1989); Salles, *E o Vale era Escravo*, pp. 177–271. On the uses of Edward Thompson's concept of moral economy in the Brazilian historiography of slavery, see Silvia Hunold Lara, *Campos da Violência. Escravos e Senhores na Capitania do Rio de Janeiro, 1750–1808* (Rio de Janeiro, 1988); Sidney Chalhoub, *Visões da Liberdade. Uma História das Últimas Décadas da Escravidão na Corte* (São Paulo, 1990); Hebe Mattos, *Das cores do silêncio. Os significados da liberdade no sudeste escravista* (Rio de Janeiro, 1995).

[22]Criminal Record for Murder, Lucio, Sebastião, Francisco and Elias, 1866, Arquivo do Tribunal de Justiça do Rio de Janeiro / IPHAN, Vassouras, Rio de Janeiro. Also see Bryan McCann, "The Whip and the Watch: Overseers in the Paraíba Valley, Brazil", *Slavery & Abolition*, 18:2 (1997), pp. 30–47; Camila Agostini, "Africanos no Cativeiro e a Construção de Identidades no Além-Mar. Vale do Paraíba, Século XIX" (Master's thesis, Universidade Estadual de Campinas, 2002), p. 44; Rafael Marquese, "African Diaspora, Slavery, and the Paraiba Valley Coffee Plantation Landscape", *Review (Fernand Braudel Center)*, 31:2 (2008), pp. 195–216, 206–210.

people, the emperor no longer applied the death penalty. Facing what they considered violations of the *moral economy of slavery*, ten enslaved men committed crimes against overseers between 1870 and 1878. At least four of them had presented themselves voluntarily to the police, preferring criminal conviction to slavery – according to the local judge. Most of them had been condemned to the galleys, a penalty criticized when applied to the enslaved. This new generation of enslaved rebels explored the contradictions of criminal law and penal reform in order to resist captivity. When Manoel and Gil surrendered themselves in 1879, Vassouras' courthouse became the political center of a social and moral crisis.[23]

The prosecutor indicted only Manoel and Gil, refusing to include the others as defendants. He was assured that they had only attacked the overseer's corpse to be released from slavery. Manoel and Gil confessed to the crime, and witnesses confirmed that they had invited others to do the same in order to "be freed" by justice. Their counsel attempted to disqualify the victim as an overseer, avoiding condemnation under the Law of 1835. Paradoxically, the defendants had different goals from their lawyer since he represented their owner. By convincing the jurors, he ensured that they would not be sentenced to perpetual galleys. After suffering 400 lashes each, Manoel and Gil returned to their plantations with irons on their necks. Their fate is unknown. However, returning to their neighborhood was not part of their plans, and it might have cost them their lives.[24]

In the 1880s, the radicalization of the abolitionist movement and of slave resistance intensified the delegitimization of slavery. In Vassouras, jurors expressed the loss of credibility in the criminal justice by acquitting or imposing minor punishments on enslaved defendants accused of capital crimes. In other cities of the Paraíba Valley, such as Paraíba do Sul and Valença, mobs broke into jails and lynched enslaved prisoners. In at least one case, the victim was kidnapped from jail and killed at the place where the original crime had happened. The spatial ritual was reversed. If enslaved people who committed crimes in their masters' domains sought refuge from state institutions in the cities, the mobs reinforced slaveholders' order by breaking into jails and performing spectacles of violence in the plantation world.[25]

The previous and following contexts reframe the significance of the crime and the trial of Manoel and Gil. Their murder was the last of a series of killings of overseers in

---

[23]On the interprovincial slave trade and the politicization of enslaved communities, see Robert Slenes, "The Demography and Economics of Brazilian Slavery: 1850–1888" (Ph.D., Stanford University, 1976); Chalhoub, *Visões da Liberdade*. On slave resistance in court, see Hebe Mattos, *Das Cores do Silêncio*; Keila Grinberg, *Liberata, a Lei da Ambiguidade. Ações de liberdade da Corte de Apelação do Rio de Janeiro no Século XIX* (Rio de Janeiro, 1994).

[24]Criminal Record for Murder, Manoel and Gil, 1879, Arquivo do Tribunal de Justiça do Rio de Janeiro / IPHAN, Vassouras, Rio de Janeiro.

[25]On lynching during the crisis of slavery in Brazil, see Ricardo Pirola, "A Lei de Lynch no Ocaso da Escravidão. Linchamentos, Justiça e Polícia (1878–1888)", in Regina Xavier and Helen Osório (eds), *Do Tráfico ao Pós-Abolição. Trabalho Compulsório e Livre e a Luta por Direitos no Brasil* (São Leopoldo, 2018), pp. 454–481; Marcelo Ferraro, "A Economia Política da Violência na Era da Segunda Escravidão: Brasil e Estados Unidos, 1776–1888" (Ph.D., Universidade de São Paulo, 2021), pp. 337–388. On abolitionism in Brazil, see Angela Alonso, *Flores, Votos e Balas. O Movimento Abolicionista Brasileiro (1868–88)* (São Paulo, 2015); Jeffrey Needell, *The Sacred Cause: The Abolitionist Movement, Afro-Brazilian Mobilization, and Imperial Politics in Rio de Janeiro* (Stanford, CA, 2020).

the 1870s. Almost all their predecessors were condemned to the galleys. This seems to have been their goal, but they were frustrated by their own lawyer and the jury. Their sentence was the first of another series of verdicts. It was the first time that enslaved defendants accused of a capital crime were not accused of violating the special Law of 1835 and were condemned to penalties milder than death or the galleys. In the subsequent trials, jurors corrupted the law to impose penalties that the local community considered fair. In the final decades of slavery, the political significance of slave resistance increased after the rise of the abolitionist movement, and the extralegal reaction of slaveholders and overseers became epidemic. Vassouras plantations and courthouses were political arenas where Manoel, Gil, and other enslaved men disputed their own notions of justice. At the same time, broken jails and lynching spectacles were violent performances of slaveholders' justice, whose world was falling apart.

Conclusion

Violence was indeed constitutive of slavery, and these findings reinforce the premise that patterns of punishment and resistance cannot be understood exclusively as the consequence of individual actions but must be viewed within broader structural conditions. The analysis of capital crimes and judicial punishment through different spatial scales (local, national, Atlantic) and over the nineteenth century contextualizes the historical significance of both enslaved peoples' resistance and state violence. Second, the comparative study of Natchez and Vassouras illuminates the differences between these racialized slave societies and their legal and political systems. The centralized monarchy established a national policy of penal reform and abolished the death penalty de facto in the Brazilian empire, while state assemblies and courts in the American South preserved it. Simultaneously, democracy encouraged the common white man not only to vote, but also to perform parallel forms of justice during insurrectionary panics in the United States. Meanwhile, oligarchical powers prevailed in rural Brazil, and extralegal violence was rarely a mob action. Therefore, these slave societies were under distinct political systems and regimes of racial violence.[26]

Despite these differences, their similarities and connections reveal an integrated history in which slavery and punishment constituted the historical experience of nation-states, liberal institutions, and the capitalist world economy in the long nineteenth century. This research identified three phases of slavery and violence in the Mississippi and Paraíba Valleys as local expressions of national and Atlantic histories. In the early nineteenth century, the expansion of the commodity frontier formed new slave societies in these regions, which matured by the 1840s and entered a declining period during the political crisis of slavery – between 1850 and 1865 in the United States and 1871 and 1888 in Brazil.

Data from Natchez and Vassouras demonstrates that in recently established plantation societies, violence expanded beyond the domestic boundaries of plantations due to the pressure on labor productivity and the lack of social bonds between enslaved people, overseers, and masters. Moreover, political divergence among free people opened possibilities for slave resistance. In response, the judiciary and the death

---

[26]For a longer version of this conclusion, see Ferraro, *A Economia Política da Violência*.

penalty became instruments of the slaveholders' hegemony in the early decades of the nineteenth century. Between the 1840s and 1850s, the decline of commodity prices and the slave trade coincided with the making of mature slave societies. Enslaved communities negotiated rights with overseers and masters, consolidating *moral economies of slavery*. At the same time, the *politics of slavery* successfully maintained a silent consensus among political parties inside state institutions in both countries, blocking antislavery agendas. During this age of political and social stability, the reform of criminal justice systems and the expansion of enslaved people's rights contributed to legitimizing these slave societies. Under such conditions, conflicts were solved on plantations, and public trials and capital punishment were rarefied.

In the second half of the nineteenth century, global economic changes stimulated cotton and coffee economies and reinforced national and local political contradictions. In the 1850s, Natchez saw more capital crimes than in previous decades. There was greater pressure on labor productivity, and the political tensions might have influenced some enslaved men to react against their overseers and owners. Nonetheless, the changing pattern of state punishment and the emergence of extralegal violence were more relevant. The secession crisis and the rise of radical abolitionism increased the political significance of slave resistance, especially through the eyes of the white community. The pressure on courts and authorities brought back the public spectacle of the death penalty. When white fears became a collective hysteria during the Civil War, whites became suspicious of the formal justice system, substituting it with inquisitorial torture and hangings – a rehearsal of the post-abolition theater of violence. The end of the Civil War in the United States isolated Brazil internationally, breaking the politics of slavery among the elites. At the same time, abolitionists and enslaved people began a systemic resistance from the bottom up. Crimes against overseers in Vassouras during the 1870s were a consequence of local tensions in the coffee fields. Simultaneously, the political divergence over slavery and the death penalty opened possibilities for a few enslaved men to seek courts as an alternative to slavery. Slaveholders and the free community lost faith in state institutions and reacted with fraudulent trials and lynchings in the 1880s.

Hence, during the crisis of slavery in the United States and Brazil, the *oligopoly of violence* became symbolically dysfunctional. Even though the criminal justice system tried all enslaved rebels, condemning most of them to harsh punishment, the resistance of the enslaved and their legal strategies destabilized the moral and institutional consensus over slavery. In turn, slaveholders' terror meant to reinforce their power locally, but the epidemic of extralegal violence became a strong argument for abolitionists, delegitimizing slavery nationally.

Abolition in Brazil and the United States did not end structural and institutional racism. Slavery was a fundamental piece in the making of criminal justice in both countries. Its legacy reshaped racial inequality and violence in later centuries through segregation, police brutality, and mass incarceration – our own peculiar institutions yet to be abolished.

Cite this article: Marcelo Rosanova Ferraro. The Political Economy of Punishment: Slavery and Violence in Nineteenth-Century Brazil and the United States. *International Review of Social History*, 68:S31 (2023), pp. 197–212. https://doi.org/10.1017/S0020859022000876

International Review of Social History, 68:S31 (2023), pp. 213–235
doi:10.1017/S0020859023000020

RESEARCH ARTICLE

The 1886 Southwest Railroad Strike, J. West Goodwin's Law and Order League, and the Blacklisting of Martin Irons

Chad Pearson

University of North Texas, College of Liberal Arts & Social Sciences, Denton, Texas, United States, e-mail: chad.pearson@unt.edu

Abstract
This article explores blacklisting practices following the massive 1886 Southwest strike staged by the Knights of Labor (KOL) against Jay Gould's railroad empire. It focuses mostly on strike leader Martin Irons and blacklisting advocate and newspaperman J. West Goodwin. The strike, which started in Sedalia, Missouri, before spreading to other states, was a disaster for the KOL. The union declined in its aftermath chiefly because of the repression unleashed by public and private forces, including businessmen-led Law and Order Leagues. After the strike, employers blacklisted many, including strike leader and Sedalia resident Martin Irons. Irons, constantly on the move, suffered from joblessness, underemployment, arrests, and broken health before he died in central Texas in 1900. Few blacklisting advocates wanted Irons to suffer more than J. West Goodwin. The Law and Order League leader and newspaperman repeatedly wrote about what he considered Martin Irons's moral lapses and shortsightedness. By focusing on Goodwin's promotion of blacklisting and Irons's post-strike struggles, this essay helps us better appreciate the underexplored dimensions of this form of punishment.

The numerous strikes that rocked the United States during the late nineteenth century triggered the wrath of powerful opponents: employers attached to various-sized businesses, local police forces, the courts, state militias, private security agencies, and vigilantes. Late nineteenth-century US history provides many examples of these repressive forces, and historians have noted the country's comparatively cruel labor relations carried out by both public and private forces.[1] Different groups of anti-labor

---

[1] David Montgomery, *Citizen Worker: The Experience of Workers in the United States with Democracy and the Free Market During the Nineteenth Century* (Cambridge, 1993), pp. 52–104; Gerald Friedman, *State-Making and Labor Movements: France and the United States, 1876–1914* (Ithaca, NY, 1998); Paul F. Lipold and Larry W. Isaac, "Striking Deaths: Lethal Contestation and the 'Exceptional' Character of the American Labor Movement, 1870–1970", *International Review of Social History*, 54:2 (2009), pp. 167–205; Robert Justin Goldstein, "*Labor History* Symposium: Political Repression of the American Labor Movement during Its Formative Years – A Comparative Perspective", *Labor History*, 51 (2010), pp. 279–280; Leo Panitch and Sam Gindin, *The Making of Global Capitalism: The Political Economy of American Empire* (London, 2012), p. 33.

forces, seeking stability, control, profits, and access to of efficient and faithful laborers, employed both hard and soft forms of repression. Hard forms included arresting, beating, and sometimes killing labor activists; softer techniques involved firing and blacklisting troublemakers. During the late nineteenth century, thousands experienced the enduring sting of the blacklist, a topic that has received far too little scholarly attention.[2]

This paper sheds light on the blacklisting process. Thousands of blacklisted men and women experienced multiple traumas, including long periods of financially ruinous and emotionally taxing forms of punishment. I will first make some general remarks about the process of blacklisting itself, noting the experiences of both victims and victimizers. Next, I will narrow my focus by exploring the tensions between two high-profile individuals involved in this process: blacklisting advocate J. West Goodwin (1836–1927) and his long-suffering victim, labor leader Martin Irons (1830–1900). Goodwin was a nationally recognized anti-labor union activist, promoter of business interests, vigorous social networker, and newspaperman; Irons was a charismatic and widely respected leader of the Knight of Labor who was responsible for calling and organizing strikes. Both men lived in Sedalia, Missouri, a modest-sized city that was one of the major centers of the 1886 strike against Jay Gould's massive railroad empire. Sedalia saw much railroad traffic and was home to the Missouri Pacific Railroad and the Missouri, Kansas, and Texas Railroad maintenance shops. The railroad shops were major employers in Sedalia, and members of the city's Board of Trade, including Goodwin, greatly appreciated how these worksites contributed to the city's overall prosperity. Exploring the colorful lives of these two men helps us more fully appreciate the personal ways that this form of managerial punishment expressed itself in practice.

Labor unrest was one of the chief impediments to the economic interests of those at the top of society, and most businessmen in Sedalia and elsewhere opposed all expressions of working-class disobedience. And managers at various levels kept close tabs on the workforce, especially during and immediately after strikes. Indeed, scholars have long noted the inordinate power of employers over workers. Political scientist Elizabeth Anderson has captured the near-absoluteness of their authority, noting that it is "sweeping, arbitrary, and unaccountable – not subject to notice, process, or appeal".[3] Firing and blacklisting were obvious ways of practicing

---

[2]The two major books about strikebreaking and unionbusting in US history say little or nothing about blacklisting as a form of punishment. Stephen H. Norwood, *Strikebreaking and Intimidation: Mercenaries and Masculinity in Twentieth-Century America* (Chapel Hill, NC, 2002); Robert Michael Smith, *From Blackjacks to Briefcases: A History of Commercialized Strikebreaking and Unionbusting in the United States* (Athens, OH, 2003). A search of "Blacklist" and "Labor" in the America: History and Life database reveals twenty-three hits, and most concern the Hollywood Blacklist of the Cold War period. For a good analysis of blacklisting on railroads, see Paul V. Black, "Experiment in Bureaucratic Centralization: Employee Blacklisting on the Burlington Railroad, 1877–1892", *Business History Review*, 51 (1977), pp. 444–459; Shelton Stromquist, *A Generation of Boomers: The Pattern of Railroad Labor Conflict in Nineteenth-Century America* (Urbana, IL, 1987), pp. 42–44; Mark Kruger, *The St. Louis Commune of 1877: Communism in the Heartland* (Lincoln, NE, 2021), p. 127.

[3]Elizabeth Anderson, *Private Government: How Employers Rule Our Lives (and Why We Don't Talk about It)* (Princeton, NJ, 2017), p. 54.

and exhibiting their control over laborers. But rather than focusing primarily on Irons's bosses – railroad supervisors who worked under Gould – this paper explores the influence of Goodwin, someone who had no direct supervisory responsibilities over Irons or any of his workmates. By highlighting Goodwin's role in reinforcing Gould's managerial interests, this paper insists that we take seriously the actions of third-party actors with respect to the question of blacklisting. Instead of examining the direct activities played by bosses in this punishment process, I investigate the pro-blacklisting actions of an urban booster who was ideologically opposed to all forms of labor militancy following the massive 1886 strike called by Irons. Goodwin saw himself as an enforcer of business power and worker subservience throughout the community and beyond. Blacklisting mutinous workers like Irons was a way to achieve what Goodwin considered community harmony, prosperity, and law and order. Goodwin's involvement in blacklisting Irons provides us with a useful and novel way of understanding the various punishing characteristics of this soft form of discipline.

The Blacklisting Process

Employers practiced blacklisting because they wanted to establish workplace control by making examples out of troublemakers in the context of labor management conflicts. Stripping men and women of their livelihoods served employers' collective and individual interests. Essentially, promoters of this form of punishment – direct supervisors and employers representing other workplaces – sought to explicitly pit unruly workers against those who conducted their duties diligently and faithfully. Blacklisting was one of the employers' foremost weapons meant to send unambiguous messages about what constituted inappropriate actions with the aim of disciplining others. Employers, irrespective of the type or size of workplaces they oversaw, desired employees who displayed unconditional loyalty, trustworthiness, and a sustained disinclination to participate in "disruptive labor actions". Blacklists starkly indicated the type of workers they did *not* want.

Unwanted workers faced many difficulties, and we must consider the multiple stages of the blacklisting process itself. For victims, it started on the last day of labor at a particular worksite and concluded elsewhere. Relatively fortunate blacklisted men and women eventually landed on their feet, finding other sources of income shortly after experiencing the traumas of termination. But not all enjoyed these somewhat positive outcomes. Whether the victim suffered in the short or long term, removal and job-seeking were deeply unpleasant experiences that produced intense feelings of anxiety. While the victims suffered their difficulties out in the open as they scrambled to find new jobs, the people responsible for their troubles conducted their work comfortably behind closed doors, where they enjoyed renewed feelings of peace of mind after firing their targets. They relished these feelings of empowerment, enjoying the authority to fire at will. They also used their power to brand their victims with the troublemaker label. The branding process generally led to long-lasting reputational damages, hurting the former employee's future job prospects and leading to a host of lingering challenges, including hunger and homelessness, as well as feelings of depression and desperation. Writing in

1885, labor activist Eugene Debs described how the "practitioners" of this form of punishment robbed wage earners of "the means of subsistence, dogging their steps for the purpose of keeping them in idleness till gaunt hunger gnaws at their vitals, until rags bespeak their degradation and blank despair shrouds their lives".[4] This managerial form of punishment hurt not only the discharged and blacklisted victims. News of terminations usually spread quickly and had profoundly chilling impacts on laborers generally. Writing about the experience of American workers in 1891, Eleanor Marx Aveling and Edward Aveling noted that many lived in fear of "The terrors of the black list".[5]

These terrors, combined with the weight of public opinion, prompted some state legislatures to ban the practice. By the early 1910s, twenty-three states barred employers' from using blacklists.[6] Yet, numerous bosses unapologetically continued this practice despite laws explicitly prohibiting it. As one writer put it: "The employer's right to discharge is absolute, and the man who is deprived of a livelihood usually has no proof against the person who supplied the information."[7] Blacklisting persisted throughout the late nineteenth and early twentieth centuries, and liberal-oriented state authorities and trade union lobbyists had little success stopping the practice.

What groups of workers experienced these terrors? Much of the evidence of blacklisting is shrouded in secrecy, but we have access to some evidence. Writing about blacklisting on the Burlington railroad in the late nineteenth century, historian Paul V. Black has listed twenty-eight reasons why employers put workmen on blacklists, including drunkenness, carelessness, incompetence, neglect of duty, laziness, and theft. At this company, strike activity was the ninth leading reason.[8] This paper is exclusively interested in blacklisting caused by acts of labor rebellion like strikes and union organizing. Indeed, people in positions of power singled out labor leaders, those responsible for challenging employers by calling strikes, organizing boycotts, building unions, or even voting for political candidates that employers loathed.[9] The men and women managers punished after outbursts of labor activism were typically well-respected working-class activists who had succeeded in building trust with the rank and file.

These individuals were generally committed to class struggle unionism, recognizing the type of leverage that strikes wielded, which included pressuring employers to increase wages, improve job security, and bargain fairly. Unlike more conservative unionists who sought to establish mutually respectful relationships with employers

---

[4]Eugene V. Debs, "The Attempted Blacklist Degradation of Employees", *Locomotive Firemen's Magazine*, 9 (1885), p. 158.

[5]Edward Aveling and Eleanor Marx Aveling, *The Working-Class Movement in America* (London, 1891), p. 46.

[6]Harry W. Laidler, *Boycotts and the Labor Struggle: Economic and Legal Aspects* (New York, 1913), p. 48.

[7]John B. Andrews, *Labor Problems and Labor Legislation* (New York, 1919), p. 101. Historian Ralph Scharnau notes that an 1888 Iowa law "was generally ignored". Ralph Scharnau, "The Knights of Labor in Iowa", *The Annals of Iowa*, 50 (1991), p. 879; David R. Berman, *Radicalism in the Mountain West, 1890–1920: Socialists, Populists, Miners, and Wobblies* (Boulder, CO, 2007), p. 135.

[8]Black, "Experiment in Bureaucratic Centralization", pp. 444–459.

[9]Gideon Cohn-Postar, "'Vote for your Bread and Butter': Economic Intimidation of Voters in the Gilded Age", *Journal of the Gilded Age and Progressive Era*, 20 (2021), pp. 480–502.

while also seeking to suppress the rebellious impulses of rank-and-filers, those committed to class struggle style unionism eagerly sought to mobilize the masses combatively, with the overarching aims of securing higher levels of power on worksites. While more moderate unionists behaved relatively diplomatically as they aimed to achieve labor-business partnerships, more radical, class struggle-style unionists were generally class-conscious and proudly defiant, recognizing the fundamentally adversarial relationships between bosses and laborers. Those who embraced the class struggle style of unionism acted in ways that challenged managers at all levels. And for these reasons, it did not take long for the most dynamic union advocates to appear on management's radar. For their part, employers, enjoying the legal right to fire whomever they wanted, took satisfaction in removing these troublemakers.

Seeking vengeance against their targets, employers embedded in various business communities received assistance from friends and strangers alike. Promoters of blacklisting generated actual lists *and* relied on the usefulness of word-of-mouth and newspaper messaging. From the employers' perspective, press coverage of dissident workers was a powerful signal of who *not* to hire.[10] Together, those responsible for the ostracization process – employers, journalists, and members of Boards of Trade in cities of various sizes – were often geographically spread out and represented different sectors of the economy. However, they shared a common interest in avoiding the type of labor problems associated with fired individuals. Some personally knew the employers responsible for firing these men and women; others learned about the supposed firebrands from discussions at business club meetings or by reading newspapers.

The employers' profoundly life-altering actions started a process that often continued for years after victims involuntarily left worksites. Receiving the news of firings from employers was an often-devastating experience. Such figures were immediately bombarded with feelings of concern, desperately asking themselves a series of nagging questions about how to move forward. How, they asked themselves, could they cover basic needs such as food, clothing, and shelter without income sources? Income loss disruptions were not merely experienced by breadwinners. Firing victims, plagued by overwhelming feelings of unease, self-doubt, and humiliation, were left unable to assist family members who often depended on their incomes. This caused growing anxiety in families, compelling members to desperately seek new forms of employment and sources of income. Additionally, employer-provoked discharges meant more than the absence of paychecks; employers involved in the termination and blacklisting process destroyed significant parts of workers' identities and sense of purpose, since victims were no longer able to engage in the familiar labor and social routines that brought them into contact with fellow employees. These routines, based mainly on their shared experiences with exploitation, led to bonds of solidarity and friendships. Vengeful employers robbed workers of much more than money.

Workplace removals following combative labor actions sent unmistakable messages about employers' core demands and interests. Naturally, managers sought to

---

[10]Mainstream newspapers were almost universally critical of labor unrest and supportive of employers during industrial disputes. Upton Sinclair, *The Brass Check: A Study of American Journalism* (Pasadena, CA, 1920).

create trouble-free and smoothly operating worksites, and punishing actions like firing and backlisting were intended to spread fear – and generating fear was designed to discipline the remaining workforce. Such actions, in short, were meant to shape the behaviors of those who continued laboring. Whether employers conveyed their messages explicitly is hard to know, but we can be confident that information circulated quickly following discharges, creating climates of insecurity. These feelings of uncertainty undoubtedly influenced the actions of many laborers, teaching them the necessity of demonstrating loyalty to their bosses and the importance of performing their duties productively without showing interest in unions or strikes. Blacklisted men and women were living examples of how *not* to behave in workplaces.

Blacklisting reached a high point in the second part of the 1880s when thousands suffered these cruelties following a series of strikes. Yet, employers were far more interested in running their businesses than addressing the traumas experienced by their victims. After discharging and blacklisting thousands of labor activists, employers hired non-unionists in their place. In 1886, employers hired 39,854 non-unionists in place of unionists. In the following year, the number of replacement laborers numbered 39,549.[11]

Goodwin vs Irons

Unfortunately, very few blacklisting practitioners or victims left documents, making it difficult for researchers to recreate the lives of those from either side of these class divides. But we know that victims' experiences were intensely upsetting, and we can patch together some relevant pieces of evidence, shedding light on both the punished and the punishers. With this goal in mind, the remaining parts of this essay explore the actions of two unusually visible figures: J. West Goodwin and Martin Irons. Goodwin was one of the nation's most prominent anti-labor union activists; he was extremely active in building employers' associations and wrote critically about union activities locally and nationally. And Irons was, for a short period, one of the country's most powerful class-conscious labor leaders partially responsible for organizing the multiline 1886 strike against the Gould system.

Both men lived interesting lives. Born in Watertown, New York, in 1836, Goodwin, a Union veteran of the Civil War and newspaperman, made his biggest mark in Sedalia. This medium-sized Missouri city was captured by Confederate troops in October 1864.[12] The city grew modestly in the years after the war, and Goodwin became a keen booster of his adopted home in the century's final years. He enjoyed connections with powerful business and political leaders, both in and outside Sedalia, and played an important part in launching the city's Board of Trade in 1870. He opened his own publishing house in Sedalia in 1868 and edited the widely read *Sedalia Bazoo*. As the owner of a one-building print shop, Goodwin quickly became an influential community voice, eagerly promoting the city as a center of business prosperity and law and order. He was an enthusiastic supporter of the engines of

---

[11]Kim Moody, *Tramps and Trade Union Travelers: Internal Migration and Organized Labor in Gilded Age America* (Chicago, IL, 2019), p. 126.

[12]Mark A. Lause, *The Collapse of Price's Raid: The Beginning of the End in Civil War Missouri* (Columbia, MO, 2016), pp. 34–39.

economic growth and established close connections with prominent businessmen; his business, for example, published documents for bankers and railroad investors.[13] He earned considerable respect among his peers active in various civic affairs; in 1891, for instance, he became the president of the Missouri Press Association. According to historian Ronald T. Farrar, his *Bazoo* "was perhaps the most widely quoted community newspaper in the state".[14] In 1902, Goodwin explained, "I have expressed my own convictions in the plainest and simplest words at my command".[15] The proud Sedalian even lobbied to make his city the state capital, hoping to deprive Jefferson City of that honor. He failed in this task but remained outspoken in drawing explicit links between business interests and community stability. This meant promoting respect for the city's businessmen against any plebeian threats – dangerous, law-breaking labor actions that were more apparent elsewhere, including in larger cities like Chicago, Pittsburgh, and St. Louis, than in Sedalia. The owner-editor sought to play his own role in discouraging such actions locally.[16] As he explained in 1879: "The newspapers are upholders of law and order."[17]

The proprietor of the J. West Goodwin Publishing Company made many lasting impressions on others, including friends and foes alike. He typically wore his signature top hat in public and was generally known for his flamboyancy and hardnosed anti-unionism, which became particularly pronounced when organizers issued him ultimatums at his worksite. In January 1885, for instance, members of the International Typographical Union (ITU) sought to organize his workers, demanding that only union members work in the *Bazoo* office. The "gang of cut throats", he later complained, "were endeavoring to break down the *Bazoo* because it would not employ Union help exclusively".[18] It is unclear if these "cut throats" were successful; at least one source suggests that the ITU had prevailed: "The boycott was a grand success, and the result was an unconditional surrender on the part of the *Bazoo* proprietor."[19] But Goodwin never admitted defeat, adamantly proclaiming that he "refused to submit".[20] Regardless of the result of this confrontation, we can, at a minimum, conclude that Goodwin sought to protect his identity as a strong-willed business owner determined to show fellow community members his uncompromisingness in the face of challenges from below.

IIn response to this conflict, a contemplative Goodwin developed a clear anti-union philosophy. The 1885 confrontation caused him to reflect, compelling him

---

[13]J. West Goodwin, *Pacific Railway Business Guide and Gazetteer of Missouri and Kansas* (St. Louis, MO, 1867); *Proceedings of the Convention of the Missouri Bankers Association Held at Sweet Springs, Mo., July 9th, 10th, and 11th, 1879* (Sedalia, 1879).

[14]Ronald T. Farrar, *A Creed for My Profession: Water Williams, Journalist to the World* (Columbia, MO, 1998), p. 40.

[15]J. West Goodwin, *Random Recollections of Forty Years in Sedalia Before the Nehemgar Club, March 20, 1902* (1902), p. 2.

[16]"Railroad Striking", *Sedalia Weekly Bazoo*, 24 July 1877, p. 4.

[17]"Davidson and the Press", *Sedalia Weekly Bazoo*, 1 July 1879, p. 4.

[18]*Sedalia Weekly Bazoo*, 27 August 1889, p. 4.

[19]W. A. Wilkinson, "Report of the Corresponding Secretary", *Thirty-Third Annual Session of the International Typographical Union* (Philadelphia, PA, 1885), p. 37.

[20]"A Few Words as to the Boycotters and Boycotting in General", *Sedalia Weekly Bazoo*, 27 January 1885, p. 8.

to outline what he considered the excessiveness and absurdities of union-imposed rules. He used his platform to warn that union demands had the potential of spilling over into other areas of society: "If these men have the same right to prescribe what a man shall eat, what a man shall wear, what church he shall attend, what prices he shall receive for his goods, whom he shall marry, when and where he shall visit and in all other things do their beck and bidding." Goodwin put his foot down, unashamedly defending his right to manage: "But the *Bazoo* denies that they have any such rights."[21]

Goodwin's significantly unpleasant experiences with pushy labor activists prompted him to think hard about the logic of closed-shop unionism – workplaces that employed union members exclusively. In his judgment, such workplaces did not merely threaten his personal interests; demands for exclusivity agreements, he reasoned, were wholly incompatible with basic American freedoms. As we will see, Goodwin believed that he had the ultimate authority to manage his workplace as he alone saw fit. He stuck to this core belief throughout his life.

Born in Dundee, Scotland, Irons had a fundamentally different outlook on life, labor, and industrial society generally. Arriving in New York City at the age of fourteen, shortly before the Civil War, Irons soon found employment in a machine shop before departing to other parts of the nation, including New Orleans. He was appalled by the working conditions he encountered in both regions, which caused him to draw revolutionary conclusions about what he considered the necessity of emancipating "my fellow-workingmen from their wage-bondage".[22] During the 1870s, Irons faced numerous difficulties navigating the job market and thus experienced periodic bouts of unemployment. Economic pressures ensured that he was often on the go, moving from different locations in the South and Midwest, settling in places like Lexington, Kentucky, Kanas City, Kansas, and Joplin, Missouri. In this decade, he became active in the Grange, an organization that promoted the rights of farmers and small businesspeople. But he did not believe that businessmen, irrespective of the size of their operations, would serve in a vanguard role in transforming industrial society. He found a more plausible vehicle for liberation when he moved to Sedalia in the early 1880s. Shortly before Goodwin faced his own labor challenges, Irons became an active member of the Knights of Labor (KOL), a mostly inclusive and largely decentralized labor union that emerged in 1869.[23]

The KOL opened membership to most workers and even invited small businessmen to join. However, it prohibited lawyers, corporate leaders, and Chinese workers from holding membership.[24] Most of all, members believed that wage earners needed to assert more control over the labor process, and participants repeatedly complained about the emergence and spread of industrial monopolies. These powerful economic

---

[21]*Ibid.*, p 8.

[22]Quoted in Charles Postel, *The Populist Vision* (Oxford, 2007), p. 216.

[23]Theresa A. Case, "Blaming Martin Irons: Leadership and Popular Protest in the 1886 Southwest Strike", *Journal of Gilded Age and Progressive Era*, 8 (2009), pp. 51–81.

[24]In the mid-1880s, its members were involved in violent anti-Chinese riots in parts of the West. Carlos A. Schwantes, *Radical Heritage: Labor, Socialism, and Reform in Washington and British Columbia, 1885–1917* (Seattle, WA, 1979), pp. 22–29; Beth Lew-Williams, *The Chinese Must Go: Violence, Exclusion, and the Making of the Alien in America* (Cambridge, MA, 2018), p. 118.

entities threatened what KOL spokespersons called the "nobility of toil".[25] The union, which essentially functioned as a labor and political organization, reached a peak membership of over 700,000 members nationally in 1886.[26] Sedalia hosted five KOL assembles at this time, numbering about 1,000, mostly railroad workers. Around this time, Irons, holding a deeply held hatred of inequality and exploitation, became a trusted leader who demonstrated a willingness to fight on behalf of the membership.[27]

KOL members staged strikes to address injustices, and sometimes the union achieved critical victories, including in March 1885, when members across multiple states halted most of Jay Gould's freight trains. This relatively peaceful affair led to wage increases and improved job security for members. Labor movement representatives, gleeful about the triumph, commented on what appeared to be a pro-union atmosphere in Sedalia following the successful work stoppage: "Work in the railroad shops is fair and the men are all well treated since the great strike." According to this May 1885 report, that strike may have motivated laborers in other sectors of the city's economy to organize: "The painters, carpenters, tailors and bricklayers have all organized within the past month, and trade unionism is fairly booming in this city."[28] Clearly, railroad victors inspired others, persuading the city's diverse set of laborers to organize with one another and seek ways to extract benefits and win respect from their bosses.

Emboldened by the strike victory against the era's quintessential robber baron the previous year, combined with the growing popularity and legitimacy of labor unionism generally, KOL members staged a second work stoppage in March 1886 because employers reneged on their contractual agreements and, in KOL members' views, unfairly fired C.A. Hall, an employee from the Texas and Pacific Railway shop in Marshall, Texas. As the KOL District Assembly 101 leader, Irons rallied members to Hall's cause and, more broadly, to the defense of union rights. Irons played an instrumental role in building and sustaining the strike during membership meetings and on picket lines. As historian Theresa Case has put it, he approached the confrontation with "determined leadership".[29] He spoke from the heart and was, by most accounts, an inspirational orator, effective motivator, and principled leader. According to historian Ruth Allen, fellow KOL members were sometimes "moved to tears by an Irons' speech" while others were entranced by "his emotional power as a speaker".[30]

---

[25]Unnamed KOL member quoted in Leon Fink, *Workingmen's Democracy: The Knights of Labor and American Politics* (Urbana, IL, 1983), p. 9; Moody, *Tramps and Trade Union Travelers*, pp. 30–36; Terence V. Powderly, *Thirty Years of Labor: 1859–1889* (New York, [1890] 1967), p. 48.

[26]Robert H. Wiebe, *The Search for Order, 1877–1920* (New York, 1967), p. 45.

[27]Michael Cassity, *Defending a Way of Life: An American Community in the Nineteenth Century* (Albany, NY, 1989), p. 134.

[28]"In Old Missouri", *The Labor Enquirer*, 16 May 1885, p. 6; Michael J. Cassity, "Modernization and Social Crisis: The Knights of Labor and a Midwest Community, 1885–1886", *Journal of American History* 66 (1979), p. 49.

[29]Theresa A. Case, "Blaming Martin Irons: Leadership and Popular Protest in the 1886 Southwest Strike", *Journal of Gilded Age and Progressive Era*, 8 (2009), p. 80.

[30]Ruth A. Allen, *The Great Southwest Strike* (Austin, TX, 1942), p. 144.

Emotion partially drove the 1886 railroad strike. The extremely disruptive and often violent affair involved roughly 200,000 participants from five states. Members from railroad towns in Missouri to Texas dropped their tools and left their stations, organized planning meetings, mobilized to prevent strikebreakers from crossing picket lines, and defaced company property. Some damaged train engines, vandalized tracks, and confronted and beat strikebreakers and supervisors while demanding that Gould and his managers bargain with the KOL and treat members with fairness and respect. The type of disorderly actions that urban boosters like Goodwin had long wanted to avoid had exploded in his beloved Sedalia.

Gould stood his ground in the face of the unrest and, with help from armed forces, chose to combat the strikers directly with the aim of undermining the union and creating workplaces where managers could more freely hire and fire employees at will. He received help from both public and private sector anti-unionists, including vigilantes active in armed, hyper-secretive Law and Order Leagues, businessmen militias that first emerged in Sedalia before spreading to other Midwestern communities. The Leagues were led by well-connected businessmen representing a diversity of worksites who systematically intimidated strikers and defended scabs at or near railroad tracks. Though membership numbers are unavailable, the Law and Order League's leadership consisted of lawyers, merchants, manufacturers, and politicians – the "best" citizens in Midwestern towns and cities. For example, E.W. Stevens, Sedalia's future mayor and a successful mule trader, was one of the organization's leaders.[31] Socioeconomically, these men fit the description of what writer Patrick Wyman called the "American gentry", those who sat "at the pinnacle of America's local hierarchies".[32] Though economically less influential than the era's extraordinarily powerful robber barons like Gould and Andrew Carnegie, they were nevertheless relatively wealthy, politically important, and supremely self-righteous who demanded that their core values – respect for private property, support for unfettered economic growth, and community stability – must predominate. As Goodwin put it in April: "Law and order is indispensable. It must and shall prevail."[33] In the face of these confrontations, Jay Gould said nothing about businessmen-orchestrated violence but shamelessly insulted strikers, whom he called a "mob" (Figure 1). Goodwin gave space to Gould's words in his paper: "At present it is only a question of the dictation of a mob against law and order."[34]

Goodwin fought the strike in two basic ways. First, as a Law and Order League participant, he was part of an organization consisting of armed men who escorted scabs, tormented strikers, and showcased their determination to impose order on the larger community. In a series of menacing actions, these men, equipped with firearms, protected trains and accompanied strikebreakers to

---

[31]M.L. Van Nada (ed.), *The Book of Missourians: The Achievements and Personnel of Notable Living Men and Women of Missouri in the Opening Decade of the Twentieth Century* (Chicago, IL, 1906), p. 98.

[32]Patrick Wyman, "American Gentry", *Atlantic*, 23 September 2021. Available at: https://www.theatlantic.com/ideas/archive/2021/09/trump-american-gentry-wyman-elites/620151/; last accessed 12 November 2022.

[33]*Sedalia Weekly Bazoo*, 6 April 1886, p. 4.

[34]Quoted in "Jay Gould on the Situation", *Sedalia Weekly Bazoo*, 23 March 1886, p. 1.

JAY GOULD'S PRIVATE BOWLING ALLEY.

Figure 1. Cartoon, "Jay Gould's Private Bowling Alley". Like other late nineteenth-century "captains of industry", Gould despised labor unions and instructed his management team to fire and blacklist strikers. A slate shows Gould's controlling holdings in various corporations, including Western Union, Missouri Pacific Railroad, and the Wabash Railroad. Illustration by Frederick Burr Opper from *Puck*, 29 March 1882, cover.
Library of Congress Prints and Photographs Division, LC-DIG-ppmsca-28461, Washington, D.C., United States.

worksites. One report pointed out that "bands of armed men" mobilized "night and day".[35] In the process, it is likely that participants established greater solidarity with one another. These direct actions inspired elites in other communities plagued with similar outbursts of labor militancy to form their own Law and Order Leagues. During the multistate strike, members of local gentries in Belleville, Illinois, Parsons, Kansas, and St. Louis, Missouri, emulating the Sedalia example, formed their own belligerent Law and Order Leagues.[36]

Second, Goodwin's newspaper served as a mouthpiece for those who opposed the belligerency of the strikers, reporting shortly after the strike's collapse that the paper had gained popularity because of "the position he [Goodwin] has taken in regard to

---

[35]"Martin Irons", *Alexandria Gazette*, 7 May 1888, p. 1.
[36]"Law and Order League", *Iron County Register*, 15 July 1886, p. 4.

the strike".[37] In Goodwin's interpretation, the paper, by opposing the strike, reflected the larger community's views. We can assume that this was a self-serving comment that mirrored the views of his class members rather than the opinion of all of Sedalia's residents, irrespective of their socioeconomic position. After all, in most communities, class consciousness had spread, union density had grown in the aftermath of the 1885 strike, and many railroaders had decided to participate in the 1886 action. For these reasons, it is improbable that the city's working-class population – most of Sedalia – had suddenly become sympathetic to the interests of their local bosses or Jay Gould, one of the nation's most despised men. Whatever the case, Goodwin ran multiple stories in his paper celebrating what he described as the fearless counter-activities of citizen anti-strike activists while denouncing the actions of the strikers and their leader.

The repressive actions carried out by the Law and Order League are noteworthy and raise questions about the actions of private armed citizens. Above all, why did these men form a vigilante organization when Sedalia had its own police force? We can speculate. Significantly, there is no evidence that spokespersons for the city's police force or state troops objected to Sedalia's Law and Order League's actions. In fact, Goodwin wholeheartedly praised the diversity of strikebreaking actors. In addition to spotlighting the decisive actions of his Law and Order League, he celebrated the actions of the deputy sheriffs who, in his words, provided "valiant service".[38] It is probable that these deputy sheriffs were also Law and Order League members. Whatever the case, the lesson was clear enough: private and public sector forces complemented, rather than competed, with one another. Public and private sector forces systematically surveilled and targeted the same groups with the central aims of protecting property, restoring order, and punishing noncompliant laborers. This point is consistent with the astute observations made by David Churchill, Dolores Janiewski, and Pieter Leloup, who have insisted that we reject "a narrow focus on 'the police'" and instead embrace "broader conceptions of 'policing' and 'security'".[39] Joint strikebreaking actions conducted during the 1886 strike, all of which served the ruling class's interests, illustrate the correctness of this line of reasoning.

But the question remains: why did Goodwin and fellow Sedalian elites – as well as businessmen in other cities – feel compelled to organize their own possies given the "valiant" services of public sector authorities? One possible reason is that they enjoyed the thrill of directly combating members of the so-called dangerous classes. A more plausible explanation is their collective realization that direct action was the most efficient way to intimidate and expel protesters, protect strikebreakers, further cement ruling-class comradeship, and ultimately end the conflict. Whatever the case, the swift emergence of the Law and Order Leagues highlights an important and often overlooked example of ruling-class self-activity.

---

[37]"Merely Sides with Law and Order", *Sedalia Weekly Bazoo*, 20 April 1886, p. 5.

[38]"Yesterday's Work", *Sedalia Weekly Bazoo*, 6 April 1886, p. 6.

[39]David Churchill, Dolores Janiewski, and Pieter Leloup, "Introduction", in *idem* (eds), *Private Security and the Modern State: Historical and Comparative Perspectives* (London, 2020), p. 2.

Indeed, the repressive forces deployed by these men ultimately led to Gould's victory. Descriptions of exactly how these "bands of armed men" conducted themselves are unavailable, which must not surprise us given the organization's commitment to secrecy. Few sources describe their gutsy actions, including their conversations with one another in meetings, the types of weapons they selected, or the precise nature of their relationships with public sector authorities like judges and police officials. But we can be sure their involvement was significant in concluding the strike on terms favorable to Gould and his management team. Years later, in a somewhat self-serving way, Goodwin reminded readers of what he deemed the Law and Order League's essentialness, writing in 1889 that it "was the most important factor in" ending the strike.[40]

Labor management relations remained extraordinarily tense following the confrontation in early May. Defeated wage earners naturally felt demoralized while also recognizing the necessity to move on; they had families to support, bills to pay, and painful memories to forget. Despite their collective feelings of bitterness, they wanted their old jobs back, recognizing that the experiences of exploitation under dictatorial bosses were far better than suffering the bite of unemployment with no income. But they faced serious stumbling blocks from grudge-holding and conflict-adverse managers, those who desired a future of relatively harmonious labor relations. For obvious reasons, hiring managers sought long-term industrial stability and thus remained unwilling to reemploy the active participants of what Gould had called "a mob".

As the strike came to an end, Goodwin used his platform to distinguish between those who had a future with the company and those who did not. Loyal men, he wrote, "will be taken back, but they must be reemployed as free men, not as blind tools of any men or set of men". In other words, Gould and his management team, led by the general manager H. M. Hoxie, with help from Goodwin, sought a union-free future in Sedalia's shops. "Free men", as opposed to demanding union members, were, from the vantage point of managers at all levels, trustworthy and unwilling to withdraw their labor power, hold membership in unions, or show any expressions of disloyalty. "Free men", in other words, had individual agency and thus emphatically rejected disruptive unions, promised to work during strikes, and demonstrated an eagerness to assist in developing and nurturing a climate of industrial stability and community harmony. "Free men" instinctively embraced independence and showed common sense. Of course, Goodwin recognized that not all accepted the idea of "free labor," and he echoed managers by insisting that KOL members avoid Sedalia's railroad shops. After a delegation of Sedalia's Law and Order League members participated in a fruitful meeting with Hoxie in St. Louis in April, Goodwin informed local jobseekers of their future prospects: "Those among the strikers of the Martin Irons type; those who have been agitators and leaders of mobs and guilty of overt acts of violence and destruction, will not be taken back on any terms."[41]

---

[40] *Sedalia Weekly Bazoo*, 1 October 1889, p. 2.

[41] "Sedalia's Success", *Sedalia Weekly Bazoo*, 20 April 1886, p. 8. By "free labor", Goodwin probably believed, as political scientist Alex Gourevitch explained, that: "The wage-laborer controlled his labor the way any property-owner controlled his property, thus wage-labor was free labor and the paradox of slavery

Goodwin was at least partially correct about the punishments that awaited labor activists. But perhaps he was overly optimistic about the overall numbers of "employable" "free men" residing in railroad communities like Sedalia. The number of those who returned to work was relatively small. According to *The Railway Age*, after the 1886 strike, one of Gould's branches, the Missouri and Pacific system, rehired fewer than 200, representing a small fraction of the 4,600 who had worked for the system before the strike.[42] Further south, thousands of other veteran strikers faced similar rejections. In his study of this labor conflict in Arkansas, historian Matthew Hild reported that about ninety-five percent of Little Rock-based railroad strikers had not returned to work following the strike's collapse, though many had wanted to.[43] Based on these numbers, we can assume that sizable numbers of jobhunters were, in fact, of the "Martin Irons type" – class-conscious men who valued combativity and solidarity over submissiveness and individualism.

Thousands of "Martin Irons" types faced uncertain futures, forced to fend for themselves in an increasingly hostile job market. Of course, many likely slipped through the cracks, ultimately securing jobs in new communities. But the most visible union activists were probably deeply unfortunate, constantly compelled to move from place to place. Meanwhile, these post-strike hardships, apparent to victims and viewers alike, offered employers an opportunity to educate the "free men", those who remained on worksites, about how *not* to behave in workplace settings. Managers sent a clear message to laborers in general: strike activity led to long-term joblessness and perhaps permanent stigmatization.[44]

Predictably, no one seemed to have suffered more than Irons himself in this repressive atmosphere of managerial revenge. Loss of income was just one of his problems, and his multiple adversaries appeared to have relished the various punishments that awaited him. For example, in August 1886, *The Railway Age* correctly predicted that this activist would spend his future in distress, incapable of venturing "with safety in some places".[45] And no one was more determined to promote this punishment than Goodwin, whose hatred for the Scottish-born labor leader lingered for years. Goodwin kept his name in the news for more than a decade after the strike, labeling him "an ignorant Englishman".[46]

---

and freedom finally resolved." See Alex Gourevitch, *From Slavery to the Cooperative Commonwealth: Labor and Republican Liberty in the Nineteenth Century* (Cambridge, 2015), p. 17. Many wage earners, victims of harsh conditions in factories, mines and on railroads, had drawn dramatically different conclusions about their place in the economy, calling themselves "wage slaves". On the contested meanings of wage labor in the years and decades after the Civil War, see Matthew E. Stanley, *Grand Army of Labor: Workers, Veterans, and the Meaning of the Civil War* (Urbana, IL, 2021).

[42]"Results of the Great Strike", *Railway Age*, 11 (12 August 1886), p. 444.

[43]Matthew Hild, *Arkansas's Gilded Age: The Rise, Decline, and Legacy of Populism and Working-Class Protest* (Columbia, MO, 2018), p. 53.

[44]Economist Michael Yates has captured the disciplinary role that fear of joblessness continues to play: "Unemployment in our society is a constant threat to the employed and a torment to those who cannot find work." Michael D. Yates, *Work, Work, Work: Labor, Alienation, and Class Struggle* (New York, 2022), p. 82.

[45]"Results of the Great Strike", *Railway Age*, 11 (12 August 1886), p. 444.

[46]J. West Goodwin, "Sedalia's Citizens' Alliance and Others", *American Industries*, 1 (1903), p. 13. For the broader context, see Case, "Blaming Martin Irons", pp. 51–81.

Many former strikers apparently shared Goodwin's anger and intolerance, and numerous people from across class lines, as historian Therese Case has shown, "blamed Martin Irons" for the strike's disastrous outcome.[47] Indeed, frequently made in newspapers and evidently repeated by ordinary citizens, disdainful name-calling had grave consequences. Goodwin and his allies wanted to isolate and demoralize Irons even before the strike ended. As the strike entered its closing stages in mid-April, Goodwin featured stories about what appeared to be Irons's deteriorating health. Irons "looked ten years older than he did before the strike", remarked an unnamed commentator in the *Bazoo* a month after the Law and Order League's emergence.[48] This was probably accurate, given the circumstances. Indeed, Irons's feelings of worry probably increased as armed Law and Order League members, perhaps including Goodwin, aggressively confronted strikers while helping armies of strikebreakers to cross picket lines. By this time, he and his fellow strikers had been thoroughly outgunned and effectively overwhelmed by well-funded and highly organized adversaries.

Irons departed Sedalia in late May, the beginning of his long decline. His experiences as a blacklisted man were, by all reports, overwhelming. This punishment was long-lasting, enforced by employers, and supported by journalists and law enforcement officials. For his part, Goodwin frequently reminded readers about the results of what he regarded as Irons's ill-informed choices. After the strike, the distraught father of five struggled to secure steady employment as a boilermaker or machinist but was repeatedly turned down by hiring managers, forced to move from community to community, where he endured years of joblessness and underemployment. In response to repeated rejections and humiliating encounters, Irons sometimes wore disguises and often changed his name, hoping to evade detection and obtain work, though observers usually outed him. Indeed, disguises offered only temporary protections – if any protection at all. Clearly, Irons was consistently on edge, forced to develop creative strategies to sustain himself financially.

Irons's blacklist-generated scars were undoubtedly visible after the strike's collapse. Newspaper reporters continued to view him as a subject of considerable interest, routinely reminding readers about his numerous post-strike defeats. A Kansas source reported in July 1886 that he was "broken in mind, pocket and spirit" while living in Rosedale, Kansas.[49] Years later, writers made similar observations, revealing that employers remained unwilling to hire him, prolonging Irons's anxiety and desperation. An unknown number of employers made their feelings clear when Irons approached them with job applications. "Whenever Martin Irons applied for work", another newspaper reported in 1888, "he was driven away with imprecations".[50] Rather than simply reject his applications, mean-spirited employers took additional steps. They treated him with total disrespect, demanding that he permanently stay away from their worksites and communities. These harrowing experiences forced Irons to travel great distances, many miles away from Sedalia. Desperate for an

---

[47] Case, "Blaming Martin Irons".
[48] "Return of Martin Irons", *Sedalia Weekly Bazoo*, 13 April 1886, p. 1.
[49] "General News", *Western Kansas World*, July 24, 1886, p. 2.
[50] "Martin Irons", *Alexandria Gazette*, May 7, 1888, p. 1.

income, Irons spent some time in St. Louis selling peanuts before moving to rural parts of Missouri and Fort Worth, Texas.[51]

The absence of a steady income was not Irons's only source of concern. As a drifter constantly job-seeking, he was vulnerable to various forms of abuse, insults, invasive monitoring, and annoying inconveniences. For example, railroad managers instructed their agents to refuse to sell him tickets, forcing Irons to travel on mostly poorly maintained rural roads on horse-drawn buggies.[52] Moreover, he enjoyed very little privacy or peace of mind. Pinkerton security agents scrutinized his movements, and policemen periodically arrested him for the "crime" of vagrancy. As an income-less person, he was forced to spend extensive amounts of time on the streets, where he was susceptible to the harassment of both public and private sector "law and order" enforcers. In addition to experiencing the precariousness of semi-homelessness, Irons dealt with the aggravations of short incarceration stays, essentially experiencing what historian Bryan D. Palmer has called "the criminalization of the out-of-work".[53] Thoroughly depressed by these traumatizing experiences, Irons sought to drown his sorrows in alcohol, which probably contributed to his declining health. In 1897, another Kansas newspaper reported rather bluntly that Irons "has had a hard struggle with the world since the great Missouri Pacific strike".[54]

But prolonged periods of living with the difficulties of financial insecurity, police harassment, and health problems did not convince him to retreat from his political commitments, which included his desire to build working-class organizations, fight oligarchs, and point out capitalism's inherent maliciousness. According to one source, he remained "more extreme than ever in his views".[55] He continued to show an inclination to participate in class struggles in his advanced age; in regions of Texas, for instance, he organized tenant farmers. Such activism showed that he was not simply a victim of the abuses unleashed by members of the capitalist class. He remained committed to advancing the class interests of ordinary people even though, in the words of one writer, "his health and spirits failed him".[56] We can assume that Irons embraced anti-capitalist views because of his experiences as a labor leader and semi-homeless person, as well as his decades-old observations of the ways the economic system adversely impacted proletarians in general; the differ-ent hats he wore had provided him with painful lessons about capitalism's innate and multifaceted cruelties. Irons's visual appearances offered plenty of evidence of how his encounters with a series of microaggressions and major setbacks had impacted him. At the end of his life, he settled near Waco, Texas, where, according to Eugene Debs, he "bore the traces of poverty and broken health".[57] Practically penniless, Irons died

---

[51]*Kansas Agitator*, October 6, 1890, p. 2.

[52]Postel, *Populist Vision*, p. 220.

[53]Bryan D. Palmer, "The *New* New Poor Law: A Chapter in the Current Class War Waged from Above", *Labour/Le Travail*, 84 (2019), p. 56.

[54]"Martin Irons Joins Debs", *Kansas Agitator*, 10 September 1897, p. 4.

[55]*Ibid.*, p. 4.

[56]"Martin Irons", *Chickasha Daily Express*, 27 December 1900, p. 6. For more on his tenant organizing in central Texas, see James R. Green, *Grass-Roots Socialism: Radical Movements in the Southwest, 1895–1943* (Baton Rouge, LA, 1978), p. 21.

[57]Eugene V. Debs, "Nailed to the Cross for Fourteen Years", *Co-Operator*, 9 (January 1905), p. 6.

in 1900. Another socialist blamed Irons's death on his old nemesis: "Jay Gould found he could not buy him, so he hounded him to death."[58]

Goodwin's Wrath

Goodwin played a critical role in helping Gould in the hounding process. Of course, he was not exclusively responsible for Irons's post-strike difficulties, but he served an important role. Indeed, the newspaperman served Gould's interest by keeping Irons's name in the news years after the strike, telling and retelling *Bazoo* readers what he considered the labor leader's moral weaknesses and imprudence. Goodwin's contempt for Irons was rooted in the newspaperman's annoying personal experiences, philosophical opposition to closed-shop unionism, and deep loathing of labor unrest and expressions of working-class insubordination generally. Perhaps his writings were also motivated by something else: the $1,000 Gould reportedly paid him annually for several years following the strike to keep Irons's name in the news. Gould and Goodwin had apparently made a deal whereby the powerful executive promised to compensate the newspaperman for reminding readers of the labor leader's supposed wickedness and error-driven ways.[59] Clearly, Gould and Goodwin wanted this blacklist to withstand the last years of Irons's life.

Goodwin did his part in at least two ways: he wrote blistering attacks on Irons and allowed others to speak about the labor leader's supposed poor choices, immorality, and general recklessness. We can identify the significance of both approaches, including the second one. After all, the words of a Law and Order League member like Goodwin likely had less of an impact on many readers than the statements of ordinary Sedalians, including former KOL members. By elevating these voices, Goodwin added credibility to the broader anti-union movement since it showed that opposition to labor leaders and their endorsement of militant activities was not restricted to business owners or managers. Instead, these people articulated their grievances from different class positions, protesting that they had been tragically misled by irresponsible men like Irons.

Consider some examples. According to a *Bazoo* article published in May 1886, one unidentified Sedalia resident denounced Irons as "a liar and scoundrel".[60] Others wrote letters to Goodwin's paper, apologizing for following Irons's instructions and participating in the disastrous strike. "I am a striker", one unnamed machinist regretted, "but here recently I have been asking myself, 'why did we strike!' and the answer comes back, 'because Martin Irons ordered it'". The consequences of the strike – led by what this commentator called "a heartless wretch at best" – led to innumerable hardships for the thousands of participants and their families. This person – if this author *was* an actual KOL member and not Goodwin or one of his Law and Order League allies – declared that Irons deserved the ultimate punishment: "The graveyard is the place for such men as Martin Irons. Six feet of rope and then drop him. Public sympathy demands it." Another sensible alternative, according

---

[58]Joseph J. Noel, "In the Industrial Arena", *Advance*, 13 April 1901, p. 2.

[59]Ruth A. Allen, *The Great Southwest Strike* (Austin, TX, 1942), p. 141.

[60]"Relating to the Rail", *Sedalia Weekly Bazoo*, 18 May 1886, p. 5.

to this writer, involved getting him "fired from our country".[61] From the standpoint of this remorseful yet outraged rank-and-filer, death or banishment constituted the best solution.

At least some KOL members remained frustrated by the strike's outcome, and many probably conveyed sincere disappointment with Irons. Yet, we can be sure that many continued to support Irons and expressed frustration with those responsible for the consequences of the industrial action, including Gould and Goodwin's Law and Order League. Obviously, Goodwin had no interest in providing a platform to anyone who raised their voices against expressions of managerial unfairness, outbreaks of repression, or the extreme inequality that characterized Gilded Age America. Clearly, Goodwin had a keen interest in keeping the public narrowly focused on Irons and reminding Sedalia's workers to show unqualified loyalty to their employers by rejecting strikes and subordinately following the orders of their supervisors. That, after all, is how "free men" behaved.

Goodwin sought to demonstrate that observers outside of Sedalia also felt justifiably outraged about Irons. One supposed "reputable citizen of Lexington, Mo" noted soon after the strike that Irons "is a man of no standing, personally or otherwise, in the community". His badly tarnished reputation predated the confrontation, according to this "reputable citizen": "Irons was considered a low man, contemptible, wife-beater, a drunken loafer."[62] The "reputable citizen", readers discovered, wanted citizens to recognize that the 1886 strike was ignited by an irresponsible man, not by structural factors or by dictatorial bosses. Moreover, Goodwin wanted readers to believe that Irons's shortcomings were not limited to his role as a labor leader, and Goodwin gave space to this "reputable citizen" to attack Irons's general character.

Goodwin wrote punchy editorials, echoing the rage supposedly conveyed by former strikers and "reputable citizens". He did so with the goal of ensuring that Irons remained incapable of securing a platform to promote his anti-capitalist opinions. "Mr. Irons had better keep still", Goodwin wrote in 1889, "as no one of respectability will believe him".[63] In Goodwin's opinion, Irons was eternally smeared with the stigma of labor rebellion, which meant that he lacked credibility in any decent society. Yet, Goodwin's words here appear that he may have harbored haunting concerns about Irons's potential influence, uneasily recalling his capacity to rally combative demonstrators in 1886. Goodwin's writings hint at the possibility that he and his colleagues remained somewhat tense, perhaps fearful of a possible repeat of disruptive industrial actions like strikes. Perhaps Goodwin dreaded the possibility of the emergence of another disgruntled labor activist. Such a person, he feared, had the potential to challenge railroad managers and thus create economic disruptions, chaos, and threats to "law and order". By highlighting Irons's misdeeds, Goodwin sought to send a clear message to others: labor rebellion led to

---

[61]"A Disgusted Striker", *Sedalia Weekly Bazoo*, 25 May 1886, p. 7. How many workers continued to "blame" Irons after the strike is a difficult question to answer. We do know that many mainstream labor unionists sympathized with him years after his death, a point Goodwin obviously did not want to highlight. In 1908, for example, the Missouri Federation of Labor sought donations to build a monument honoring Irons. "Notes from the Labor World", *Lewiston Evening Teller*, 17 January 1908, p. 2.

[62]"All About an Agitator", *Sedalia Weekly Bazoo*, 18 May 1886, p. 2.

[63]*Sedalia Weekly Bazoo*, 1 October 1889, p. 2.

livelihood-destroying outcomes. Workers could avoid this punishment by demon-strating total devotion to their jobs. In Goodwin's view, self-respecting workers rejected labor unions and became "free men". According to this logic, free men eagerly and efficiently toiled without holding labor union memberships.

Half a decade after the strike's collapse, Irons painfully acknowledged Goodwin's role in contributing to his misery when a Sedalia resident described a short meeting he had with the legendary drifter. Irons wanted to know about his former commu-nity: "He wanted to know if the *Bazoo* was still in the land of the living and published for the people now on earth. I told him 'by a large majority'." Irons responded with a "grunt".[64] This response illustrates Irons's pent-up aggravation and demonstrates that Goodwin had obviously achieved one of his objectives. While Goodwin was obviously not solely responsible for Irons's years of unhappiness, the labor leader clearly acknowledged that the newspaperman played a part in his punishment.

Achieving the goals of punishing Irons in particular, intimidating wage earners generally, and advancing the interests of managers and "free men" required considerable efforts on Goodwin's part. The enthusiastic urban booster was left feeling vulnerable and perhaps a bit embarrassed during the 1886 strike; this enormously disruptive job action was especially troubling to him because a fellow Sedalian had led it. That strike and the growth of labor unionism in the city in the mid-1880s threatened the interests that he and his fellow Board of Trade members deeply cherished: business prosperity, managerial control, and the presence of a community that obeyed the law. Goodwin was, first and foremost, a champion of business interests, and this newspaperman, booster, and law and order advocate took extraordinary steps in the areas of labor and public relations: helping to build Sedalia's Law and Order League, denouncing strikes in the pages of the *Bazoo*, tarring Irons's name during the labor leader's final years of life, and inviting "free men" to labor in the city's workplaces. By routinely drawing attention to what he considered Irons's offenses in the years after the strike, Goodwin illustrated his critical role in the blacklisting process.

Goodwin and the Ongoing Fight Against Labor

Irons's death did not cause Goodwin to stop advocating for business interests or cease his efforts against organized labor in the name of law and order. And the notorious blacklisting of Irons hardly stopped the labor movement (Figure 2). In the early twen-tieth century, when growing numbers of skilled and unskilled workers across different industries staged strikes and protests for union recognition, Goodwin led several recruitment trips to cities around the country to convince businessmen to join the anti-labor union open-shop movement. Most notably, he was one of the chief orga-nizers of the Citizens' Alliances, a collection of extremely secretive organizations that brought together employers, lawyers, judges, journalists, and clergymen in cities throughout the nation. By 1910, there were over 500 chapters of these organizations. In 1903, Goodwin boasted that he was "the Christopher Columbus" of this second movement and was "probably more responsible for the formation of the first

---

[64]"Dr. White's Find", *Sedalia Weekly Bazoo*, 26 May 1891, p. 5.

Figure 2. Cartoonist Thomas Nast echoed railroad officials in casting the Southwest strikers as foes of the free labor system, caught in the ideological "grip" of Missouri union leader Martin Irons and the voluntary "slavery" of unionism. In the cartoon, the choices exercised by white labor baffle a freedman. Nast's depiction ignored the widespread participation in the strike by both black and white railroaders and the popular support on Gould's roads for the union strike order. *Harper's Weekly*, 17 April 1886.

Citizens' Alliance than any other man on this soil".[65] In these years, Goodwin inspired employers and policed labor well beyond Sedalia's borders. Like those from the mid-1880s, Citizens' Alliance members during the misnamed "Progressive Era" discussed managerial techniques, condemned closed-shop unionism, shared

---

[65]J. West Goodwin to E. J. Phelps, 11 September 1903, M465 Citizens Alliance of Minneapolis Records, 1903–1953, Roll 1, Minnesota Historical Society, St. Paul, Minnesota.

blacklists of union members, and pitted labor activists against "free men" – scabs willing to cross picket lines.[66]

In writing about his history of anti-labor union organizing during the new century, Goodwin touted his community's involvement in unionbusting during the 1886 railroad strike. The mobilization of KOL strikers coincided with the development of, as he put it in 1903, "an uprising on the other side": the growth of the Law and Order League movement. In his immodest telling, Sedalia's "people flocked to the organization in great numbers". Together they helped to put down "lawlessness" while "restoring peace to the communities and compelling the due observance of property rights".[67] Goodwin's contributions to direct strikebreaking, combined with his promotion of anti-labor propaganda more than a decade before employers' active in organizations like the National Association of Manufacturers launched a vicious open-shop movement, help us understand why large numbers of union haters throughout the nation requested his assistance in building Citizens' Alliances and battling labor activists in their communities.

Conclusion

Why does the conflict between Goodwin and Irons matter? Most significantly, Goodwin's actions help us understand how a powerful individual on the sidelines assisted in making Irons's life precarious while helping to undermine the labor movement generally. We can draw meaningful lessons from their experiences during and after the 1886 railroad strike. The strike and its aftermath had pitted one of the country's most visible strike leaders against one of the nation's most vocal anti-labor spokespersons. That both men lived in a relatively small city is perhaps coincidental. Observers of the so-called labor problem had their eyes set on events in this city during and immediately after the confrontation. As an influential opinion maker with close ties to employers and journalists throughout the Midwest, Goodwin was in a privileged position to shape the narrative of the strike and its aftermath while inspiring anti-union figures from other cities to form their own unionbusting organizations. Goodwin's self-serving narratives, repeatedly articulated in the pages of the *Bazoo*, were, essentially, simple morality tales: the city's heroic citizens, seeking to protect the interests of "free men" and resume commerce, had helped to put down a lawless strike led by an irredeemable man. As a journalist with a significant reach, Goodwin played a key, though far from exclusive, part in punishing Irons.

---

[66]One of Goodwin's colleagues in the open-shop movement, William H. Pfahler, made this case especially explicit in a short article. See William H. Pfahler, "Free Shops for Free Men", *Publications of the American Economic Association*, 4 (1903), pp. 183–189. Also see A. O. Wharton, "Why is This Thus?", *Machinists' Monthly Journal*, 17 (1905), p. 222; James W. Byrkit, *Forging the Copper Collar: Arizona's Labor-Management War of 1901–1921* (Tucson, AZ, 1982); William Millikan, *A Union Against Unions: The Minneapolis Citizens' Alliance and Its Fight Against Organized Labor, 1903–1947* (St. Paul, MN, 2001), p. 70; Chad Pearson, *Reform or Repression: Organizing America's Anti-Union Movement* (Philadelphia, PA, 2016), p. 174, 187–215; Aaron Goings, *The Port of Missing Men: Billy Gohl, Labor, and Brutal Times in the Pacific Northwest* (Seattle, WA, 2020); Vilja Hulden, *The Bosses' Union: How Employers Organized to Fight Labor Before the New Deal* (Urban, IL, 2023).

[67]J. West Goodwin, "Sedalia's Citizens' Alliance and Others", *American Industries*, 1 (1903), p. 13.

That significant numbers followed Goodwin's actions demonstrates that employer organizing, employee surveillance, blacklisting, and the trash-talking of rebellious wage earners were not limited to Sedalia. The many men who joined Goodwin in Law and Order Leagues in the 1880s and Citizens' Alliances at the turn of the century illustrate the growing importance that members of the nation's occupationally diverse ruling classes placed on building and sustaining counter-organizations, monitoring workers, bad-mouthing disobedient former employees, and employing punishing techniques like firing and blacklisting. Powerful businesses continue these vile practices today. We can, for example, draw comparisons between Amazon's disrespectful treatment of labor leader Chris Smalls with how members of the ruling class and their agents treated Irons. While Goodwin condemned Irons as "ignorant", Amazon's arrogant managers and lawyers have referred to Smalls – the proud, grassroots organizer fired for leading a walkout in early 2020 at one of the retail giant's massive warehouses in New York City – as "not smart or articulate". Two years after staging this dramatic action and months after helping to successfully organize that same warehouse, Smalls – whose determination to improve the conditions of his workmates mirrors the demands articulated more than a century ago by Irons – cannot secure work at Amazon.[68] The unremorseful objective remains consistent: smear leaders with the aim of punishing them while discouraging others from following their examples.

Plenty of others uninvolved in employers' associations, both past and present, have played junior roles in this form of managerial punishment. Employers with disproportionate power over workers have never needed to look far to discover the perks of blacklisting troublesome workers. After all, joblessness often led to countless other challenges, including financial insecurity, hostile meetings with law enforcement officials, poor health outcomes, and probably early deaths. Blacklisting, Irons's life reveals most clearly, was the punishment that kept punishing – and an illustration of how to terrify workers into submission.

This form of punishment undoubtedly shaped broader workplace and community environments, where countless other laborers experienced what Eleanor Marx Aveling and Edward Aveling identified as the "terrors of the black list". Indeed, the presence of blacklists communicated broader messages to workers considering challenging their employers. That people like Irons and many others faced years of financial precarity, emotional abuses, and occasional physical attacks – revealed in numerous news sources – surely convinced sizable numbers to think twice before joining unions and participating in labor actions; how many chose to reject or abandon unions, labor diligently, and avoid conflicts with their bosses is impossible to measure with exactness, but we can be confident that many picked the path of least resistance. Blacklisting helped impose greater amounts of market discipline on

---

[68]Paul Blest, "Leaked Amazon Memo Details Plan to Smear Fired Warehouse Organizer: 'He's Not Smart or Articulate'", *Vice*, 2 April 2020. Available at: https://www.vice.com/en/article/5dm8bx/leaked-amazon-memo-details-plan-to-smear-fired-warehouse-organizer-hes-not-smart-or-articulate; last accessed 12 November 2022; Shirin Ghaffary, "Amazon Fired Chris Smalls: Now the New Union Leader is One of its Biggest Problems", *Vox*, 7 June 2022. Available at: https://www.vox.com/recode/23145265/amazon-fired-chris-smalls-union-leader-alu-jeff-bezos-bernie-sanders-aoc-labor-movement-biden; last accessed 12 November 2022.

the workforce and, in the process, revealed the enormous power wielded by employers and their allies. Blacklisting did not end class conflicts, but this method of managerial punishment injured the most impassioned labor activists and, in the process, sent worrying messages to others considering challenging their bosses.

Cite this article: Chad Pearson. The 1886 Southwest Railroad Strike, J. West Goodwin's Law and Order League, and the Blacklisting of Martin Irons. *International Review of Social History*, 68:S31 (2023), pp. 213–235. https://doi.org/10.1017/S0020859023000020

International Review of Social History, 68:S31 (2023), pp. 237–251
doi:10.1017/S0020859023000044

RESEARCH ARTICLE

Caught In-Between: Coerced Intermediaries in the Jails of Colonial India*

Michaela Dimmers

Max Weber Forum for South Asian Studies, Delhi, India; Centre for Modern Indian Studies,
Modern Indian History, Georg-August University, Göttingen, Germany, e-mail: michaela.dimmers@
cemis.uni-goettingen.de

Abstract

This article analyses the role coerced intermediaries had on colonial power and authority
in the prisons of British India. Coerced intermediaries in this context were convicts placed
in positions of control by the colonial prison administration as warders, overseers,
and night watchmen and night watchwomen, summarized here under the term "convict
officers". These convict officers were employed by the colonial authorities to maintain a
coercive order and became essential to the exercise of colonial authority and control in
the prisons of British India. The article argues that with their employment, the colonial
administration created a third group within its prisons, situated between the colonial
administration and the inmates. This contradictory practice blurred the lines of
colonial control and authority and raises larger questions about intermediation by unfree
and coerced people in unfree and coerced colonial contexts. The focus here is not so much
on what intermediation is but on what it does. At the same time, the article relates the
system of convict officers as intermediaries to the theoretical concepts used by Foucault
and Goffman and questions the binarity used in most of their theories.

This article studies the exercise of colonial power and authority as well as its reliance –
partially but substantially – on intermediate groups. It does so by observing the system of convict officers, examining how the colonial state used convicts and how, at
the same time, the system could be utilized by convicts for their own purposes within
the colonial prison system.[1] The question asked here is not so much what

---

*I am grateful to Ravi Ahuja and Christian G. De Vito for their comments and insights. Adam Fagbore,
Douglas E. Haynes, Indivar Kamtekar, Nabhojeet Sen, Samita Sen, the participants of the Modern Indian
History Research Seminar at the Centre for Modern Indian Studies, University of Göttingen, and of the
interdisciplinary conference "Punishment, Labour, and the Legitimation of Power", organized by the
Bonn Center for Dependency and Slavery Studies, University of Bonn, 18–19 February 2021, as well as
the reviewers, added greatly with their comments and perspectives. Sebastian Schwecke endured endless
discussions and read numerous draft versions. All comments gave form and shape to this article. This
work would not have been possible without the generous support of the Deutsche
Forschungsgemeinschaft (DFG).

[1] "Convict officers" for the purpose of this article includes convict night watchmen and watchwomen,
convict overseers, and convict warders. The sources sometimes also include convict teachers, convict clerks,

intermediation *is* but rather what it *does*. Moreover, it examines *how* the colonial state exercised its authority in an institution emblematic of colonial coercion. To maintain this authority, it is argued, the colonial regime engaged in a contradictory practice of employing convicts, the very people it convicted of crimes and incarcerated, in order to control the prison population and maintain a coercive order, thus blurring the lines of colonial control and authority.[2] This system was not specific to a colonial context. A system of coerced people watching and exerting control over other coerced people existed in diverse oppressive regimes, such as slavery,[3] and contexts of incarceration, such as concentration camps, gulags, labour camps, or penal settlements. In the nineteenth-century London Newgate prison, the post of wardsman existed, an individual "chosen by the keeper or by the prisoners" to maintain "a rough sort of order", distribute bread and water, and settle disputes among prisoners.[4] This system was disallowed in 1865[5] but was available as a model for the employment of convict officers in colonial India. In Vietnamese colonial prisons in the nineteenth and twentieth centuries, convict officers were called *contremaîtres* or *caplans*.[6] Nazi concentration camps employed so-called *Funktionshäftlinge* or *Kapos*; that is, *Kameradschaftspolizei*, or comradeship police. *Kapos* had different positions within the German concentration camps, including heads of labour squads and camp institutions, as well as foremen.[7] These are just a few examples. In each context, slaves and inmates employed in such or similar positions constituted an intermediate layer between coercers and coerced. As such, they can be defined not only as coerced intermediaries, but also as coerced coercers. The existence of such groups also questions the binarity in the theoretical concepts used by Foucault and Goffman on total or disciplinary institutions.

---

etc. in the term convict officers. There was no distinction made between jails and prisons in colonial India. This article will limit itself to the prisons of colonial India in the North-Western Provinces, later United Provinces.

[2] For criticism of this system, see Government of India, "Report of the Indian Jail Conference assembled in Calcutta in January–March 1877, under the Orders of His Excellency the Governor General in Council: With Appendices", IOR/V/27/170/2 (IOR = India Office Records) (Calcutta, 1877), pp. 70–72 (for the whole discussion on convict officers, see pp. 69–75); David Arnold, "The Colonial Prison: Power, Knowledge and Penology in Nineteenth-Century India", in *idem* and David Hardiman (eds), *Subaltern Studies VIII: Essays in Honour of Ranajit Guha*, 6th edn (New Delhi, 2008), pp. 148–187, 154; for more criticism, see e.g. Government of India, "Report of the United Provinces Jails Inquiry Committee", IOR/V/26/170/5 (Allahabad, 1929), pp. 105–108. Sofsky has argued that the employment of inmates in concentration camps was "blurring the line of distinction between personnel and prisoners"; see Wolfgang Sofsky, *The Order of Terror: The Concentration Camp*, 2nd edn (Princeton, NJ, 1999), p. 98.

[3] William E. Wiethoff, "Enslaved Africans' Rivalry with White Overseers in Plantation Culture", *Journal of Black Studies*, 36:3 (2006), pp. 429–455; Timothy Walker, "Slaves or Soldiers? African Conscripts in Portuguese India, 1857–1860", in Indrani Chatterjee and Richard Maxwell Eaton (eds), *Slavery & South Asian History* (Bloomington, IN, 2007), pp. 235–261.

[4] Michael Ignatieff, *A Just Measure of Pain: The Penitentiary in the Industrial Revolution, 1750–1850* (London, 1978), pp. 39–40.

[5] United Provinces Jails Inquiry Committee Report, 1929, p. 114.

[6] Peter Zinoman, *The Colonial Bastille: A History of Imprisonment in Vietnam, 1862–1940* (Berkeley, CA, 2001), esp. ch. 4.

[7] Lutz Niethammer, *Der gesäuberte Antifaschismus. Die SED und die roten Kapos von Buchenwald. Dokumente* (Berlin, 1994). A *Funktionshäftling* was an "operational inmate" or an inmate with certain functions within the concentration camps of Nazi Germany. Sofsky, *Order of Terror*.

Taking the point of departure of studying the convict officer system raises issues not only of intermediation in unfree and coerced colonial contexts but also of labour, outlining the limits of coercive systems relying on intermediation and the possibilities of carving out a certain level of freedom for coerced labourers in such contexts.

Coerced Intermediation

The convict officer system was introduced in mainland India in the North-Western Provinces and was, according to the report of the Jail Conference of Inspectors-Generals of 1877, fully developed there in British India.[8] Even though the reasons given in the governmental sources for introducing and retaining such a system vary somewhat, it is primarily budgetary justifications that are specified throughout.[9] The first textual trace of convicts holding supervisory powers over their fellow inmates in these provinces dates from a report published in 1861, which describes a system of punishment for prison offences that was put in place in Agra Central Jail and developed into a shift system for sentry duties by prisoners in their barracks.[10] From its inception, the convict officer system was expanded to other central jails in the province and adapted to the colonial regime's changing needs in carceral punishment and labour. Rules were laid out, marking the beginning of a regulated convict officer system, at least on paper. With the exception of the regulation of timings for meals and head counts, these rules appear to have been almost the same as for the staff guards, regulating their uniform, privileges, salary, selection, and duties.[11] Within a few years, this system became an established part of the prison complex, so much so that by 1867, the Superintendent of Benares Central Jail stated that he was looking "forward to the time when the Jail will be entirely guarded by

---

[8]Report of the Indian Jail Conference, January–March 1877, p. 69; even though the sources show clearly that the system was introduced in the North-Western Provinces into mainland colonial India, the report of the Indian Jails Committee of 1919–1920 states otherwise: Government of India or East India, "Report of the Indian Jails Committee 1919–1920 (Contents: Sir A.G. Cardew chairman. Vol. I Report)", I (Report and Appendices) (London, 1921), p. 68; for earlier convict systems outside the Indian mainland, see e.g. Clare Anderson, *Legible Bodies: Race, Criminality and Colonialism in South Asia* (Oxford, 2004), pp. 29–30; David Arnold, "Labouring for the Raj: Convict Work Regimes in Colonial India, 1836–1939", in Christian G. de Vito and Alex Lichtenstein (eds), *Global Convict Labour* (Leiden, 2015), pp. 199–221, 217; John Frederick Adolphus McNair, *Prisoners Their Own Warders: A Record of the Convict Prison at Singapore in the Straits Settlements Established 1825, Together with a Cursory History of the Convict Establishments at Bencoolen, Penang and Malacca from the Year 1797* (Westminster, 1899).

[9]See e.g. Government of Bengal, "Proceedings of the Third Conference of Inspector-General of Prisons held at Calcutta, 1927", IOR/L/PJ/6/1961, File 2014 (Calcutta, 1928), p. 16.

[10]S. Clarke [presumably Inspector-General of Prisons Stewart Clark, mentioned in the next footnote], "Prison Returns of the North Western Provinces, for 1860 [1859]", IOR/V/24/2029 (Allahabad 1861), p. 8. In the following, these yearly reports will be abbreviated as ARCMJ (Annual Report, with tabular statements, for the year *x* on Condition and Management of the Jails in the North-Western Provinces (later the United Provinces)), as these reports were titled from the report for the year 1861 onwards. Shelf mark, archive, and page numbers will follow in that order.

[11]ARCMJ, 1863, IOR/V/24/2030, British Library, pp. 18–21; Report of the Indian Jail Conference, January–March 1877, pp. 69–70. Even though the jail manual of 1863 for the province did not mention convict officials, the jail administration report for the same year introduced rules for convicts employed as officers. See Stewart Clark, *A Manual of Jail Discipline and Economy for the Use of Officers in Charge of Jails in the North-Western Provinces* (Agra, 1863).

prisoners; for there can be no doubt that only under such a system will the Jail discipline ever become perfect".[12] By 1888, convict officers guarded work gangs inside and outside the prisons, in workshops and factories, to such a degree that by then, "[t]he whole watch and ward by day and night, the overseeing of the factories and workshops, and the control of the out-door gangs is practically carried out by the convict warders, superintended by the free warders".[13] This practice was confirmed by Sardar Sahib Bhai Ganda Singh, jailor of Benares Central Jail, during an interview with members of the Indian Jails Committee 1919–1920, in which he stated that "[a]ll the gates and all the factories are in the hands of convict officers". Ganda Singh answered in the affirmative when asked if "the jail is practically run by convict officers".[14] In 1896, the duties for three grades of convict officers were described as follows: (1) the *convict night watchman*, considered the lowest rank, who worked "as an ordinary prisoner during the day and keeps watch for two hours during the night in the barrack"; (2) *convict overseers*, responsible for labour crews or gangs, who worked during daytime; and (3) *convict warders*, who took "the place of a paid warder in case of a vacancy". Only one convict warder for every eight or nine staff warders was supposed to be employed. The number of convict overseers was officially limited to "5 per cent. of the jail population". Convict night watchmen, however, could be employed in an unlimited number and on an ad hoc basis.[15] A female convict warder had to be employed in every central and district jail, but her duties were not defined in the jail manuals. Like her male counterparts, she received a salary and so-called remission marks. She was supposed to be given accommodation outside the female barracks for the night and call for – presumably male – assistance when needed.[16] The duties of all ranks of convict officers were adapted throughout the years.

As they occupied a crucial role within the colonial jails of British India, their service became an intrinsic and essential element of the penal system on which the colonial prison administration became reliant in guarding prisoners, overseeing labour, enforcing discipline, and maintaining control. Their employment constituted

---

[12]ARCMJ, 1867, IOR/V/24/2031, British Library, Appendix No. III: Reports of the Superintendents of Central Prisons in the North-Western Provinces, Annual Report of the Benares Central Prison for the year 1867, Hooper, Superintendent, p. 71. Not everyone within the echelons of the prison administration was in favour of the system. However, dissenting voices were rare. For criticism of the system from within the prison administration, see Report of the Indian Jail Conference, January–March 1877, pp. 70–72. In this connection, see Arnold, "Colonial Prison", p. 154. For more criticism, see United Provinces Jails Inquiry Committee Report, 1929, pp. 105–108. The members of the Indian Jails Committee 1919–1920 were divided in opinion concerning the system: the voiced general criticism can be found in Indian Jails Committee 1919–1920 Report, 1921 (Cardew Vol. I Report), pp. 68–69.

[13]ARCMJ, 1888, IOR/V/24/2036, British Library, p. 8.

[14]Government of India, "Indian Jails Committee, 1919–20, Volume V, Minutes of Evidence taken in the United Provinces, The Punjab and the North-West-Frontier Province, Calcutta, Superintendent Government Printing, India", IOR/L/PARL/2/407 B, 1922, p. 1305.

[15]ARCMJ, 1896, IOR/V/24/2037, British Library, p. 12. The Jail Committee of 1889 had also complained that different terms were used in different provinces and found that there was a variation in grades: W. Walker and Alfred Swaine Lethbridge, "Jail Administration in India (Walker and Lethbridge) Committee 1889: Report", IOR/V/26/170/2 (Calcutta, 1889), p. 50.

[16]Major Charles MacTaggart, "Rules for the Management and Discipline of Prisoners in the N.-W. Provinces and Oudh", IOR/V/27/171/91 (Allahabad, 1902), p. 278.

a specific part of the broader prison labour system. Their power over fellow inmates was comparable with that of prison officers recruited from the extramural population. Convicts employed in this unfree labour system occupied a privileged position but remained imprisoned inside the system, situated between staff members and prisoners, occupying an ambivalent position in the microcosm that was the colonial prison system. This ambivalent position could create a rupture within the prison population, as convicts in such positions had to invariably adjust their loyalties towards their fellow prisoners and the prison administration, de facto and de jure their employer. At first glance, the convict officer's position could be seen as that of an intermediary agent or intermediary, comparable or equal to those working in such positions in free(er) contexts, who, as numerous studies of intermediaries in colonial India have shown, were employed in a multitude of areas and came from all strata of the colonized society.[17] David Arnold portrays the system of convict warders as "a replication within the prison order of a factor common in Indian labour organization – the use of foremen, known by such terms as *sardars* and *maistries*, to supervise the work of others".[18] However, it can be argued that there were intrinsic differences, for example in the power of negotiation, between intermediaries such as *sardars* or *maistries* (and other intermediaries for that matter) and convict warders, or convict officers as such, for the simple fact that free intermediaries could change employers or end their contract, where applicable. Divergence in the disciplining power merits consideration as

---

[17]See e.g. Ravi Ahuja, "Networks of Subordination: Networks of the Subordinated: The Ordered Spaces of South Asian Maritime Labour in an Age of Imperialism (c. 1890–1947)", in Ashwini Tambe and Harald Fischer-Tiné (eds), *The Limits of British Colonial Control in South Asia: Spaces of Disorder in the Indian Ocean Region* (London, 2009), pp. 13–48; Crispin Bates and Marina Carter, "Sirdars as Intermediaries in Nineteenth-Century Indian Ocean Indentured Labour Migration", *Modern Asian Studies*, 51:2 (2017), pp. 462–484; Rana P. Behal and Prabhu P. Mohapatra, "'Tea and Money versus Human Life': The Rise and Fall of the Indenture System in the Assam Tea Plantations 1840–1908", *Journal of Peasant Studies*, 19:3–4 (1992), pp. 142–172; Rajnarayan Chandavarkar, "War on the Shopfloor", in Rana P. Behal and Marcel van der Linden (eds), *India's Labouring Poor: Historical Studies, 1600–2000* (Cambridge, 2012), pp. 265–278; Eugene F. Irschick, *Dialogue and History: Constructing South India, 1795–1895* (Berkeley, CA and London, 1994); Amit Kumar Mishra, "Sardars, Kanganies and Maistries: Intermediaries in the Indian Labour Diaspora During the Colonial Period", in Sigrid Wadauer, Thomas Buchner, and Philip R. Hoffmann-Rehnitz (eds), *The History of Labour Intermediation: Institutions and Finding Employment in the Nineteenth and Early Twentieth Centuries* (New York, 2015), pp. 368–387; Norbert Peabody, "Cents, Sense, Census: Human Inventories in Late Precolonial and Early Colonial India", *Comparative Studies in Society and History*, 43:4 (2001), pp. 819–850; idem, "Knowledge Formation in Colonial India", in Douglas M. Peers and Nandini Gooptu (eds), *India and the British Empire* (Oxford, 2012), pp. 75–99; Tirthankar Roy, "Sardars, Jobbers, Kanganies: The Labour Contractor and Indian Economic History", *Modern Asian Studies*, 42:5 (2008), pp. 971–998; Sebastian Schwecke, "Merchants, Moneylenders, Karkhanedars, and the Emergence of the Informal Sector", in Harald Fischer-Tiné and Maria Framke (eds), *Routledge Handbook of Colonial South Asia* (Routledge, 2021), pp. 145–155; Samita Sen, *Women and Labour in Late Colonial India: The Bengal Jute Industry* (Cambridge, 1999); idem, "Making Coolies: Labour Brokerage and the Tea Industry in India, 1830–1930", digital presentation given to the German Historical Institute London, 28 April 2020; idem, "Commercial Recruiting and Informal Intermediation: Debate over the Sardari System in Assam Tea Plantations, 1860–1900", *Modern Asian Studies*, 44:1 (2010), pp. 3–28; Lakshmi Subramanian, "Banias and the British: The Role of Indigenous Credit in the Process of Imperial Expansion in Western India in the Second Half of the Eighteenth Century", *Modern Asian Studies*, 21:3 (1987), pp. 473–510. Just to name a few.
[18]Arnold, "Labouring for the Raj", p. 217.

well. Free(er) intermediaries could more often than not determine the level and space of intermediation they could occupy within societal hierarchies, which most convict officers could not do due to the coercive space they were situated in. Considering the coercive and unfree contexts they were detained in, they cannot be put on a par with intermediaries in free(er) circumstances per se, even if some of the functions of their role were similar to, or even the same as, those of free(er) intermediaries. The unfree and coerced context in which they worked made their position intrinsically different from intermediaries outside the prison. This suggests an overarching question: how can people in an unfree context, here incarceration, be considered intermediaries within or between the system of oppression and the oppressed? The same could be asked, for example, about enslavement and indentured labour.[19]

Ambiguous Alliances

There were at least three structural levels of inmate control in the colonial prison that comprised primarily physical and psychological control: (1) *disciplinary control*: guards and rules, constituting the administration's disciplining intentions, which could have been officially or unofficially enforced;[20] (2) *spatial control*: architectural features, such as walls, bars, doors, and gates that could be locked and unlocked at the administration's will; and (3) *taxonomical control*: bureaucratic procedures and forms of administrative control, manifested by registration and documentation of the prison population, permeating a prisoner's personality and history, being part of a wider taxonomical project by the colonial regime.[21]

Disciplinary control was an essential part of power since it wielded authority over people's movements, labour, food, speech, sleep, hygiene, and health, encompassing all aspects of everyday life. Convict officers had an evident power over their fellow prisoners since they played a central role in the everyday mechanisms of inmate management and constituted a large part of the control mechanisms of everyday life exercised in the name of the colonial state. They were placed – or perhaps caught – between the prison administration and the prison population. As shown below, when illicit behaviour became known, they held complex and discretionary forms of power over the prisoners as they could decide what information to pass on to the prison administration and what to withhold, at times being caught between the two groups, as the notion of "hopelessness", cited below, partly exemplifies.[22] Being part of the

---

[19]I am grateful to Christian G. De Vito, Nabhojeet Sen, and Samita Sen for the discussion and their insights on the topic.

[20]David Arnold considers colonial medicine as "an agency of disciplinary control". Arnold, "Colonial Prison, p. 180.

[21]On taxonomy, see e.g. Anderson, *Legible Bodies*; Arjun Appadurai, "Number in the Colonial Imagination", in Carol A. Breckenridge and Peter van der Veer (eds), *Orientalism and the Postcolonial Predicament: Perspectives on South Asia* (Philadelphia, PA, 1993), pp. 314–339; Nicholas B. Dirks, *Castes of Mind: Colonialism and the Making of Modern India* (Delhi, 2004); Peabody, "Cents, Sense, Census"; *idem*, "Knowledge Formation in Colonial India"; Radhika Singha, "Settle, Mobilze, Verify: Identification Practices in Colonial India", *Studies in History*, 16:2 (2000), pp. 151–198; Richard Saumarez Smith, "Rule-By-Records and Rule-By-Reports: Complementary Aspects of the British Imperial Rule of Law", *Contributions to Indian Sociology*, 19:1 (1985), pp. 153–176.

[22]For the notion of the enabler and the traitor, see David Turnbull, "Boundary-Crossings, Cultural Encounters and Knowledge Spaces in Early Australia", in Simon Schaffer, Lissa Roberts, Kapil Raj, and

prison population, they had an intrinsic insight not only into the prisoners' intra-mural lives but also into mechanisms of resistance against the prison administration. This gave them some control over the prison administration as informants and, possibly as mediators between the inmates and the prison administration. As they were part of both the administration and the inmate population, they could or had to choose to whom to be loyal: the former, the latter, or themselves. They had to or could constantly determine with whom to collaborate and with whom not, be it during escapes, riots, and disturbances, or when it came to other breaches of jail dis-cipline. This power, be it to inform on other prisoners, prevent or aid escape attempts, or even to decide who was allowed to get up at night, exemplifies the control these convicts could exert and epitomizes the ambivalences in loyalty convict officers could have towards both fellow prisoners and the administration. Evidence about these convicts' relationship or standing with other (free) staff and other convicts is scarce in the sources. In one report Inspector-General of Prisons Clements alluded to a tense relationship between prisoners and convict officials:

> Control of the convicts is mainly vested in convict officials. Some of the convicts in our jails are not amenable to discipline and resent being ordered about by fellow convicts and they give trouble if the shoe pinches too tight. This was a direct factor in the genesis of two disturbances in the central prisons, one at Benares and the other at Lucknow, and recently there was a third riot in the Allahabad central prison. Some convicts received serious injuries and as a result four died.[23]

Unsurprisingly, the available sources remain generally opaque concerning the question of why such breakdowns in jail discipline occurred. Was it due to general dissatisfaction with prison conditions or policies that boiled over, singular changes in policies, or certain events that led to protests and clashes between prisoners and staff, including convict officers?[24] The account just cited suggests that assaults had

---

James Delbourgo (eds), *The Brokered World: Go-Betweens and Global Intelligence, 1770–1820* (Sagamore Beach, MA, 2009), pp. 387–428.

[23]ARCMJ, 1927, IOR/V/24/2040, British Library, p. 21.

[24]For examples of breakdowns of jail discipline due to changes in the prison policies, see Clare Anderson, *The Indian Uprising of 1857–8: Prisons, Prisoners and Rebellion* (London, 2007), pp. 37–54; David Arnold, *Colonizing the Body: State Medicine and Epidemic Disease in Nineteenth-Century India* (Berkeley, CA, 1993), pp. 110–111; *idem*, "India: the Prisoners' Revolt", *IIAS Newsletter*, 39 (2005); *idem*, "India: The Contested Prison", in Frank Dikötter and Ian Brown (eds), *Cultures of Confinement: A History of the Prison in Africa, Asia and Latin America* (London, 2007), pp. 147–184, 163–165; *idem*, "Colonial Prison", pp. 150–152, 171–172; Rachna Singh, "Messing, Caste and Resistance: The Production of 'Jail-Scapes' and Penal Regimes in the Early 1840s", in William Andrew Pettigrew and Mahesh Gopalan (eds), *The East India Company, 1600–1857: Essays on Anglo-Indian Connection* (Abingdon/New York, 2019), pp. 193–217; Radhika Singha, "'No Needless Pains or Unintended Pleasures': Penal Reform in the Colony, 1825–1845", *Studies in History*, 11 (1995), pp. 29–76; *idem*, *A Despotism of Law: Crime and Justice in Early Colonial India* (Delhi, 1998), pp. 278–284; Anand A. Yang, "Disciplining Natives: Prisons and Prisoners in Early Nineteenth Century India", *South Asia: Journal of South Asian Studies*, 10:2 (1987), pp. 28–45; *idem*, "Of Lotahs and Men: Confronting of the Body (Politics in the Lotah Emeutes of 1855", in James H. Mills and Satadru Sen (eds), *Confronting the Body: The Politics of Physicality in Colonial and Post-Colonial India* (London, 2004), pp. 102–117.

taken place, at least on this occasion, due to a resentment of the power and privileges convict officers had. While there is no a priori reason to presuppose an overriding sense of solidarity between prisoners, nor that they would have worked together as a unified group against the prison administration, it can be assumed that power relations, hierarchy, class, and caste played a large, if not dominating, role in the way prisoners, confined in a limited space, lived together. David Arnold has suggested that some of these power relations at play outside the prison walls might have differed inside the prison, as some convict officers considered low caste could have held positions of power over higher caste inmates; in other words, this system may have inverted caste hierarchies.[25]

Alliances appear to have been constantly forged, renegotiated, and broken. At times, the convict officers were on the side of the prison administration, as is illustrated by examples that include an incident in which a convict officer killed a fellow convict to protect a head jailor,[26] as well as instances of extrajudicial ill-treatment of other prisoners or the prevention of attempted escapes. At other times, they were on the side of the prisoners, especially when facilitating escapes, or not reporting infractions of jail rules. MacTaggart, Inspector-General of Prisons, stated that even though convict officers could "generally be trusted to prevent serious breaches of discipline such as assaults and escapes as far as they can" and were always "loyal to jail superintendents in emergencies", they would "not report minor breaches of discipline", would "do little or nothing to prevent prisoners having forbidden articles", and could not "reasonably be expected to do so".[27] Consequently, their use of discretionary powers to maintain jail discipline, on the one hand, and balancing any kind of allegiance between their fellow prisoners and the prison administration, on the other, seem to have been tolerated by at least parts of the prison administration. At the same time, rules in the jail manuals prescribed that special remission was to be given to any convict for collaborating with or aiding the prison administration in certain ways, for example, by "protecting an officer of the prison from attack". This reveals that breakdowns in prison discipline, perceived or real, were anticipated.[28] One obvious form of collaboration with the prison administration concerned the organized ill-treatment of prisoners. Allegations that the higher echelons of the prison administration were witnesses to or ordered convict officers to perpetrate extrajudicial ill-treatment were voiced in the interviews of the Jail Committee

---

[25]Arnold, "India: The Contested Prison", p. 172. This could also be the case with intermediaries such as the *kangani*, as Crispin Bates and Marina Carter point out, referring to Peebles: see Bates and Carter, "Sirdars as Intermediaries", p. 465.

[26]Government of India, House of Commons, "Death of an Indian Prisoner Detained in Benares Central Jail: Result of a Post-mortem; Parliamentary Enquiries", IOR/L/PJ/6/1946, File 2745, 1927.

[27]ARCMJ, 1910, IOR/V/24/2039, British Library, p. 9. For another example, see ARCMJ, 1881, IOR/V/24/2035, British Library, p. 8.

[28]MacTaggart, "Rules for the Management", p. 266; Government of the United Provinces of Agra and Oudh, "United Provinces Jail Manual, Revised Edition 1927", IOR/V/27/171/93 (Allahabad, 1927), p. 37; Government of the United Provinces, "United Provinces Jail Manual: Containing the Rules for the Superintendence and Management of Jails in the United Provinces, Revised Edition 1941", IOR/V/27/171/95 (Allahabad, 1942), p. 57. The jail manuals for the years 1927 and 1941 prescribe that in this and other cases special remission was to be given to those who were eligible for "ordinary" remission and with some exceptions to those not being eligible for remission.

Report of 1919–1920.[29] In a later report, the United Provinces Jail Inquiry Committee of 1929 reported having looked into such allegations. The committee stressed that no evidence of alleged ill-treatments, such as beating inmates with a shoe or putting them into stress positions, could be found. Even though it admitted that "unauthorized punishments" would occur, the committee believed this was not common or severe in the provinces.[30] Sachindra Nath Sanyal, incarcerated in connection with the Benares Conspiracy and Kakori Train Dacoity cases,[31] reported to the committee instances of ill-treatment by convict officials, but not by other officials. Convict officials, he is quoted in the report, would "pick up quarrels with the prisoners over whom they want to exercise overlordship" and beat them. Allegations by other convicts were voiced as well.[32] Jawaharlal Nehru, who was to become the first prime minister of India after independence and was incarcerated multiple times during the independence struggle, also described the ill-treatment of a prisoner who had allegedly bitten an assistant jailer and who was severely beaten presumably by convict warders and guards, whom he called *"pukkas, lambardars &c."*, on the order of the assistant jailer. He further asserted that convict officers would beat convicts "just to please the jailer".[33] But Nehru also described instances of solidarity among convict officers with other prisoners; for example, when during a hunger strike by inmates that also involved a labour strike in Naini Prison, convict officials asserted that even though they would perform their usual or official tasks, they would not mistreat fellow inmates if ordered.[34] These examples exemplify not only the violence prevalent in colonial prisons and breakdowns in prison discipline, but also the fine line of loyalty between the administration and prisoners that convict officials apparently tried to tread. This fine line put the convict officers, especially higher ranking ones, at an intersection of the regulated and the regulator.[35]

---

[29]Indian Jails Committee 1919–1920 Report, 1922 (Vol. V Minutes of Evidence), p. 1324. Not everyone who gave evidence for this report confirmed this (see below).

[30]United Provinces Jails Inquiry Committee Report, 1929, pp. 158–162, 281–285. However, the chairman of the Jail Inquiry Committee and the Committee believed there would be "some" extra-legal ill-treatment, as found in the registers for staff, who were punished for beating prisoners, but prisoners in interviews in the absence of jail officials had apparently not alleged ill-treatment. The chairman of the committee stated that he believed prisoners would not consider a slap in the face or beatings with a stick or cane as "very serious", or worth a complaint. He considered such treatment as "most wrong and most improper" and did not condone any "infliction of unauthorised punishments by members of the staff". Not all committee members shared his opinion. According to another member, any superintendent of a jail who would not detect severe ill-treatment would "fail his duty". See United Provinces Jails Inquiry Committee Report, 1929, pp. 159–161, 284–285.

[31]On the Benares Conspiracy case, see e.g. Government of India, "Benares Conspiracy Cases: Judgments of the Special Tribunal", IOR/L/PJ/6/1434, File 1381, 1915–1918; On the Kakori case, see Government of India, "The Kakori Train Dacoity Case: High Court Proceedings and Judgments; Newspaper Extracts", IOR/L/PJ/6/1910, File 2226, 1925–1927.

[32]United Provinces Jails Inquiry Committee Report, 1929, p. 280. For descriptions of other attacks, see pp. 166–169.

[33]Jawaharlal Nehru, *Selected Works of Jawaharlal Nehru* (New Delhi, 1973), IV, p. 342.

[34]*Ibid.*, p. 366.

[35]For the concept of "the regulated and the regulator", see Chitra Joshi, "Public Works and the Question of Unfree Labour", in Alessandro Stanziani (ed.), *Labour, Coercion, and Economic Growth in Eurasia, 17th–20th Centuries* (Leiden, 2013), pp. 273–287.

Disciplining Loyalties

Privileges and punishment were not only used to ensure loyalty; both were also indicators of carceral power structures and hierarchical differences between convict officers and inmates within the colonial prisons, using, in effect, the divide-and-rule approach that was so characteristic of colonial authority. Control over the labouring inmate body was thus ensured by incentivized labour through privileges and mechanisms of punishment. The prison administration evidently felt that privileges were important to maintain "a high standard of discipline and encouraging good work" as the "safe custody of prisoners" would depend "to a great extent on the reliability and steadfastness of these officials".[36] Privileges for convict officials included a salary, an official tobacco allowance, or being allowed to purchase and smoke tobacco, wearing shoes, being paraded and sleeping separately from other inmates, not wearing fetters, and being allowed to grow a beard and their hair "to such extent as the Superintendent may think sufficient as a mark of distinction from the ordinary Convicts", having better or different food and cooking for oneself, as well as keeping pets.[37] Their special status was also reflected in the frequency of the heavily regulated meetings with the outside world. By 1902 prisoners could, as per the jail manual, have only one to two interviews per year; convict officers could have one per month.[38] However, the most important privilege seemed to have been the increased good conduct or remission marks they received, which meant they could gain certain privileges and an earlier release. Other convicts received good conduct marks and some of these privileges as well, but generally, convict officials received them to a much greater extent.[39] The contraposition of privileges was punishments, which could include revoking privileges and "warning, forfeiture of good conduct remission, suspension, fine and dismissal",[40] putting the prison administration into an even more powerful position as the possibility of punishment was presumably ever looming. Such punishment within punishment constituted an effective tool of control not only for convict officers, but for all labouring convicts. As the ARCMJ reports show and David Arnold has established, staff officers committed infractions, just as convict officers did.[41] Staff

---

[36] ARCMJ, 1925, IOR/V/24/2040, British Library, p. 10.

[37] ARCMJ, 1863, IOR/V/24/2030, British Library, p. 20; ARCMJ, 1889, IOR/V/24/2036, British Library, p. 8; ARCMJ, 1895, IOR/V/24/2037, British Library, p. 10; MacTaggart, "Rules for the Management", p. 278; United Provinces Jail Manual (Rev. Edn 1927), pp. 46–47; United Provinces Jails Inquiry Committee Report, 1929, p. 67; United Provinces Jail Manual (Rev. Edn 1941), p. 68. The ARCMJ and the Jail Committee's recommendations give an insight into the application of these rules in the everyday life. See also Arnold, "India: The Contested Prison", p. 172. On pets, see Jawaharlal Nehru, An Autobiography, 6th ed. (Delhi, 1988), p. 358.

[38] MacTaggart, "Rules for the Management", pp. 217–219. The rules mention only interviews with friends and do not specify if for interviews with families the same rules would apply. See also Indian Jails Committee 1919–1920 Report, 1922 (Vol. V Minutes of Evidence), p. 1290.

[39] On remission marks, see ARCMJ, 1889, IOR/V/24/2036, British Library, p. 8; convict warders could earn double the remission marks of an "ordinary" convict. For statistics on prisoners who received an additional thirty good conduct marks for "good service as Lumberdars", and those prisoners who received fifty additional good conduct marks for "good service as Warders", see ARCMJ, 1869, IOR/V/24/2032, British Library, pp. 68A–69A.

[40] ARCMJ, 1925, IOR/V/24/2040, British Library, p. 61A, as just one example. The ARCMJ also include documentation and statistics for the punishment of all prisoners and staff, see also footnote 42.

[41] Arnold, "India: The Contested Prison", pp. 171–172; Arnold, "Colonial Prison", pp. 154–155.

warders could be punished with demotion, fines, dismissal, and imprisonment, and were, as the statistics provided in the ARCMJ reports suggest, punished on a higher level than convict officers.[42] This accentuates the notion that convict officers were more reliable than staff warders, who were considered "mostly men of inferior class and in many instances untrustworthy".[43] However, the language of reliability, trustworthiness, and loyalty used in the government reports changed gradually. If convict officers were described in the ARCMJ report of 1863 as "superior in trust-worthiness and efficiency", they were by 1901 believed to be "fairly trustworthy" and carried out their duties "very fairly satisfactorily".[44] By 1907, their behaviour was considered still "on the whole very good", but at the same time, it was held that they

> undoubtedly very frequently connive at or, wilfully shut their eyes to the intro-duction of prohibited articles, especially tobacco, but it is doubtful if in this respect they are much worse than many of the paid warders. The convict over-seer no doubt generally discovers the hopelessness of his position in opposing himself against the united determination of his fellow prisoners to obtain such articles.[45]

The passage illustrates, on the one hand, the compromises the prison administra-tion was willing to make to keep this system in place and, on the other, that convict officers were not mere instruments of the jail administration but navigated the prison system and the various pressures with which they were confronted. They did so also in order to tap into the structures of privilege and incentives offered by the admin-istration for compliance with its needs. In turn, the colonial state maintained these structures of privilege and incentives by these same needs, in effect granting convict officers an extraordinary form of power in part due to their ambivalent intermediate position. Even though a lack of sources echoing their voices directly makes it difficult to analyse in detail how they negotiated this nexus of power and powerlessness, it is apparent that they could use the trust placed in them to their advantage.[46] Preventing escapes could lead to an immediate release, a reward that was given, for example, to one convict warder who, by holding the inner prison gates closed, had prevented an escape attempt involving a convict overseer. Two other convict warders, who came to his help, received "two months special remission".[47] At the same time, if an infraction against prison rules was detected or even suspected, the punishment could be swift

---

[42]See ARCMJ for the years 1887, p. 25; 1888, pp. 8, 26; 1889, pp. 8, 29; 1890, pp. 8, 21 (all IOR/V/24/2036, British Library); 1891, pp. 17, 39; 1892, pp. 23, 50; 1893, pp. 9, 31; 1894, pp. 10, 46; 1895, pp. 11, 52; 1896, pp. 12, 33; 1897, pp. 20, 83; 1898, pp. 13, 36 (all IOR/V/24/2037, British Library); 1899, pp. 14, 36; 1900, pp. 13, 39 (both IOR/V/24/2038, British Library).

[43]ARCMJ, 1898, IOR/V/24/2037, British Library, p. 10.

[44]ARCMJ, 1863, IOR/V/24/2030, British Library, p. 12D (Simson, Secretary to the Government of the North-Western Provinces, No. 1876 A. of 1864, dated 27/06/1864); cf. ARCMJ, 1901, IOR/V/24/2030, British Library, p. 4.

[45]ARCMJ, 1907, IOR/V/24/2038, British Library, p. 7.

[46]For example ARCMJ, 1891, IOR/V/24/2037, British Library, p. 16.

[47]ARCMJ, 1921, IOR/V/24/2039, British Library, p. 7.

and severe. Considering that the post of convict officer elevated its holder to the legal status of a public servant, they were punished not as convicts but as employees of the colonial state if they broke rules in their capacity as convict officers. Most infractions for which details were documented in the ARCMJ reports were related to escapes, for example, the case of a convict warder and a staff warder who were both suspected of aiding two convicts to escape and were sentenced to "four years' imprisonment".[48] In another case, a convict warder escaped with a convict, aided by a "convict overseer on duty outside", who was sentenced for his involvement to "one year's simple imprisonment and Rs. 100 fine or three months more simple imprisonment". Other officials apparently involved in the case were also punished.[49] More rarely documented infractions committed by convict officers included the case of two convict officers who were transferred from Benares to "Agra Jail for insubordination", one of whom had apparently tried to kill a European officer and was sentenced to "ten years additional imprisonment".[50]

With this system, the colonial state created an elite group of convicts within its prisons that was expected to be overall loyal to the state and prison administration. As shown, incentives, mainly in the form of privileges, were offered to retain this loyalty in order to establish and maintain a system of carceral power structures exerting control and punishment over the prison population that was cost-effective and could affirm, either in reality or as a conjecture, the reasoning of convict reform. With it, the colonial regime had constructed a powerful mechanism for coercion, control, and jail discipline in its prisons and, considering the extent of incarceration, for a large part of the colonized population.[51] Both the prison administration and the convict officers benefited from this system. The benefits to the colonial regime seem to have been much greater since the convict officer system gave it the resources to control parts of the colonized population, thus if not enabled then at least helped it to expand, develop, consolidate, and maintain its control over colonial India.[52] Convict officers were used to ensure parts of this imperial order. Their employment helped the colonial regime establish a high level of control over the prisoners. Yet, by putting convict officers in effect in charge of jail discipline, the colonial prison could serve as an illustration of how the British empire was, indeed, "an ultimately precarious shifting and unruly formation, quite distinct from its self-projected image as an orderly behemoth".[53]

---

[48] ARCMJ, 1912, IOR/V/24/2039, British Library, p. 6.

[49] ARCMJ, 1922, IOR/V/24/2040, British Library, p. 8.

[50] ARCMJ, 1864, IOR/V/24/2030, British Library, p. 50c.

[51] See also Yang, "Disciplining Natives", pp. 30–31.

[52] See also *ibid.*, p. 30.

[53] Ashwini Tambe and Harald Fischer-Tiné, "Introduction", in *idem, The Limits of British Colonial Control in South Asia: Spaces of Disorder in the Indian Ocean Region* (London, 2009), pp. 1–10, 3. For the colonial prison as a visualization of colonial power, see e.g. Clare Anderson and David Arnold, "Envisioning the Colonial Prison", in Dikötter and Brown (eds), *Cultures of Confinement*, pp. 304–331; Arnold, "India: The Contested Prison"; Mira Rai Waits, "Imperial Vision, Colonial Prisons", *Journal of the Society of Architectural Historians*, 77:2 (2018), pp. 146–167; Singha, *Despotism of Law*.

Conceptual Observations

The very existence of such an intermediate group complicates Foucault's and Goffman's theories. It adds to the already established critique of their work that suggests a more complex understanding of how power was exercised, for example, in institutions such as the colonial prison.[54] Both Foucault and Goffman based their analyses of institutions such as prisons on a binary structure comprising the administration/staff and the inmates and did not consider any third group, such as convict officers.[55] Goffman even speaks of a "staff-inmate split" as "one major implication of the central features of total institutions".[56]

When it comes to an intermediate inmate group, constituted of coerced coercers, punished labourers, and punishing labouring inmates, the axiom of the resulting binary theorem of prison organization as total institutions (Goffman) or of *institutions disciplinaires* (Foucault) must be developed and extended.[57] Foucault's approaches to, for example, docile bodies and heterotopia also fail to take into account such intermediary groups and thus the complexities of actual sociopolitical systems, in this case, colonial prisons. His vision of the docile body, which can be "subjected, used, transformed and improved",[58] seems somewhat doubtful in light of the examples about convict officers. Since the colonial regime's approach to convict officers aimed to exploit their labour as a means to economize budgets, those convict officers were certainly "subjected" and "used" too. It cannot be denied that there was also, at least officially, an intention to "reform". The question here is how disciplined and docile people put into the position of discipliner (and at the same time constituting a disciplined entity) were on a pendulum constantly swaying between disciplining and being disciplined, subject and object of the prison administration, hence of control and power? At the same time, the Foucauldian analysis of power, especially his critique of the binary formation of power, helps to understand these complex and constantly adapted power relations. In his discussion on "power and strategies", Foucault shows that "one should not assume a massive and primal condition of domination, a merely binary structure with 'dominators' on one side and 'dominated' on the other", but rather "a multiform production of relations of domination".[59] Convict

---

[54]See also Peabody, "Knowledge Formation in Colonial India", p. 98, on the need of expansion of the binary categories used in the wider colonial context. I am grateful to Douglas E. Haynes for his comments and insights (not only) in this regard.

[55]For the colonial Indian prison and the critique of Foucault see the work of Clare Anderson, David Arnold, Radhika Singha, and others.

[56]Erving Goffman, "Characteristics of Total Institutions", in Walter Reed Army Medical Center, National Research Council (eds), *Symposium on Preventive and Social Psychiatry* (Washington DC, 1958), pp. 43–93, 47; Erving Goffman, *Asylums: Essays on the Social Situation of Mental Patients and Other Inmates* (Harmondsworth, 1961), p. 9.

[57]Goffman, *Asylums*; Michel Foucault, *Surveiller et punir. Naissance de la prison* (Paris, 1975). In these works, Foucault and Goffman apply a fundamental binary character (i.e. inmates and staff) of total/disciplinary institutions.

[58]Foucault, *Surveiller et punir*, p. 138 (English translation by Alan Sheridan, *Discipline and Punish: The Birth of the Prison* (New York, 1979), p. 136). I am grateful to Indivar Kamtekar for his comments on this and other topics.

[59]Quoted in Colin Gordon (ed.), *Power/Knowledge: Selected Interviews and Other Writings 1972–77 – Michael Foucault* (New York, 1980), p. 142. See page 62 for a discussion on "agents of liaison".

officers were part of this "multiform production of relations in domination" as they were simultaneously the dominators and the dominated. The dependency of the colonial state on convicts to ensure the intramural security of their prisons and enforce discipline among the inmates implies a more nuanced picture of how power and control worked, relying in part on intermediation with specific features arising from its unfree settings, which, in turn, were partially shaped by the colonial context. It shows that absolute control was not always in the hands of the colonial state but perforated with different actors who had – at times – differing interests.

While it might seem self-evident that convict officers were intermediaries, it is not self-evident whether their functional role was that of agents of colonial or penal intermediation, or both.[60] As mentioned, convicts employed in this manner were considered public servants by law. They were not mere passive subordinates but active participants in this system, constituting an elevated position within the hierarchy and using their position for their own purposes to gain privileges and freedoms in an otherwise unfree and coercive environment.[61] As the example of convict officers demonstrates, rather than being a static process, this intermediation could be a vastly complicated and complex maze of shifting loyalties, privileges, and negotiations.

Conclusion

Convict officers negotiated the seemingly contradictory state of having great power and being simultaneously powerless; they disciplined yet were disciplined, were controlled yet were agents of control over their fellow prisoners. They constituted an in-between group within the prison hierarchy, considered their benefits and used the system to their advantage, but also negotiated a pendulum of loyalty to the prison administration and their fellow prisoners. Even though only institutional records could be used here, and the voices of those who constituted the larger part of convict officers are rarely heard, it becomes clear that at least some without a voice outside the prison walls might have had some power inside them. The unique position they had can be defined as an intermediary coerced body that fulfilled some functions of intermediation between the colonial prison administration and their fellow inmates, though without possessing the full range of characteristics associated with colonial intermediaries in free(er) contexts – underlining the differences between various forms of intermediation. What is dealt with here comprised different registers of intermediation, between which a fine balance had to be struck by convict officers to avoid punishment by the prison administration and hostility from fellow prisoners. The colonial prison administration had to tolerate sporadic breakdowns in its authority to ensure the broader need for prison discipline and, by way of punishment, could, for the most part, hold this breakdown of authority in check.

Overlooked in Foucault and Goffman's concepts on total or disciplinary institutions, such an in-between group challenges and calls for a loosening of their binary

---

[60]This notion is derived from Corsín Jiménez in the completely different context of trust. Alberto Corsín Jiménez, "Trust in Anthropology", *Anthropological Theory*, 11:2 (2011), pp. 177–196, 178–179.

[61]MacTaggart, "Rules for the Management"; United Provinces Jail Manual (Rev. Edn 1927); United Provinces Jail Manual (Rev. Edn 1941). For last three sources, see Section 23 of the Prisons Act, Act IX of 1894, in the respective jail manuals.

approach. It complicates their theories and suggests a more complex understanding of how power was exercised in an institution such as the colonial prison.[62] Adding the layer of coerced coercers challenges their binary theorems, but combining it with the Foucauldian analysis of power and its "multiform production of relations in domination" shows the complexity of power relations in the everyday and the omnipresent need for *compromise* in coerced contexts, be it in the colonial prison, penal settlements, or other coercive institutions. In essence, the logics of power had to be constantly assessed, not only by the coerced coercers, but also by the coercers themselves. Looking at how these additional layers of domination worked in such contexts not only sheds light on the logics of such coercive institutions; it also shows that it could lead to significant and often unforeseen or even unforeseeable ramifications on the processes of exercising this authority and its impacts.

Moreover, registers of penal intermediation and colonial intermediation were, at times, at odds. What intermediation precisely *does* is rarely captured in its conceptual understanding, which tends to highlight aspects of collaboration and divide-and-rule techniques of exercising authority and often neglects to inquire into its actual outcomes. A more nuanced approach to the question of carceral labour, punishment, intermediation, and the term intermediary itself, seems necessary. Convict officers were undoubtedly able to exert power over prisoners and were thus part of the executive force of the colonial punishment regime, but were at the same time subjugated to the same regime. The convict officer system in North Indian colonial jails thus exemplifies the need to look into the manifold forms of intermediation and its complex and nuanced results, especially when it is connected to questions of punishment and labour. The issue of intermediaries in unfree and coercive circumstances within South Asia and beyond needs further research to identify the finer textures of not only such intermediation but also modes of power and control in order to better understand the complex structures of labour and punishment in such contexts.

---

[62] I am grateful to Douglas E. Haynes for his comments and insights here.

Cite this article: Michaela Dimmers. Caught In-Between: Coerced Intermediaries in the Jails of Colonial India. *International Review of Social History*, 68:S31 (2023), pp. 237–251. https://doi.org/10.1017/S0020859023000044